1975

Later

MEDIEVAL

ENGLISH PROSE

GOLDENTREE BOOKS

R. C. BALD, SAMUEL H. BEER & WILLIAM C. DEVANE
Series Editors

THOMAS E. CONNOLLY, Editor
Joyce's "Portrait": Criticisms & Critiques

C. DAY LEWIS, Editor
English Lyric Poems, 1500–1900

O. B. HARDISON, JR., Editor
Modern Continental Literary Criticism

O. B. HARDISON, JR., Editor
English Literary Criticism: The Renaissance

SAMUEL HYNES, Editor
English Literary Criticism: Restoration and 18th Century

DANIEL G. HOFFMAN and SAMUEL HYNES, Editors
English Literary Criticism: Romantic and Victorian

KATHERINE LEVER
The Novel and the Reader

MILTON MARX
The Enjoyment of Drama, 2nd Edition

WILLIAM MATTHEWS
Later Medieval English Prose

HAROLD OREL, Editor
The World of Victorian Humor

ROBERT L. PETERS, Editor
Victorians on Literature & Art

EDWARD STONE, Editor
Henry James: Seven Stories and Studies

WILLIAM MATTHEWS
University of California at Los Angeles

EDITOR

Later
MEDIEVAL
ENGLISH PROSE

New York

APPLETON-CENTURY-CROFTS

Division of Meredith Publishing Company

ACKNOWLEDGMENTS

IT IS A PLEASURE to express here my thanks and gratitude to the following persons and bodies (and their secretaries and librarians) who have generously given me permission to publish selections from works listed in the first part of the bibliography at the end of this book: G. Brodin and J. van Zutphen; the Oxford University Press and the Cambridge University Press; the Bodleian Library and the British Museum Library; the Early English Text Society, the Scottish Text Society, and the Royal Historical Society. To the various editors and publishers whose permission I did not seek, on the score that the editions from which I selected were out of copyright, I also tender my thanks and gratitude.

W.M.

CONTENTS

Contents

Later

MEDIEVAL

ENGLISH PROSE

Introduction

Apart from *Owl and Nightingale,* Layamon's *Brut,* and a small group of religious pieces—*Ancrene Riwle, Sawles Warde,* and some others—there is little in English literature between the end of the eleventh century and the beginning of the fourteenth to spark any critic's enthusiasm. Indeed, from all that long stretch of time, there is not much English writing at all, good or bad.

The reason is simple enough. It is not merely that English was the language of a subject people whose rulers spoke French. English was also a provincial tongue that offered no advantage—except for local purposes—to writers who belonged to the international coterie of learned men. That native imagination, learning, wit, and skill in composition had not fled the island is clear from the work of Geoffrey of Monmouth, Matthew Paris, Walter Map, Alexander of Hales, Nigel Wireker, John of Salisbury, Grosseteste, Thomas of Kent, Roger Bacon, Gerald of Wales, William of Ockham, Duns Scotus, to name only names still well known. But such writers, most of them aiming at a wider intellectual public than England afforded, preferred to use Latin, the lingua franca of medieval scholarship and art, or on occasion the one modern language, French, that had acquired something of the same status. Rather than a relapse from the practice of Anglo-Saxon years, this procedure was in fact normal.

It is rather the abundance of English prose *before* the Norman Conquest that needs special explanation. And that explanation is not far to seek. King Alfred, personally responsible for most of the earliest English prose, explains that translation was the readiest way to repair the breakdown of Latin education wrought by the Viking invasions. Begun from necessity, continued mostly for the convenience of the "Latinless," Anglo-Saxon prose was, for all its achievement, largely a stop-gap. The post-Conquest re-estab-

1

lishment of English education and its later affiliation with the cathedral schools and the new universities of France and England joined with Norman supremacy in England to restore a learned tradition that even in Alfred's time had not completely been broken.

The recrudescence of English literature in the fourteenth century and the renewal of English prose in particular is in part a response, shared with other European countries, to general movements that led to a crumbling of the theocratic social order, the emergence of sectarianism, the rise of a mercantile bourgeoisie, and a consequent sharpening of the sense of democratic and national identities. In part, however, it also reflects a resolution of local rivalries that made English once again a language worthy of English pens and French an enemy language to be learned painfully in classroom or abroad.

The mileposts in this change of status are familiar: shortly before 1350, John Cornwall began to teach Latin at Oxford through the medium of English; in 1362, the Statute of Pleading generalized a prescription that had been adopted six years before in London, that English should replace French in all legal proceedings. Such formal steps followed the bellwether of popular preference among a reading public that was increasing in size and was also ill at ease in any language but its own. In 1385, John Trevisa, speaking of native teaching, declared that grammar-school children now knew no more French than their left heels; in 1387, the same writer translated the *Polychronicon* for a noble patron who claimed to know Latin well but still found English more comfortable; and in 1422, one of the reasons given by the Brewers Company for turning to English in their records was that although many of the Craft could read and write English, Latin, or French "they do not in any wise understand."

The release of native literary talent that coincided with this restoration of English to prime status in all but the most scholarly matters is familiar through its poetry: the work of Gower, Chaucer, Langland, and the *Pearl*-poet alone establish the later fourteenth century as one of the high-tides of our literature. What has not been so well recognized is the achievement of English prose at this time, and also in the next century, the dog-days for poetry that followed the Chaucerian spring. In our generation, R. W. Chambers and his scholarly progeny have redeemed from neglect the splendid prose of the English mystics; there have long been voices to praise and readers to read Mandeville and Malory; and even Caxton, Fortescue, Pecock, and the Pastons have not lacked admirers.

But save for H. S. Bennett and an occasional thesis-writer, literary historians or critics have paid little heed to the abundant prose of other kinds and other authors, even though much of it is not devoid of literary interest and some might well be held to rival the classics of the time in both form and content. Scholarship itself is not immune from fashion or deep-frozen ideas, and, although the earlier Middle Ages have been redeemed from Gothick contempt, the fifteenth century continues to pay a melancholy tribute to Renaissance revolt and to scholarly patterns of cultural deaths and rebirths.

One hope that has inspired the present anthology is to redeem from quasi-oblivion a number of medieval prose works that can still give pleasure, by setting them among writings with which an adventurous reader may already be familiar. The other is to present an array of medieval prose-styles and a representation of the ideas and subjects with which people were preoccupied in the late Middle Ages. Wherever feasible, justice to content as well as to composition has been sought by choosing short works that could be presented completely or chapters that form understandable units in the logic of larger works. Linguistic study not being the primary objective of the collection, the pieces have been accorded a modernity that somewhat parallels the sort of modernity they had when they were composed: punctuation has been altered to suit recent habit; spelling (the chief stumbling-block to easy reading) has been modernized; words like *ilka, thir, quhilk, hem, her* (their), *tho, thilk* (that), and *n*-inflections are replaced by our own equivalents: these changes have been indicated in the text by using italics for added letters. Syntax, morphology, vocabulary are otherwise very little altered; but obsolete words have been glossed. The changes are fewer than in some fifteenth-century modernizations of earlier English, but although they leave some pleasing obscurities of a social or semantic nature, it is likely that the reader will be impressed that, linguistically, John Bull new-suited is John Bull much the same then and now.

No important pioneering in subject or genre accompanied the linguistic freedom afforded English writers by the adoption of their native tongue. Medieval literary practice stressed variation and incrementation rather than radical originality, even the most brilliant imaginations being largely content to make over existing work with embroidering detail, new styles, and new applications. The splendid poetry of fourteenth-century England is closely tied to French or Latin or Italian originals, and the new English prose is dominated by a simple purpose to make available in English standard matter for the reading of a growing public that included not only monolingual merchants but also "Latinless" parish priests, nuns, and physicians. Much original prose there is, but three-quarters of the work, a larger proportion than at any other period of English literature, is translated.

Throughout the period, books of piety and necessary information claim most attention, their range of subject increasing as the generations go by. Standard works on natural science, Christian behavior, universal and national history, are gradually supplemented by treatises on medicine, manners, sport, palmistry, political philosophy, pedagogy, by biographies of holy men and women, and at length by tales and romances. The intellectually important writings of the Middle Ages were left untranslated, however, reserved for the study of those qualified to read them. Except for Pecock, Fortescue, and John of Ireland, writers on weighty subjects rarely stooped to the vernacular for their original work.

Nor was the still lowly status of English the only impediment. Verse, which had been the normal medium for vernacular writings, was slow to relinquish its sway. Original prose is restricted to business, history, political philosophy, and religion. Even subjects that had already been treated in Latin or French prose continued to be turned into verse: nearly all the English poems on Troy, for example, are adapted from Guido delle Colonne's Latin prose, and several of Lydgate's and Chaucer's poems follow the prose versions in French. In general, English prose remained a second-best affair, appropriate mainly to simple works for unscholarly readers.

Nevertheless, by the end of the fifteenth century, prose was the medium of more than three hundred books and treatises, some brief, some extremely long, that deal with most subjects of medieval interest. The range of Caxton's many translations and publications—books of history, science, moral philosophy, pious biography, fables, religion, manners, romance, the bulk of them in prose—reveals the status prose was beginning to command. The public to which scribes and printers catered was far from being either large or democratic. But by 1500, partly because of the very abundance of prose-translations from French and Latin prose, even more because of the commonly-expressed belief that prose is briefer and plainer than verse and easier to understand, English prose was well on its way to achieving the role it now fills—the expected form for works of fact, fiction, and argument addressed primarily to the reason or fancy of the commonalty of Englishmen.

But if it was plainly headed towards assurance in its status, as much cannot be claimed about its developments in style. Prose, it has been well said, is a social institution, far more subject to law and convention than poetry. In modern centuries, any prose writer ambitious enough to publish a book or article may fairly be expected to command a language and a rhetoric conventionally associated with his subject and aims. In the late Middle Ages, however, few English writers owe much to any native convention or law concerning prose other than the inescapable laws of the language itself.

An initial reason for this must be that English prose was really new for most men: few can have known the *Ancrene Riwle* and still fewer the works of Aelfric or Wulfstan. A more important and continuing reason lies in the limited distribution of English books and the small reading of them. Despite some impressive figures, such as the nearly five hundred texts that contain one or another of Rolle's writings, manuscript copies were normally few and seldom available for general reading. Caxton, apparently still thinking in terms of manuscripts, never envisaged the large public that printed books were soon to command: his editions rarely went above a hundred copies, it would seem. Some manuscripts passed from hand to hand and their raggedness bears witness to the loans, but many may have gone no farther than the patrons who ordered them to be composed or translated.

Literature was half-private, the book trade in its cradle, authors professionally uncoordinated. Seven or eight translations were made of St. Bridgit's *Revelations* and *Life,* and as many of Friar

Laurent's *Somme des Vices et des Vertus,* four of both *Secreta Secretorum* and *The Life of Alexander,* three of *Mandeville's Travels, The Imitation of Christ,* and so on, each successive translator either unaware or unconcerned, apparently, that his labors had already been done. As for the public, whose expectations are all-important when prose assumes its place as a social institution, it was probably even less knowledgeable than the authors about what works were being written. Wills and inventories mention beds far more often than books, and the earliest indications that some people in secular life were beginning to make small book collections—most of them in French or Latin—occur in the later fifteenth century. The mainstay of the book-trade was copying for college and monastery libraries.

One effect of this small distribution of books is that English prose-writers seem to be tackling the problems of translation and original composition without much benefit of prior English example. No new theory evolves from all their work in translation and little consistency in general practice. The statements of the word-for-word and meaning-for-meaning formulae, which go back at least to St. Jerome, are just as conventional as the standard assertions of the translator's inadequacy—it is seldom a translator holds himself prisoner to his declaration. But there is no consensus on subtler matters, no practical agreement as to how the difficulties of matching or suitably varying alien linguistic structures might be met, no informal sense of the hierarchy of words, no conventions as to what kinds of works might best be expanded, abbreviated, or left as they were, no protocol on the ranking of original and translation. In original composition, matters are much the same. In some few areas there is evidence of continuity and of tacit agreement about the style proper to certain subjects: succession of office ensures the continuing plainness of company records, the traditional terse formulae in wills, and the persistence of the magniloquence that writers of official letters first learned from the *artes dictaminis.* Wycliffe's pungent bareness in controversial sermons and treatises seems to form a model for Lollard writing. The comparative ease of Caxton's later prefaces indicates that he learned much from his numerous adventures with that high-style genre, and the successive versions of *The Brut* and the various chronicles that draw upon those versions share a style that interestingly moves toward ampler descriptions and more extended and logical sentence structures.

And in the mystical branch of devotional prose there was enough reading, copying, and imitation for a lengthy stylistic tradition to develop. Between the rhetoric of Aelfric, *Ancren Riwle*, Rolle, Hilton, Nicholas Love, Julian of Norwich, Margery Kempe, and Sir Thomas More there are marked differences, some the product of differences in personality and intent, others resulting from various foreign models. Nevertheless, there is a core of sentence arrangement, diction, illustration, rhythm that these writers tend to share, one which reinforces similarities proceeding from their common subject. But there are few signs that one tradition influenced any other stylistically or that they were taken as models by the many other prose-writers of their time. Pastons, Celys, Stonors and their like write with primitive simplicity, only an occasional member influenced by the formulae of legal style or the architectonics of Latin. Translators follow the styles of their sources, but in their own composition they may write quite differently. Among the originals, Usk owes a debt to Chaucer's style in the *Boethius*, but generally walks his own flowery way. So too do Pecock, Fortescue, John of Ireland, Capgrave, perhaps even Malory, each of them forging his own English style, seemingly oblivious of what any compatriot might have done in similar affairs.

Despite this disconnectedness in the literary scene and the consequent lack of a body of theory or conventions, either tacit or expressed, the period was not without distinguished stylistic achievements, and there is one obvious common ground in its various prose styles.

As for achievement: among the originals, Hilton, the anonymous author of *The Cloud of Unknowing*, Lavenham, Margery Kempe, Fortescue, each in his own fashion, must be reckoned among the minor masters of English prose style. Rolle, although he is uneven, is sometimes crystalline in exposition or lyrical in exhortation; Capgrave writes history and pious-biography with some eloquence; and even Pecock's legal crabbedness is not without its peculiar merits. The anonymous translators of *Mandeville's Travels, The Knight of the Tower, The Imitation of Christ,* and *The Golden Legend* are skillful in matching the styles of their varied sources, and sometimes they even improve on them. Nicholas Love, as much an original as a translator, is in Hilton's company as an exemplar of controlled eloquence. And Malory's outstanding contribution to romance, the means by which his version of the Arthurian story has so long outlived the sources from which he took it, is the vitality of his narrative style. These are the best, but there are not a few others who write clearly, simply, and with unpretentious honesty, intent on their matter, instinctively preferring the familiar speech of their time to any floridity they may have known from books.

As for the common ground in style, it is almost as obvious as the common grounds in the prose of later periods. Part of it stems from the structure of the English language itself; part from the nature of the foreign works that English writers used as their sources or models. These are matters that may now claim our consideration.

In the course of its long history, English has amplified its vocabulary vastly: from many languages, words which have their own colorations have entered English; words have dropped into limbo, developed new meanings, acquired new associations; pronunciation, and with it spelling, has altered greatly in some ways; and the system of inflections that was once operative (though the syntactical variations it might have made possible were little exploited) is now largely gone. Nevertheless, the basic patterns of the language have changed very little in over a thousand years. Perhaps the best way of illustrating this apparent paradox is to quote some samples of the earliest English prose and to translate them as literally as current usage will allow.

The first sample is taken from King Alfred's report of the conversation he had with his Norwegian visitors, Ohthere and Wulfstan:

He waes mid þaem fyrstum mannum on þaem lande; naefde he þeah ma þonne twentig hryþera ond twentig sceapa ond twentig swyna; ond þaet lytle þaet he erede he erede mid horsan. Ac hyra ar is maest on þaem gafole þe þa Finnas him gyldaþ. þaet gafol biþ on deora fellum and on fugela feþerum ond hwales bane, and on þaem sciprapum þe beoþ of hwaeles hyde geworht and of seoles. Aeghwyle gylt be his gebyrdum.

He was among the first men in the land; he had not, though, more than twenty cattle and twenty sheep and twenty swine; and the little that he ploughed he ploughed with horses. But their income is mostly in the tribute that the Finns yield them. That tribute is in animals' skins and in fowls' feathers and whales' bone, and in the ship-ropes which are of whale's hide made and seal's. Each gives according to his ranks.

The second comes from the *Anglo-Saxon Chronicle* for 963 and is a fair spokesman for the general run of that work.

On þes oþer gear syþþon he waes gehalgod. þa makode he feola minstra. and draf ut þa clerca of þe biscop rice. forþan þaet hi noldon nan regul healden. and saetta þaer muneca. He macode þaer twa abbotrice. an of muneca oþer of nunna. þaet waes eall wiþinnan Wintanceastra. Syþþan þa com he to se cyng Eadgar. bed him þet he scolde him giuen ealle þa minstre þa haeþene men haefden aer tobrocon.

In this second year after he was hallowed then made he many minsters, and drove out the clerks from the bishopric, because they would no rule hold, and set there monks. He made there two abbacies, one of monks, the other of nuns. That was all within Winchester. After that, came he to the king Edgar; bade him that he should him give all the minsters the heathen men had earlier destroyed.

The translations, childish as they are in style, are not unacceptable as English. Apart from an odd word and a few differences in word-order (which could have been the same in the original without offending a common usage), the language is the spittenimage of the Old English. All four pieces are cut to the same pattern: a diction bare of ornament and not venturing beyond familiar words; a syntax in which modifying words and phrases occupy set positions and the subject-verb-object order is standard, despite all the chances for variation afforded by early English inflections; a grouping that is paratactic, the statements, short and of even length, set end to end or linked by a few conjunctions—with only an occasional clausal subordination lending its formal aid to the logic of the matter itself.

So unconsidered a style is impersonal and scarcely artistic, but it is the basis of English prose—the nearest literary representation of ordinary speech. As such it has been a norm for everyday informal writing during the whole history of English. Nourished by convention, cultivated by rhetoric, it has been seemingly transformed into flowers of unending shapes and hues, prim, rambunctious, sly, stately, contorted, coy, severe, orchidaceous—all the prized blooms of the anthologist's posy. But outlasting all such hybrids of rhetoric, the parent stock persists, perdurable, hardly changing. In letters and diaries, even in autobiographies, it is the staple prose-style, down to the present day. Restricting ourselves to the period with which this book deals, here, for example, are three pieces of fifteenth-century prose, all original; the first from the Paston Letters, the second from a London chronicle, the third, which shows some modicum of rhetorical cultivation, from a treatise on the ten commandments. Little in the passages has been changed but the spelling:

A. On Thursday the wall was made yard high, and a good while before evening it rained so sore that they were fain to helle [cover] the wall and leave work. And the water is fallen so sore that it standeth under the wall a foot deep to Ball's ward. And on Friday, after sacring, one came from church ward, and shove down all that was thereon, and trod on the wall and broke some, and went over; but I cannot yet wit who it was. And Warren King's wife, as she went over the stile, she cursed Ball, and said that he had given away the way, and so it proved by John Paston's words.

B. Also in this same year, the Duchess of Gloucester was arrested and put in hold, for she was suspect of treason. And a clerk that was longing to her, which was cleped Roger, which was taken for sorcery against the king. And he was put in the Tower of London, and after he was brought into Paul's, and there he stood up on high on a scaffold against Paul's Cross on a Sunday, and there he was arrayed in his garments, and there was hanged round about him all his instruments, which were taken with him, and so showed all the people.

C. Therewith cometh in Pride and sitteth him in the middle of all, and then he beginneth to boast and ruse himself of many things that he hath not, ne could, and all say it is sooth. Then Covetise heareth that, and then cometh he in boldly, and he cheereth them all, and anon he beginneth for to bargain, and then lacketh not great oaths and swearings, and then is each of them about to beguile other. Then cometh in Lechery and he looketh all about the house, and then he setteth him down on the bench and then beginneth he to speak and bring in old stories of women and of lusts and ribaldry.

These samplings are true to a good part of the prose of the revival: the first to family letters and other informal documents; the second to the earlier chronicles and to things like the Brewers'

Book; the third to much of the simple literary prose, sermons, exemplary stories, medical books, the translated ones as well as original compositions. Their small differences from the prose of five centuries before are a feather's weight in comparison with their similarities in diction, structure, and rhythm. And what this similarity establishes is that the paramount continuity in English prose is the continuity of the English language. The paucity of English prose in the twelfth and thirteenth centuries, like the paucity of English verse, is primarily the result of political and social considerations that dictated what languages should be written. But of English speech there was no paucity. French and Latin may have been the high horses, but it would be astonishing to learn that the ordinary thirteenth-century Englishman was any more learned than the fifteenth-century Brewers who, knowing no language but their own, jumped at the chance offered by Henry V's example to read and write in their native tongue. Given a similar sanction, the average Englishman, brewer, baker, candlestick maker, would have done the same in the thirteenth century and his style would have been a pea from the same pod.

Some branches of medieval prose, sermons, saints' lives, and kindred genres, were intended for oral delivery, and much of the rest was expected to reach its larger audience by means of reading aloud. That so much of it is simple and unvaried, that the phraseology and constructions of colloquial English are so close to the surface of the writing, that anecdotes abound, that dialogue is prevalent in matter that would now be treated wholly in the third person, and that much of it has the air of a simple conversation, is scarcely surprising. Nevertheless, even in the Middle Ages, speech seldom appeared in literature completely unadorned. There are sections of the *Anglo-Saxon Chronicle* far more maturely constructed than the sample we have already quoted; Alfred, in translating from Latin works that themselves varied strikingly in composition and rhetoric, attempted several styles, most of them ornate, complex, and not a little confused; and in the original work of Aelfric and Wulfstan and such translations as *Apollonius of Tyre* there is Old English prose of considerable variety, maturity, and eloquence.

Such developments from the basic style are outcomes of more literary sophistication than the ordinary man can command. Wulfstan's vehement and often lengthy sentences, with their paired synonyms, serially balanced phrases, antitheses, alliteration, and chanting rhythms, are grounded on Latin and Biblical exhortation. Aelfric's cautious exploitation of the possibilities that Old English grammar offered for hypotactical constructions and positional variations; his judicious interplay of simple sentences with complex ones no longer than English taste prefers; his clarity, point, and gentle eloquence—all these must stem from his long study of Latin prose, narrative prose particularly, and his own extensive experience in composing it. *Apollonius,* first among English romances but stylistically akin to Aelfric's homilies, is even more directly an heir to Latin practice: here and there, native linguistic habit led the translator to break up the fairly simple constructions of his source, but his success lies in the skill with which he could normally match the short Latin periods, phrase for phrase, clause for clause, and still be English.

To devise any style more subtle than that of everyday English speech, to find effective substitutes for the intonations, stresses, separations, and paces of speech, or its obbligato of gesture and bearing, writers needed to go to school, and the schools to which all their training led them were the manuals of Latin rhetoric and the patristic and medieval Latin prose that was the normal study and reading of educated men. There, and also in French prose, it was that they learned the principles and practice of maintaining a consistent tone and point of view throughout a lengthy utterance and of combining statements into larger units which reflected formally the logical relationship of the components. There too they discovered the many means for giving emphasis where needed and all the subtleties of rhetoric, the rules for adjusting style and diction to subject, audience, or occasion, and the tropes and figures—*conversio, transgressio, compar, sententia, similitudo, transitio,* and all the rest—that could be used to manipulate a language into combinations that would serve well a writer's purposes of instructing, moving, or persuading his reader, and of expressing or hiding his own thoughts and feelings. Not until the sixteenth century had built up a large body of original English prose did native models commonly replace those of Latin and French, and even then foreign influence remained strong.

The Latin that served as both source and model for the new

English prose was as varied in form and quality as the vastness of medieval Latin prose would suggest. Between Boethius's *Consolations*, St. Gregory's *Homilies*, the histories of Jerome's Bible, Bede, Geoffrey of Monmouth, and Martinus Polonus, the devotional treatises of Dionysius the Areopagite, Hugh of St. Victor, St. Bonaventura, Suso, the scientific writings of Vincent of Beauvais and Bartholomew the Englishman, or the narratives of Petrus Alfonsus, *Gesta Romanorum*, Jacques de Vitry, and Legenda Aurea—to name only a scintilla of the popular sources—there are as wide divergencies as might be expected from the differences in their subjects, objectives, and audiences, and from the qualities of the writers. Medieval Latin prose ranges from near-Ciceronianism in the complexity of its sentence structures to paratacticism not far removed from that of the naïve English that has already been quoted; in over-all organization it varies from mathematically-logical to associational-rambling; and its lexicon and rhetoric display every shade from excessive ornateness to severity. Nevertheless, most of it adheres in some measure to the traditions of classical composition and rhetoric embodied in the writings of Jerome, Augustine, and other early Fathers, and in such technical treatises as the grammars of Donatus and Priscian and the *Rhetorica ad Herennium*, and there is not a little that is patterned on Seneca, Suetonius, and Cicero himself. At its best it offered models almost as sophisticated as classical Latin prose; even at its simplest it was structurally more mature and rhetorically more varied than the basic styles of the vernaculars.

What these models meant to English writers may best be seen in translation, one of the chief means by which they came, in the Middle Ages and later, to realize the linguistic and rhetorical means to a mature prose. Here for example is a chapter from a translation of the *Mystica Theologia* of Dionysius:

Also, we, ascending and beginning our denyings and our doings away at the highest of understandable things, say that he is neither soul, nor angel, nor hath fantasy, nor opinion, nor reason, nor understanding; nor He is reason nor understanding; nor He is said nor understood. And—that we run from these high things by means to the last things—he is no number, nor order, nor greatness, nor littleness, nor equality, nor likeness, nor unlikeness; nor he standeth, nor he moveth, nor he holdeth no silence, nor he speaketh. And—that we turn again to

the highest things, and end our denyings at things most high—we say
that he hath no virtue, nor he is virtue, nor light, nor he liveth, nor He
is life, nor he is substance, nor age, nor time, nor there is any understandable touching of him, nor he is knowledge, nor truth, nor kingdom, nor one, nor unity, nor Godhead or goodness; nor he is spirit, as
we understand spirit; nor sonhood, nor fatherhood, nor any other thing
known by us or by any that be; nor he is anything of not-being things,
nor anything of being things; nor any of those things that be-know
him as he is; nor He knoweth those things that be as they be in themselves, but as they be in him; nor there is any way of reason or of understanding for to come unto Him; nor name, nor knowing of Him; nor he
is darkness, nor he is light, nor he is error, nor he is truth. Nor (knit-
tingly to say) there is of Him no setting nor doing away; but, when we
affirmingly set or denyingly do away, all or any of those things that be
not he, him we may neither set nor do away, nor in any understandable
manner affirm him, nor deny him. For the perfect and singular Cause
of all must needs be without comparison of the most high height above
all, both setting and doing away, and his not-understandable overpass-
ing is understandably above all affirming and denying.

This passage, surely as sustained and subtle a specimen of English prose as could be hoped for at this time, is a mirror-image of
the Latin original: the vocabulary has been completely anglicized,
word-pairs have occasionally been substituted for single words,
and there are some differences in detail; but the sentence constructions, the rhetorical devices, the length of clauses and their
rhythms are in almost every respect those of the Latin.[1] The same
is true of the following passage, the opening paragraph in a translation of the Latin life of *St. Elizabeth of Spalbeck:*

In the province of Leody, beside a famous abbey of nuns of Cistercians order that is called Herkenrod, six mile or seven from the city of
Leody, there was a maiden that hight Elizabeth, in whom our merciful
Lord hath shewed marvellous miracles of his blessed Passion that may
stir all Christian people to devotion. The which marvellous works of our
Lord, when I, Don Philip of Clairvaux, heard, what time that I visited
houses of mine order in that country, I gave no credence to them that
told me, till time that I came myself and saw and proved that I had not
heard the half.

---

[1] The Latin or French originals of the passages quoted in this section of
the introduction will be found in the Appendix. The only changes made in
the English quotations are orthographical.

In addition to unremitting care, success in translation depends upon the translator's knowledge and sense of his own language as much as upon his ease in the foreign tongue. The habit of many medieval English translators was to work clause by clause, substituting equivalent English words and constructions without very much regard to the sequence. Lacking any English dictionary or book of usage, they were entirely dependent on their own linguistic resources; their tendency was to use the most familiar English words and the commonest of syntactical patterns—although some regarded their work as a means of enriching the language, and a few had a larger sense than the rest of what was both possible and natural in English. The two samples that we have quoted represent the more competent and careful work: utilizing the necessary minimum of independence, the writers have managed to match Latin periods and rhetorical devices with an educated, but not newfangled, vocabulary and periodic constructions that give no offense to English usage or to an English sense of rhythm.

Such care and skill was not every translator's, as may be seen from two English versions of a single passage from Higden's *Polychronicon*, the first Trevisa's, the second that of an anonymous later writer:

A. Also that year, Conradus the emperor, Louis [the Seventh], King of France, the Earl of Flanders, and many other that had y-taken the cross to the Holy Land, chose the land way and not the water way, and passed by Hungary, and were betrayed by fraud of the Emperor of Constantinople, for many of them tasted meat, and y-meddled with lime, and died, and many others were dead by sword of war, and hanged for robbing and reaving, and lechery. Louis, King of France, came homeward out of the Holy Land, and worth [became] sick for long covetise and default of women, as leeches said, and leeches and prelates counselled him to take a wench, for he was far from the Queen. "Me is liefer to die," quoth he, "chaste, than live in spousebreach." And so he all put in God's hand, and was whole anon. In that time a clerk came to him and brought with him privilege of the Pope that he should in every cathedral church of his realm have the first benefice that voided, with the fruit and profits in the meantime. Anon he threw the letter into the fire, and said that him were liefer burn such letters than have his soul y-tormented in hell.

B. In which year, Conradus the Emperor, the King of France, the Earl of Flanders, and many other noble men took their way by Hungary to the Holy Land, which were betrayed by treason of the Emperor of Constantinople, for many men, eating bread mixed with lime, died thereof. Some men were slain, some men died for extortion and sin. Lodovicus, King of France, returned from the Holy Land, labored in great infirmity caused by continence, as physicians said; wherefore he was moved to use some maid. To whom he said, "I have liefer die in chastity than live in adultery," and after that he was recured again. A clerk bringing to the said king the privilege that he should rejoice the investitures of prelates and the fruits of their churches for their vacation, he took the letters then that his soul should be punished in hell therefor. [A clause has been dropped from the last sentence by the medieval copyist]

Between them, the two passages illustrate the more prevalent weaknesses in English prose at the time: an elementary and often hurried approach; a tendency to tackle each clausal unit separately and thus to fall either into anacoluthon, illogicality, imbalance, and incompleteness in periodic sentences, or into the paratacticism and strung-out compounds of basic English; a habit, less common than the first, of imitating Latin constructions without regard to native linguistic usage; a fashion for amplitude in vocabulary.[2]

This fashionable amplitude, or augmentation, imitated from the French and Latin and justified by a notion that English was an inadequate language in comparison with French and Latin, is not so prevalent in medieval writing as it is among Elizabethans. But many authors cannot resist the attractions of word-pairs, and a few were besotted with circumlocutions and polysyllabic Latinisms.[3]

[2] Other common defects, arising from differences between English and Latin syntax, are the ellipsis of pronoun-subjects and the introduction of them where English has no need for them.

[3] Notable as augmenters are Lydgate, Caxton, Skelton, some writers of official letters, and for different reasons, Pecock.

The beginnings of the Elizabethan cliché about the inadequacy of English are represented by Skelton's complaint that the language was rude, rusty, dull, and lacking in polished terms; by a Bishop of Durham's characterization of "our gross native language;" by Caxton's apologies for his simple style and his broad and rude English; and possibly by Trevisa's sharp contempt for the English dialects. Although Caxton testifies that some scholars preferred a simple, familiar English to the augmented language he himself used, there can be little doubt that the opinion lent strength to the rhetorical fashion for an augmented style. The opinion is superficially persuasive and even modern critics incline to accept it, with the historical explanation that English had been neglected for so long that it needed new words for ideas and practices

Not all the translations were from Latin, however; many were made from French, a language more generally familiar to Englishmen and more akin to English in its constructions. French prose begins effectively with Nicolas de Senlis's translation of the *Pseudo-Turpin Chronicle,* put into prose rather than into verse *"parceque la rime amène l'addition de mots qui ne sont pas dans le latin."* From that time, late in the twelfth century, the shift toward prose was rapid, and by the middle of the next century almost every literary genre except the lyric was amply represented in the medium. Many of these works are translations from Latin; others, such as the prose versions of the Arthurian romances and the stories of Charlemagne and his peers, are adapted from earlier poems; not a few, especially in the areas of history and religion, are original. The styles in which these books and their abundant followers are written vary greatly. The earliest works, the prose-sections of *Aucassin et Nicolete,* Robert de Clari's history, or the *Memoirs* of Philip de Novarre, for example, are not dissimilar in style to the *Anglo-Saxon Chronicle.* Much of the prose that follows, however, has benefited from Latin example, and some has suffered from it. Alain Chartier, father of French eloquence, as he has been called, writes rhetorical prose with exemplary skill; his contemporary, Christine de Pisan, is just as rhetorical but crabbed and overdense. Perhaps the finest general achievement is the narrative style found in history and romance—one unpretentious in vocabulary, loose but rarely illogical in sentence-structure, the rhythm gently flowing, the manner easy, the narrative evenly disposed between dialogue and exposition. Following the meanderings of the plots or the historical events with which this narrative

---

that had arisen since the twelfth century. How far this applies to augmentation, however, is questionable. The still-familiar French words that seemingly cascaded into English literature in the fourteenth and fifteenth centuries are likely to have been current in spoken English long before, and that English had any crying need for the more recherché importations of the augmenters or for the circumlocutions and pleonasms that accompanied them, is made dubious by the record. The evidence of the Oxford English Dictionary indicates that a great part of the Latinate loans, Elizabethan and Jacobean as well as medieval, immediately died on the vine. The overwhelmingly native vocabulary and the terseness of Hilton, Malory, Fortescue, and others also shows beyond cavil that unaugmented English was thoroughly adequate to matters for which French or Latin was the normal medium, and in the right hands could also be made eloquent.

style deals, it may often seem wordy, spineless, or naïve; yet, in fact, few styles are more lucid and assured or better adjusted to their subjects. Some of these French styles, naturally enough, are less mature and effective than others, but taken as a whole, French prose, in the two or three centuries of its continued history, had learned many of the lessons that English had yet to master.

French syntax and vocabulary presented far fewer difficulties than did Latin for an English translator, but whenever French prose was rhetorical and Latinate its impact upon a clause-by-clause translator was very much the same as Latin's. Gilbert Hay in translating Christine's Latinate sentences is betrayed into endless grammatical non-sequiturs and a polysyllabic utterance. Caxton, although he learned much in the course of his ceaseless translating, never completely mastered the syntax of a complicated sentence nor relinquished the *rhétoriqueurs'* fashion of fumosity in words.[4] Here, for example, is a sample from one of his later translations, the *Fayttes of Armes*, 1489.

Now have we in this first chapter touched shortly how wars and battles by good right emprised is a thing just, then is it to be taken heed, sith they be of right, it appertaineth to every man to do just and rightful work. If it be lawful to any person to emprise war for to keep his right, then it should seem by this reason that without to mesprise every man may so do it. But for to declare the truth to them that in this point might err, it is to wit that without to make any doubt, after the determination of right and of the laws, it appertaineth to none to emprise war or battle for any manner case, but if it be to kings, dukes, and other lords terriens, which be merely principal heads of jurisdictions temporal, ne to a baron whatsomever he be, ne to any other, be he never so great, without license, congee, and volunty of his sovereign lord.

Christine's French is complicated enough: Caxton's literalness has produced a confusion which resembles the spider's web after the bee has crashed into it.

More competent in adapting a balanced and rhythmical style to English linguistic structures is the anonymous translator of Chartier's *Quadrilogue Invéctif*. Only the Gallic use of the definite

---

[4] Caxton's excuse for his inadequacy is that he was brought up in Kent, where English was rude, and that he had been so long abroad that he had almost forgotten English. It is difficult to agree with scholars who accept the explanation: adults who go abroad just don't forget their native tongues, especially when they are associated with fellow-countrymen, as Caxton was.

article (and the chanting eloquence of the whole) would betray the fact that the following specimen—the reply of the People to the Aristocracy—was not originally composed in English:

> Thou sayest that I am cause of this cursed war and that I have purchased it through the impatience of the high prosperity of peace. Thou sayest that my mad error and the parties that I have holden be causers of this confusion and unhappy mischief. Wherefor, I answer thee, that the folly of the poor people is founded upon the outrage of the great men, and that the sins and disordinate governance be descended from the greatest to the lowest. For, as the princes and high men maintain themselves in their living and estate, the people taketh of them rule and example, be it good or ill, of peace or of slander.

As with Latin, however, it was the narrative style that translators found most comfortable: its simpler vocabulary and its modest constructions, part-way between basic paratacticism and the extended hypotacticism of the rhetoricians, presented a minimum of linguistic problems. Even Caxton learned to do quite well with such a prose, and the translator of the *Book of the Knight of Tour-Landry,* helped by his greater independence, does excellently. In average example we may quote a passage from the anonymous *Merlin,* chosen partly because it is so close to the French and partly because of its relevance to Malory:

> Now saith the story, that when the twelve messengers were departed from the king Arthur, the king and his barony abided still, full wroth and angry for the mandment of Luce the emperor.
>
> And Merlin said, "Sir, send for your people hastily, for the emperor appareleth him right fast."
>
> "Merlin, friend," said the king, "I shall meet with him sooner than he would."
>
> "He shall you meet," said Merlin, "to his damage! And abide here in joy, for I go to make the message to the barons."
>
> With that he vanished, that Arthur ne wist where he became. And Merlin went first into Orcany and did the message to the King Lot: that within fifteen days he should be at Logres with all his power. And then Merlin departed.
>
> Wherefore should I make you long tale? He warned all the princes and barons that of the King Arthur were holding to be the fifteenth day at Logres, save only the King Ban of Benoic and the King Bohors of Gannes. And after that he returned again and found the King Arthur in

his chamber, and said, "Your message is done to all the barons, and they shall be ready here from hence fifteen days."

The French prose that determines this English style is also the source for Malory's *Le Morte Darthur*, and it would be a confident judge who could be sure that any short sample of the anonymous translation was not Malory's work. This is not to deny that Malory's own tastes and his technique of drastic abbreviation by jumping from one key statement to the next did not lend distinctive qualities to his book and his style: a somewhat synoptic narrative that stresses action more than description or analysis and so achieves greater energy and directness (and also occasional confusion); an emphatic manner that accompanies his fondness for front-positioning adverbials; slightly more dialogue; a less involved characterization and interpretation; an Englishry that proceeds from these simplifications as well as from his strong preference (despite a sprinkling of Gallicisms) for native vocabulary; and a personal cast of language that comes from the reiteration of favorite words and phrases. Such traits, however, become obvious only with extended reading. The bases of his style, like the matter itself, come from the French romances[5]—the forms of the sentences and their continuing even rhythms, the simplicity in diction, the ordering of events and their disposition between exposition and dialogue—these are almost as much indebted to the French sources as is the style of the unadventurous translation of the *Merlin*, as the following random quotation will show:

Now saith the tale, after Sir Gawain departed he rode many journeys, both toward and froward. And at the last he came to the abbey where Sir Galahad had the white shield. And there Sir Gawain learned the way to sue after Sir Galahad, and so he rode to the abbey where Melyas lay sick. And there Sir Melyas told Sir Gawain of the marvellous adventures that Sir Galahad did.

"Certes," said Sir Gawain. "I am not happy that I took not the way that he went. For, an I may meet with him, I will not depart from him lightly, for all marvellous adventures Sir Galahad enchieveth."

"Sir," said one of the monks, "He will not of your fellowship."

"Why so?" said Sir Gawain.

"Sir," said he, "for ye be wicked and sinful, and he is full blessed."

[5] It will be evident that I am of Andrew Lang's and W. P. Ker's opinion about the source of Malory's style, not of Eugène Vinaver's.

So, right as they thus talked, there came in riding Sir Gareth, and then they made great joy, either of other. And on the morn they heard mass and so departed, and by the way they met with Sir Ywain le Avoutres. And there Sir Ywain told Sir Gawain that he had met with none adventures sith he departed from the court.

Even though separation of writers and small distribution of their works precluded the development in the late middle ages of a body of theory, convention, and linguistic usage, extensive practice of translation must have played some part in the maturing of English prose which may be detected here and there. In the sixteenth century, certainly, when printing vastly enlarged the reading public and so broke down the writer's separation, translation was a major means in the development of the techniques of English composition.

As for the original English prose of the later middle ages, it would be impossible in most cases to prove that any of the contemporary translations was a model. But that does not preclude a probability that translation of another kind, the processes of imitating or expanding from Latin or French prose, was an important influence. Almost without exception, the original prose-writers of the time were competent in Latin or French—all habitual readers in those languages, some of them writers.[6] And behind their writings usually lie similar works in foreign tongues. Much of Nicholas Love's *Life of Christ*, one of the most eloquent pieces of medieval prose, follows the style of its Latin original; but the abundant interwoven commentary, which is Love's own composition, involves no break in the texture, for it maintains the same rhythm, sentence structures, and lexicon.

Sir John Fortescue's treatise on government is adapted from the Latin work he wrote on the same subject, and although his vocabulary is predominantly English, his sentence patterns and rhetorical devices bear the stigmata of their origin. Capgrave, reputed to be the most learned Englishman of his time, wrote mostly in Latin prose and this long experience is evident in the more developed sections of his English history. Caxton's prefaces, when they

---

[6] The obvious exceptions, Julian of Norwich and Margery Kempe, are more apparent than real, for it seems likely that their lives were written, not by themselves, but by confessors who may have been familiar with the many similar documents in Latin.

are not translations from French prefaces, are manifestly in the rhetorical, periodic style that Frenchmen considered proper to such occasions—his normal cumbrousness bears witness to the difficulties with which the style presented him. Concerning Pecock, no critic has ever doubted that his dense style, with its Latinisms and neologisms, its many-claused sentences, and its mathematical organization, is a result of his long study and writing of Latin theology. Among his thirty lost works, ten were certainly in Latin, and perhaps seven more.

As for the fourteenth-century mystics—Rolle, Hilton, and the anonymous author of *The Cloud of Unknowing*—although it is often difficult to pin their works to particular sources, numberless references and quotations testify to their familiarity with Latin devotional treatises, particularly those of Augustine, Gregory, Bernard, Dionysius, Bonaventura, and the Victorines. The author of *The Cloud* in all likelihood was also the translator of Dionysius's *Mystica Theologica*. Rolle wrote abundantly in Latin as well as in English. And although their styles owe something to a native tradition from the *Ancren Riwle*, they probably owe a great deal, in their several varieties, to the prose of Latin theologians as well. Rolle, at least, hints so himself, when he declares in his English Psalter: "In this work I seek no strange English, but lightest and commonest and such that is most like unto the Latin."[7]

To support these claims specifically is not easy: a general or instinctive familiarity with rhetorical device, a natural or trained logic or associationalism might produce Latinate effects without deliberate imitation. But, apart from the probability raised by the Latin compositions of the writers with whom we are now concerned, it might be possible to suggest that they approached Eng-

---

[7] Chambers' famous argument for the continuity of a native English prose from Aelfric to More, winning as it is, is not quite so dispassionate as most critics, particularly in America, have thought it. In part it is an apologia against attacks upon the philological approach to literature that found support in *The Teaching of English in England*, 1921, with its assertion that it might be sensible to begin with Chaucer and to study foreign literatures rather than Anglo-Saxon as a background. In other part it is a manifestation of the religious love and patriotism that went into Chambers' work on More and on the *Ancrene Riwle*. It is through these lenses that he looks at early English prose, and if they explain much of the attractiveness of the essay they also explain some of its idiosyncratic emphases and its many blind spots.

lish writing through habits formed on Latin by showing the fre-
quency with which they fall victim to the same difficulties that
beset translators: how to contrive grammatical balance, how to
sidestep the vernacular tendency toward paratactic constructions,
how to maintain logical subordinations and to secure necessary
emphases throughout a lengthy sentence. To cite an example from
one of the better writers, this is the way that Nicholas Love begins
his book on the life of Christ:

And so forasmuch as in this book be contained divers imaginations on
Christ's life, the which life, fro the beginning unto the ending evermore
blessed and withouten sin, passing all lives of all other saints, as for a singular prerogative may worthily be cleped the blessed life of Jesu Christ.
The which also, because that it may not be fully described as the lives
of other saints, but in the manner of likeness as the image of a man's
face is shewed in the mirror, therefore, as for a pertinent name to this
book it may skillfully be cleped *The Mirror of the Blessed Life of Jesu
Christ.*

So stumbling a style (fortunately not common in Love's book) is
akin to Caxton's when in his prefaces he is imitating the lofty constructions and vocabulary of French forewords.

Another line of proof would be to compare translation with
original writing. Instances of exact correspondence in subject
matter are not common, but here is part of a fifteenth-century
translation of Rolle's *Emendatio Vitae* and also Rolle's own English treatment of the topic in *The Form of Living:*

A. There be three degrees of the love of Christ, in the which he that
is chosen to love styeth [rises] up from one of them to the other. The
first is called the degree that may not be overcome; the second degree
is that may not be departed; and the third is a singular degree. Then is
love in the first degree when it may not be overcome with other loves,
but casteth away gladly all things that should let it. It slaketh all fleshly
desires, and it suffereth patiently all manner of disease for Christ's love.
All manner travail is light to a lover, and travail may not be better overcome than by love. Then is love in the second degree when a soul is
wonderly burnt in love, so that it leaneth and cleaveth upon Christ with
a steadfast thought that it may not be departed from Him. It suffereth
Him not to be a moment out of mind, but it bindeth Him so to it as with
a rope. It desireth to be bound in His love that the fetters of deadly
kind might be broken, that it might see Him clearly whom it loveth and

desireth; and he that is in this degree worshippeth and loveth this name Jesu so much that it resteth alway in his heart and in his soul.

B. Three degrees of love I shall tell thee, for I would that thou might win to the highest. The first degree is called insuperable, the second, inseparable, the third is singular. Thy love is insuperable when no thing that is contrary to God's love overcomes it, but is stalwart against all fandings [temptations] and stable, whether thou be in ease or in anguish, or in heal or in sickness, so that thee think that thou would not for all the world, to have it without end, wrath God any time; and thee were liefer, if either should be, to suffer all the pain and woe that might come to any creature ere thou would do the thing that should mispay him. In this manner shall the love be insuperable, that nothing may down bring, but springing on height. Blessed is he or she that is in this degree; but yet are they blesseder that might hold this degree and win into the other, that is inseparable.

Inseparable is thy love when all thy heart and thy thought and thy might is so wholly, so entirely, and so perfectly fastened, set, and stabled in Jesu Christ that thy thought comes never off him, never departed fro him, out-taken sleeping; and as soon as thou wakens thy heart is on Him, saying *Ave Maria* or *Gloria tibi Domine* or *Pater Noster* or *Miserere mei Deus* if thou have been tempted on thy sleep, or thinking on his love and his loving, as thou did waking, when thou may no time forget him, whatso thou dost or sayst, then is thy love inseparable.

Rolle's original English version has been expanded by rhetorical devices, but the sentence patterns and their rhythms, the vocabulary, and the composition of the whole are much the same as in the independent translation from his Latin. Manifestly, his Latin composition determined the form of his English discussion. And where similar means are available for other writers, similar results can be shown: Capgrave's Latin history is close in style to the developed sections of his English history; Caxton's own prefaces continue the style of the ones he translated; Fortescue's *De Natura Legis Naturae* and *De Laudibus Legum Angliae* contain arguments that are presented in very much the same form and manner in *The Governance of England;* the prose of the original preface to the *Life of St. Elizabeth* and the translated life is the same, though the preface is less assured.

So far, this introduction has been concerned with fundamental aspects of prose as an instrument: the problems presented by the

language, the sources from which writers sought solutions, the social status of prose. But these aspects are not the only ones of importance; the construction and rhythm of prose throughout a
whole work, the matter and the spirit in which it is treated are no
less significant.

It has been argued that the practice of reading aloud and the
resultant slow progress through a book were responsible for the
division of medieval books into short chapters and for the seeming
non-sequiturs that sometimes characterize their sequence. More
significant, however, is the obvious fact that the over-all constructions and the over-all rhythms of medieval prose differ with the
subjects and the traditions that affect them. History, though it occasionally takes on integrated patterns, is traditionally a journal-
istic form, organized as annals or chronicles, with no unit larger
than the matter of a year or event, the entries assembled like un-
sorted beads on the string of time. Short stories are set out simply
but clearly: chronological in arrangement of the detail, they usually move to an end-climax without delay of any kind.

Romances and other long narratives occasionally employ the
technique of the short story, merely amplifying the detail and the
embroidery of settings and occasions, but often they follow a complicated technique. One hero or one event suggests others, the
narrative moves from highway to byways and, although it always
comes back, its progress inevitably strikes the modern reader as a
casual meander; the manner is even less direct when there are two
main heroes, two main highways that cross and recross and only
eventually unite. Casual as it may now seem and subject as it is to
disproportion and blind alleys, the technique is deliberate and has
its own unity and rhythm, its objective being a larger human scene
and a wider range of values than could be achieved by straight-
line narrative. Biography varies considerably: saints' lives con-
centrate upon miraculous events, and many merely string together
the more wonderful stories that were associated with the individual heroes; biographies of more recent subjects share this emphasis and have a tendency toward episodic construction, but they
are usually fuller, more balanced, and more complete in their
pattern of birth to death.

The loose construction which is common in narrative genres is
not so apparent in the argumentative forms. Sermons are built on

the firm patterns prescribed by the preaching manuals, and even if pedagogical repetition and illustrative stories hold up the progress, the sequence of the argument is normally logical and clear. Religious handbooks such as *Vices and Virtues* are rigidly ordered on the scheme of the moral values and their recognized subdivisions, and although the sections differ in length and completeness of detail, the design is transparent, even mathematical. In a less mechanical way, this schematic pattern is characteristic of the devotional treatises: chapter by chapter they take up the sins and virtues, the active and contemplative lives, and the steps on the ladder of contemplation, each unit self-contained but leading logically to the next. And in secular matters, the philosophy of Boethius and the political treatises of Bonet, Christine, Chartier, Fortescue, and John of Ireland proceed in well-ordered fashion from generalizations or definitions to the relevant details and summations.

Just as the lowliness of prose in medieval England and the modesty of its objective preclude anything manifestly original in language or form, just so they ensure that prose is seldom a vehicle for anything essentially new in thought or imagination. Montaigne's ideal of "a natural, simple, and unaffected speech . . . so written as it is spoken, and such upon the paper as it is in the mouth" is approached more nearly by these stylistically self-effacing medieval writers than by those Elizabethans who strut and preen in prose. Their syntax, vocabulary, and idiom is largely colloquial and of their own time; nouns and verbs predominate over adjectives and adverbs; deliberate archaism is almost non-existent; and writers who ape the circumlocutions, ornamentations, and magniloquent latinity of the *florida verborum venustas* are fortunately few. Nevertheless, no one would assert that medieval plainness on unambitious topics was equal in vitality to the linguistic excess that Elizabethans favored in their brave new world of ideas and fancies.

Such negative generalizations, however, are not the whole story, particularly for the general reader. Much medieval English prose was secondhand; but secondhandedness is seldom apparent to readers who do not know the originals. Topics that may seem clichés to the scholar whose life is devoted entirely to reading medieval books may have been fresher to a less sated medieval audience, and to the modern amateur these topics may appear strange and rare. And such a work as *Mandeville's Travels* is witness that interesting matter and personal commitment may convert a trivial style and rambling arrangement into a thing of delight. Among the medieval writers who are represented in this volume only a few can be said to be excellent stylists or in any way original, yet to the generous taste by which literature lives few of them can seem dull. The sturdiness with which Fortescue upholds the habits of Englishmen; the urbanity of the Knight of the Tower's treatise on social ethics; Mandeville's eager curiosity about strange lands and strange people; the contentiousness of Pastons; John Arderne's self-satisfaction; the strident energy of Margery Kempe; the controlled passion of William Thorpe's defence; Thomas Usk's sham elegance; the accepted wonder of the saints' lives; the commitment to heavenly love that is quiet or fervent in so many devotional treatises; Pecock's intellectualism; the gusto that goes into an anonymous description of a quintessential cure-all; or the vigor and nostalgia that permeate Malory's romance of chivalry—these and other personal attitudes lend individual colors to matters which are not only interesting of themselves but may also be romantically colored by the patina of time.

The present collection, since it is the first of its kind, bears the pioneer duty of representing medieval English prose in most of its varieties. More than most books that deal with a large subject, it enjoys the advantage that its subject is not very well known, and the compiler's hope is that the samplings will give enough pleasure to lead the reader into further explorations and finer discriminations.

Historians

◄◊◊►

AFTER THE *Anglo-Saxon Chronicle* petered out in 1154, more than two centuries passed before historians readopted English prose. During those centuries, and even in the fifteenth century, although some romantic chronicles were composed in English verse, the linguistic medium that historians normally used for the recording and interpreting of *res gestae* was Latin. Historical writing in English prose is resumed with translation of major Latin works, such as John Trevisa's 1387 version of Higden's *Polychronicon,* and then, by slow degrees, with original works of popular type.

An outstanding exception to this general practice is the incomplete *Chronicle of England* that was composed by John Capgrave (1393–1464) towards the end of his life. Born at Lynn in Norfolk, where English prose was beginning to flourish, and educated at Cambridge apparently, Capgrave passed his life as an Austin-Friar at Lynn, and in his last years was director of the friary there. On the basis of numerous books in both Latin and English, he was often described as the most learned Englishman of his times. The paradox that so learned a man should have written history in English may be explained by its being produced, like others of his English works, for local patrons who knew no Latin.

Beginning with the Creation and general world history, the chronicle focuses on England after the Anglo-Saxon conquest; from Henry III's accession English affairs are its major concern. The exposition varies similarly: the earliest section consists of brief notes taken from Martinus Polonus's very popular epitome of world history; for a few decades before 1417, when it breaks off, it is a full and independent report on events connected with Henry IV, Henry V, Wycliffe, and the Lollards. In these later sections the writing is full and cultivated, highly personal but judicious in opinion, vigorous in description, pleasingly varied in the sentence constructions. Our selection is the entry for 1415, the year of the great English victory at Agincourt.

Much less sophisticated in outlook and style is *The Brut,* a full survey of English history that, to judge by the many manuscripts, was the most popular English chronicle of the fifteenth century. From the literary viewpoint, however, it is surpassed in interest by several minor chronicles, some of them local records compiled for London and the larger provincial towns, others partisan narratives set down by persons who took part in the civil wars. Among the liveliest is the chronicle that is attributed to William Gregory, a skinner who was Mayor of London in 1451-52. Among its original sections, the report on Jack Cade's rebellion which has been chosen for this anthology is outstanding for the sprightliness of its narrative, the downright, merchant-based opinions, and the vigorous, colloquial, and at times emotionally incoherent language.

There is no classic among these English prose-chronicles: they are too derivative, too close to journalism, too undeliberate for that. Yet, like the old *Anglo-Saxon Chronicle,* they sometimes respond to the excitement of particular events or passions and, aided by an unsophisticated, direct language, contrive to fix the spirit of their time.

John Capgrave

"CHRONICLE OF ENGLAND"

IN THE YEAR of the world 6611 and of our Lord Jesu 1413, was Henry the Fifth crowned at Westminster on Passion Sunday. And after his coronation he was even turned unto another man and all his motions inclined to virtue . . .

[handwritten note: Shakesp. H. IV I & 2 and H. V Henry gave up Falstaff]

In this same time [1414] the Lollards, that condemned the preaching of the prophets, the Gospel, and the apostles, set up bills on the church doors, in which bills was contained that a hundred thousand were ready for to rise and destroy all *t*hem that would not consent to *t*heir sect and *t*heir opinions. They trusted much on the wit and on the power of a certain knight they clept Sir John Oldcastle. He was clept Cobham, for he had wedded a woman nigh of the lord's kin. A strong man in battle he was, but a great heretic and a great enemy to the church. For his cause, the archbishop gathered a council at London, for he sent out priests for to preach which were not admitted by no Ordinary, and he was present at *t*heir sermons, and all they that said again*st* his priests was he ready to smite with his sword.

[handwritten left margin note: Falstaff link]

[handwritten bottom note: Lollards too straitlaced for ordinary men — like Puritan in Shakesp's time]

For these causes and many more because he was a knight of the king's household, the archbishop complained of him to the king. After much labour to his amendment, the king wrote to the archbishop that he should summon him to appear and answer. The knight lay that time in his castle, clept Cowling. The messenger that was sent was warned that he should not enter his castle but if he had leave. Then entered into the castle one John Butler, that was Usher of the King's Chamber, and he asked the knight whether the summoner should come to him or he should send him the letter. The knight refused both. Then was the summons set on the monastery doors in Rochester, but three mile fro him. And at day assigned, the archbishop, in the castle of Leeds, cursed him for contumacy and great fautor [supporter] of heretics.

After this, on a Saturday after the feast of St. Matthew, apostle and evangelist, the archbishop sat in Paul's chapter-house, and with him Harry of Winchester and Richard of London, bishops. And Sir Robert Morley—at commandment of the king—then keeper of the Tower, brought this knight Oldcastle unto the presence of these bishops.

There the bishop rehearsed that for contumacy he stood accursed, and if he would meekly submit him to the church he would assoil [absolve] him. Oldcastle stood and would none ask, but took out of his bosom a bill indented, and when he had read it, took it to the bishops.

Then said the archbishop, "Lo, Sir John. Here be many good things in your bill, but ye must answer to other things that be put on you, touching the sacrament of the altar and the power of the church and much other thing."

He said to this that he would give no other answer than was written in his bill.

Then the archbishop took him certain articles in a bill, to which he assigned him that he should answer on the Monday following. And when the day was come, the archbishop inquired of him if he would be assoiled after the form of the church. He said nay; he looked after no absolution but of God. And of the sacrament of the altar, he said thus: "Even as Christ, while He went here, was God and Man—the manhood might men see but not the godhead —so in this sacrament is Christ's body and bread. The bread may men see but not Christ's body." He said more, "That the determination of the church and the doctors, that say the reverse, are plainly against holy scripture."

For the sacrament of penance, he said: "That what man is in grievous sin and could not rise fro his sin, it is full necessary that he have a wise priest to tell him the manner of his amendment. But that a man should be shriven to his proper priest, or to another priest, it is no need. For contrition without confession purgeth all sin."

For worshipping of the cross, he said: "That Body that hung on the cross should be worshipped, and nothing but He." And when they asked him what worship he would do to the image on the cross, he said he would wipe it and keep it clean.

Then they asked him what he said of the pope. He said, "The pope is antichrist; bishops be his members; and friars be his tail."

The archbishop saw no other amendment in this man, condemned him for a heretic, and left him to the secular hand. And then went he to the king and told him all the process, praying the king to grant him life forty days, that he might do penance.

But this indulgence turned unto great mischief. For within those forty days he brake out of the Tower and sent letters unto his sect. For all that time, fro his evasion about Michaelmas unto the Epiphany, he made him strong to destroy the king and many other. And they that were gathered to go with him, if they made question to what intent they should rise, this answer had they: "It skills you not [no reason], so ye have good wages and truly paid."

The king kept Christmas at Eltham; and Cobham, with his retinue, had thought to fulfill his intent. The king was warned of this matter by certain men that had conscience [knowledge] and were of counsel with Cobham, and suddenly the king removed unto Westminster.

The Lollards were warned that they should gather in St. Giles's Field, for there should come to them out of London 50,000, as was behight [promised] them. But the king was ware of all this, and commanded London Gates to be sperred [shut] and kept. He sent out eke [also] men-of-arms by divers ways, which apposed [challenged] them that came running in haste, "Whither they should go?" And they said, "To Cobham." Thus were taken and slain thousands. The king was in the field soon after midnight. This espied Cobham. He fled, and many with him. Many of his

were taken and hung and drawn and burnt. One was there of
Dunstable, a special scholar of this sect—they clept him William
Morley. Oldcastle had behight him that he should be a knight.
And in proof of that behest, they found with him two steeds and
gilt spurs in his bosom . . .

In this time, [1415], after many treaties betwixt this land and
France—and nothing that they proferred was according to reason
—the king made ready his ships at Southampton, to speed him to
his conquest. And there were three notable men that had con-
spired his death. One was Harry Scrope, on whom the king
trusted most and by whose counsel all thing was done. Sober was
the man in work and cheer, and under that hypocrisy had he a
full venomous heart. He had a fellow consenting unto him, Richard, Earl of Cambridge, and Thomas Gray, a knight of the North.
But ere they brought about their conclusion, they were detected,
condemned by their peers, and dead . . .

The king with his navy took the sea, and landed at Caux, with
a thousand ships and five hundred. He entered the land on a
Wednesday which was the vigil of Assumption of Our Lady
[August 14], and on the Saturday after he laid siege to the town
of Harfleur, he by land, the ships by the water. And this siege
lasted till the Sunday before Michaelmas. In the Tuesday before
that Sunday, the lords that were keepers of the town sent out a
man unto the Duke of Clarence, praying him entirely that they
might treat with the king, and that he should make his gunners to
cease, for it was to them intolerable. The names of them were
these: the Lord Goncourt, the Lord Stuteville, the Lord Boute-
ville, and the Lord Clare.

The Duke of Clarence spake for them to the king, and the king
sent to them the Earl of Dorset and Sir Thomas Erpingham to
know their desire. They prayed the king meekly that he should
cease of his shot unto Sunday, and if the King of France came not
by that time they should deliver him the town. They proferred
him eke that, if he would give them leave and safeconduct to ride
to the King of France, they should lay pledges twenty-two knights,
with the best of the town.

So the Lord Hacqueville and twelve persons had leave to ride
through the host. And on the Wednesday, early, came out of the
town the lords, twenty-two knights, squires, and burgesses of the
town. And against them the king sent a solemn procession of prel-

ates and priests, and the sacrament, and after following, lords, knights, and the people. When they had made a solemn oath, they went to meat into the king's tent, but they saw not the king. After meat, they were commanded for to go with certain lords that should keep them. On the Sunday came the messengers again, without any help of king or dauphin. Therefore, they that were in the town submitted them unto the king, and they that were with the king, sent by the French king to keeping of the town, remained as prisoners.

In this siege many men died of cold in nights and fruit-eating—eke of stink of carrions [corpses]. He died there, Master Richard Courtney, Bishop of Norwich, in whose place the monks chose John Wakering. There died Michael de la Pole, The Duke of Clarence, the Earl of March, the Earl Arundel, and the Earl Marshal took great sickness there.

The king, after this conquest, purposed to go to Calais, with footmen for the most part. For all his host was not accounted passing eight thousand, so many were left sick at Harfleur. Marvel it was that he, with so few, durst go through all the thick woods in that country. For the French party in all this time had made an host of an 140,000. Victuals were kept fro them, that eighteen days they had walnuts for bread. And flesh had they some; but their drink was water.

So, in the 23rd day of October, the hosts met, not a mile asunder. The king comforted greatly his men, that they should trust in God, for their cause was rightful. The French part stood on the hill and we in the vale. Betwixt them was a land new-harrowed, where was evil footing. Short for to say, the field fell unto the king and the French lost it, for all their number and their pride.

There were dead, the Duke of Lausanne, the Duke of Brabant, the Duke of Bavaria, five earls, the Constable eke of France, and a hundred lords; knights and squires, 4069; the common people was not numbered. These were taken: the Duke of Orleans, the Duke of Bourbon, the Earls of Eu and Vendome, Arthur, the Duke's brother of Brittany which claimeth to be Earl of Richmond, and a knight they clept Boucicaut, Marshal of France. And others were taken there, of coat-armour, into a seven hundred. On our side were dead: Edward, Duke of York; the Earl of Suffolk; four knights, a squire, Davy Gamme; of the commons, twenty-eight.

In the time of the battle, the brigands of the French side took the king's carriage and led it away, in which they found the king's crown. They made the bells to ring and men for to sing, "Te Deum laudamus," telling verily that the king was dead. But within a few hours after, their joy was changed.

The king rode to Calais, and over the sea to Dover. And in the 23rd day of November came to London, and there was received in the best manner.

William Gregory

CHRONICLE

[1450] AND AFTER THAT the commons of Kent arose with certain other shires, and they chose them a captain, the which captain compelled all the gentles to arise with him. And at the end of the Parliament they came with a great might and a strong host unto the Black Heath beside Greenwich, the number of 46,000. And there they made a field, diked and staked well about as it be in the land of war, save only they kept order among them, for as good was Jack Robin as John at the Oak, for all were as high as pigsfeet, unto the time that they should come and speak with such states and messengers as were sent unto them. Then they put all their power unto the man that named him captain of all their host, and there they abode certain days to the coming of the king fro the Parliament at Leicester.

And then the king sent unto the captain divers lords, both spiritual and temporal, to wit and to have knowledge of that great assembling and gathering of that great and misadvised fellowship —the captain of them sending word again unto the king that it was for the weal of him our sovereign lord, and of all the realm, and for to destroy the traitors being about him, with other divers points, that they would see that it were in short time amended. Upon which answer that the king, thither sent by his lords, did make a cry in the king's name of England that all the king's liegemen of England should avoid [quit] the field. And upon the night after they were all voided and a-gone.

Upon the morn after, the king rode armed-at-all-pieces from St. John's-beside-Clerkenwell through London, and with him the most part of temporal lords of this land of England, in their best array. After that, they were, every lord with his retinue, to the number of 10,000 persons, ready as they all should have gone to battle into any land of Christendom, with bends [heraldic devices] above their harness that every lord should be known from other. And in the forward, as they would have followed the captain, was slain Sir Humfray Stafford and William Stafford, squire, one the manliest man of all this realm of England, with many more other of mean persons at Sevenoaks in Kent, in their outraging fro their host of our sovereign lord's the king, Harry the Sixth. And the king lodged that night at Greenwich, and soon after every lord with his retinue rode home into their country.

And after that, upon the first day of July, the same captain came again as the Kentish men said; but it was another that named himself the captain, and he come to the Black Heath, and upon the morrow he come with a great host into Southwark, and at the White Hart he took his lodging. And upon the morrow, that was the Friday, against even, they smote asunder the ropes of the draught-bridge and fought sore *and* manly, and many a man was murthered and killed in that conflict—I wot not what to name it for the multitude of riff-raff. And then they entered into the city of London as men that had been half beside their wit, and in that furyness they went, as they said, for the commonweal of the realm of England, even straight unto a merchant's place named Philip Malpas of London. If it were true as they surmised after their doing, I remit me to ink and paper—*Deus scit et ego non*—but well I wot that every ill beginning most commonly hath an ill ending, and every good beginning hath the very good ending. *Proverbium: Felix principium finem facit esse beatum.* And that Philip Malpas was alderman, and they despoiled him and bare away much goods of his and in special much money, both of silver and gold, the value of a notable sum, and in special of merchandise, as of tin, wood, madder, and alum, with great quantity of woollen cloth and many rich jewels, with other notable stuff of feather beds, bedding, nappery, and many a rich cloth of arras, to the value of a notable sum—*nescio, set Deus omnia scit.*

And in the evening they went with their simple captain to his lodging, but a certain *number* of his simple and rude meinie abode there all the night, weening to them that they had wit and wisdom for to have guided or put in guiding all England, all so soon as they had got the city of London by a mishap of cutting of two sorry cords that now be altered, and made two strong chains of iron unto the draught-bridge of London. But they had other men with them, as well of London as of their own party, and by them of one part and of that other part they left nothing unsought and they searched all that night.

And in the morn he came in again, that sorry and simple and rebellious captain, with his meinie. That was Saturday and it was also a Saint Martin's Day, the dedication of Saint Martin's in the Vintry, the fourth day of July. And then divers quests were y-sommed [gathered] at the Guildhall, and there Robert Horne, being alderman, was arrested and brought into Newgate. And that same day William Crowmer, squire and sheriff of Kent, was beheaded in the field without Aldgate at the mile's-end beside Clopton's place. And another man that was named John Bayley was beheaded at the White-Chapel. And the same day, afternoon, was beheaded in Cheap, afore the Standard, Sir James Fynes, being that time the Lord Saye and Great Treasurer of England, the which was brought out of the Tower of London unto the Guildhall. And there of divers treasons he was examined, of which he acknowledged of the death of that notable and famous prince the Duke of Gloucester. And then they brought him unto the Standard in Cheap, and there he received his chevise [business] and his death. And so forth all the three heads that day smitten off were set upon the bridge of London, and the two other heads taken down that stood upon the London Bridge before. And at the coming of the captain into Southwark, he let smite off the head of a strong thief that was named Haywardyn, and upon the morrow, the Sunday, at high mass time, he let to be headed a man of Hampton, a squire, the which was named Thomas Mayne.

And that same even, London did arise and came out upon them at ten of the bell, being that time their captains the good old Lord Scales and Mathew Gough. And from that time unto the morrow, eight of *the* bell, they were ever fighting upon London Bridge, and many a man was slain and cast in Thames, harness, body, and all. And among the press was slain Mathew Gough and John

Sutton, alderman. And the same night, anon after midnight, the captain of Kent did fire the draught-bridge of London, and before that time he brake both King's Bench and the Marshalsea and let out all the prisoners that were in them.

And upon the morrow betimes came my lord the Cardinal of York and my lord of Canterbury and the Bishop of Winchester, and they treated between the Lord Scales and that captain, that the sore conflict and skirmish was ceased; and gave the captain and his meinie a general charter for him and for all his company in his name, calling himself John Mortimer—and through that means they were avoided, the most part. And the sixth day after that, the Saturday at even, the three heads were taken down off London Bridge, that is to say, the Lord Saye's head, Crowmer's, and the bailey's, and the other two heads set up again that stood upon London Bridge before; and the bodies with heads were buried at the Greyfriars at London.

And upon the 12th day of July, the year aforesaid, the said captain was cried and proclaimed traitor, by the name of John Cade, in divers places of London and also in Southwark, with many more, that what man might or would bring the said John Cade to the king, quick or dead, should have of the king a thousand mark. Also, whosomever might bring or would bring any of his chief counsellors or of affinity that kept any state or rule or governance under the said false captain, John Cade, he should have to his reward of the king five hundred mark.

And that day was that false traitor the Captain of Kent y-taken and slain in the Weald in the country of Sussex, and upon the morrow he was brought in a car all naked, and at the Hart in Southwark there the car was made stand still, *so that* the wife of the house might see him if it were the same man or no that was named the Captain of Kent, for he was lodged within her house in his peevish time of his misrule and rising. And then he was had into the King's Bench, and there he lay from Monday at even unto the Thursday next following at even, and within the King's Bench the said captain was beheaded and quartered, and the same day drawn upon a hurdle in pieces, with the head between his breast, from the King's Bench throughout Southwark, and then over London Bridge, and then through London unto Newgate. And then his head was taken and set upon London Bridge.

Biographers and Autobiographers

☙🙐❧

THE SECULAR BIOGRAPHY, although it constitutes a major element in many chronicles, rarely appears in medieval literature as an independent form. Latin and French lives of great rulers—Charlemagne, Alfred, St. Louis and their like—tend toward hagiography. In English, biographical sketches of kings and magnates are embodied in most chronicles, but with the loss of Caxton's translation of a life of Robert, Earl of Gloucester, there is no independent secular biography before Sir Thomas More's life of Richard III: merely John Shirley's translation of a short Latin report on the assassination of James I of Scotland and some passages in the first English life of Henry V that may be near-contemporary reminiscences.

Secular autobiographies were even fewer, and in English they were non-existent. But just as chronicles reveal biographical interest, just so dedications and prefaces to prose-works often reflect the autobiographical fashion that is so marked in poetry of the later middle ages—Caxton is a notable example. Sometimes such prefaces verge on being informal short autobiographies, and one of these provides our first selection, the preface to John Arderne's *Fistula in Ano*. This medical treatise, with its preface, was written in Latin in 1376, when Arderne was sixty-nine, and translated early in the fifteenth century. Before going into the grisly details of his subject, the author sketches his career and appropriates, with abundant additions from his own experience, the criteria of a good physician that appear in Lanfranc's treatise on surgery. The whole introduction forms a self-contented self-portrait of a medical specialist —its pungent, drumfire short sentences, with hardly a word wasted, admirably suited to the bumptious shrewdness of the writer.

Literary concern with private lives was just beginning in the late middle ages, but in religious matters it had a long history. For over a thousand years it had been the church's habit to dim pagan heroes and enhearten the converted with stories of the sufferings and victories of the soldiers of Christ, the martyrs, saints, and champions of the church. Singly and in collections, there is an abundance of these short biographies in English, the outstanding prose-collections being two versions of the *Legenda Aurea*—one an anonymous translation made early in the fifteenth century; the second compiled by Caxton on the basis of a Latin text, a French translation, the earlier English version, and the Vulgate Bible.

To represent this characteristic medieval compilation, we choose from Caxton's text of the earlier translation of the *Legenda* the *Life of Saint Thomas à Beckett*. This selection is more nearly contemporary with its subject than most saints' lives and comes closer to our own notions of biography. The narrative is comprehensive and logically organized, the technique is familiar and realistic, the theme is medieval politics. Nevertheless, in its focus upon martyrdom and miracle, its black-and-white characterization, its objective of upholding clerical values, it is at one with the rest of hagiography.

The translation from which this life-sketch is taken has been ascribed, unconvincingly, to Osbern Bokenham. Whoever did the job was an able writer: some admirers even put him on Malory's pedestal as a master of narrative prose. Here, too, is assured sentence construction, economy and vigor in phraseology, firm rhythms, and a nice disposition of exposition and dialogue. Over a long stretch, the short sentences, mostly of one pattern, and the narrative formulae would become wearisome, but for these short lives and their uncomplicated purpose of invoking religious wonder, the diction and composition are admirable. Caxton's rehandling touches this simple style with latinity, but the original lucidness shines through, making Caxton's text the best of all his works as English prose.

Among later hagiography, the lives of the women-mystics have a special interest for English letters. These ladies, most of them Germans or Netherlanders, include such famous personalities as Hildegard of Bingen, the two Mechthilds, Angela of Foligno, Brigid of Sweden, and Catherine of Sweden among the autobiographers, and Marie d'Oignies, Elizabeth of Hungary, Katherine of Sweden, and Joan of Arc among the subjects of biographies. Two English lives belong to the same tradition—those of Julian of Norwich and Margery Kempe.

No one familiar with hagiography will doubt that there is a tradition and a rhetoric in these lives, in the lived as well as the literary form. Taking example from Thais, Mary of Alexandria, and the desert fathers, probably, and encouraged by the writings of the Victorines, St. Bernard, St. Bonaventura, Suso, Tauler, Rolle, or Hilton, the ladies' lives were written in plain awareness of appropriate precedent—quite as they lived.

Some of the continental Lives circulated widely in England, and the Life of Margery Kempe reveals the author's knowledge of several of them. Mostly the texts were Latin, although there were several translations of the life and revelations of St. Brigid, and an English version of the life of St. Catherine of Siena may also have been available before Margery arranged for the writing of her own life. So, too, may have been a collection of lives that was compiled and translated by a Carthusian monk from Beauvale in Nottinghamshire.

This monk's collection, comprising short biographies of Catherine of Siena and three Belgian saints of the thirteenth century—Elizabeth of Spalbeck, Christine the Marvelous, and Marie d'Oignies—is a remarkable document. The matter of the lives recalls the experiences and behavior of Margery Kempe: visions, conversations with Christ, Mary, and the saints, asceticisms, ecstasies, weepings, conversions, miracles. The style, however, is highly individual. The translator, who worked at the command of his prior, declares that he met the difficulties of Latin vocabulary and syntax by using English approximations and a glosing (interpretive) method of translation. Actually, he did more, for although he correctly matches the sentence forms of his originals, he also endows them with his own manner.

That manner is a much-heightened variety of the poetic prose that is sometimes found in association with alliterative verse—Aelfric's in the tenth century, the *Ancren Riwle* in the thirteenth, and Nicholas Love's in the early fifteenth, for example. Parallel constructions piled up into lengthy periods, heavy alliteration, poetic inversion, symbolism, insistent imagery, set descriptions, word pairs, word play, and fervent rhythm are its obvious features. The writer may have been the simpleminded man he said he was, but either by feeling or design he fitted his style to his matter: the same ecstasy characterizes both. To represent his work—which should be better known than it is—we have taken sections from the beginning and the end of the life of St. Marie of Oignies, originally written in Latin by her confessor.

The earlier of the two indigenously English examples is the autobiography of Dame Julian of Norwich (*c*.1342–*c*.1416), an anchoress at St. Julian in Norwich and by her own statement "a simple person unlettered." In 1373, at the point of death, she experienced a swift succession of sixteen visions or "shewings" and twenty years later was graced by an inward teaching that enabled her to understand more fully these shewings. *Revelations of Divine Love*, which may have been set down by an amanuensis, is her account of this dual experience—part autobiography, part reflection. The alliance of these two elements confuses chronology, but in other respects the work is finely written, remarkable for the blending of mystical feeling with rugged common sense, for precision in description, and for eloquence in sentence construction and vocabulary (possibly modelled on Walter Hilton) that conveys the tranquil recollections of her earlier emotion. Our selection is a slightly shortened form of the first shewing.

In strong contrast, as regards its attitude and variety, is the life of her neighbor and acquaintance, Margery Kempe (born *c.* 1373). Both for its manner and its matter this is one of the most astonishing personal documents in English.

The matter is the experience of a woman who claimed more direct revelations of Christ and the saints than have been granted, perhaps, to any other creature of English stock. Her "stirrings," both spiritual and physical, her evangel, miracles, pilgrimages and other travels, and the troubles that her claims and behavior brought upon her provide a narrative that, although similar in substance to some others of its time, has no peer for verve and variety. Nor has it a match for the incidental depiction of religious and social life and of a host of her friends and foes—who appear with all the frustration, anger, sympathy, and bewilderment that Margery's goings-on will-nilly forced them into.

The narrative, which is written in the third-person, hovers between biography and autobiography. Margery was illiterate and her book was set down, between 1430 and 1436, by two amanuenses: the first an Englishman who had lived in Germany, possibly her own son; the second a priest who revised and added further episodes. As we have the book, its grammar and spelling are probably the priest's. But the matter was contributed by Mistress Kempe herself, and how much of the art and cunning of the narrative is hers, how much the amanuenses', is uncertain. Her behavior and attitude owe much to literary predecessors, notably the autobiography and revelations of St. Brigid, which were particularly popular in East-Anglia. No less familiar was she with the New Testament or with sermons that rammed home their points with proverbs, catch-phrases, and lively yarns. The speaking voice of a simple but adroit creature is discernible throughout the Life, and not only in her own speeches.

But beyond this first-person quality there is also a cultivated manner, both in the style of writing and in the point of view, that suggests more art and more tolerance than she, as one may guess, could have commanded. The simple formulae of the sentences are ingeniously varied and balanced; antitheses, inversions, parallelisms, repetitions support the syntactical emphases and rhythms with calculated skill. And this subtlety of language is matched by the frequent understanding of other views than Margery's own. Predominantly, the book represents Margery's conviction that hers was the Lord's side, but not seldom it mirrors dramatically the many shades of feeling of those whom she rubbed the wrong way. Mistress Kempe, for all her hysteria, exhibitionism, and arrogant humility, was a woman of talent; but it would be surprising to know that her talent included such civilized understanding as this work shows. But one never knows. To this day she is as baffling as she was to the archbishop who examined her at York. Autobiographies set down by ghosts are many, and usually there is small difficulty in estimating how large is the ghost's contribution. Here, in the classic of the ghosted autobiography, the matter remains a mystery.

The incidents are set down chronologically in a series of scenes, and we have selected some sections that represent its chief types of activity: the chastity-compact she made with her husband, a brush with the monks of Canterbury, part of her pilgrimage in Jerusalem, and her examination before Henry Bowet, Archbishop of York, in 1417.

See Introd. to this section
for Latin, 1376. Arderne then bg. Transl. early 15 c.

John Arderne

"FISTULA IN ANO," PREFACE

I, JOHN ARDERNE, fro the first pestilence, that was in the year of our Lord 1349, dwelled in Newark in Nottinghamshire unto the year of our Lord 1370, and there I healed many men of *fistula in ano*. Of which, the first was Sir Adam Everingham of Laxton-in-the-Clay beside Tewkesford. Which Sir Adam, forsooth, was in Gascony with Sir Henry, that time named Earl of Derby (and after was made Duke of Lancaster), a noble and worthy lord. The foresaid Sir Adam, forsooth, suffering *fistulam in ano,* made for to ask counsel at all the leeches [physicians] and surgeons that he might find in Gascony—at Bordeaux, at Bergerac, Toulouse, and Narbonne, and Poitiers, and many other places—and all forsook him for uncurable. Which see*n* and heard, the forsaid Adam hasted for to turn home to his country. And when he come home, he did off all his knightly clothings and clad mourning-clothes, in purpose of abiding dissolving or losing of his body, being nigh to him. At last I, foresaid John Arderne, sought and covenant made, come to him and did my cure to him, and (our Lord being mean*s*) I healed him perfectly within half a year. And afterward, whole and sound, he led a glad life by thirty year and more, for which

note that he attributes cures 1st to God

Criteria of a good physician approper. from Lanfranc's treatise on surgery, with abundant additions from A.boon's experience

"Fistula in ano," Preface 43

cure I got much honor and loving [praise] through all England, and the foresaid Duke of Lancaster and many other gentles wondered thereof.

Afterward I cured Hugh Darling of Fowick, of Balne-by-Snaith; afterward I cured John Sheffield of Brightwell-aside-Tickhill; afterward I cured Sir Reynald Grey, Lord of Wilton in Wales and Lord of Shirland-beside-Chesterfield, which asked counsel at the most famous leeches of England, and none availed him. Afterward I cured Sir Henry Blackburn, clerk, treasurer of the Lord Prince of Wales. Afterward I cured Adam Humfrey of Shelford-beside-Nottingham and Sir John, priest of the same town, and John de Holle, of Shirland, and Sir Thomas Hamelden, parson of Langer in the Vale of Beauvoir. Afterward I cured friar Thomas Gunny, custod*ian* of the friar-minors of York.

Afterward, in the year of our Lord 1370, I come to London, and there I cured John Colin, Mayor of Northampton, that asked counsel at many leeches. Afterward, I healed or cured Hugh Denny, fishmonger of London, in Bridge Street; and William Pole and Ralph Double; and one that was called Thomas Brown, that had fifteen holes by the which went out wind with egestious odor —that is to say, eight holes of the one part of the arse and seven on the other side; of which some holes was distant fro the tewell [funnel] by the space of a handbread*th* of a man, so that both his buttocks was so ulcerat*ed* and putrefied within that the quiture [discharge] and filth went out each day as much as an eggshell might take.

Afterward I cured four friars-preachers; that is to say, friar John Writell, friar John Hacket, friar Peter Brown, friar Thomas Apperley, and a young man called Thomas Voke. Of which foresaid, some had only one hole, distant from the tewell by one inch or by two or by three, and other*s* had four or five holes proceeding to the cod of the testicles, and many other manners, of which the telling were full hard. All these foresaid cured I afore the making of this book. Our Lord Jesu, blessed God, knoweth that I lie not; and therefore *let* no man doubt of this, though-all old famous men and full clear in study have confessed them that they found not the way of curation in this case. For God, that is dealer or rewarder of wisdom, hath hid many things fro wise men and sly which he vouchsaf*ed* afterward for to shew to simple men.

Therefore, all men that are to come afterward, wit they that old masters were not busy ne pertinacious in seeking and searching of this foresaid cure; but for they might not take the hardness of it at the first front, they cast it utterly behind their back. Of which, forsooth, some deemed it wholly for to be incurable; others applied doubtful opinions. Therefore, forasmuch in hard things it speedeth to studiers for to persevere and abide and for to turn subtly their wits (for it is opened not to them that are passing but to them that are persevering); therefore, to the honor of God Almighty that hath opened wit to me that I should find treasure hid in the field of studiers—that long time and with panting breast I have sweated and travailed full busily and pertinaciously *in diu avidius,* as my faculty sufficeth, without fair speaking of enditing —I have brought for to shew it openly to them that cometh after, our Lord being means and this book. Not that I shew myself more worthy of loving [praise] of such a gift than other, but that I grieve not God, and for the drachm that he hath given to me that I be not constrained for treason.

Therefore, I pray that the grace of the Holy Ghost be to this work, that he vouchsafe for to speed it, that those things which in working truly I am ofttimes expert I may plenerly [fully] explain them in this little book. And this I say: that I know not in all my time, ne heard not in all my time, of any man, neither in England ne in parts beyond the sea, that could cure *fistula in ano*—outtake a friar-minor that was with the Prince of Wales in Gascony and Guienne, which rosed and boasted him that he had cured the foresaid sickness. And at London he deceived many men; and when he might not cure some men, he made suggestion to them that no man might cure them. And that affirmed he with swearing that if the fistula were dried, that the patient at the next should not escape death—which, forsooth, left and forsaken of him, I cured perfectly.

And to remove false opinions of ignorant men, for witness I put experience. Avicenna, forsooth saith, "Experience overcometh reason." And Galen in *Pantegni* saith, "No man ought for to trust in reason alone but-if it be proved of experience;" and he saith in another place, "Experience without reason is feeble, and so is reason without experience fast unto him." Nevertheless, I affirm not that I might heal all *fistulae in ano,* for some be uncurable, as it shall be said more fully within when I shall treat of them.

First, it behoveth him that will profit in this craft that he set God afore evermore in all his works, and evermore call meekly with heart and mouth his help, and sometimes visit of his winnings poor men, after his might, that they by their prayers may get him grace of the Holy Ghost. And that he be not found temerarious or boastful in his sayings or in his deeds; and abstain he fro much speech, and most among great men; and answer he slyly to things asked, that he be not taken in his words. Forsooth, if his works be ofttime known for to discord fro his words and his behests, he shall be holden more unworthy and he shall blemish his own good fame. Wherefore, saith a versifier; *vincat opus verbum, minuit iactantia famam:* "Let work overcome thy word, for boast lesseneth good laus [praise]."

Also, be a leech not much-laughing ne much-playing, and, as much as he may without harm, flee he the fellowship of knaves and of unhonest persons. And be he evermore occupied in things that beholdeth to this craft: either read he, or study he, or write or pray he, for the exercise of books worshipeth [honors] a leech. For-why he shall both be holden and he shall be more wise. And, above all these, it profiteth to him that he be found evermore sober, for drunkenness destroyeth all virtue and bringeth it to nought. As saith a wise man: *Ebrietas frangit quicquid sapiencia tangit;* "Drunkenness breaketh whatso wisdom toucheth." Be he content in strange places of meats and drinks there found, using measure in all things. For the wise man saith: *Sicut ad omne quod est mensuram ponere prodest, sic sine mensura deperit omne quod est;* "As it profiteth to put measure to all thing that is, so without measure perisheth all thing that is." Scorn he no man, for of that it is said: *Deridens alios non inderisus abibit;* "He that scorneth other men shall not go away unscorned." If there be made speech to him of any leech, neither set he him at nought ne praise him too much or commend him; but thus may he courteously answer: "I have not very knowledge of him, but I learned not ne I have not heard of him but good and honest." And of this shall honor and thankings of each party increase and multiply to him: after this, honor is in the honorer and not in the honored.

Consider he not over-openly the lady or the daughters of other fair women in great men's houses, ne proffer them not to kiss, ne touch not privily ne apertly their paps, ne their hands, ne their share [pubes], that he run not into the indignation of the lord ne none of his. Inasmuch as he may, grieve he no servant, but get he their love and their good will. Abstain he him fro harlotry as well in words as in deeds in every place, for if he use him to harlotry in privy places, sometime in open place there may fall to him unworship of evil usage. After that it is said: *Pede super coles pedes ubi pedere nolles;* "Fart upon hills, and thou shalt fart where thou would not, against thy will." And it is said in another place: "Shrewd speech corrupteth good manners."

When sick men, forsooth, or any of them beside cometh to the leech to ask help or counsel of him, be he not to them over-fell [rough] ne over-homely, but mean [moderate] in bearing, after the askings of the persons: to some reverently, to some commonly. For after wise men, overmuch homeliness breedeth despising. Also, it speedeth that he have seemly excusations—that he may not incline to their askings without harming or without indignation of some great man or friend or for necessary occupation; or feign he him hurt, or for to be sick, or some other convenable cause by which he may likely be excused.

Therefore, if he will favor to any man's asking, make he covenant for his travail, and take it beforehands. But advise the leech himself well that he give no certain answer in any cause but [unless] he see first the sickness and the manner of it. And when he hath seen and assayed it, though-all him seem that the sick may be healed, nevertheless he shall make prognostication to the patient the perils to come if the cure be deferred. And if he see the patient pursue busily the cure, then, after that the estate of the patient asketh [suggests], ask he boldly more or less; but ever be he ware of scarce askings, for over-scarce askings setteth at nought both the market and the thing. Therefore, for the cure of *fistula in ano* when it is curable, ask he competently: of a worthy man and a great, an hundred mark or forty pound, with robes and fees of an hundred shilling, term of life by year; of less men, forty pounds, or forty mark ask he without fees. And take he nought less than a hundred shillings, for never in all my life took I less than a hundred shilling for cure of that sickness. Nevertheless, do another man as him-think better and more speedful. And if the patients or their friends or servants ask by how much time he hopeth to heal it, evermore let the leech behight the double that he supposeth to speed by half; that is, if the leech hope to heal the

patient by twenty weeks—that is the common course of curing—
add he so many over. For it is better that the term be lengthened
than the cure, for prolongation of the cure giveth cause of despair-
ing to the patients when trust to the leech is most hope of health.
And if the patient consider or wonder or ask why that he put him
so long a time of curing, sith [since] that he healed him by the
half, answer he that it was for that the patient was strong-hearted
and suffered well sharp things, and that he was of good complexion and had able flesh to heal; and feign he other causes
pleasable to the patient, for patients of such words are proud and
delighted.

Also, dispose a leech him that in clothes and other apparelings
be he honest, not likening himself in appareling or bearing to
minstrels; but in clothing and bearing shew he the manner of
clerks; for-why it be-seemeth any discreet man clad with clerks'
clothing for to occupy gentlemen's boards. Have the leech also
clean hands and well-shapen nails and cleansed fro all blackness
and filth. And be he courteous at lords' boards and displease he
nought in words or deeds to the guests sitting by. Hear he many
things, but speak he but few; for a wise man saith, "It be-seemeth
more to use the ears than the tongue" and in another place, "If
thou had been still thou had been holden a philosopher." And
when he shall speak, be the words short and, as much as he may,
fair and reasonable and without swearing. Beware that there be
never found double words in his mouth, for if he be found true in
his words, few or none shall doubt in his deeds.

Learn also a young leech good proverbs pertaining to his craft
in comforting of patients. Or if patients 'plain that their medicines
be bitter or sharp or such other, then shall the leech say to the
patient thus: "It is read in the last lesson of matins of the nativity
of our Lord that our Lord Jesus Christ came into this world for
the health of mankind to the manner of a good leech and wise.
And when he cometh to the sick he sheweth him medicines, some
light and some hard, and he saith to the sick man, 'If thou wilt be
made whole, these and these shall thou take.' Also, in another
place in an homily upon the gospel of the sons of Zebedee, where
the mother asked saying, 'Lord, say that my two sons sit in thy
kingdom, the one on the right hand and the tother on the left.'
And Jesus answering said, 'Ye wot never what ye ask.' Then said

he to the sons of Zebedee, 'May ye drink the chalice that I am to drink?' They said to him, 'We may,' as if he said to them, 'If your soul or mind covet what delighteth, drink the first that sorroweth or acheth.' And so by bitter drinks of confection it is come to the joys of health . . ."

Also it speedeth that a leech can talk of good tales and of honest, that may make the patients to laugh, as well of the Bible as of other tragedies, and any other things of which it is nought to charge whilst that they make or induce a light heart to the patient or the sick man.

Discover never the leech unwarely the counsels of his patients, as well of men as of women; ne set not one to another at nought, though-all he have cause, that he be not guilty of counsel. For if a man see thee hele [hide] well another man's counsel, he will trust better in thee. Many things, forsooth, be to be kept of a leech, without these that are said afore, that may not be noted here for overmuch occupying. But it is not to doubt that if the foresaid be well kept, that they shall give a gracious going to the user to the height of worship and of winning, for Cato saith, *Virtutem primam puta esse compescere linguam:* "The first virtue trow you to be to refrain the tongue."

After all these, it behoveth that he know the names of the instruments that pertaineth to the cure of the fistula, without which a leech may not well speed him.

collection of saints' lives

From Caxton's text of the earlier transl. "LEGENDA AUREA" — *orig. author was Jacobus Arer*

"LIFE OF SAINT THOMAS À BECKET" *d. 1171*

THE MARTYR SAINT THOMAS was son to Gilbert Becket, a burgess of the city of London, and was born in the place where as now standeth the church called St. Thomas of Acres. And this Gilbert was a good devout man, and took the cross upon him and went on pilgrimage to the Holy Land, and had a servant with him. And when he had accomplished his pilgrimage, he was taken homeward by the heathen men and brought in prison of a prince named Amurath, where long time he and his fellowship suffered much pain and sorrow. And the prince had great affection towards this

Closer to tone of subj. than others; closer to modern notion of biog. comprehensively + logically org. Technique familiar + realistic; theme is med. politics but focus on martyrdom + miracle, black-+-white characterization + its objective upholding of clerical values it is one with rest of hagiog.

Gilbert and had often communication with him of the christian faith and of the realm of England. By which conversation it fortuned that the daughter of this prince had especial love unto this Gilbert and was familiar with him. And on a time she disclosed her love to him, saying, if he would promise to wed her she should forsake friends, heritage, and country for his love, and become christian. And after long communication between them he promised to wed her if she would become christian, and told to her the place of his dwelling in England. And after, by the purveyance of God, the said Gilbert escaped and came home.

And after this it fortuned so, that this prince's daughter stole privily away, and passed many a wild place and great adventure, and by God's purveyance came at the last to London, demanding and crying "Becket! Becket!"—for more English could [knew] she not. Wherefore the people drew about her, what for the strange array of her as for that they understood her not, and many a shrewd boy. So long she went, till she came before Gilbert's door. And, as she stood there, the servant that had been with Gilbert in prison, which was named Richard, saw her and knew anon that it was the prince's daughter that had them in prison. He shewed it to his master and told to him how that this maid stood at his door. And anon he went forth to see her. And as soon as she saw him she fell into a swoon for joy, and Gilbert took her up and comforted her, and brought her into his house. And sith [after] went to the bishops, which then were six at Paul's, and rehearsed all the matter. And after they christened her and forthwith wedded her unto Gilbert Becket. And within time reasonable and accustomed was brought forth between them a fair son named Thomas.

And after this, yet the said Gilbert went again to the Holy Land and was there three years ere he came again. And this child grew forth till he was set to school, and learned well and became virtuous. And when he was twenty-four year old, his mother passed out of this world. And after this he served a merchant of London a while in keeping his charge and *ac*counts, and from him he went to Stigand, archbishop of Canterbury, and he was in so great favor with him that he made him archdeacon and chief of his counsel. And well executed he his office in punishing the culpable and cherishing the good people, and divers times went to Rome to support and help holy church.

And after this, Henry II, that was the emperor's son, was made

king of England, and he ordained this Thomas chancellor, and
had great rule and the land stood in prosperity. And St. Thomas
stood so greatly in the king's favor that the king was content with
all that he did, and when the king went into Normandy he betook
the governance of his son and the realm into the rule of St.
Thomas, which he wisely governed till his return again.

And anon after died Theobald, the archbishop of Canterbury,
and the king gave his nomination to St. Thomas; and by the chapter was elect in the year of his age, forty-four, and was full loath
to take that great charge on him. And so at last, had his bulls, he
was sacred [consecrated] and stalled and became an holy man,
suddenly changed into a new man, doing great penance, as in
wearing hair with knots and a breech of the same down to the
knees. And on a Trinity Sunday he received his dignity, and there
was at that time the king with many a great lord and sixteen
bishops. And fro thence was sent the abbot of Evesham to the
pope with other clerks for the pall, which he gat and brought to
him, and he full meekly received it. And under his habit he ware
the habit of a monk, and so was he withinforth a monk, and outward a clerk, and did great abstinence, making his body lean and
his soul fat. And he used to be well served at his table and took
but little refection thereof, and lived holily in giving good example.

After this, many times the king went over into Normandy, and
in his absence always St. Thomas had the rule of his son and of
the realm, the which was governed so well that the king could
[gave] him great thanks, and then abode long in this realm. And
when so was that the king did anything against the franchises and
liberties of holy church, St. Thomas ever withstood it to his power.
And on a time, when the sees of London and of Winchester were
vacant and void, the king kept them both long in his hands for to
have the profits of them. Wherefore Thomas was heavy and came
to the king and desired him to give those two bishoprics to some
virtuous men. And anon the king granted him his desire and ordained one master Roger, bishop of Winchester, and the Earl of
Gloucester's son, bishop of London, named Sir Robert. And anon
after, St. Thomas hallowed the abbey of Reading, which the first
Harry founded. And the same year he translated St. Edward, king
and confessor, at Westminster, where he was laid in a rich shrine.

And in some short time after, by the enticement of the devil, fell great debate, variance, and strife between the king and St. Thomas, and the king sent for all the bishops to appear tofore him at Westminster at a certain day. At which day they assembled tofore him; whom he welcomed, and after said to them how that the archbishop would destroy his law and not suffer him to enjoy such things as his predecessors had used tofore him. Whereto St. Thomas answered that he never entended to do thing that should displease the king, as far it touched not the franchise and liberty of holy church. Then the king rehearsed how that he would not suffer clerks, that were thieves, have the execution of the law. To which St. Thomas said that he ought not execute them, but they belong to the correction of holy church, and other divers points to which St. Thomas would not agree. To the which the king said, "Now I see well thou wouldst foredo the laws of this land which have been used in the days of my predecessors, but it shall not lie in thy power." And so the king, being wroth, departed.

Then the bishops all counselled St. Thomas to follow the king's intent, or else the land should be in great trouble. And in like wise the lords temporal that were his friends counselled him the same. And St. Thomas said, "I take God to record it was never mine intent to displease the king or to take anything that longeth to his right and honor."

And then the lords were glad and brought him to the king to Oxford, and the king deigned not to speak to him. And then the king called all the lords spiritual and temporal to him and said he would have all the laws of his forefathers there new confirmed. And there they were confirmed by all the lords spiritual and temporal. And, after this, the king charged them for to come to him in Clarendon to his parliament at a certain day assigned, on pain to run in his indignation. And at that time so departed. And this parliament was holden at Clarendon the eleventh year of the king's reign and the year of our Lord 1164.

At this parliament were many lords which were all against St. Thomas. And then the king, sitting in his parliament in the presence of all his lords, demanded them if they would abide and keep the laws that had been used in his forefathers' days. Then St. Thomas spake for the part of holy church and said, "All old laws that be good and right and not against our mother, holy church, I grant with good will to keep them."

And then the king said that he would not leave one point of his law, and waxed wroth with St. Thomas. And then certain bishops required St. Thomas to obey to the king's desire and will, and St. Thomas desired respite to know the laws and then to give an answer. And when he understood them all, to some he consented but many he denied and would never be agreeable to them. Wherefore the king was wroth and said he would hold and keep them like as his predecessors had done before him, and would not diminish one point of them.

Then St. Thomas said to the king, with full great sorrow and heavy cheer, "Now, my most dear lord and gracious king, have pity on us of holy church, your bedemen [plaintiffs], and give to us repite for a certain time."

And thus departed every man, and St. Thomas went to Winchester and there prayed our Lord devoutly for holy church and to give him aid and strength for to defend it, for utterly he determined to abide by the liberties and franchise. And fell down on his knees, full sore weeping and said: "O good Lord, I knowledge that I have offended, and, for mine offence and trespass this trouble cometh to holy church: I purpose, good Lord, to go to Rome to be absolved of mine offences"—and departed toward Canterbury.

And anon the king sent his officers to his manors and despoiled them, because he would not obey the king's statutes. And the king commanded to seize all his lands and goods into his hands. And then his servants departed from him, and he went to the seaside for to have gone over sea, but the wind was against him. And so thrice he took his ship, and might not pass. And then he knew that it was not our Lord's will; that yet he should not depart, and returned secretly to Canterbury. Of whose coming his men made great joy. And on the morn came the king's office for to have seized all his goods, for the noise was that St. Thomas fled the land. Wherefore they had despoiled all his manors and seized them into the king's hand.

And when they came, they found him at Canterbury, whereof they were sore abashed, and returned to the king, informing him that he was yet at Canterbury. And anon after, St. Thomas came to the king at Woodstock for to pray him to be better disposed toward holy church. And then said the king to him in scorn, "May not we two dwell both in this land? Art thou so sturdy and hard of heart?"

To whom St. Thomas answered, "Sire, that was never my thought, but I would fain please you and do all that you desire, so that ye hurt not the liberties of holy church, for them will I maintain while I live, ever to my power."

With which words the king was sore moved and swore that he would have them kept, and in especial, if a clerk were a thief he should be judged and executed after the king's law and by no spiritual law. And said he would never suffer a clerk to be his master in his own land. And charged St. Thomas to appear before him at Northampton and to bring all the bishops of this land with him. And so departed. St. Thomas besought God of help and succour, for the bishops which ought to be with him were most against him.

After this, St. Thomas went to Northampton where the king held then his great council in the castle with all his lords. And when he came before the king, he said, "I am come to obey your commandment, but before this time was never bishop of Canterbury thus entreated. For I am head of the church of England and am to you, Sir King, your ghostly father. And it was never God's law that the son should destroy the father which hath charge of your soul. And by your stirring hath made all the bishops that should abide by the right of the church to be against holy church and me. And ye know well that I may not fight, but am ready to suffer death rather than I should suffer to lose the right of holy church."

Then said the king, "Thou speakest as a proud clerk, but I shall abate thy pride ere I leave thee, for I must reckon with thee. Thou understandest well that thou were my chancellor many years, and once I lent to thee £500, which thou never yet hast repaid: which I will that thou pay me again, or else incontinent thou shalt go to prison."

And then St. Thomas answered, "Ye gave me that £500, and it is not sitting [suitable] to demand that which ye have given." Notwithstanding, he found surety for the said £500 and departed for that day.

And after this, the next day, the king demanded £30,000 that he had surmised on him to have stolen, he being chancellor. Whereupon he desired day to answer. At which time he said that when he was archbishop he set him free therein, without any claim or debt before good record, wherefore he ought not to answer unto the demand. And the bishops desired St. Thomas to obey the king, but in no wise he would not agree to such things as should touch against the liberties of the church. And then they came to the king and forsook St. Thomas, and agreed to all the king's desire. And the proper servants of St. Thomas fled from him and forsook him. And then poor people came and accompanied him. And in the night came to him two lords, and told to him that the king's meinie had emprised to slay him. And the next night after he departed, in the habit of a brother of Sempringham, and so chevissed [contrived] that he went over sea.

And in the meanwhile, certain bishops went to Rome for to complain on him to the pope, and the king sent letters to the king of France not to receive him. And the King Louis said: though a man were banished and had committed there trespasses, yet he should be free in France. And so, after when this holy St. Thomas came, he received him well and gave him license to abide and do there what he would.

In this meanwhile, the king of England sent certain lords to the pope complaining on the archbishop Thomas, which made grievous complaints. Which when the pope had heard said, he would give none answer till he had heard the archbishop Thomas speak, which would hastily come thither. But they would not abide his coming, but departed without speeding [success] of their intents, and came into England again.

And anon after, St. Thomas came to Rome on St. Mark's day at afternoon, and when his caterer should have bought fish for his dinner because it was fasting-day, he could get none for no money, and came and told to his lord St. Thomas so. And he bade him buy such as he could get, and then he bought flesh and made it ready for their dinner. And St. Thomas was served with a capon roasted and his meinie with boiled meat. And so it was that the pope heard that he was come and sent a cardinal to welcome him. And he found him at his dinner eating flesh, which anon returned and told to the pope how he was not so perfect a man as he had supposed— "for contrary to the rule of the church he eateth this day flesh." The pope would not believe him, but sent another cardinal, which for more evidences took the leg of the capon in his kerchief and affirmed the same, and opened his kerchief before the pope—and he found the leg turned into a fish called a carp. And when the pope saw it, he said they were not true men to say such things of this good bishop. They said, faithfully, that it was flesh that he ate. And after this, St. Thomas came to the pope and did his reverence and obedience. Whom the pope welcomed, and after certain communications, he demanded him what meat he had eaten. And said "Flesh," as ye have heard before, because he could find no fish, and very need compelled him thereto. Then the pope understood of the miracle that the capon's leg was turned into a carp, and of his goodness granted to him and to all them of the diocese of Canterbury license to eat flesh ever after on St. Mark's day when it falleth on a fish day, and pardon withal. Which is kept and accustomed unto this day.

And then St. Thomas informed the pope how the king of England would have him consent to divers articles against the liberties of holy church, and what wrong he did to the same, and that for to die he would never consent to them. And when the pope had heard him, he wept for pity and thanked God that he had such a bishop under him that had so well defended the liberties of holy church. And anon wrote out letters and bulls commanding all the bishops of Christendom to keep and observe the same. And then St. Thomas offered to the pope his bishopric into his hands, and his mitre with the cross and ring. And the pope commanded him to keep it still, and said he knew no man so able as he was. And, after, St. Thomas said mass before the pope in a white chasuble; and after mass he said to the pope that he knew by revelation that he should die for the right of holy church and, when it should fall, the chasuble should be turned from white to red.

And after, he departed from the pope and came down into France unto the abbey of Pontigny, and there he had knowledge that when the lords spiritual and temporal which had been at Rome were come home and had told the king that they might in no wise have their intent, that the king was greatly wroth and anon banished all the kinsmen that were belonging to St. Thomas, that they should incontinent void his land, and made them to swear that they should go to him and tell him for his sake they were exiled. And so they went over sea to him to Pontigny, and he being there was full sorry for them.

And after, there was a great chapter in England of the monks of Cîteaux, and there the king desired them to write to Pontigny that they should no longer keep ne sustain Thomas the archbishop, for if they did he would destroy them of that order being in England. And, for fear thereof, they wrote so over to Pontigny, that he must depart thence with his kinsmen. And so he did; and was then fully heavy and remitted his cause to God.

And anon after, the king of France sent to him that he should abide where it pleased him, and dwell in his realm, and would pay for the costs of him and his kinsmen. And he departed and went to Sens, and the abbot brought him on the way. And St. Thomas told him how he knew by a vision that he should suffer death and martyrdom for the right of the church, and prayed him to keep it secret during his life.

After this, the king of England came into France and there told the king how St. Thomas would destroy his realm; and then said how he would foredo such laws as his elders had used before him. Wherefore, St. Thomas was sent for and they were brought together. And the king of France labored sore to set them at accord, but it would not be; for that one would not *di*minish his laws and accustoms, and St. Thomas would not grant that he should not do contrary the liberties of holy church. And then the king of France held with the king of England against St. Thomas, and was wroth with him and commanded him to void his realm with his kinsmen.

And then St. Thomas wist not whither to go, but comforted his kinsmen as well as he might, and purposed to have gone into Provence for to have begged his bread. And as he was going, the king of France sent for him again, and when he came he cried him mercy and said he had offended God and him, and bade him abide in his realm where he would, and he would pay for the dispenses of him and all his kinsmen.

And in the meanwhile the king of England ordained his son king and made him to be crowned by the archbishop of York and other bishops, which was against the statutes of the land, for the archbishop of Canterbury should have also consented and also have crowned him. Wherefore, St. Thomas got a bull for to accurse them that so did against him, and also on them that occupy the goods *be*longing to him.

And yet, after this, the king labored so much that he accorded the king of England and St. Thomas. Which accord endured not long, for the king varied from it afterward. But St. Thomas, upon this accord, came home to Canterbury, where he was received

Henry II, Henry Beauclaire, in other respects a good king. It might be that people close to the king thought they were doing the king's will and killed Thomas.

"Life of Saint Thomas à Becket"   57

worshipfully, and sent for them that had trespassed against him;
and, by the authority of the pope's bull, openly denounced them
accursed unto the time they came to amendment. And when they
knew this they came to him and would have made him to absolve
them by force, and sent word over to the king how he had done.
Whereof the king was much wroth and said, "If he had men in his
land that loved him, they would not suffer such a traitor in his
land alive."

And forthwith, four knights took their counsel together and
thought they would do the king a pleasure, and emprised to slay
St. Thomas. And suddenly departed and took their shipping toward England. And when the king knew of their departing, he
was sorry and sent after them; but they were on the sea and departed ere the messengers came; wherefore the king was heavy
and sorry.

These be the names of the four knights: Sir Reynold Beareson, *All greater but not of highest*
Sir Hugh Morville, Sir William Tracy, Sir Richard de Breton.

On Christmas day, St. Thomas made a sermon at Canterbury in
his own church, and, weeping, prayed the people to pray for him, *Passed*
for he knew well his time was nigh. And there executed the sen- *sentence*
tence on them that were against the right of holy church. And *of excommun.*
the same day, as the king sat at meat, all the bread that they han- *(Interdiction*
dled waxed anon mouldy and hoar, that no man might eat of it, *all rites? Ch.*
and the bread that they touched not was fair and good for to eat. *stopped.)*
And these four knights aforesaid came to Canterbury on the Tuesday in Christmas week about evensong time, and came to St.
Thomas and said that the king commanded him to make amends
for the wrongs that he had done and also that he should absolve
all them that he had accursed anon—or else they would slay him.

Miracle? What could have explain perhaps not.

Then said Thomas, "All that I ought to do by right, that will I
with a good will do; but as the sentence that is executed, I may not
undo but-that they will submit them to the correction of holy
church, for it was done by our holy father the pope, and not by
me."

Then said Sir Reynold, "But-if thou absolve the king and us,
understanding the curse, it shall cost thee thy life."

And St. Thomas said, "Thou knowest well enough that the king
and I were accorded on Mary Magdalene's day and that this curse
should go forth on them that had offended the church."

Then one of the knights smote him as he kneeled before the

altar on the head. And one Sir Edward Grim, that was his crossier, put forth his arm with the cross to bear off the stroke. And the stroke smote the cross asunder and his arm almost off. Wherefore, he fled for fear and so did all the monks, that were that time at compline. And then smote each at him, that they smote off a great piece of the skull of his head, that his brain fell on the pavement. And so they slew him and martyred him, and there cruelly—that one of them brake the point of his sword against the pavement.

And thus this holy archbishop St. Thomas suffered death in his own church for the right of holy church. And when he was dead they stirred his brain, and after went into his chamber and took away his goods and his horse out of his stable, and took away his bulls and writings and delivered them to Sir Robert Broke to bear into France to the king. And as they searched his chamber, they found in a chest two shirts of hair made full of great knots. And then said, "Certainly he was a good man!" And, coming down into the churchward, they began to dread and fear that the ground would not have borne them, and were marvellously aghast, for they supposed that the earth would have swallowed them all quick. And then they knew that they had done amiss.

And anon it was known all about how that he was martyred. And anon after took this holy body and unclothed him, and found bishop's clothing above and the habit of a monk under. And next his flesh a hard hair, full of knots, which was his shirt. And his breech was of the same. And the knots sticked fast within the skin and all his body was full of worms: he suffered great pain.

And was thus martyred the year of our Lord 1171, and was fifty-three year old.

And soon after tidings came to the king how he was slain. Wherefore the king took great sorrow and sent to Rome for his absolution.

Now, after that St. Thomas departed from the pope, the pope would daily look upon the white chasuble that St. Thomas had said mass in. And that same day that he was martyred he saw it turn into red, whereby he knew well that that same day he suffered martyrdom for the right of holy church, and commanded a mass of requiem solemnly to be sung for his soul. And when that the choir began for to sing requiem, an angel on high above began the office of a martyr—*Laetabitur justus*—and then all the whole choir followed, singing forth the mass of the office of martyr. And then the pope thanked God that it pleased him to show such miracles for his holy martyr.

At whose tomb, by the merit and prayers of this holy martyr, our blessed Lord there hath showed many miracles. The blind have recovered there their sight, the dumb their speech, the deaf their hearing, the lame their limbs, and the dead their life.

"LIFE OF ST. MARY OF OIGNIES"

Wän gay

IN THE BISHOPRIC of Luettich, in a town that is called Nivelle, there was a young maiden, in life and name glorious, the which hight Mary, come of father and mother that were of commoners. And though they abounded in riches and many worldly goods, nevertheless worldly goods never enticed her mind to them fro she was a child, so that well-nigh from her mother's womb she was cast into our Lord. And never, or else full seldom, she played her as others do, nor she was fellow with such damsels that fare all with phantom; but keeping her soul fro all covetise and vanity, shewing through God's ordinance in her childhood what she should be in elder age. Wherefore, often in her youth she kneeled before her bed and offered to our Lord orisons that she had learned, as first fruits of her life. Insomuch, soothly, fro a child little, grew with her mercy and pity and, as with a natural pity, loved religion, so that when there came brethren of Citeaux's order otherwhile by her father's house, she, looking up, followed after privily and had wonder of their habit. And when she had no more that she might do, for desire she set her feet in the steps of the converses or monks. Also, when her father and mother, as manner is of seculars, would have arrayed her with delicate garments and gay, she was sorry and forsook them, as if she had read, impressed naturally in her mind, what Saint Peter saith of women, thus: "Whose array of clothing be not withoutforth tressing and tiffing of hair or attire of gold or gowns." And also Saint Paul saith, "Not in crumpled locks or gold or pearls or precious cloth." Wherefore, her father and mother, laughing and scorning the maiden, said, "What manner woman shall our daughter be?"

Her goal different to that of parents. Great humanity shown in contrast

This reveals much of extraordinary movement of personal mysticism which passed over Continent in 13-14 centuries, Meister Eckhardt on Cont., lge. groups like the Beguines (?) + Beckhards (?) devoted to mysticism. This particular portrait shows Eng. interest in Cont. mystics.

And, therefore, they, having envy at her gracious deeds, when she was fourteen year old married her to a young man.

So then she, removed fro father and mother, was kindled in so passing fervor, and with so great fighting chastised her body and brought it underneath, that often, when she had travailed with her own hands muckle part of the night, after labor she was full long in her prayers. And that other deal [part] of the night, as often as it was leaveful to her, she slept but little and that upon a few slats, the which she had privily hid at her bed's feet. And for she had not openly power of her own body, she bare privily under her smock a full sharp cord, with the which she was girded full hard.

I say not this praising the excess, but telling the fervor. In this and many other that she wrought by privilege of grace, let the discreet reader take heed that privilege of a few maketh not a common law. Follow we her virtues: the works of her virtues, without special privilege, follow may we not. Soothly, though the body be to be constrained to serve the spirit, though we ought to bear in our body the wounds of our Lord Jesu Christ, nevertheless we wot that the King's worship loveth law and right, ne sacrifice of ravine [rapture?] pleaseth not our Lord. Certainly, necessaries are not to be withdrawn fro the poor flesh, but vices are to be refrained. And, therefore, that that we read some saints have done by familiar and homely counsel of the Holy Ghost we shall rather marvel than follow.

And when she so a good while had lived with John, her spouse, in matrimony, our Lord beheld the meekness of his maiden, and graciously heard her prayers. For John was inspired to have Mary as taken-to-keep whom he had had first as wife. He made the chaste man tutor of his maiden, that she should have solace of her keeper, and left to her a true purveyor that she might more freely serve our Lord. And also before, of a natural goodness, the same John again-said not the holy purpose of his wife, as a custom is of other men, but full goodly suffered and compassion had of her labours. And visited was of our Lord, that he deserved not only *celibacy* and very angels' life by continence and chastity, but also to give all that he had for Christ's love to poor men and to follow his fellow departed from her by carnal affection, the nearer was he knit to her in holy purpose and holy religion. For ever the further he was by love of spiritual spousehood.

Wherefore our Lord appeared after in vision to his maiden and behight [promised] that as reparelled [restored] matrimony he would give again to her in heaven her fellow, the which for love of chastity withdrew him fro fleshly lust in earth. Therefore, wretched lechers, fouling them-own-selves out of wedlock with unleaveful commixions, may be shamed and feared, sith [since] both these blessed younglings, abstaining fro leaveful halsings [embraces] for God's love, overcame the hard heat of burning youth through fervor of religion. For they deserved crowns for the prize: to whom our Lord gave in his house and in his walls place and name better than sons and daughters, sith of a blessed kind of martyrdom, in fire not burning, where lust abounded their own lust slaying, near the flood thirsting, and among meats hungering, they stuck their fleshes with nails of God's dread. Yea, not setting by themselves for our Lord's love, they served some while to some mesels [lepers] beside Nivelle, in a place that is named Villambrose.

This is the kind of compact descriptive statement that is representative of the whole.

paradox means by which mystical experience is described

coffin in olig. times meant "cheat"

Devils saw and envied, seculars and cousins saw and with teeth against them gnashed. Whom first they worshipped rich; after, they despised and scorned for Christ's love made poor. Vile and abject they were accounted for God; upbraidings had they many for our Lord's sake. Dread thou not, Christ's maiden, to go wilfully with thy Christ unto contumelous scorns of the cross and set aside the joy and this world's worship. It better is to be abject and not set by in the house of our Lord, than dwell in halls and chambers of sinners. Thou hast lost grace of cousins; but thou hast found Christ's grace. Hast thou lost thy cousins' love? Nay! For certainly they loved thee never, but by chattle. Flies follow honey, wolves the carrion, and thieves their prey—not the man.

the element of preaching in this that is not in T. Beckett.
This is like a "Tract for the Times."

Lord, thou art full good to them that trust in thee, thou art true to them that abide thee. Thy maiden hath despised the realm of the world and all the worship thereof for thy love. Soothly, thou hast given her again the hundredfold in this world and everlasting life in that that is to come. Then look we, with how great stones of virtues, as a sad and whole vessel of gold honored with every precious stone, thou hast arrayed and attired thy full dear friend; with how great miracles thou hast worshipped her, that abject and scorned of seculars.

Invocation to the Lord
Passage is heavily emotional.

full

The beginning of her conversation with thee, first fruits of her life, was thy cross and thy passion. Thy hearing she heard and

30-fold — good married people
60 widows who remain so chaste
100 virgins & martyrs — St. Jerome.

dreade*d*; she beheld thy works and was afeared. For-why, upon
a day when she, prevent [forewarned] and inspired of thee, considered the benefits that thou mercifully shewed in flesh to mankind,
she found so muckle grace of compunction, so great plenty of
tears, thrust out in thy passion with the pressure of thy cross,
that her tears, copiously down running on the *church* pavement,
shewed where she yede [walked].

Wherefore, long time after this visitation of her, she might not
behold an image of the cross, ne speak ne hear other folk speaking
of the passion, but-if she fell into a swooning for high desire of
heart. And therefore, otherwhile*s*, to temper her sorrow and to
withhold abundance of tears, she left the manhood of Christ and
held up her mind to the Godhead and Majesty, that she might
find comfort in his unsufferability. But whereas she enforced her
to restrain her weeping, there increased marvelously tears more
and more. For when she took heed how great he was that suffered
for us so muckle despite, her sorrow was eft renewed and her soul
with new tears was refreshed by a sweet compunction.

It was upon a day before Good-Friday, near Christ's passion,
when she had offered herself to our Lord with muckle water of
tears, sobbings, and sighings, a priest of the kirk, as with pleasance blaming her, bade that she should pray softly and let be her
weeping. She, soothly, as she ever was shamefast and in all things
simple as a dove, did her busyness to obey. Then she, knowing her
unmight, went privily out of the church and hid her in a privy
place far fro all folk, and got grant of our Lord with tears that he
would shew to the same priest that it is not in man's power to
withhold the strong stream of tears when a great blast bloweth
and the water floweth. Wherefore, that priest, the while he sang
mass that same day, was so overcome with abundance of tears
that his spirit was well-nigh strangled, and the more that he
busied him to refrain his tears the more not only he, but also the
book and the a*l*tar-clothes were wet with water of weeping, so
that he, una*d*vised-man; he, that blamer of Christ's maiden,
lear*n*ed with shame by experience what he should do that he
would not first know by meekness and compassion. For after many
sobbings, pronouncing many words unordinately now and now, at
last unnethes [with difficulty] he scaped fro peril, and he bore
witness that both saw and knew—and we wot that his witness is
true . . .

Christ's maiden *sur*passed and was excellent by so great grace
of fasting that those days in the which her behoved to have recreation of body, she went to meat as to medicine. She ate once and
a little in the day, in summer at even, in winter at the first hour of
the night. Wine drank she none, she used no flesh, and fish ate
she never, but seld*om* small fishes; and she was sustained with
fruits of trees, herbs, and pottage. And long time she ate full black
bread and full sharp, that dogs unnethes might eat of, so that
for overmuckle sharpness and hardness her chavels [jaws] were
flay*ed* within-forth, and blood came out of the wounds. But thinking of Christ's blood made it sweet to her, and with wounds of
Christ her wounds were lockened [cured], and the sharpness of
full-hard bread was sweetened with softness of heavenly bread.
Upon a day while she ate, she saw the old enemy, all bepained
with envy: and when he had no more that he might do, he scorned
her and said, "Lo, thou glutton! Thou filleth thee overmuch!". . . .

Composition of bearing of her outward and furthermore parts
shewed the inward making of her mind, and the seemliness of her
seemlin*g* [face] would not let the joy of her heart be hid. Forsooth, in a marvellous measure she tempered the sadness of her
heart with gladness of cheer, and somewhatly covered the mirth
of her mind with simpleness of shame of visage. And for the
apostle saith, "Women shall pray with heled [covered] head," the
white veil that hid her head hung before her eyes. She went
meekly with a slow and easy pace, her head louting [bowed] and
her face looking to the earth. Insomuch, soothly, the grace of her
soul shined in her visage of plenty of her heart, that many, of the
self [very] looking of her, were g*h*ostly refreshed and stirred to
devotion and weeping; and reading in her cheer the unc*t*ion of
the Holy Ghost as in a book, knew that fro her came virtue.

And so it fell on a day that a goodly man, familiar and friend
of religious persons, Guy, sometime chanter of the church Cam-
eracense, turned out of his way to visit her. Then one of his fellows, the which haply unto then knew not by experience how
much visitation and humbleness of good folk may do to meek
minds, as in scorning the goodly labor of the foresaid devout man,
said, "For God's love, sir chanter, what seek ye? Why leave ye
your way? Wherefore will ye follow and take flies and flying butterflies with child*re*n?"

He, soothly, that was meek, mild, and suffering, left not his way that he purposed for such words, but devoutly went to Christ's maiden, of whose presence another time he had not a little comfort. And while he spoke to her, his fellow, as secular manner is, set little by such words, and on another side was occupied with divers and idle words. Then when he was full and irked of abiding, he came to the chanter to bid him that he should hie in haste. And haply, as he looked rudely in the visage of Christ's maiden, suddenly and marvelously he fell into so great weeping of tears that unnethes he might be brought a long time after fro that place and presence of her.

Then the chanter, though he would for shame have holden counsel, taking heed and knowing the chance, was glad and scorned his fellow again and said, "Go we hence, what stand we? In hap [perhaps] ye will drive and chase butterflies?"

And he, after many sighings and tears, unnethes at last he might be pulled thence, saying, "Forgive me, father, for I wist not what I said before. Now, soothly, I have percevied by experience God's virtue in this woman.". . . .

But for we have shewed the precious brooches of this King's daughter and the sweet-savoring clothes of this spouse of Christ —though not sufficiently, nevertheless after our power—now go we to the hems of her clothes, that is to say, to her blessed passing, that we offer with the head the tail of our host.

When she had long time sacrified herself to our Lord at the foresaid place that is cleped Willambroc, she, that coveted to give herself to God alone, might no longer suffer muckle recourse of men that came to her often of devotion, for because she was so near the next town, that is cleped Nivelle. And when she had besought our Lord oftentimes with many prayers that he would purvey to his maiden a covenable place to her purpose and persons that meekly would agree them to her desire, the place of Oignies was shewed to her, that she saw never before, sith also that for newness and poverty of the house unnethes was then any mention thereof among men. And long advising herself, she wist not what manner place this should be. Forsooth, she, trusting of our Lord's behest long ere she came to the place, as daughter of obedience took leave of John her husband and of his brother, Master Guy her ghostly father, to visit that place and to dwell there if her list. Soothly, they, lest they should make her sorry whom they loved in charity, granted her lightly leave. . . .

After that through our Lord's bidding she was gone fro her own country and kindred; after that she had sat the more privily, the more easily, under the ombre of him that she desired, I suffice not to conceive with thought ne tell with word how great things our Lord wrought for her in that place. How often, more plenteous than before, he visited her with comfort of angels. How often she had homely speakings together in the church with our Lord's Mother. How often our Lord himself presencially appeared to her. For ever the more the term that she desired and the last year of her temporal life nighed, our Lord shewed to her the more abundant treasures of his largesse.

And when the last year that our Lord behight was near—the which herself might not hide for joy, for six year before she named it to Master Guy; also she prophesied to us often both the year and the time of her passing, but she expressed not the day —nevertheless, when she might no longer contain herself, she panted, sighed, and for desire cried, as no longer suffering till she should clip [embrace] our Lord, "Lord, I will not thou go without me; I covet no more here to abide; I will go home!" And in a marvellous manner, while she so out-ravished was anguished with huge desire, for plenty of heart she seemed well-nigh all to burst in body. And when she was turned to herself she might not stand on her feet long time after.

Also, for fervor of spirit, while she crying was drawn out of herself, she seemed as *if* fiery in visage, and (*that* the more marvel is) while she was in that excess of mind she might behold the compass of the material sun with the sight of her eyes unsmitten again. Then she, moisted with mirth, might not be still but cried, "It is said to me of our Lord that I go *in sancta sanctorum,* that is to say into holy things. O so sweet a word! Tell me Cleanness, what is *sancta sanctorum?*"—for Cleanness hight [was the name of] her maiden of whom for ghostly drunkenness she asked signification of the word, that they neither wist. Nevertheless, that word she rehearsed often, for it savored sweetly to her heart.

Then when she turning to herself marvelled that she was ravished above herself more hugely than before, it was said to her, "Marvel thou not; this is the last year! Now ha*st* thou no more time.! And she heard a voice of our Lord, cleping [calling] her and saying, "Come thou, my friend, my dove, and thou shalt be crowned.". . . .

Then the time behight was near the which she had desired before with many tears and asked with many sobbings and sighs. And lo! suddenly was made a sound fro heaven and a turtle's voice heard in our church, voice of joying and confession, as noise of one eating and gladding, as noise of high God in heaven. For our Lord shook away all weeping fro the eyes of his maiden and filled her heart with mirth and her lips with modulation [music]. Soothly, she began to sing with a high voice and clear, and ceased not the space of three days and three nights to love God, to do thankings, and to set together a full sweet cantilena and melody with dulcet note and rhyme of God, of saints, of our Lady, of other holy things, of her friends, and of holy writ. And she advised her not to find sentence, ne abode to set them together that were found; but as they had been written before her, our Lord gave her into that hour what she should say. Joying with continual cry, nor she in thinking labored ne disturbed her mind in disposing and setting of her words. For, as her seemed, one of the seraphim, that is a burning angel, spread his wings above her breast; by whose ministering and sweetly by-standing that rhymed ditty was inspired to her without all difficulty or hardness. And when she had all day cried unto night, her cheeks were made hoarse [rough], so that in the beginning of the night unnethes she might put forth any voice.

Then the prior of our house was fain [glad], for-because on the morn, that was Sunday, secular men of the country are wont to come to our church, the which in hap [perhaps], if they heard her sing without cease with so sharp and small voice, might be slandered thereby and count her as a fool . . . And at morn our timberer [singer] began to harp higher and clearer than before, for our Lord's angel that night did away all hoarseness fro her throat, putting into her breast anointment of wondrous suppleness. And so, her artery-veins reparalled and voice renewed, wellnigh all day she ceased not and men heard loving [praising] of God, voice of gladness, and merry notes of melody. Soothly, the doors were stuck and all shut out and our prior and the holy woman's maiden abode in the church; but they might not understand many things that she said of heavenly privities; and some they understood, but —woe the while!—they heled [concealed] not a few.

At the first she began her anthem fro the highest tone, that is fro the Holy Trinity, loving full long time the Trinity in unity, unity in Trinity, setting among to her sweet song marvelous things and unspeakable of the holy Trinity; also some things of holy writ, newly and wonderly expounding of the gospel, with psalms of the Old Testament and the New, shewing subtly muckle that she never heard. From the Trinity, soothly, she came down to the manhood of Christ; from thence to our Lady; from thence pronouncing many things of holy angels, of the apostles, and other saints following. Then, as in the last point and lowest, she said much of her friends that yet are in the world and commending them to our Lord *each* after other by row, prayed to God for them with many orisons. And all this she said in rhyme and Roman tongue. . . .

Soothly, the same Saturday at even when the day of joy and mirth was near, day that our Lord made, day that our Lord purveyed and behight to his maiden, our Lord's day, day of resurrection, day of the vigil of St. John Baptist, in the which also, as men saith, Saint John Evangelist passed fro this world, though his feast be holden another time, then Christ's maiden, that had eaten no manner meat two and fifty days, began with a sweet voice to sing alleluiah, and wellnigh all that night, as bidden to a feast, she was in joy and mirth.

Soothly, the fiend appeared on the Sunday and vexed her greatly, for she began somewhat to dread and to ask help of them that stood about. But then she, taking again trust of our Lord and strongly breaking the dragon's head and shielding herself with the sign of the cross, "Go aback!" quoth she, "Thou filth and foulness" —for she called him not foul but foulness. Then, the fiend fleeing away, she began to sing and thanked God of his great grace. And then certainly, when the even came near, before the feast of Saint John Baptist, about that hour that our Lord yielded the ghost on the cross, that is, the hour of noon, she soothly passed to God, never changing for any sorrow of death gladness of seeming or visage of joying. Nor I have mind that in health she had more gladness of cheer and more likeness of life. Nor, as custom is after death, she seemed brown or blue in face, but with an angel's countenance and dovely simpleness, white and clear in visage, in her dying and after her death she stirred many to devotion.

Also many were moisted sweetly in her obit with plenteous

flood of tears, and they perceived themselves visited of God through her prayers, as a holy woman saw before of the Holy Ghost and said before: that they that came together at her passing should receive muckle comfort of our Lord.

Forsooth, when her holy body should be washed in her obit, she was found so small and lean through infirmity and fastings that the ridge-bone of her back was clung to her womb, and as under a thin linen-cloth the bones of her back seemed under the little skin of her belly. She forsook them not after her death whom she loved in her life, but to some she came again. Also she spake often to holy women and of proved life, and she taught her friends what they should do, and warned them in perils, putting away all doubt fro their hearts by certain privy tokens. Also she got of our Lord with prayers to some of her friends both grace of wisdom and fervor of charity. Whereby to say: a monk of Cistercians' order saw in sleepings after the passing of Christ's maiden that a golden chalice went out of her mouth, with the which he gave drink to some of his friends. Another told me that he saw in sleepings her body borne as into a full bright precious stone.

Soothly, in the year of incarnation of Christ a thousand, two hundred and thirteen, the ninth calends of July, in the even of Saint John Baptist, the Sunday about noon, the precious pearl of Christ, Mary of Oignies, about six and thirty year of her age, was borne into the palace of the everlasting King, where is life without death, day without night, truth without falseness, joy without sorrow, sureness without dread, rest without travail, everlastingness without end; where the heart is not anguished with business, where the body is not diseased with sorrow, where the river of lust [desire] filleth all things and stops with spirit of full freedom, where we shall know as we are known, when God shall be all in all and shall give realm [rule] to God the Father, our lord Jesus Christ, that with the Father and the Holy Ghost liveth and reigneth, without end. Amen.

Here endeth the book written in the year of grace a thousand, two hundred and fifteen, that is to wit, of the life of Saint Mary of Oignies, endited in Latin of Master James, Bishop of Aachen.

[handwritten marginalia] Extremely close detail — again photos eyewitness account

[handwritten marginalia] died July 1213

[handwritten marginalia] a writer

[handwritten note at bottom] Cistercians made contrib to story of Holy Grail; lance as that of Centurion; Chalice as that of Last Supper and many other Xian points are added to tale of Grail through the Cistercians.

Characteristic of many points

Dame Juleanis of the more controlled, orthodox mystics; more orderly, decorous quality here but also deep feeling.

Dame Julian of Norwich

"REVELATIONS OF DIVINE LOVE"

HERE IS A VISION shewed by the goodness of God to a devout woman, and her name is Julian, that is recluse at Norwich and yet is on life, Anno Domini, 1413; in the which vision are full many comfortable words and greatly stirring to all them that desires to be Christ's lovers.

I desired three graces by the gift of God. The first was to have mind of Christ his passion; the second was bodily sickness; and the third was to have of God's gift three wounds. For the first come to my mind with devotion: methought I had a great feeling in the passion of Christ, but yet I desired to have more by the grace of God. Methought I would have been that time with Mary Maudeleine and with others that were Christ's lovers, that I might have seen bodily the passion of our Lord that he suffered for me, that I might have suffered with him as others did that loved him, notwithstanding that I believed sadly [fully] all the pains of Christ, as Holy Kirk shews and teaches, and also the paintings of crucifixes that are made, by the grace of God, after the teaching of Holy Kirk to the likeness of Christ's passion, as far forth as man his wit may reach. And naughtwithstanding all this true belief, I desired a bodily sight, wherein I might have more knowing of bodily pains of our Lord our Saviour and of the compassion of Our Lady and of all his true lovers that were believing his pains, that time and sithen [since]. For I would have been one of them and suffered with them. Other sight of God, ne shewing, desired I never none till that the soul were departed from the body, for I traist soothfastly that I should be safe. And this was my meaning, for I would, for cause of that shewing, have the more true mind in the passion of Christ.

For the second come to my mind with contrition, freely, withouten any seeking a willful desire to have of God's gift a bodily sickness; and I would that this bodily sickness might have been so hard as to the death, so that I might in the sickness take all my ritings [rites] of Holy Kirk, weening myself that I should die and that all creatures that saw me might ween the same, for I would have no comfort of no fleshly, neither earthly, life. In this weakness, I desired to have all manner of pains, bodily and ghostly, that I should have if I should die; all dreads and tempests of fiends and all manner of their pains, save of the out-passing of the soul. For I hoped that it might be to me a speed when I should die, for I desired soon to be with my God.

These two desires of the passion and of the sickness I desired them with a condition, for methought that it passed the common course of prayers, and therefore I said: "Lord, thou wot what I would, if it be thy will that I have it. Grant it me; and if it be nought thy will, good Lord, be not displeased, for I will nought but as thou will.

This sickness desired I in my thought, that I might have it when I were not thirty year elde. For that, the third, I heard a man tell of Holy Kirk of the story of Saint Cecilia: in the which shewing I understood that she had three wounds with a sword in the neck, with the which she pined to the death. By the stirring of this, I conceived a mighty desire, praying our Lord God that he would grant me three wounds in my lifetime: that is to say, the wounds of contrition, the wound of compassion, and the wound of willful longing to God. Right as I asked the other two with a condition, I asked the third withouten any condition. This two desires beforesaid passed fro my mind, and the third dwelled continually.

And when I was thirty winter old and a half, God sent me a bodily weakness, in the which I saw three days and three nights; and on the fourth night I took of my rightings of Holy Kirk and weened nought till [to] have lived till day. And after this, I languored forth two days and two nights; and on the third night I weened ofttimes to have passed, and so weened they that were about me. In this, I was right sorry and loath; thought for to die, but for nothing that was in earth that me liked to live for, nor nothing that I was afeared for, for I trusted in God. But it was for I would have loved God better and lang time, that I might, by the grace of that living, have the more knowing and loving of God in the bliss of heaven. For, methought, all the time that I have lived here, so little and so short in the regard of endless bliss, I thought thus: Good Lord, may my living be no langer to thy worship. And

I was answered in my reason and by the feelings of my pains, that I should die. And I assented fully, with all the will of my heart, to be at God his will.

Thus I endured till day; and by then I was in my body dead, fro the midst downward, as to my feeling. Then was I stirred to be set uprights, leaning; with clothes to my head, for to have the more freedom of my heart to be at God's will and thinking of him, whiles my life would last. And they that were with me sent for the parson, my curate, to be at mine ending. He come and a child with him, and brought a cross. And by then I had set mine eyen and might nought speak. The parson set the cross before my face, and said, "Daughter, I have brought thee the image of thy savior. Look thereupon and comfort thee therewith, in reverence of him that died for thee and me." Methought then that I was well, for mine eyen were set upward unto heaven, whither I trusted for to come. But, nevertheless, I assented to set mine eyen in the face of the crucifix if I might, for to endure the longer in the time of mine ending, for methought I might longer endure for to look evenforth than upright.

After this, my sight began to fail and it was all dark about me in the chamber, and mirk as it had been night; save in the image of the cross there held a common light and, I wist never how, all that was beside the cross was ugly to me, as if it had been mickle occupied with fiends. After this, the over-party of my body began to die as to my feeling. My hands fell down on either side. And also, for unpower, my head settled down to one side. The most pain that I feeled was shortness of wind. And, failing of life, then weened I soothly to have been at the point of death.

And in this, suddenly all my pain was away fro me and I was all whole, and namely [especially] the over-party of my body, as ever I was before or after. I marvelled of this change, for methought it was a privy working of God and nought of Kind. And yet, by the feeling of ease, I trusted never the more that I should live, ne the feeling of this ease was ne full ease to me, for I thought I had liefer be delivered of this world, for my heart was willful thereto.

And suddenly come into my mind that I should desire the second wound of our Lord's gift and of his grace, that he would fullfil my body with mind of feeling of his blessed passion, as I had before prayed. For I would that his pains were my pains, with compassion; and afterward, longing to God, thus thought me: that I might, with his grace, have his wounds that I had before desired. But in this I desired never ne bodily sight ne no manner shewing of God but compassion, as me thought that a kind soul might have with our Lord Jesu, that for love would become man, with him desired to suffer living in deadly body, as God would give me grace.

And in this, suddenly I saw the red blood trickle down fro under the garland all hot, freshly, plentifully and lovely, right as methought that it was in that time that the garland of thorns was thrusted on his blessed head. Right so, both God and man, the same suffered for me. I conceived truly and mightily that it was himself that shewed it me, withouten any mean [middleman], and then I said, "Benedicite, domine!" This I said vehemently in my meaning, with a mighty voice and full. Greatly I was astonied for wonder and marvel that I had that he would speak humbly with a sinful creature living in the wretched flesh.

Thus I looked it for that time, that our Lord Jhesu of his courteous love would shew me toforth, before the time of my temptation. For methought it might be well that I should, by the sufferance of God and with his keeping, be tempted of fiends ere I died with the sight of his blessed passion; with the godhead that I saw in mine understanding, I saw that this was strength enough to me; yea, unto all creatures living, that should be safe against all the fiends of hell and against all ghostly enemies.

In this same time that I saw this bodily sight, our Lord shewed me a ghostly sight of his holy loving. I saw that he is to us all thing that is good and comfortable to our help. He is our clothing for love: waps [embraces] us and winds us, halses [greets] us, and all teaches us: hangs about us for tender love that he may never leave us.

And so in this sight I saw soothly that he is all thing that is good as to mine understanding, and in this he shewed me a little thing, the quantity of a hazelnut lying in the palm of my hand, and to my understanding that it was as round as any ball. I looked it upon and thought, "What may this be?" and I was answered generally thus: "It is all that is made."

I marvelled how that it might last. For methought it might fall

suddenly to nought for little. And I was answered in mine understanding: "It lasts, and ever shall: for God loves it. And so hath all
thing the being through love of God." In this little thing I saw
three parties; the first is that God made it, the second is that he
loves it, the third is that God keeps it.

But what is that to me? Soothly, the maker, the lover, the
keeper, for to I am substantially oned to him. I may never have
love, rest, ne very bliss: that is to say, that I be so fastened to him
that there be right nought that is made betwixt my God and me.
And who shall do this deed? Soothly, myself by his mercy and his
grace, for he has made me thereto and blissfully restored.

In this, God brought Our Lady to mine understanding. I saw
her ghostly in bodily likeness: a simple maiden and a meek, young
of age, in the stature that she was when she conceived. Also, God
shewed me in part the wisdom and the truth of her soul. Wherein
I understood the reverent beholding that she beheld her God that
is her maker, marvelling with great reverence that he would be
born of her that was a simple creature of his making. For this was
her marvelling: that he that was her maker would be born of her
that was a simple creature of his making. And in this wisdom and
truth, knowing the greatness of her maker and the little heed of
herself, that is made, made her meekly for to say to the angel
Gabriel: "Lo me, here, God's handmaiden!"

In this sight I saw soothfastly that she is more than all that God
made beneath her in worthiness and in fulheed. For, above her is
nothing that is made but the blessed manhead of Christ. This little
thing that is made, that is beneath Our Lady, Saint Mary, God
shewed it unto me, as little as it had been a hazelnut: methought
it might have fallen for little.

In this blessed revelation God shewed me three noughts. Of
which noughts, this is first that was shewed me. Of this, needs ilk
man and woman to have knowing that desires to live contemplative. That him may like not all thing that is made, to have the love
of God that is unmade. For this is the cause why they that are occupied wilfully in earthly business and evermore seeks worldly
weal are nought here of his in heart and in soul if they love and
seeks their rest in this thing that is so little, where no rest is in, and
knows not God that is all-mighty, all-wise, and all-good, for he is
very rest. God will be known, and him likes that we rest in him;

M. a.
Tremendous freedom of action but considerable control of thought
Today
Freedom of thought but control of action (Ex. cars at cloverleaf

for all that are beneath him suffices not to us. And this is the cause why no soul is rested till it be noughted of all that is made. When he is noughted for love to have him that is all that is God, then is he able to receive ghostly rest.

Margery Kempe

"THE BOOK OF MARGERY KEMPE"

ANOTHER TIME, as this creature prayed to God that she might live chaste, by leave of her husband, Christ said to her mind, "Thou must fast the Friday both fro meat and drink, and thou shalt have thy desire ere Whitsunday, for I shall suddenly slay [strike] thine husband."

Then, on the Wednesday in Easter week, after her husband would have had knowledge of her as he was won*t* before and when he gan [did] nigh her, she said, "Jesus, help me!" And he had no power to touch her at that time in that wise, ne never after with no fleshly knowing.

It befell on a Friday before Whitsun Even, as this creature was in a church of St. Margaret at N*orwich* hearing her mass, she heard a great noise and a dreadful. She was sore astoni*s*hed, sore dreading the voice of the people which said God should take vengeance upon her. She kneeled upon her knees, holding down her head and her book in her hand, praying our Lord Christ Jesu for grace and for mercy. Suddenly fell down from the highest part of the church-vault, fro under the foot of the spar, on her head and on her back a stone which weighed three pound and a short end of a tree weighing six pound, that her thought her back brake asunder and she feared as she had b*een* dead *in* a little while. Soon after, she cried, "Jesu, mercy!" and anon her pain was gone.

A good man which hight John of Wereham, seeing this wonder-case and supposing that she *had* been greatly dis-eased, came and pulled her by the sleeve and said, "Dame, how fare ye?"

The creature, all whole and sound, thanked him of his cheer and his charity, much marveling and greatly a-wondered that she felt no pain and had felt so much a little before. Ne twelve weeks after she felt no pain. Then the spirit of God said to her soul, "Hold this for a great miracle and, if the people will not *be*lieve this, I shall work much more.". . . .

Soon after, this creature was moved in her soul to go to visit certain places for ghostly health, inasmuch as she was cured and might not without consenting of her husband. She required her husband to grant her leave and he, fully trusting it was the will of God, soon consenting, they went together to such place as she was moved.

And then our Lord Christ Jesu said to her, "My servants desire greatly to see thee." Then was she welcomed and much made of in divers places. Wherefore she had great dread of vainglory and much was afeared. Our merciful Lord Christ Jesu—worshipped be his name—said to her, "Dread thee not, daughter, I shall take vainglory fro thee. For they that worship thee, they worship me; they that despise thee, they despise me; and I shall chastise *t*hem therefor. I am in thee; and thou in me. And they that hear thee, they hear the voice of God. Daughter, there is no so sinful man in earth living, if he will forsake his sin and do after thy counsel, such grace as thou behestest him I will confirm for thy love."

Then her husband and she went forth to York and to other divers places.

It befell upon a Friday, on Midsummer Even in right hot weather, as this creature was coming fro York-ward, bearing a bottle with beer in her hand, and her husband a cake in his bosom, he asked his wife this question: "Margery, if here came a man with a sword and would smite off mine head lest than I should commune kindly [naturally] with you as I have d*one* before, say the truth of your conscience—for ye say ye will not lie— whether, would ye suffer mine head to be smit off, or else suffer me to meddle with you again as I did some time?"

"Alas, sir!" she said, "Why move ye this matter, and have we been chaste this eight weeks!"

"For I will wit the truth of your heart."

And then she said with great sorrow: "Forsooth, I had liefer see you be slain than we should turn again to our uncleanness."

And he said again: "Ye are no good wife."

And then she asked her husband what was the cause that he had not meddled with her eight weeks before, since she lay with

him every night in his bed. And he said he was so much afeared
when he would *have* touched her that he durst no more do.

"Now, good sir, amend you and ask God mercy, for I told you
near three year since that ye should be slain suddenly; and now is
this the third year and yet I hope I shall *have* my desire. Good
sir, I pray you grant me *t*hat I shall ask and I shall pray for you
that ye shall be saved through the mercy of our Lord Jesu Christ
and ye shall have more mede in heaven than if ye weared an hair-
shirt or an habergeoun. I pray you, suffer me to make a vow of
chastity in what bishop's hand that God will."

"Nay," he said, "That will I not grant you, for now may I use
you without deadly sin and then might I not so."

Then she said again: "If it be the will of the Holy Ghost to fulfil
*t*hat I have said, I pray God ye may consent thereto. And if it be
not the will of the Holy Ghost, I pray God ye never consent
thereto."

Then went they forth to Bridlington-ward in right hot weather,
the foresaid creature having great sorrow and great dread for her
chastity. And as they came by a cross, her husband set him down
under the cross, cleping [calling] his wife unto him and saying
these words unto her: "Margery, grant me my desire and I shall
grant you your desire. My first desire is that we shall lie still together in *one* bed as we *have* *done* before; the second, that ye
shall pay my debts ere ye go to Jerusalem; and the third, that ye
shall eat and drink with me on the Friday as ye were wont to do."

"Nay, sir," she said, "To break the Friday I will never grant you
while I live."

"Well," he said, "Then shall I meddle *with* you again."

She prayed him that he would give her leave to make her prayers; and he granted it goodly. Then she kneeled down beside a
cross in the field and prayed in this manner, with great abundance
of tears: "Lord God, thou knowest all thing; thou knowest what
sorrow I have had to be chaste in my body to thee all this three
year; and now might I have my will and I dare not for love of
thee. For, if I would break that manner of fasting which thou
commandest me to keep on the Friday, without meat or drink, I
should now have my desire. But, blessed Lord, thou knowest I
will not contrary thy will, and mickle now is my sorrow *unl*ess
tha*t* I find comfort in thee. Now, blessed Jesu, make thy will

known to me unworthy, that I may follow thereafter and fulfil it with all my mights."

And then our Lord Jesu Christ with great sweetness spake to this creature, commanding her to go again to her husband and pray him to grant her *what* she desired—"and he shall have *that* he desireth. For, my dearworthy daughter, this was the cause that I bade thee fast, for thou shouldest the sooner obtain and get thy desire—and now it is granted thee. I will no longer thou fast; therefore I bid thee in the name of Jesu eat and drink as thine husband doth."

Then this creature thanked our Lord Jesu Christ of his grace and his goodness, *and* sith [after] rose up and went to her husband, saying unto him, "Sire, if it like you, ye shall grant me my desire and ye shall have your desire. Granteth me that ye shall not come in my bed, and I grant you to quit your debts ere I go to Jerusalem. And maketh my body free to God, so that ye never make no challenging in me to ask no debt of matrimony after this day while ye live, and I shall eat and drink on the Friday at your bidding."

Then said her husband again *to* her: "As free may your body be to God as it hath been to me."

This creature thanked God greatly, enjoying that she had her desire, praying her husband that they should say three pasternosters in the worship of the Trinity for the great grace that he had granted them. And so they did, kneeling under a cross. And sithen they ate and drank together in great gladness of spirit. . . .

On a time, as this creature was at Canterbury, in the church among the monks, she was greatly despised and reproved for cause she wept so fast, both of the monks and priests and of secular men, near all a day, both aforenoon and afternoon—also in so much that her husband went away fro her as he had not a-known her and left her alone among *them*—choose her as she could, for other comfort had she none of him as that day.

So an old monk, which had been treasurer with the queen while he was in secular clothing, a rich man and greatly dread of much people, took her by the hand, saying unto her, "What canst thou say of God?"

"Sir," she saith, "I will both speak of him and hear of him"— rehearsing the monk a story of scripture.

The monk said, "I would thou were closed in an house of stone, that there should no man speak with thee."

"Ah, sir!" she said, "Ye should maintain God's servants, and ye are the first that hold against them. Our Lord amend you!"

Then a young monk said to this creature, "Either thou hast the Holy Ghost or else thou hast a devil within thee, for that thou speakest here to us it is holy writ, and that hast thou not of thyself."

Then said this creature, "I pray you, sir, give me leave to tell you a tale."

Then the people said to the monk, "Let her say what she will."

And then she said, "There was once a man that had sinned greatly against God, and when he was shriven his confessor enjoined him, in part of penance, that he should one year hire men to chide him and reprove him for his sins, and he should give them silver for their labor. And on a day he came among men, great men, as now be here—God save you all—and stood among them as I do now among you, despising him as ye do me, the man laughing or smiling and having good game at their words. The greatest master of them said to the man, 'Why laughest thou, brothel [wretch], and art thou greatly despised?' 'Ah, sir, I have a great cause to laugh, for I have many days put silver out of my purse and this day I may keep my silver in my purse, and hired men to chide me for remission of my sin; and this day I may keep my silver in my purse, I thank you all.' Right so I say to you, worshipful sirs. While I was at home in mine own country, day by day with great weeping and mourning I sorrowed, for I had no shame, scorn, and despite, as I was worthy. I thank you all, sirs, highly for what, forenoon and afternoon, I have had reasonably this day, blessed be God thereof."

Then she went out of the monastery, they following and crying upon her, "Thou shalt be burnt, false lollard. Here is a cartful of thorns ready for thee, and a tun to burn thee with."

And the creature stood without the gates at Canterbury, for it was in the evening, much people wondering on her. Then said the people, "Take and burn her!" And the creature stood still, trembling and quaking full sore in her flesh, without any earthly comfort, and wist not where her husband was become.

Then prayed she in her heart to our Lord, thinking on this manner, "Hither came I, Lord, for thy love. Blessed Lord, help me and have mercy on me!" And anon, after she had made her prayers in her heart to our Lord, there came two fair young men and said to her, "Damsel, art thou no *heretic* ne no lollar?"

And she said, "No, sirs. I am neither *heretic* ne lollar."

Then they asked her where was her inn. She said she wist never in what street: nevertheless it should be at a Dutchman's house. Then these two young men brought her home to her hostel and made her great cheer, praying her to pray for *them*. And there found she her husband . . .

And when this creature saw Jerusalem, riding on an ass she thanked God with all her heart, praying him for his mercy that, like as he had brought her to see this earthly city Jerusalem, he would grant her grace to see the blissful city Jerusalem above, the city of heaven. Our Lord Jesu Christ, answering to her thought, granted her to have her desire.

Then, for joy that she had and the sweetness that she felt in the dalliance of our Lord, she was in point to a-fallen off her ass, for she might not bear the sweetness and grace that God wrought in her soul. Then two pilgrims of Dutchmen went to her and kept her fro falling, of which the one was a priest. And he put spices in her mouth to comfort her, weening she had been sick. And so they helped her forth to Jerusalem. And when she came there she said, "Sires, I pray you be not displeased though I weep sore in this holy place where our Lord Jesu Christ was quick and dead."

Then went they to the temple in Jerusalem and they were let in on the one day at evensong-time and abode therein till the next day at evensong-time. Then the friars lifted up a cross and led the pilgrims about fro *one* place to another where our Lord had suff-ered his *penance* and his passions, every man and woman bearing a wax candle in *their* hand; and the friars alway, as they went about, told *them* what our Lord suffered in every place.

And the foresaid creature wept and sobbed so plenteously as though she had seen our Lord with her bodily eye suffering his passion at that time. Before her in her soul she saw him verily by contemplation, and that caused her to have compassion. And when they came up onto the Mount of Calvary, she fell down that she might not stand ne kneel, but wallowed and wrest*l*ed with her body, spreading her arms abroad, and cried with a loud voice as though her heart should a-burst asunder, for in the city of her soul she saw verily and freshly how our Lord was crucified. Before her face she heard and saw in her ghostly sight the mourning of our Lady, of St. John, and Mary Magdalene and of many other that loved our Lord, and she had so great compassion and so great pain to see our Lord's pain that she might not keep herself fro crying and roaring, though she should a-been dead therefor. And this was the first cry that ever she cried in any contemplation; and this manner of crying endured many years after this time, for ought that any man might do, and therefor suffered she much despite and much reproof. The crying was so loud and so wonderful that it made the people astonished less than [unless] they had heard it before or else that they knew the cause of the crying. And she had them so often-times that they made her right weak in her bodily mights, and namely if she heard of our Lord's passion. And sometimes, when she saw the crucifix, or if she saw a man had a wound or a beast whether it were, or if a man beat a child before her or smote an horse or another beast with a whip, if she might see it or hear it, her thought she saw our Lord be beaten or wounded like as she saw in the man or in the beast—as well in the field as in the town; and by herself alone as well as among people.

First when she had her cryings at Jerusalem, she had them often-times—and in Rome also. And when she came home into England, first at her coming home it came but seldom, as it were once in a month, sithen once in the week, afterward quotidianly, and once she had fourteen on one day, and another day she had seven, and so as God would visit her—sometime in the church, sometime in the street, sometime in the chamber, sometime in the field when God would send them, for she knew never time ne hour when they should come. And they came never without passing great sweetness of devotion and high contemplation. And, as soon as she perceived that she should cry, she would keep it in as much as she might, that the people should not a-heard it for annoying of them. For some said it was a wicked spirit vexed her; some said it was a sickness; some said she had drunken too much wine; some banned [cursed] her; some wished she had been in the haven; some would she had been in the sea in a bottomless boat. And so each man as him thought. Other ghostly men loved her and favored her the more. Some great clerks said our Lady cried never so, ne no saint in heaven; but they knew full little what she felt, ne they would not believe but that she might have abstained her fro crying if she had willed. . . .

On the next day she was brought into the chapter-house of Beverley, and there was the Archbishop of York and many great clerks with him, priests, canons, and secular men. Then said the archbishop to the said creature, "What, woman, art thou come again! I would fain be delivered of thee."

And then a priest brought her forth before him, and the archbishop said, all that were present hearing: "Sirs, I had this woman before me at Cawood, and there I with my clerks examined her in her faith and found no default in her. Furthermore, sirs, I have sithen that time spoken with good men which hold her a perfect woman, and a good woman. Notwithstanding all this, I gave one of my men five shillings to lead her out of his country, for quieting of the people. And, as they were going in their journey, they were taken and arrested; my man put in prison for her; also, her gold and her silver was taken away fro her with her beads and her ring; and she is brought here again before me. Is here any man can say anything against her?"

Then other men said, "Here is a friar can [knows] much thing against her."

The friar came forth and said that she dispraved [disparaged] all men of holy church, and much ill language he uttered that time of her. Also he said that she should have been burnt at Lynn had his order, that was Friar-Preachers', ne been. "And, sir, she saith that she may weep and have contrition when she will."

Then came those two men which had arrested her, saying with the friar that she was Combomy's [Cobham's?, i.e. Sir John Oldcastle's] daughter, and was sent to bear letters about the country. And they said she had not been at Jerusalem ne in the Holy Land no on other pilgrimage, like as she had been in truth. They denied all truth and maintained the wrong, as many other had done before. When they had said enough, a great while and a long time, they were in peace.

Then said the archbishop to her, "Woman, what saist thou hereto?"

She said, "My Lord, save your reverence, it are lesings [lies], all the words that they say."

Then said the archbishop to the friar, "Friar, the words are no heresy; they are slanderous words and erroneous."

"My Lord," said the friar, "She can [knows] her faith well enough. Nevertheless, my lord of Bedford is wroth with her, and he will have her."

"Well, friar," said the archbishop, "And thou shalt lead her to him."

"Nay, sir," said the friar, "It falleth not for a friar to lead a woman about."

"And I will not," said the archbishop, "that the Duke of Bedford be wroth with me for her." Then said the archbishop to his men, "Taketh heed to the friar till I will have him again," and commanded another man to keep the said creature also till he would have her again another time when he liked.

The said creature prayed him of his lordship that she should not be put amongst men, for she was a man's wife; and the archbishop said, "Nay, thou shalt none harm have."

Then he that was charged with her took her by the hand and led her home to his house, and did her sit with him at meat and drink, shewing her goodly cheer. Thither came many priests and other men eftsoon to see her and speak with her, and much people had great compassion that she was so evil-fared with.

In short time after, the archbishop sent for her, and she came into his hall. His meinie was at meat, and she was led into his chamber, even to his bed's side. Then she, obeying, thanked him of his gracious lordship that he had shewed to her before-time.

"Yea, yea!" said the archbishop. "I am worse informed of thee than ever I was before."

She said, "My Lord, if it like you to examine me, I shall be a-know [avow] the truth and if I be found guilty I will obey your correction."

Then came forth a Friar-Preacher which was suffragan with the archbishop, to whom the archbishop said, "Now sir, as ye said to me when she was not present, say now while she is present."

"Shall I so?" said the suffragan.

"Yea," said the archbishop.

Then said the suffragan to the said creature, "Damsel, thou were at my Lady Westmoreland."

"When, sir?" said she.

"At Easter," said the suffragan.

She, not replying, said, "Well, sir?"

Then said he, "My Lady her own person was well pleased with thee and liked well thy words, but thou counseledest my Lady Greystoke to forsake her husband, that is a baron's wife and daughter to my Lady of Westmoreland, and now hast said enough to be burnt for." And so he multiplied many shrewd words before the archbishop—it is not expedient to rehearse them.

At the last, she said to the archbishop, "My lord, if it be your will, I saw not my Lady Westmoreland this two year and more. Sir, she sent for me ere I went to Jerusalem and, if it like you, I will go again to her for record that I moved no such matter."

"Nay," said they that stood about, "Let her be put in prison, and we shall send a letter to the worshipful Lady, and, if it be truth that she saith, let her go quit without danger." And she said she was right well a-paid that it were so.

Then said a great clerk which stood a little beside the archbishop, "Put her forty days in prison and she shall love God the better while she liveth."

The archbishop asked her what tale it was that she told the Lady of Westmoreland when she spake with her.

She said, "I told her a good tale of a lady that was damned for she would not love her enemies, and of a bailliff that was saved for he loved his enemies and forgave what they had trespassed against him, and yet he was held an evil man."

The archbishop said it was a good tale. Then said his steward, and many more with him, crying with a loud voice to the archbishop, "Lord, we pray you let her go hence at this time, and, if ever she come again, we shall burn her ourselves."

The archbishop said, "I believe there was never woman in England so fared withal as she is and hath been." Then he said to the said creature, "I wot not what I shall do with thee."

She said, "My lord, I pray you let me have your letter and your seal into record that I have excused me against mine enemies and nothing is attied [charged] against me, neither error ne heresy that may be proved upon me, thanked be our Lord—and John, your man, again to bring me over the water."

And the archbishop full goodly granted her all her desire—our Lord reward him his mede!—and delivered her purse with her ring and her beads, which the Duke's men of Bedford had taken fro her before. The archbishop had great marvel where she had goods to go with about the country, and she said good men gave it her for she should pray for them. Then she, kneeling down, received his blessing; and took her leave with right glad cheer, going out of his chamber.

And the archbishop's men prayed her to pray for them. But the steward was wroth, for she laughed and made good cheer, saying to her, "Holy folk should not laugh."

She said, "Sir, I have great cause for to laugh, for the more shame I suffer and despite, the merrier may I be in our Lord Jesu Christ."

Then she came down into the hall, and there stood the Friar-Preacher that had caused her all that woe. And so she passed forth with a man of the archbishop, bearing the letter which the archbishop had granted her for a record. And he brought her to the water of Humber, and there he took his leave of her, returning to his lord and bearing the said letter with him again. So she was left alone without knowledge of the people.

All the foresaid dis-ease fell her on a Friday, thanked be God of all.

Social Writers

AMONG MANY INDICATIONS that English prose had been reinstated as the normal medium for ordinary writing and that a basic style was common property are the family letters, courtesy books, and treatises on sport that crop up at the end of the fourteenth century and become fairly numerous in the fifteenth. Before then, such writings, so far as they existed at all, were in French or even in Latin.

The earliest collections of family letters belong to the fifteenth century—written by the Celys, a merchant family that did business in London and Flanders; the Stonors, another merchant family, settled near Henley in Oxfordshire; and the Pastons, lawyers and estate-owners in Norfolk. Contributed by several generations, the letters touch on an infinity of local and personal matters as well as on business, law, quarrels, courtships, marriages, and domestic affairs; they are written by persons whose command of English prose ranged from high skill to near illiteracy.

From this diversity we have selected a few letters on love and marriage by some of the more accomplished writers: first, a whimsically-bothered letter that Thomas Betson, partner to Sir William Stonor, wrote to his partner's stepchild, little Katherine Rich, the thirteen-year-old child whom he married two years later; second, a gossipy complaint that Betson sent to the girl's mother; third, a few letters that passed between John Paston and Margery Brews before and after their marriage; fourth, the *cri-de-coeur* that Richard Calle, a bailliff who had been presumptuous enough to elope with his employer's sister, Margery Paston, wrote to his wife just after their secret marriage. All the letters belong to the 1470-80's.

For the convenience of such families as the Pastons and the guidance of youngsters in training in noble households, books of manners, translated from Latin or French, become common in the later fifteenth century. Most are in verse, either from old tradition or for easier memorization. *The Marshall in Hall* from which our selection is taken differs in being directed toward an important particular office—the one that Chaucer's Host was said to be fitted for—but its social code is similar to the rest, a formal politeness more ceremonial than ours but not different

85

in kind. Described as "A general rule to teach every man that is willing
for to learn to serve a lord or a master in everything to his pleasure," it
seems to be an independent composition, written about 1475, and its
style is as formally precise as its prescription.

The earliest sporting manual in English, *The Master of Game*, was
compiled shortly after 1406 from a French book written by Gaston,
Comte de Foix, the southern nobleman whose impressive self-indulgence is described so elegantly in Froissart. The English compiler was
Edward, second Duke of York, then in prison for his part in a plot
against Henry IV. Among its successors was one of the few fifteenth-
century books printed outside London, *The Book of St. Albans*, 1486,
often attributed to Dame Juliana Berners (born about 1386), a prioress.
The little treatise deals with hawking, hunting, and heraldry, and must
have been written soon after the Duke of York's work, to which it is a
kind of appendix. Our selection, a short treatise on fishing, is a supple-
ment to this appendix, for it first appears in Wynkyn de Worde's reprint
of 1496. Whoever wrote it had the Walton touch, for he was a fishing-
devotee who was able through simple language to call others to his own
passion.

LETTERS ON LOVE AND MARRIAGE

THOMAS BETSON TO KATHERINE RICH
JUNE, 1475

MINE OWN heartily-beloved cousin Katherine,

I recommend me unto you with all the inwardness of mine
heart. And now lately ye shall understand that I received a token
from you, the which was and is to me right heartily welcome, and
with glad will I received it. And, over that, I had a letter from
Howlake your gentle squire, by the which I understand right
well that ye be in good health of body and merry at heart. And I
pray God heartily to his pleasure to continue the same, for it is to
me very great comfort that ye so be, so help me Jesu. And if ye
would be a good eater of your meat alway, that ye might wax and
grow fast to be a woman, ye should make me the gladdest man of
the world, by my troth. For when I remember your favor and
your sad, loving dealing to me-wards, forsooth, ye make me even

very glad and joyous in my heart. And, on the tother side again, when I remember your young youth and see well that ye be none eater of your meat, the which should help you greatly in waxing, forsooth, then ye make me very heavy again. And, therefore, I pray you, mine own sweet cousin, even as you love me, to be merry and to eat your meat like a woman. And if ye so will do for my love, look what ye will desire of me, whatsoever it be, and by my troth I promise you, by the help of Our Lord, to perform it to my power. I can more no say now, but at my coming home I will tell you much more between you and me and God before.

And whereas ye, full womanly and like a lover, remember me with manifold recommendation in diverse manners, remitting the same to my discretion to depart [share] them there as I love best, forsooth, mine own sweet cousin, ye shall understand that with good heart and good will I receive and take to myself the one half of them—and them I will keep by me. And the tother half, with hearty love and favor, I send them to you, mine own sweet cousin, again, for to keep by you. And, over that, I send you the blessing that Our Lady gave her dear son, and ever well to fare.

I pray you, greet well my horse. And pray him to give you four of his years to help you withal, and I will at my coming home give him four of my years—and four horse-loaves to amends. Tell him that I prayed him so. And, cousin Katherine, I thank you for him—and my wife shall thank you for him hereafter—for ye do great cost upon him, as it is told me.

Mine own sweet cousin, it was told me but late, that ye were at Calais to seek me, but ye could not see me nor find me. Forsooth, ye might have come to my counter [shop], and there ye should both find me and see me, and not have faulted of me. But ye sought me in a wrong Calais, and that ye should well know if ye were here and saw this Calais—as would God ye were, and some of them with you that were with you at your gentle Calais.

I pray you, gentle cousin, commend me to the clock and pray him to amend his unthrift manners. For he strikes ever in undue time, and he will be ever afore—and that is a shrewd condition. Tell him, without he amend his condition, that he will cause strangers to avoid and come no more there. I trust to you that he shall amend against mine coming, the which shall be shortly, with all hands and all feet with God's grace.

My very faithful cousin, I trust to you that, though all I have not remembered my right worshipful mistress, your mother, afore in this letter, that ye will of your gentleness recommend me to her mistress-ship as many times as it shall please you. And ye may say, if it please you, that in Whitsun week next I intend to the mart-ward. And I trust you will pray for me—for I shall pray for you and, so it may be, none so well. And almighty Jesu make you a good woman and send you many good years and long, to live in health and virtue to his pleasure.

At great Calais on this side on the sea, the first day of June, when every man was gone to his dinner and the clock smote nine and all our household cried after me and bade me come down—"Come down to dinner at once!" And what answer I gave them, ye know it of old.

By your faithful cousin and lover, Thomas Betson.

I sent you this ring for a token.

THOMAS BETSON TO
DAME ELIZABETH STONOR
JULY 1478

RIGHT HONORABLE and my right singular good lady,

I recommend me unto your good ladyship. And, madam, if it like you, sith [since] I came home to London I met with my lady, your mother, and God wot she made me right sullen cheer with her countenance whiles I was with her—methought it long till I was departed. She brake unto me of old far-years, and specially she brake to me of the tale I told her between the vicar-that-was and her. She said the vicar never fared well sith, he took it so much to heart. I told her a light answer again, and so I departed from her. I had no joy to tarry with her. She is a fine, merry woman, but ye shall not know it nor yet find it, nor none of yours, by what I see in her.

Mother midwife told me that neither my lady your mother, my Lady Stoker, nor her husband came once to see my cousin Anne sith she came to her, nor yet asked once how she fared. And if my lady, your mother, meet my cousin Anne, she will say no more but

"God's blessings have ye and mine!" and so go her way forth, as though she had no joy of her. When ye come to London I shall tell you more.

My cousin Anne hath been with me here at home, and she is hale and right well amended and as a woman should be—there is no fault, Our Blessed Lord be thanked and his blessed mother. Good Madam, by the next *th*at comes, let her have all her clothes. She hath need unto them, and that knoweth Our Lord, who ever preserve you Madam, and all yours, in long health and virtue to His pleasure.

At London, the last day of July, Anno supra, by your servant, Thomas Betson.

JOHN PASTON TO MARGERY BREWS
1476

MISTRESS,

Though so be that I, unacquainted with you as yet, take upon me to be thus bold as to write unto you without your knowledge and leave, yet, mistress, for such poor service as I now in my mind owe to you, purposing—ye not displeased—during my life to continue the same, I beseech you to pardon my boldness and not to disdain, but to accept this simple bill to recommend me to you in such wise as I best can or may imagine to your pleasure.

And, mistress, for such report as I have heard of you by many and divers persons, and specially by my right trusty friend Richard Stratton, bearer hereof—to whom I beseech you to give credence in such matters as he shall on my behalf commune with you of, if it like you to listen him. And that report causeth me to be the more bold to write unto you so as I do. For I have heard oft times Richard Stratton say that ye can and will take everything well that is well meant, whom I believe and trust as much as few men living, I ensure you by my troth. And, mistress, I beseech you to think none otherwise in me but that I will and shall at all seasons be ready, with God's grace, to accomplish all such things as I have informed and desired the said Richard on my behalf to give you knowledge of, but—if it so be that against my will it come of you that I be cast off from your service, and not willingly

by my desert, and that I am and will be yours and at your commandment in every wise during my life.

Here I send you this bill, written with my lewd hand and sealed
with my signet, to remain with you for a witness against me, and
to my shame and dishonor, if I contrary it. And, mistress, I beseech you, in easing of the poor heart that sometime was at my
rule, which now is at yours, that in as short time as can be, that
I may have knowledge of your intent and how ye will have me
demeaned in this matter. And I will be at all seasons ready to perform, in this matter and all others, *at* your pleasure, as far forth as
lieth in my poor power to do, or in all theirs that aught will do for
me, with God's grace—whom I beseech to send you the accomplishment of your most worshipful desires, mine own fair lady.
For I will no further labor but to you, unto the time ye give me
leave, and till I be sure that ye shall take no displeasure with my
further labour.

MARGERY BREWS TO JOHN PASTON
FEBRUARY 1477

RIGHT REVEREND and worshipful, and my right well-beloved Valentine,

I recommend me unto you, full heartily desiring to hear of your
welfare, which I beseech Almighty God long for to preserve unto
his pleasure and your heart's desire.

And, if it please you to hear of my welfare, I am not in good
health of body nor of heart, nor shall be till I hear from you:

For there wots no creature what pain that I endure
And for to be dead, I dare it not discure [discover]

And my lady, my mother, hath labored the matter to my father
full diligently, but she can no more get than ye know of, for the
which God knoweth I am full sorry. But if that ye love me, as I
trust verily that ye do, ye will not leave me therefore. For, if that
ye had not half the livelihood that ye have, for to do the greatest
labor that any woman alive might, I would not forsake you:

And if ye command me to keep me true wherever I go,
Iwis, I will do all my might you to love, and never no mo.

> And if my friends say that I do amiss,
> They shall not me let [stop] so for to do.
> Mine heart me bids evermore to love you
> Truly over all earthly thing.
> And if they be never so wroth,
> I trust it shall be better in time coming.

No more to you at this time, but the Holy Trinity have you in keeping. And I beseech you that this bill be not seen of none earthly creature save only yourself, etc.

And this letter was endited at Topcroft, with full heavy heart, etc., by your own Margery Brews.

RIGHT WORSHIPFUL and well beloved Valentine,

In my most humble wise I recommend me unto you, etc. And heartily I thank you for the letter which that ye sent me by John Bickerton, whereby I understand and know that ye be purposed to come to Topcroft in short time, and without any errand or matter but only to have a conclusion of the matter betwixt my father and you. I would be most glad of any creature alive, so that the matter might grow to effect. And thereas ye say, an ye come and find the matter no more toward than ye did aforetime, ye would no more put my father and my lady my mother to no cost nor business for that cause a good while after—which causeth mine heart to be full heavy. And if that ye come and the matter take to none effect, then should I be much more sorry and full of heaviness.

And as for myself, I have done and understood in the matter what I can or may, as God knoweth. And I let you plainly understand that my father will no more money part withal in that behalf, but £100 and 50 marks, which is right far from the accomplishment of your desire.

Wherefore, if that ye could be content with that good [sum] and my poor person, I would be the merriest maiden on ground. And if ye think not yourself so satisfied, or that ye might have much more good (as I have understood by you afore)—good, true, and loving Valentine, that ye take no such labor upon you as to come more for that matter, but let it pass and never more to be spoken of, as I may be your true lover and beadswoman during my life.

No more unto you at this time, but Almighty Jesus preserve you both body and soul, etc.,

By your Valentine, Margery Brews.

MARGERY PASTON (BREWS) TO JOHN PASTON DECEMBER 1484

RIGHT WORSHIPFUL HUSBAND,

I recommend me unto you.

Please it you to wit that I sent your eldest son to my Lady Morley, to have knowledge what sports were used in her house in Christmas next following after the decease of my lord her husband. And she said that there were none disguisings, nor harping, nor luting, nor singing, nor none loud disports; but playing at the tables, and chess, and cards. Such disports she gave her folks leave to play and none other. Your son did his errand right well, as ye shall hear after this.

I sent your younger son to the Lady Stapleton, and she said according to my Lady Morley's saying in that, and as she had seen used in places of worship thereas she hath been.

I pray you that ye will assure to you some man at Caister to keep your butter, for the man that ye left with me will not take upon him to breve [make accounts] daily, as ye commanded. He saith he hath not used to give a reckoning, neither of bread nor ale, till at the week's end. And he saith he wot well that he should not condeneth [give satisfaction]. And, therefore, I suppose he shall not abide, and I trow ye shall be fain to purvey another man for Simon, for ye are never the nearer a wise man for him.

I am sorry that ye shall not at home be for Christmas. I pray you that ye will come as soon as ye may. I shall think myself half a widow, because ye shall not be at home, etc.

God have you in his keeping. Written on Christmas even, *1484,*
By your, *Margery Paston.*

RICHARD CALLE TO MARGERY PASTON
1469

MINE OWN LADY and mistress, and before God very true wife,

I, with heart full sorrowful, recommend me unto you, as he that can not be merry, nor nought shall be, till it be otherwise with us than it is yet. For this life that we lead now is neither pleasure to God nor to the world, considering the great bond of matrimony that is made betwixt us and also the great love that hath been and, as I trust, yet is betwixt us, and as on my part never greater. Wherefore, I beseech almighty God comfort us as soon as it pleaseth him, for we that ought of very right to be most together are most asunder. Meseemeth it is a thousand year ago since that I spake with you. I had liefer than all the goods in the world I might be with you.

Alas, alas, good lady! Full little remember they what they do that keep us thus asunder. Four times in the year are they cursed that let [hinder] matrimony. It causeth many men to deem in them they have large conscience in other matters as well as herein. But what lady suffers as ye have done? And make you as merry as ye can, for y-wis [surely], lady, at the long way God will of his righteousness help his servants that mean truly and would live according to his laws, etc.

I understand, lady, ye have had as much sorrow for me as any gentlewoman hath had in the world, as would God all that sorrow that ye have had had rested upon me, so that ye had been discharged of it. For y-wis, lady, it is to me a death to hear that ye be entreated otherwise than ye ought to be. This is a painful life that we lead. I cannot live thus without it be a great displeasure to God.

Also like you to wit that I had sent you a letter by my lad from London, and he told me he might not speak with you, there was made so great await upon him and upon you both. He told me John Thresher came to him in your name and said that ye sent him to my lad for a letter or a token which I should have sent you. But he trusted him not; he would not deliver him none. After that, he brought him a ring, saying that ye sent it him, commanding him that he should deliver the letter or token to him; which I conceive, since by my lad it was not by your sending, it was by my mistress and Sir James's advice. Alas! what mean they? I suppose they deem we be not insured [betrothed] together. And, if they do so, I marvel, for then they are not well advised, remembering the plainness that I brake to my mistress at the beginning, and I suppose by you both [too], an ye did as ye ought to do of very right. And if ye have done the contrary, as I have been informed ye have done, ye did neither consciencely nor to the pleasure of God, without ye did it for fear and for the time, to please such as were at that time about you. And if ye so did it for this service, it was a reasonable cause, considering the great and importable calling upon that ye had and *that* many an untrue tale was made to you of me, which God knoweth I was never guilty of.

My lad told me that my mistress your mother asked him if he had brought any letter to you. And many other things she bare him on hand and, among all other, at the last she said to him that I would not make her privy to the beginning, but she supposed I would at the ending. And, as to that, God knoweth she knew first of me and none other. I wot not what her mistress-ship meaneth, for, by my troth, there is no gentlewoman alive that my heart tendereth more than it doth her, nor is loather to displease, saving only your person, which of very right I ought to tender and love best, for I am bound thereto by the law of God and so will do while that I live, whatsoever fall of it.

I suppose, an ye tell them sadly [fully] the truth, they would not damn their souls for us. Though I tell them the truth, they will not believe me as well as they will do you. And, therefore, good lady, at the reverence of God, be plain to them and tell the truth. And if they will in no wise agree thereto, betwixt God, the devil, and them be it; and that peril that we should be in, I beseech God it may lie upon them and not upon us. I am heavy and sorry to remember their disposition. God send them grace to guide all things well, as well I would they did. God be their guide, and send them peace and rest, etc.

I marvel much that they should take this matter so hardly as I understand they do, remembering it is in such case as it cannot be remedied. And my desert upon every behalf, it is for to be thought there should be none obstacle against it. And also, the worship [honor] that is in them is not in your marriage: it is in their own marriage, which I beseech God send them, such as may be to their worship and pleasure to God and to their hearts' ease—for else were it great pity.

Mistress, I am afraid to write to you, for I understand ye have showed my letters that I have sent you before this time. But I pray you let no creature see this letter. As soon as ye have read it, let it be burnt, for I would no man should see it in no wise. Ye had no writing from me this two year, nor I will not send you no more. Therefore, I remit all this matter to your wisdom.

Almighty Jesu preserve, keep, and *give* you your heart's desire, which I wot well should be to God's pleasure.

This letter was written with as great pain as ever wrote I thing in my life. For, in good faith, I have be*en* right sick and yet am not verily well at ease. God amend it, etc.

"THE MARSHALL IN HALL"

Pge of habits and activities

THE MARSHAL in the morning ought to come into the hall and see that it be clean of all manner thing that may be found unhonest therein: the stools, trestles, or else forms, if any be, that they be set in their own places—at meals at the board, and afore and after meals in corners farthest from all encumbrance; and all the hallings and coasters [tapestries] dressed in their kind [proper] places, and shaken or beaten with rods if need be; and that no hounds be abiding in the hall from morn to even. And to perform these things said afore, he shall charge the usher and the groom of the hall therewith.

Also in winter-time, the said groom, by the oversight of the usher, shall bring into the hall as much wood and coals as shall be spent daily in the hall, and bear out the ashes and all other filth of the hall. The said groom shall also keep the key of the wood and coal and deliver it out daily by tally to the kitchen, hall, and liveries, and bring the said tally to the steward at the week's end. The said groom shall also continually be in the hall at the first meat or supper, to bear away dishes and keep out hounds and fetch sauces, and to obey all other commandments of the head officers, that is to say of steward, marshal, and usher.

Marshall later in France, a military leader under napoleon

Also, half an hour ere the lord go to meat or supper, the marshal shall take the rod in his hand and command the panter and ewer [pantryman and water-server] to cover and make ready for the lord and for the household: and as soon as it is made ready the marshal shall command the sewer [waiter] to a-wait when the cooks be ready; and then shall the sewer go to the ewery and take a towel upon his shoulder, and the marshal and he to go together and shew afore the lord, so that he may know thereby when his meat is ready. And when it liketh the lord to ask water, then shall the esquires and the marshal and sewer go by and be next the lord's basin and even at [by] the lord. The sewer shall deliver the towel to the worthiest that be about him and go straight to the kitchen with all the men that shall serve.

The marshal then shall uncover the basin if it be covered, and hold it in his hands also unt*il* the lord have washe*d,* and then make a salutation and take it to the squire that brought it thither, and he to bear it to the ewery and anon command water for all them that shall sit at the lord's board, and go with the lord to be set and their asketh him how his board shall be set.

And the yeomen and grooms, or groom of the chamber if it be there, or the usher or grooms or groom if it be there, shall set up boards and make ready the stools afore meat and have *t*hem ready at the setting of boards, and bring them ready to the marshal when he calleth, and also after meat bear away the boards, trestles, and stools. And when the lord is set, and the other boards in his presence, the marshal shall fetch in his courses with the sewer by and by. The marshal and sewer shall make a salutation when they come almost at the board—and none other that beareth meat or drink at that time till he be delivered of that that he beareth.

And when all the lord's mess is sewed [served], then shall another esquire next the hand sew the other messes at the board or in his presence. And anon forthwith the almoner shall bring in the alms-dish, with a loaf therein, and set it beneath the lord's salt or else upon the cupboard if no room be upon the board. And a little afore the second course, the almoner shall take of every standard of great meat that comes before the lord at the first course a certain [portion], with the help of the carver, and put it in the alms-dish and send the void [empty] dishes to the kitchen. And all this meanwhile the marshal shall look both in the chamber and the hall that there lack neither bread, ale, wine, ne meat there as it ought to be served, and the sewer shall look that there lack no sauce in the lord's presence.

And when the second course is ready, the sewer shall come and warn the marshal, and the marshal all esquires and yeoman-waiters, to go to the kitchen. And like as the marshal and sewer did at the first course, so shall they do at the second; and when the marshal seeth time, that is to say, within three-quarters of an hour that the last mess be set in the hall, the marshal shall command to take-up and all the broken meat and broken bread to be cast into the alms-vessel. And when it cometh to the usher yeomen of the chamber, or gentlemen, then the ewer to be there, ready for to deliver to the groom of the hall or men's servants waiters' towels for them that shall wash, and some men to be there ready with voiders for to take up trenchers and broken bread. And as soon as they have washed, that the ewery be borne away and the hall new-covered for the later meat. . . .

Also, that the marshal, sewer, or esquires-waiters at mealtimes make honest cheer with soft speech to strangers sitting at the lord's board or in his presence, if they may goodly come to them and as they see time. Also, that in the lord's presence such silence be kept that there be no loud speech, save only of the lord and such as he speaketh to; and in the hall such low communication be had that the head-officer's voice be heard unto all other officers; and that no groom's head be covered serving at meals yeoman, ne yeoman gentleman, ne gentleman the steward. Also, that the gentlemen and yeoman serve all those in the lord's presence; and out of the lord's presence yeomen serve gentlemen and set down yeomen and grooms serve them, set grooms and pages to serve them.

Then the marshal in a lord's house is gentleman-harborer [dispenser of lodgings] and the usher of the hall yeoman of the same; and after the usher of the chamber, if any be, or yeoman of the chamber in his absence, have taken up lodging for his lord and for himself in his own manor or in other places, the marshal or the usher in his stead shall assign all other men to their lodgings, as well strangers as men of household; and also he shall assign them bread, ale, wine, wax, tallow, and fuel to their lodging, after the season of the year and their degrees, and reckon for it daily and weekly as the lord's books be made.

Then the marshal and usher shall daily reckon all the messes within the house, that is to say the lord for two messes, and every lord in the same wise at the board; afterward, every man at the board for one mess; and then after through the house, gentlemen, yeomen, grooms, and pages, every two to one mess. And in the same wise bring then daily and weekly to the clerk of the kitchen as they be asked and the books made.

Also, the marshal hath power to correct all such as doth great offences within the house or without, as in fighting, horrible chiding, making of debates, drawing of knives, and stealings, affrays, and such other: to put them into the porter's ward or in stocks, in all wise as far-forth as the steward, save in putting out of the house. And in all these points, in like wise the usher hath the same power in the marshal's absence—all this to be thus understood: the steward above all the gentlemen, the marshal above yeomen, the usher above grooms and pages. . . .

Also, at every time that the lord commandeth drink, the marshal or usher shall warn esquires or yeoman to await thereon, and they shall go with him and command it at every office. And in case there be so many lords and strangers that there shall need pots with wine, then shall the marshal call every lord's squire or assign other squires of his own lord's for them, and then deliver cups to the said squires for the said lords, covered or uncovered as that the case requireth, at the cellar door; and he himself shall take as many cups void, each within other betwixt his hands with his rod, as he supposeth to serve the remnant of the house, and so shall he go afore. All the other cups void save the chief lord's, follow him, and last of all the butler with the cupboard-cloth on his shoulder and pots of wine in his hands. And when they come into the place there as the lords be, the marshal, carver, cupbearers shall make a salutation and go straight to a bay-window, a form, or cupboard at the lower end of the house, if any be there, and stand there in order, like as they were delivered at the cellar door, till the cups be filled. Then shall the butler lay down his cupboard-cloth and set the pots thereon, and the marshal all the cups that he beareth in like wise. Then shall the marshal call the squires with the cups and do fill them by order after their estates [ranks], and when all the cups be filled he shall command them to go forth to the lords, and forthwith he shall call other gentlemen or yeomen of the chamber or waiters, and deliver them cups such as he brought, as many as he supposeth will serve the house, and tell them where they shall serve. And when they have all drunken, the marshal shall take again all the cups that he brought himself, putting the wine left in them, if any be, in a void pot of such as the butler brought. And when he hath again all the said cups, he shall take *t*hem in like wise as he brought *t*hem, and the butler cast his cloth again upon his shoulder and take the pots in his hands; and forthwith the marshal shall give a warning to the carver and cupbearers, and all together shall make a salutation and therewith depart, the carver first, the cupbearers next, the marshal with the cups after them, and last of all the butler with the pots of wine.

Reasons for hunting birds Macchiavelli says a great deal should hunt to keep in arms & enhance warfare 1: to get food 3: to destroy the vermin (foxes)

Dame Juliana Berners

"THE BOOK OF SAINT ALBANS"

Now THEN WILL I describe the said disports and games, to find the best of them as verily as I can, albeit that the right noble and full worthy prince, the Duke of York—late called Master of Game— hath described the mirths of hunting like as I think to describe of it and of all the others.

For hunting, as to mine intent [understanding], is too laborious, for the hunter must always run and follow his hounds, travailing and sweating full sore. He bloweth till his lips blister, and when he weeneth it be an hare, full oft it is an hedgehog. Thus he chaseth, and wot not what. He cometh home at even rainbeaten *and* pricked, and his clothes torn, wet-shod, all mirey; some hounds lost, some surbate [foot-sore]. Such griefs and many others happeth unto the hunter, which, for displeasance of them that love it, I dare not report. Thus truly meseemeth that this is not the best disport and game of the said four.

The disport and game of hawking is laborious and *an*noyous also, as meseemeth. For often the falconer loseth his hawks, as the hunter his hounds. Then is his game and his disport gone. Full often cryeth he and whistleth till that he be right evil a-thirst: his hawk taketh a bough, and list not once on him regard; when he would have her for to fly, then will she bathe; with mice-feeding she shall have the fronce, the rye, the cray, and many other sicknesses that bring them to the souse [rise]. Thus by proof, this is not the best disport and game of the said four.

The disport and game of fowling meseemeth most simple. For in the winter season the fowler speedeth not but in the most hardest and coldest weather, which is grievous. For when he would go to his gins, he may not for cold. Many a gin and many a snare he maketh, yet sorrily doth he fare. At morn-tide, in the dew he is wet-shod unto his tail. Many other such I could tell; but dread of maugre [ill-will] maketh me for to leave.

Thus, meseemeth that hunting and hawking and also fowling be so laborious and grievous that none of them may perform nor be [the] very means that induce a man to a merry spirit which is cause of his long life, according unto the said parable of Solomon. Doubtless then, followeth it that it must needs be the disport of fishing with an angle—for all other manner of fishing is also laborious and grievous, often making folks full wet and cold, which many times hath been cause of great infirmities. But the angler may have no cold nor no dis-ease nor anger, but-if he be causer himself. For he may not lose at the most but a line or an hook, of which he may have store plenty of his own making, as this simple treatise shall teach him. So then, his loss is not grievous and other griefs may he not have, saving but if any fish break away after that he is taken on the hook or else that he catch nought. Which be not grievous, for if he fail of one he may not fail of another if he doth as this treatise teacheth—but-if [unless] there be nought in the water.

And yet at the least he hath his wholesome walk and is merry at his ease. A sweet air of the sweet savor of the mead-flowers— that maketh him hungry. He heareth the melodious harmony of fowls; he seeth the young swans, herons, ducks, coots, and many other fowls with their broods—which meseemeth better than all the noise of hounds, the blasts of horns, and the screech of fowls that hunters, falconers, and fowlers can make. And if the angler take fish, then surely is there no man merrier than he is in his spirit.

Also, whoso will use the game of angling, he must rise early. Which thing is profitable to man in this wise, that is to wit; most to the heal*th* of his soul, for it shall cause him to be holy; and to the heal*th* of his body, for it shall cause him to be whole; also to the increase of his goods, for it shall make him rich. As the old English proverb saith in this wise, "whoso will rise early shall be holy, healthy, and zealy."

Thus have I proved in mine intent that the disport and game of angling is the very mean and cause that induceth a man into a merry spirit, which, after the said parable of Solomon and the said doctrine of physic, maketh a flowering age and a long. And, therefore, to all you that be virtuous, gentle, and free-born, I write and make this simple treatise following: by which ye may have the full craft of angling to disport you at your list, to the intent that your age may be the more flowery and the more longer to endure.

Some indications, with documentation, that clergy weren't permitted to hunt because their noble lords didn't want competition (Mr. Utley) rather than because of Church ideas.

Business Documents

THERE IS NO surer proof of the sound foundations and the general command of common English prose in this early period than the simple clarity and assurance of many of the business documents in English that begin at the end of the fourteenth century and grow common in the fifteenth. Utilizing only the basic patterns of English syntax and sentences, they set out instructions and reports without fuss, achieving clear communication in spite of the handbooks for correct writings, the *artes dictaminis* which were the counterparts of our own manuals of business writing. These "arts" set down for the guidance of clerks and secretaries the rules for clerkly composition and models for all occasions, the manners rhetorically suited to the various matters, but all magniloquent. Some shreds of their formulae may be traced in the high-sounding greetings of late medieval letters, even of letters sent by fathers to sons, and their influence was heavy upon the correspondence of town and university officials when, early in the fifteenth century, they turned from Latin to English. But in some of the wills of the same time, in guild reports, and in the minutes of the city companies, what sits in the literary saddle is a robust English, true to everyday speech in vocabulary, true to practical written communication in sentence and paragraph, a style that is the workaday cousin of Malory's or Hilton's.

Three pieces have been selected to represent these styles. The first piece is the will that was made by Robert Folkingham in July 1399. The second is taken from the minutes of the London Brewers Company for 1422, and was probably written by William Porland, their clerk. In simple English that bears only a trace of the Latin clerical style, the minutes record the attempts of the Brewers to slip the curbs that had been placed upon their manoeuvers to raise the profits on ale. The extract describes their meeting with the new mayor, Robert Chichele, where they were arraigned at the instance of an old mayor, Richard Whittington. The last piece is a letter that the mayor and aldermen of London sent to Henry V in 1419, which contrasts violently with Porland's style by virtue of its Latinism in vocabulary and sentence constructions and its pretentious windiness.

102

t days – Written in Eng.; growth of vernacular / *earliest* First major legal document in Eng. was under Edw. III in 14th century. Actual use of law-Fr not finally abandoned until time of Elizabeth.

A Will 103

Robert Folkingham

A WILL

IN THE NAME of almighty Jesu, I, Robert Folkingham, being in whole and clear mind, the 6 day of July, the year of Our Lord 1399, make my testament and my last will in this manner.

First, I betake my soul into the hands of almighty God, beseeching to Our Lady, St. Mary, and to all the whole company of heaven, to pray for mercy and grace for me. Also I bequeathe my wretched sinful body to be here in earth, abiding the dreadful doom of God, in such place and manner as it liketh to his wise endless purveyance. Also I will that at mine interment there be about my body but tway [two] tapers of wax and four torches of wax, the which torches I will *to* be given to burn at the *e*levation of the sacrament while they will dure, in the same church that I shall be buried in. Also I will that, in all the haste that it may be d*o*ne after my death, there be said a thousand masses for my soul, and for all Christian souls.

Also I bequeath, to be done in alms after discretion of mine executors, in all the haste for my soul, for the souls of my father, mother, and of all *t*hem that I am indebted to by way of kind, by way of friendship, or by way of restitution, for the good I have had of *t*heirs by any way, forty pound of gold, and, over that, that they have part of all the prayers, good deeds, and alms that I have d*one* or ordained to be d*one*, as well in this testament as tofore in all my life.

Sithen [next], I give to William Flete, my cousin, forty mark of gold and all mine horses, a blue bed of Arras work, tway pair sheets, my best habergeoun, my pisane [neck-armour], my kettle-hat, and mine arming-sword of Bordeaux. Also I bequeath to John of Bruges an habergeoun, a basinet [steel headpiece], a long dagger of Bordeaux harnessed with silver in manner of a sword. . . . Also I bequeath to Thomas Heighelme a gown of black worsted, furred with beaver.

Also, I will that all the debts that any man can reasonably ask,

that they be paid. And the remnant of all my goods, whereso it be
in the hands of my debtors or else, I bequeath it to Jonet my wife,
to govern and sustain with, her and Eleanor my daughter, and
eke [also] to do in alms for me, and for her, and for all them that
we be indebted to do for by any way, as she may reasonably, not
diminishing greatly her livelihood ne her poor estate.

The execution of which things abovesaid after my last will to be
done and fulfilled, I make mine executors Jonet my wife, [etc.],
praying to them for God's sake, for charitable deeds of alms, and
for the sovereign trust I have in them, that they will take this
charge on them and refuse it by no manner way.

Written the day and year tofore named, with mine own hand, in
witness of my last will, and ensealed with my seal.

William Porland

BOOK OF LONDON BREWERS COMPANY

AND WHEN THE foresaid brewers came before the mayor and the
aldermen, John Fray, at that time being recorder of the said city,
said to the brewers in this wise:

"Sirs, ye be accused here that ye sell dear ale and set your ale at
a greater price than ye should do, without leave of this court. And,
moreover, ye be bound in this court in a recognisance of £20: at
what manner *of* price that malt is sold, ye shall sell your best ale
out of your houses to your customers for *three-halfpence* [per gal-
lon], that is, a barrel for 42 pence, and no dearer." And after this,
the mayor asked of Robert Smith how he sold a barrel of his best
ale. And he answered: "For five shillings, and some barrels for
four shillings and tenpence." And on this manner said the most
part of the brewers that were at that time there present.

And the mayor shewed them divers examples of malt in the
same court, to the which malt the brewers answered that they
could make no good ale thereof. For there was an example of malt
of Norfolk, one quarter for four shillings, the which was in a ship
at Billingsgate. And the same malt was so good cheap that the

mayor, Richard Whittington, and the aldermen and the most part of the commons of the city, said that it was a false thing to sell *t*heir ale so dear while they might have malt so good cheap. But men said at that time that brewers were cause of the dearth of malt, with *t*heir riding into divers countries to buy malt. And also men said that the multitude of brewers would have dear malt for the profit of the rich brewers of London. And by motion of Richard Whittington, there being present, he said to the brewers that they had ridden into the country and forstalled [cornered] malt; wherefor it caused malt to be so dear. For one quarter of malt was at that time at seven shillings and sixpence, and within little time before one quarter of malt was sold in the market for eight shillings and eightpence, and some for nine shillings.

And after this the mayor commanded John Carpenter, clerk of the Guildhall, to read the same ordinance that was made in the time of Richard Whittington, Mayor of London. And when it was full read before the mayor and aldermen and before the brewers, then said the mayor and all the aldermen that they were condemned in their bond of £20. Wherefore, the foresaid recorder said these words and gave open judgment afore the mayor and the aldermen: "That the craft of Brewers should pay to the work of the Guildhall £20, for they kept not the ordinance that was ordained upon them. Wherefore, the mayor ordaineth and commandeth that the foresaid masters of brewers' craft, that is to wit, Robert Smith and his fellows, should be kept in the ward of the chamberlain of the Guildhall, in prison, unto the time that the foresaid masters of brewers' craft had found surety for to pay the same £20, or else to pay it ere they go out of prison." And thus they did abide, upon the grace of the chamberlain, still in the Guildhall into the time that the mayor and aldermen were gone homeward to *t*heir meat. And after this, the said masters yeden [went] to the chamberlain and to John Carpenter to wit what they should do. And the said chamberlain and John Carpenter did command them to go home to *t*heir houses, and so John Carpenter behight [promised] *t*hem at that time that they should no more harm have, neither of prisonment of *t*heir bodies ne of loss of £20, for well they wist and knew that all the foresaid judgment of the mayor and aldermen was not done at that time but for to please Richard Whittington—for he was cause of all the foresaid judgment.

MAYOR AND ALDERMEN OF LONDON TO HENRY V

AN OFFICIAL LETTER

OUR MOST DREAD and most sovereign earthly lord, we recommend us unto the sovereign excellence of your kingly majesty in the most humble and lowly wise that any poor or simple lieges can best imagine or devise, lowly thanking your sovereign excellence and noble grace of the right gracious and right comfortable letters which ye liked late to send us fro your town of Nantes by John Palyng. The which letters, with all manner of honor and lowly reverence we have meekly received and understood.

And truly, most dread and sovereign lord, gladder ne more comfortable tidings might never have come, nor in better time, for to satisfy and refresh the fervent desire of your poor lieges, that have long thirsted after knowledge of your prosperity, than were your said gracious letters, the which, amongst all other special graces most principally for our heartly comfort, contained the sovereign health and perfect prosperity of your most sovereign and gracious person. The which Christ of his sovereign mercy and noble pity please alway to keep in all manner of worship and joy.

Our most dread and most sovereign earthly lord, when we remember us how that your kingly might and power, grounded in the true peace of God, is so virtuously sounded with the spirit of meekness in devout and continual thanking of God in all his sonds [acts] and trust of good prayers of your people—as your said letters make gracious mention—truly we are moved by as great consideration and as reasonable cause as ever were liegemen to pray, as we have and shall if God will, for the good and gracious speed [success] of your most excellent and gracious person, and to thank God lowly that ever he sent us so gracious and so virtuous a sovereign lord to reign and have lordship upon us.

Our most dread and most sovereign lord, if it like your sovereign highness to hear of the estate of your City of London, please it your kingly majesty to conceive that in more quiet ne peaceabler rest, as farforth as absence of you that are our most gracious and most sovereign lord may suffer, was never earthly city nor place, blessed be God.

Our most dread and most sovereign lord, we lowly beseech God, the king of peace whose grace exceedeth the merit of *them that pray, that he vouchsafe your kingly majesty *establish in all virtue, and evermore keep your most excellent and sovereign person in all joy and prosperity to his pleasaunce.

Written at your said City of London, under the seal of mayoralty thereof, the 6th day of September. To the King, our most dread and most sovereign lord, your poor and humble lieges, the mayor, sheriffs, aldermen, and commons of your City, London.

Translators of Holy Writ

≈§§≈

TRANSLATION OF THE Bible into the vernacular was acceptable to French clerics in the later Middle Ages, but their English colleagues inclined to view the procedure with horror. According to Wycliffites, friars and their partisans asserted it was "heresy to write thus God's law in English and make it known to lewd men." Henry of Knighton, canon of Leicester, roundly abused the translations that the reformers made in despite of opposition: "In this way the pearl of the Gospel is scattered broadcast and trodden under foot by swine." Through the dust of the argument, however, it is apparent that opposition was not complete. In addition to versions intended for Lollards, there were in the late fourteenth century several orthodox translations of parts of the gospels, Paul's epistles, the psalter, and the apocrypha. Some of these orthodox translations are akin to the mystical treatises of the time, meant for nuns—whose modest Latinity accounts for many "Englishings" of materials that the church might have preferred to keep in Latin.

To represent this body of translation, the following have been selected: Two passages from the second Wycliffite version of the Bible, c. 1388. This version, credited largely to John Purvey, is a competent piece of English prose, far superior to the distressingly awkward and literal earlier version. A passage from an orthodox translation of parts of the *New Testament*, contemporary with Purvey's and addressed to a nun: somewhat less accurate than the Wycliffite version, much of it is far more assured in its command of English structure, idiom, and rhythm. A translation of a short text of the *Vision of St. Paul*, one of the many apocalyptic narratives that were excluded from the Vulgate but continued popular throughout the Middle Ages: there are at least six different versions of it in Middle English, the present one probably made a little before 1400.

From Vulgate. men later went back to Greek and Hebrew

SECOND WYCLIFFITE BIBLE

THE WORKERS IN THE VINEYARD. The kingdom of heaven is like to an husbandman that went out first early, to hire workmen into his vineyard.

Forsooth, the covenant made with workmen, of a penny for the day, he sent *t*hem into his vineyard. And he, gone out about the third hour, saw other*s* standing idle in the cheaping [market]. And he said to *t*hem, "Go and [also] ye into my vineyard, and that that shall be rightful I shall give to you. Soothly, they wenten forth.

Forsooth, eftsoon he went out about the sixth hour and the ninth, and did in like manner. But, about the eleventh hour, he went out and found other*s* standing, and he said to *t*hem, "What standen ye here idle all day?"

They sayen to him, "For no man hath hired us." He saith to *t*hem, "Go and ye into my vineyard."

Forsooth, when evening was made, the lord of the vineyard saith to his procurator, "Clepe [call] the workmen and yield to *t*hem their hire, beginning at the last till to the first."

Therefore, when they weren come that camen about the eleventh hour, and they took singular pence. Truly, and the first coming, deemeden [judged] that they weren to take more, truly and they tooken each one by himself a penny. And they, taking, grouched again*s*t the husbandman, saying, "These last diden work one hour and thou hast made *t*hem even to us that ha*v*e borne the charge of the day and heat."

And he, answering to one of *t*hem, said, "Friend, I do thee no wrong; whether [I ask whether] thou hast not accorded with me for a penny? Take away that that is thine and go. Forsooth, I will give and to this the last man as and to thee. Whether it is not lawful to me for to do that that I will? Whether thine eye is wicked for I am good? So there shall be the last men the first and the first men the last, for many be cleped but few chosen." *St. Matthew,* XX, 1–16.

THE GOOD SAMARITAN. Soothly, Jesus beholding, said, "Some man came down fro Jerusalem into Jericho and fell among thieves, which also robbeden him and—wounds put in—wenten away, the man left half quick [alive].

Forsooth, it befell that some priest came down in the same way and, him seen, passed forth. Also, forsooth, and a deacon, when he was beside the place and saw him, passed forth. Forsooth, some man Samaritan, making journey, came beside the way, and he, seeing him, was stirred by mercy.

And he, coming nigh, bound together his wounds, heelding [pouring] in oil and wine. And he, putting on his horse, led into a stable and did the cure of him. And another day he brought forth twenty pence and gave to the keeper of the stable, and said, "Have thou the cure of him, and whatever thing thou shalt give over I shall yield to thee when I shall come again."

Who of these three seemeth to thee to have been neighbour to him that fell among the thieves?

And he said, "He that did mercy on him."

And Jesu saith to him, "Go thou and do thou in like manner." *St. Luke* X, 30–37.

ORTHODOX VERSION OF THE BIBLE: CORINTHIANS

If that I speak with men's tongues or with angels' tongues, and I ne have not charity, I am made as brass that soundeth or a cymbal that soundeth. And if I have every prophecy and know all privities, and if I have every cunning and every faith, so that I may move hills from their places, if I ne have no charity, I ne am nought. And if I deal all my chattel into poor men's livelihood, and give my body to burn, and I ne have no charity, it profiteth me nothing.

Charity is patient and benign; charity ne hateth no man, ne doth not wickedly, ne is not blown with pride. He ne is not covetous; he ne seeketh not his own things; he ne is not wrathed; he ne thinketh none evil, ne joyeth not upon wickedness, but joyeth to truth. All things he suffreth, all things he believeth, all things he hopeth, all things he abideth.

Charity ne falleth never away, whether that prophecies shall be voided away or languages shall cease or cunning shall be destroyed. For a part we knoweth and a part we prophecieth. But when that cometh that is perfect, then it shall be voided—that thing that ne is but a part.

When I was a little child, I spake as a little child and I thought as a little child and I savoured as a little child. But when I was man I voided away those things that were of childhood.

We see now through a mirror in darkness; but then we shall see face to face. Now I know a part; but then I shall know right as I am known myself.

And now dwelleth these things: faith, hope, and charity. But the greatest of these is charity. *1st Corinthians*, XIII.

"THE VISION OF ST. PAUL"

PAUL AND MICHAEL prayed to our Lord Jesu Christ of his great grace to shew the pains of hell to his disciple Paul, that he might declare them in opening [preaching] to Christian people. Wherefor, our Lord granted him power by the leading of his angel Michael for to see the pains of souls punished in that fearful place.

And the angel Michael brought Paul before the gates of hell for to see the pains of hell, and there Paul saw before the gates burning trees, and in those trees sinful souls tormented and hanged, all burning, some by the hair, some by the neck, some by the tongue, some by the arms. And furthermore, Paul saw a furnace all burning, in the which souls were punished with seven manner of pains: the first, snow; the second, frost; the third, fire; the fourth, adders; the fifth, lightning; the sixth, stench; the seventh, sorrow without end. And in that furnace be souls punished the which did no penance by their life-day and every-each is punished after his deeds that he had in this world wrought, wherein is sorrowing, weeping, waymenting [lamenting], burning, seeking of death. This place is to be dreaded, in the which is sorrow of adders and sorrow without gladness, in the which is plenty of pains with burning wheels, and in every wheel a thousand crooks [hooks], smitten a thousand times with devils, and in every crook hanging a thousand souls.

And furthermore, he saw an horrible flood with many devils therein for to torment souls and thereupon a bridge, by the which shall pass rightful souls and evil souls, thus to be punished after *t*heir trespass; and there be dwelling-places of sinful souls. And there Paul saw souls falle*n*, some to the knees, some to the navel, some to the lips, some to the top of the head.

And therefore Paul sore gan weep, and then said Michael, "These that be falle*n* to the knees be such as speak fair tofore and doth evil behind; these be tho*se* that be fallen to the navel, the which that did avoutery and fornication and did no penance in their life; these be tho*se* that be fallen to the lips, the which did *de*bating in holy church and heard nought the word of God; these be tho*se* that be fallen to the top of the head, that be glad of *t*heir neighbours' harm."

And thereof Paul wept bitterly and said, "Is this grievous pain ordained to them?"

And after that he saw a place full of souls hanging by the tongues, and then said the angel, "These be fenerators [money-lenders] and usurers."

And then he saw a place in the which were all pains; and there were black maidens with black clothes, in pitch and brimstone, with fiery clothes, dragons, and adders hanging about their necks, and four devils going about *t*hem and saying to them, "Ye know-eth nought God's son that bought you!"

And then said Paul, "What souls be these?"

"These be souls of maidens the which were not chaste to *t*heir wedding, and tho*se* that dealt with *t*heir kin, and overlay their children and slew them."

And after he saw women upon camels, and afore them much fruit, but they ne might none take. "These be tho*se* that broke *t*heir fast before time."

And then he saw an old man between four devils, weeping, and he asked what he was. The angel said, "This was negligent, the which kept nought the law of God, ne was not chaste of body ne of word*s* ne of works, but was proud and covetous. And therefore he shall suffer this into the day of doom."

And then wept Paul. And the angel asked, "Why dost thou weep upon this man? For yet thou shalt see more greater pains." And he shewed him a pit locked with seven locks, and said to him, "Stand outer, so that thou might suffer the savour and the stench!" And he opened the pit and there came out a strong stench, worst above all pains. And then said Michael, "Whosoever cometh into this pit, there shall never be made mind [mention] of him in heaven before God ne his angels. And into this pit shall be thrown those souls the which that believe not that the Son of God took flesh and blood of Saint Mary, ne troweth nought in the sacrament of the altar."

And he saw in another place men and women, and worms and adders eating them. And there lay soul upon soul, as though it were frogs in a strong storm, and that place was as deep as it is fro heaven to earth. And there he heard great weeping and groaning and grinding of teeth, as it were a thunder. And then he saw a sinful soul between seven devils, weeping and sorrowing, leading that soul that same day fro the body. And angels cried against that soul, saying to him, "Thou wretched soul, what hast thou done in earth?" And there they read his charter, in the which all his sins were in. And there he was thrown into the deep pit, into the deepest darkness.

And in the same while, angels led another soul fro the body into heaven, and there they heard a thousand thousand of glad angels saying to that soul, "Araise we him up afore God, for he hath chosen his blessed works!" And after that, Saint Michael put him into Paradise, and there all angels worshipped that soul. And sinful souls, that lay in pain, they cried and said, "Have mercy on us, Michael and Paul, the which that is most beloved with our Lord God. Prayeth for us!"

And then said the angel Michael, "Now kneel down on your knees and prayeth with us!"

And that heard those that were in hell. Then with one voice they cried, the which that were in hell, and said, "Have mercy on us, Christ, God's son and man!"

And they looked up ruefully to heaven, and they saw suddenly God's son, saying to them, "For you I was crucified, stung with a spear, with nails nailed, with thorns crowned, and eisel [vinegar] and gall ye gave me to drink: and I gave for you mine own body to the death. What might I more do to you? And ye to me were never good; but wicked and shrewd; and never did good in your life, but wickedness and shrewdness in your life. But, for the prayer of Michael and of Paul and for my blessed resurrection, I grant you to have rest from Saturday at noon into the rising of the sun the Monday."

And then they were glad of that grant, all that were in hell, and they cried with one voice, "Blessed may thou be, God's son, the which that hath granted us this refreshing! For it is to us more remedy of this day and this night than was all the refreshing that we had on earth all our life while we were on earth. For whoso keepeth the Sunday, he shall have peace, rest, and joy with angels."

And Paul asked of the angel how fele [many] pains were in hell. The angel answered and said, "Almost there be forty hundred and four thousand. And if there were an hundred men speaking from the beginning of this world to the day of doom, and thereto every man had four tongues of iron, *one* ne might not tell how fele sorrows there be in hell."

And so suddenly they went fro that place.

Devotional Manuals
and Sermons

❦

IN 1281, A LAMBETH COUNCIL summoned by John Peckham, archbishop of Canterbury, issued a vigorous directive to parish priests: at least once a quarter they should instruct their flocks—in English—in the articles of the creed, the ten commandments, the two angelic precepts, the seven works of mercy, the seven deadly sins and their progeny, the seven chief virtues, and the seven sacraments. This decree was in line with a continental campaign toward the reform of the regular clergy from the laxness always apt to be charged against it by monastics.

A treatise that admirably subserved this program of instruction was the *Somme des Vices et des Vertus,* 1279, written by the Dominican friar, Lorens d'Orleans. Simply, but completely, it detailed standard doctrine on most of the matters listed in the Lambeth decree, and, for fuller measure, also provided an Art of Dying. In English alone there are nine translations or adaptations of this work, ranging from Dan Michel's *Ayenbite of Inwyt,* 1340, to Caxton's *Royal Book, c.* 1486. From *Vices and Virtues, c.* 1400, the most widely diffused of these translations, we have chosen the paragraphs that discuss usury, the first bough of Covetousness. They present standard doctrine on profit and interest and are presented in a style that well represents pedagogical prose of the period, mathematically organized, impersonal, unornamented save for its familiar symbolism and stories, simple and native in syntax and vocabulary—a competent though dull manner of prose.

In addition to versions of Lorens' work, there was an abundance of similar treatises, some original, most translated. In fact, as one pious writer complained, there were so many that "this small life shall rather have an end of any man than he may either study or read them." Both because it is an original English composition (though the matter is standard) and because it is better written than the rest, we have chosen Richard Lavynham's little treatise on the sins to represent these devotional treatises. The author was an inmate of the Carmelite house at Ipswich, took a prominent part in the Wycliffite controversy, and died

This body of material contrasts with that of mystics 115
which followed. Parochial instruction on morals + Emphasis on work rather
than on faith (?)

at Bristol in 1383. His treatise, which survives in fourteen copies, is a concise, well-balanced discussion, set out in clear, scholarly English. Our selection consists of the short introduction and the section on envy.

Akin to these treatises are the medieval sermons, a large body of writing which is mostly unprinted.

Sermons, like drama, live along the boundaries of speech and literature. Although they have their own rhetorical tradition, they often employ a style that comes close to the idiom of contemporary speech, and they are clear and direct from necessity. This is one of the major attractions of the English sermons that begin to be numerous in the later fourteenth century. Another is that, in a period when most English prose was translation, these pieces are largely independent composition.

As instruments in the reform of the parish clergy, manuals of basic doctrine were compiled, also collections of stories that might be used to point and enliven that doctrine. A more comprehensive device was the sermon complete in both doctrine and stories, of which there are several collections in English. Typical of them is John Mirk's *Festial*, *c.* 1400 from which we have selected one sermon. Mirk was a canon-regular at the monastery of Lilleshul in Shropshire, His book, serviceable enough to survive in nine manuscripts and nearly a score of printings up to 1532, contains sermons for all the feast-days of the year. It was compiled, Mirk states, for the use of priests whose excuse for their defects was "default of books and simpleness in literature." The congregations it envisages were even more unsophisticated.

Marvellous stories, mostly miracles wrought by the various saints, form a disproportionate part of the sermons in *Festial;* the doctrine seldom transcends fundamentals and is hammered home by repetition. The writing is popular, but in its own way very effective: rarely touched by pulpit eloquence, it is clearly constructed, both in sentence and in whole, its syntactical patterns are neatly balanced and varied, the vocabulary is native and familiar, and proverbs and traditional phrases add salt to the direct vigor and ease.

"VICES AND VIRTUES"

THERE BE ONE manner of usurers-lenders that lendeth silver to be paid again of the chattel [property]; and above the chattel they take more, as in silver, or in horses, or in corn, or in wine, or in wool or in fruit, or in land, and that taketh they as a deed-wed

[handwritten marginal note:] Med. view of usury, which can apparently extend them many uses. Making money with [money]. Ezra Pound uses usury – with shifted meaning – as one of the fundamental betrayals of the world. Zane not particularly signif.

[pledge], for they will not account the profit that they have the whiles it is in their hand; and, yet worse, they will account twice or thrice to make the usury wax, and yet they will have at every term a profit above all this, and maketh oft of usury principal debt. These be despitous and foul usurers.

But other lenders-courteous, that lend without any covenant-making, nonetheless they look after profit—either in silver, or in horses, or in cups of silver or gold, or cloth, or robes, or tuns of wine, or swine, or pigs, or hens, or capons, or such other things, or service, or certain men for nought, or of cart, or of his plough, or to get his son a provender [prebend] or a church, or of any manner of thing of usury.

The second manner of usurers be such that lendeth not themselves; but that that their fathers or their mothers, their wives, or their ancestors won by usury they hold and ne will not yield it again. The third manner of usury is in them that will not lend by their own hands; but they make their servants and their prentices, or other men, lend their chattel. That be the master-usurers. Of that sin be not these great lords clean that holdeth and sustaineth Jews and Saracens that lendeth about in country and destroyeth the people—and the lords take the gifts and the amends, and otherwhiles they ransom them, and all that is the chattel of poor men of the country. The fourth manner is of them that lendeth of other men's chattel or borrow for little cost and lendeth forth for a greater cost. That be scholars of usurers that learneth that foul craft.

The fifth manner of lending is in merchandise, when a man selleth dearer his chaffer than it is worth, for he must give day of payment. And yet is well worse when he seeth a man at mischief [in trouble]: then will he sell all the dearest—yea, twice or thrice more than it is worth—and that is against the statute of merchants. Such folk doth much harm, for because of term of payment that they giveth they destroyeth the people, and namely [particularly] poor knights and squires, and also great lords that be young and go to jousting and tournaments and over the Great Sea and into Prussia[1], for they take them oft their lands and rents and great heritages in wed [pledge] and in deed-wed as mortgage, and by letters of sale, that be lost for evermore, for they may not quit them

[1] To the crusades in the Holy Land and against the Slavs.

at the term. The others sinneth in buying of things, as corn or wine or other things, for half that they be worth, and that for that they payeth tofore; and after they selleth them again for twice so much as they cost. And others buyeth things when they be least worth (as, in harvest, corn; in vendage time, wine or other such things), for to sell twice so dearer. Some buy the corn in grass, or wine when it bloweth, when it sheweth fair. Yea, and to such covenant that they have their chattel saved what-so befall.

The sixth manner is in those that taketh their silver to merchants so that they may be fellows to the winning and not to the losing; or that taketh their beasts to farm, so that they be always stoor [strong], that is to say, if they die the farmer shall find others as good. The seventh manner is in them that set their poor neighbors in works for they have lent them silver or corn, or any other thing done for them. And when they see them poor and needful, then make they covenant with them to do their works, and for a little silver or corn that they take them to-fore, they have and take threepenny-worth of work for one penny. And these be the boughs that waxeth of the shrewd [wicked] branch of usury.

Richard Lavynham

"A LITTLE TREATISE ON THE SEVEN DEADLY SINS"

TWO THINGS I HAVE purposed, through God's grace, to do in this little treatise. First, to shew shortly the common conditions of the seven deadly sins, as by figure and example in general. And afterward, to rehearse by process and by order what branches and boughs growen out of them in special. As touching the first matter, an holy man writeth in his book (*et est Sanctus Thomas secundum quosdam vel Albertus secundum alios in compendio theologie, libro tertio*). "The seven deadly sins," he saith, "be likened to seven sundry beasts: as Pride to the lion, Covetise to the urchin, Wrath to the wolf, Envy to the hound, Sloth to the ass, Gluttony to a bear, and Lechery to a swine." Of which figures and examples I think to touch in each of the seven deadly sins by themselves. . . .

Envy is the sorrow which that one creature hath that another fareth well, or the gladness that he fareth evilly. Therefore is the envious man likened to the hound. For right as it grieveth the hound that a man goeth by the way, though that man do him none harm—and else would he not bark upon him?—right so it grieveth an envious man that another go beside him, though he that goeth beside him do him none harm—and else would not the envious man backbite his neighbor and speak evil of his even-Christian? There is some hound of this condition: he will while a man is present fawn upon him with his tail, but anon as that man turneth his back that same hound will bite him by the heel. Right so, an envious man in presence of him that he hateth will speak fair with the tongue, but anon as that same man turneth back the envious man is ready to backbite him and to speak evil of him in his absence.

And therefore it is always good to flee the company of the envious man, as Solomon counseleth in his book of proverbs, and saith thus: *Non commodas cum homine inuido et ne desideres cibos illius, Proverbiorum* 23; "Eat thou nought with the envious man, ne desire not his meats." But here may be asked a demand: how a man might so shape his life that no man should have envy with him? This same asked Plato of his master Socrates, as a clerk rehearseth (*et est Petrus Blesensis, epistola* 69). And Socrates answered and said again to his disciple: *Esto inquit miser quia sola miseria caret inuidia*: "if thou wilt live," he saith, "without envy, be a wretch [exile], for there liveth no man without envy but only the wretch."

Out of envy springeth four branches, the which be here entitled, as: gladness of another man's mischief; heaviness of his bonchief [good fortune]; backbiting; sowing of discord.

Gladness of another man's mischief is when a man seeth his brother lose his goods, forego his friends, fall in sickness or in danger of lordship, in poverty, in slander, or in any other dis-ease, and is thereof glad and joyful in his heart. Of that man speaketh Solomon, and saith thus: *Qui in ruina alterius letatur non erit impunitus, Proverbiorum* 18: "Who that is glad that another man falleth in mischief shall not escape that he ne shall be punished therefor."

This branch of envy hath a condition contrarious to charity. For

*Uses metaphor of tree — 4 branches.
Sound, carefully analytical morality.*

it fareth by tho*se* men that love *t*hem together and accord in charity as it doth by the strings in the harp that accord together in
tune. For Saint Gregory saith thus (*et est in prologo Moralium*),
that when the harp is well set in tune, let one string be touched
thereof and anon shall another string, that is his consonant and
according with him in tune, stir and be moved at the touch of his
fellow. Right so it fareth ghostly [spiritually]: let one good Christian man be touched with sickness bodily or with any other mischief, anon is there another good Christian man thereby stirred
and hath thereof ruth and pity in his heart. Thus fared Saint Paul
when he said thus: *Quis infirmatur et ego non infirmor. Secunda
ad Corinth. xi*: "Who is sick," he saith, "and I am not sick also?"
And this manner of perfection he taught other men when he said
thus: *Gaudete cum gaudentibus et flete cum flentibus, ad Ro-
manos 12*: "Be ye glad with them that be glad and joyful and weep
ye with them that weep and be sorrowful."

Heaviness of a man's bonchief is when a man seeth his brother
increase in virtue, in richesse, in good loos [praise], in getting of
good love [reputation], in winning of worship, or in any other
good hap, and is heavy in his heart thereof and casteth cautels
[tricks] to hinder him and to appair [harm] his name. Of this
branch of pride speaketh the wise man Socrates: (*et ponitur in
proverbiis philosophorum*) and saith thus: "So would God that envious men had *t*heir eyes and *t*heir ears in all great cities and
towns, that *t*heir hearts might the more be dis-eased and the more
full of care through seeing and hearing of other men's welfare."

Backbiting is when a man appaireth his brother by way of slander, be it sooth, be it false—feigning false tales and bearing false
tidings about, discovering counsel that should be hid and hiding
the truth that should be know*n*, praising him that is vicious and
lacking him that is virtuous, turning each good word and each
good deed of him that he hateth to the worst intent. Of this branch
of envy, that is full common among*s*t worldly men, toucheth the
law *canon, sexta, quarta parta Deteriores,* where it is said that a
backbiter is worse than a thief or a robber of men's good*s*, and the
skill [reason] is: for it is worse to be nome [taken] a man's good
loos than his chattel and his good*s*. For Solomon saith thus in his
book: *Melius est inquit nomen bonum quam diuicie multe, Proverbiorum 22*: "Better is a good name than many riches."

Sowing of discord is when a man goeth and maketh them at the debate that have been fellows or friends, by telling of tales for privy envy and enmity to some of the parties. Of this manner of envy speaketh Solomon in the book of his proverbs (*et est prouerbiorum 6*), where he saith that, after all other wicked men that God hateth, he loatheth greatly and hateth specially that man the which soweth discord among his brethren. What man, therefore, so soweth the seed of dissension, he is the Fiend's child doubtless, forwhy [because] he is contrarious to Christ, prince of peace, which that saith thus in the gospel: *Beati pacifici quoniam filii dei vocabuntur: Mt. 5,* "Blessed be they," saith Christ, "that be makers of peace, for they shall be cleped [named] God's children for their goodness."

John Mirk

"FESTIAL"

Hortamur vos, ne in vacuum graciam Dei recipiatis. Corinthians VI.

GOOD MEN AND WOMEN, these words that I have said in Latin be thus to say in English: "We admonish you that ye take not the grace of God in vain." These be the words of St. Paul, Christ's holy apostle, that be read in the epistle of this day. By the which word this holy apostle chargeth all good people that they take heed what grace God sendeth them and that they taken not that grace in vain. God giveth grace to man all times; but, for a man needeth more his grace this time than another, therefore, of his high mercy, he giveth nowadays more abundance of Lent than any other time. The which grace he parteth in three ways; that is to say, in way of gracious abiding, in way of gracious deeming [judging], and in way of gracious amends-making. These three ways God sendeth his grace to you.

Wherefore, right as St. Paul admonisheth his disciples, right so I admonish you that be my children in God, that ye take not this grace of God in vain.

Ye have a common saying among you and say that God's grace

But because imbedded in middle of sto sermons are exempla — tale told in midst of exhortation to illustr. the point.

is worth a new fair. Then taketh heed how much worth God's
grace is. For, though any of you had as much gold as a fair is
worth, but he had God's grace with it, it should turn him more
into shameship than into worship. Thus ye may see by very reason that God's grace is more worth than any fair. But yet ye shall
know further. For, though a man had never so much riches and
prosperity here, that cometh all of God's grace. But-if [unless]
he take that grace well and please his God withal, it shall turn
him into damnation.

But, for the poor plaineth on the rich and say they be unkind to
God and do not as God biddeth them do and full elder [quickly]
see a mote in another man's eye that cannot see a beam their own;
therefore, ye shall know well that it is a special grace of God when
he maketh a man rich and some man poor. He maketh them rich
that they with their riches should succour the poor in their need,
and so with their goods buy them heaven. And some he maketh
poor that their poverty shall be their salvation. For God knoweth
well, if they were rich they would forget their God and so spill
[destroy] themself.

Wherefore, we admonish you, both rich and poor, that ye take
not this grace of God in idle nor in vain. But he that is rich, set not
his heart thereupon, but ever be in dread, lest he misspend it, and
thank God of his grace. And he that is poor, grouch he not against
his God, ne deem he not the rich, but take his poverty in patience,
and thank God of his grace; for, at the last he shall have that for
the best.

But a man, be he rich or be he poor, if he have grace of God to
see how much he taketh of God and how little he giveth again,
very reason will tell that he is more worth damnation than salvation. But, for God is full of grace and sheweth his grace to all his
handiwork, and for he knoweth our frailty, he hath compassion
of us and giveth us his grace in abiding of amendment. That is:
though thou trespass sore against him, he will not smite anon,
but graciously abideth, for he hath much liever for to do grace
than vengeance. And that is for two causes, as St. Augustine saith.

One is: if God had done vengeance, anon the world had been
ended many a day ago, and so many had been unborn that now be
holy saints in heaven.

That other cause is: for to shew how full he is of grace, and how fain he will do grace and mercy to all that will leave the evil and take the good. Wherefore he saith thus by his prophet: *Nolo mortem peccatoris, sed ut magis convertatur et vivat*: "I will not," he says, "that a sinful man be dead, but I will rather that he turn to good life."

Thus ye heareth how gracious God is in abiding. Wherefore, I *ad*monish you that ye take not this grace in vain, but thinketh well how he hath spared you from Easter hitherto, *w*hereas he might, by right, have smitten you with his sword of vengeance each day. For, as St. Anselm saith, the least sin that a man doth, it unworshippeth [dishonoreth] God. Then, if a man did anything that unworshipped his worldly king, he were worthy to take his death, much more is a man worth the death that unworshippeth him that is King of Heaven and lord and king over all kings. But, right as he passeth all in dignity, right so he passeth all in grace and bounty. But, though ye feelen him gracious, be never the bolder to lie in sin, but hieth you for to cleanse you thereof. For though he abide long, at the last He will smite such that will not amend *t*hem. And when he smiteth, he smiteth sore.

I read that there was a knight that had no rents of his own, but he had gotten much good in wars. And, when he had all spent out, he yode [went] and wedded a lady of that country that was rich enough. And though he was poor, he was a seemly man of person.

She said to him thus: I wot well that thou art a seemly man of body, but for thou art poor I may not, for shame, take thee but-if thou have much gold or many rents. But for thou hast no gold, do as I teach thee, and get gold. Go into such a place there many rich merchants come, and get thee gold, and then thou shalt have me."

Then went he thi*th*er. And it happened that there came a rich merchant that way. And he anon took him, and bare forth his gold, and slew him and buried him. And then after came to the lady and said, "Lo!—the sum of gold I have gotten of such a man, and buried him there!"

Then said the lady, "Go again tonight and look if thou aught hear."

Then yede he that night and stood by the dead *man's* grave. And at midnight there came a light from heaven down to the grave, and then the grave opened, and the cor*p*se sat up and held up his hands to God, and said, "Lord that art righteous ju*d*ge, *do* thou wreke [avenge] me upon this man that hath thus falsely slain me for my true chattel."

And therewith came a voice from heaven and said, "This day thirty winter thou shalt have vengeance." And then the corpse thanked God and lay down in his grave again.

Then was this knight sore afeared, and went to this lady and told her all, and how the voice said how, that day thirty winter, he should have vengeance.

Then said the lady, "Yea," quoth she, "Much may fall in thirty winter! Go we together and be wedded!"

So they lived y-fere [together] twenty year, in prosperity and weal. But ever this knight was adread of this vengeance, and said to the lady, "Now twenty year be passed, and the ten will hie fast. What is thy best counsel?"

Then she said, "We will make this castle as secure and as strong as we may. And, that same day, we shall gather all our friends and stuff [provide] us with men enow, and so we shall scape well enough.

And so they did. When the day came, they gathered a great sum of men into the castle, and set them to the meat, and made all the mirth that they could. Then was there a harper, and harped always at the meat.

But, for there may no wicked spirit come there ne have no powsty [power] as far as the harp is heard, there came out of the kitchen a brothel [low fellow], bawded with grease, and rubbed his strings with his bawdy hands. Then was this harper wonder wroth, and with his harp would have smitten this brothel. But, for he flew fast away, the harper sued [followed] him out of the castle. And, when he came out, this brothel vanished away.

Then this harper turned again—and saw this castle sink into the earth, all afire.

Thus ye may see, though God abide long, at the last he smiteth sore. Wherefore, I admonish you that ye take not his grace of abiding in vain, but bethinketh you well of your misdeeds and cometh betimes and cleanseth you. For God giveth you all an high grace of deeming, for thereas he is truth and righteousness, and he may not deem but with righteousness. And then shall none scape undamned [unjudged], for, as Job saith, "Though we would strive with him, we may not answer of one good deed for a thousand that he giveth us."

Mystics

❧❧❧

THROUGHOUT THE MIDDLE AGES it was the opinion that the highest form of Christian life was one in which the believer sought through solitary contemplation to bring himself toward direct spiritual union with God. This was the motivation for the spiritual treatises of St. Augustine of Hippo, and Dionysius the Areopagite, and for the abundant mystical works of the later medieval centuries that set out directions for contemplation or recounted the visions and other psychic phenomena that their authors had experienced in their own attempts to lose and find themselves in the life of the spirit.

The extension of this form of piety beyond the monasteries and the hermit-holds and with it the composition of popular mystical treatises are striking manifestations of the last medieval centuries. It is to this tendency, European in its scope, that we owe most of the many mystical writings that were produced in England in the fourteenth and fifteenth centuries. Autobiographical and biographical, didactic, cautionary, lyrical, this literature is varied in form, and much of it is excellent in style. Here it is represented by a few outstanding pieces—three other pieces that belong to the same movement have been included in the section on biography and autobiography.

Richard Rolle (c.1300-1349), hermit of Hampole in Yorkshire, was the earliest and most famous of these mystics: his abundant writings, in Latin and English, prose and verse, survive in several hundred copies. Following the tradition of St. Augustine, the Victorines, and St. Bonaventura, these works set out the stages of mystical experience, offer counsel to nuns and seculars, or relate his own aspirations and revelations. The earlier of them are composed in rhetorical, mannered Latin. His English writings, generally less mannered in style, range from the restless, ornamented prose of his commentary on the Psalms to the plain prose of his schematically-ordered treatise, *The Form of Living*.

As a prose-stylist Rolle has received high praise from some modern critics, and it is certain that at his best he writes very well, expressing his fervency clearly and with a driving force by means of careful construction and a familiar native vocabulary. But this assurance and con-

125

St. Aug. gave the 4-fold interpr. (Dante in letter to Can'Grande) literal, allegorical, tropological (moral) and anagogical (4 last things)

trol is fitful: too often he hovers uncertainly between the rhythms and diction of poetry and prose, too often he leaps without warning from conversational plainness to the encrusted decoration of pulpit rhetoric. Resourceful as he is, he lacks the firm sense of the essential nature of prose that characterizes the work of some of his followers. Our selection from his work consists of one short autobiographical piece and an abbreviated text of Chapters VII and VIII of his most famous treatise, *The Form of Living*, an oft-copied work that was originally written for Margaret Kirkby, one of the author's recluse-disciples in Yorkshire.

The individualism and intensity of mystical experience tends towards personal lyricism in style: mystics are often poets, and sometimes they compose the same work in both verse and prose. A notable example of this tendency is the series of prayers entitled *A Talking of the Love of God*, *c.* 1380, which was written by one of Rolle's disciples: its ecstasy in feeling and style reach an intensity rare among English writers. Sensual imagery (much of it from the Song of Songs), repetitions, archaisms, rimes, puns, word-play, sentences that consist of gatherings of short units arranged as cadenzas, with the rhythms emphasized by rhetorical syntax, parallel phrasing, antitheses, and abundant alliteration—all feed a prose-style that would be overwrought even in verse. The reflex of its author's own ecstasy, it was nevertheless calculated for its effect on a listening audience, directed to their emotions. It was "made for to stir them that it read," states the writer. "It falleth for to read it easily and soft, so as men may most in inward feeling and deeply thinking savour find." After reading our selection—taken from the middle of the work—few readers are likely to share Horstmann's view that it is one of the pearls of old English literature; but it is a fascinating work and it exemplifies in extreme the sophistication that sometimes varies the normally plain style of later medieval prose.

The Cloud of Unknowing, *c.* 1350, from which we select Chapters III-V, is one of the greatest products of the mystic school in both spirit and style. The treatise takes its inspiration from the negative mysticism of Dionysius—among other anonymous treatises ascribed to the same author is a translation of Dionysius' *Mystica Theologia*. As against Augustinian mysticism, this vein of contemplation insists upon the unknowableness of God and directs itself toward a "cloud of unknowing" that lies between man and his creator. In embroidering this theme for the benefit of a young man of twenty-four the author of *The Cloud* proceeds judiciously, aware of the perils of so specialized a life as well as of its intense satisfactions, and scornful of pretenders who aped the externals of contemplation. His style is one neatly tailored to the situation and to this blend of emotion and reason—a gentleman's prose in which reason and emotion are subserved by precise statements, and by vocabulary, idiom, and rhythm which are native and sensitively ordered to the feeling and thought. First-person in statement, it has the impress of dignified conversation.

The most influential member of the school, however, and to some tastes the best writer among them, is Walter Hilton. Little is known of his life beyond the facts that he was an Augustinian canon attached to the priory of Thurgarton in Nottinghamshire, and that he died there in 1396. His major work is *The Scale of Perfection,* which visualizes the soul's progress up a Jacob's ladder set between earth and heaven. Almost immediately upon its appearance in the later fourteenth century it became a devotional classic, often copied in manuscript and printed eight times before 1533. Among his minor works, *A Treatise to a Devout Man,* addressed to a rich lord, applies the teaching of *The Scale.* Describing the nature of both the active and the contemplative lives, this treatise advises the lord to follow a mixed life, one blending good works with contemplation.

Of Angels' Song, a brief masterpiece which is here given in full, discusses with Hilton's persuasive good sense one of the major phenomena of mystical rapture. Its first-person tone; the precise thought; the well-formed periods, balanced, logical and cleanly ordered; the sensitive choice of sentence length and variations in syntactical pattern to achieve well-considered rhythms and emphases; the discriminating use of a wide range of the English lexicon; and the graceful ease of his manner—all these qualities combine with Hilton's reasonableness and clarity in an emotional subject to produce one of the best of English prose-styles.

Even more widely diffused was *The Mirror of the Blessed Life of Christ,* written about 1410 by Nicholas Love, prior of the Charterhouse of Mount Grace in Yorkshire, and a fervent admirer of Hilton. It survives in some two dozen manuscripts and in four printings between 1486 and 1494, and is an item often mentioned in fifteenth-century wills. This substantial book, which narrates events in the life of Christ and furnishes each with an exegesis directed toward piety, was translated for "lewed men and women and hem that ben of symple understondynge," seemingly as a rival to Wycliffite translations of the Bible.

The Latin source for Love's book (wrongly attributed to Saint Bonaventura) is in the normal homiletic tradition, amply furnished with dicta from the church fathers and with allegorical interpretations of Biblical details. Love's translation is freely abbreviated and expanded, and is made relevant to contemporary England. Stylistically, it belongs to the school of Rolle and Hilton, of which it is one of the most distinguished products. Less perfect in control than Hilton, Love sometimes stumbles in intricate periodic sentences, but normally he writes easily in the elegant, learned, but familiar manner of his master. Our selection is Chapter 33, dealing with Martha and Mary, Leah and Rachel, traditional symbols of the active and contemplative lives.

Richard Rolle

"NARRATION"

WHEN I HAD taken my singular purpose, and left the secular habit and I began more to serve God than man, it fell on a night, as I lay in my rest, in the beginning of my conversion, there appeared to me a full fair young woman, the which I had seen before and the which loved me not little in good love.

And when I had beholden her and I was wondered why she came so on night in the wilderness, suddenly, without any more speech, she laid her beside me. And when that I feeled her there, I dreaded that she should draw me to evil, and said that I would rise and bless us in the name of the holy trinity.

And she strained me so stalwartly that I had no mouth to speak, ne no hand to stir. And when I saw that, I perceived well there was no woman, but the devil in shape of woman. Therefore I turned me to God, and with my mind I said, "Ah, Jesu, how precious is thy blood!"—making the cross with my finger in my breast.

And all so fast she waxed weak, and suddenly all was away. And I thanked God that delivered me. And, soothly, fro that time forth I forced me for to love Jesu, and ay the more I profited in the love of Jesu, the sweeter I found it, and to this day it went not fro my mind. Therefore, blessed be the name of Jesu in the world of worlds. Amen, Amen, Amen! Jesu, the son of the glorious virgin: Now Lord have mercy on all thine. Amen, amen! Pour charité. Amen!

"THE FORM OF LIVING"

AMORE LANGUEO. Thir [these] two words are written in the book of love, that is called the song of love, or the Song of Songs. For he that mickle [greatly] loves, him list [desires] oft sing of his love, for joy that he or she has when they think on that that they love, namely if their lover be true and loving. And this is the English of these two words: "I languish for love." Sere [different] men in earth have sere gifts and graces of God, but the special gift of those that leads solitary life is for to love Jesu Christ. Thou says me, "All men loves him that holds his commandments." Sooth it is. But all men that keeps his bidding keeps not also his counsel, and all that do his counsel are not also fulfilled of the sweetness of his love, ne feel not the fire of burning love of heart. Forthy [therefore], the diversity of love makes the diversity of holiness and of meed [reward]. In heaven, the angels that are burningest in love are nearest God. Also men and women that most have of God's love, whether they do penance or none, they shall be in the highest degree in heaven; they that love him less, in the lower order. If thou love him mickle, mickle joy and sweetness and burning thou feels in his love; that is thy comfort and strength night and day. If thy love be not burning in him, little is thy delight. For him may no man feel in joy and sweetness but if they be clean and filled with his love, and theretill shall thou come with great travail in prayer and thinking, having such meditations that are all in the love and in the loving of God. And when thou art at thy meat, love ay God in thy thought at each a morsel, and say thus in thy heart:

> Loved be thou, king,
> And thanked be thou, king,
> And blessed be thou, king.
> Jesu, all my joying,
> Of all thy gifts good,
> That for me spilt thy blood
> And died on the rood,
> Thou give me grace to sing
> The song of thy loving.

And think it not only whiles thou eatest, but both before and after, ay but when thou prayest or speakest. Or if thou have other thoughts that thou hast more sweetness in and devotion than in those that I lere [teach] thee, thou may think *them*. For I hope that God will do such thoughts in thy heart as he is paid [pleased] of and as thou art ordained for. When thou prayest, look not how mickle thou sayest, but how well, that the love of thy heart be ay upward and thy thought on that thou sayest, as mickle as thou may. If thou be in prayers and meditations all the day, I wot well that thou mon [may] wax greatly in the love of Jesu Christ and mickle feel of delight, and within short time.

Three degrees of love I shall tell thee, for I would that thou might win to the highest. The first degree is called insuperable, the second inseparable, the third is singular.

Thy love is insuperable when no thing that is contrary to God's love overcomes it, but is stalwart against all fandings [trials] and stable, whether thou be in ease or in anguish or in heal or in sickness, so that thee think that thou would not for all the world, to have it withouten end, wrath God any time; and thee were liefer, if either should be, to suffer all the pain and woe that might come to any creature, ere thou would do the thing that should mispay [displease] him. On this manner shall thy love be insuperable, that nothing may down bring, but springing on height. Blessed is he or she that is in this degree, but yet are they blesseder that might hold this degree and win into the other, that is inseparable.

Inseparable is thy love when all thy heart and thy thought and thy might is so wholly, so entirely, and so perfectly fastened, set, and stabled in Jesu Christ that thy thought comes never off him, never departed fro him, outtaken [apart from] sleeping, and as soon as thou wakenest thy heart is on him, saying, "Ave Maria," or "Gloria tibi Domine," or "Pater noster," or "Miserere mei Deus," if thou have been tempted in thy sleep, or thinking on his love and his loving, as thou did waking. When thou may no time forget him, whatso thou dost or sayest, then is thy love inseparable. Full mickle grace have they that is in this degree of love, and methink thou, that hast naught else to do but for to love God, may come theretill if any may get it.

The third degree is highest and most ferly [wondrous] to win, that is called singular, for it has no peer. Singular love is when all comfort and solace is closed out of thy heart, but of Jesu Christ alone. Other joy list it not, for the sweetness of him in this degree is so comforting and lasting in his love, so burning and glading, that he or she that is in this degree may as well feel the fire of love burning in their soul as thou may feel thy finger burn if thou put it in the fire. But that fire, if it be hot, is so delightable and wonderful that I cannot tell it. Then thy soul is Jesu loving, Jesu thinking, Jesu desiring, only in the covetise of him aneding [breathing], to him singing, of him burning, in him resting. Then the song of loving and of love is come. Then thy thought turns into song and into melody, then thee behoves sing the psalms that thou before said, then thou mon [may] be long about few psalms, then thee will think the death sweeter than honey, for then thou art full sicker [sure] to see him that thou lovest, then may thou hardily say, "I languish for love," then may thou say, "I sleep, and my heart wakes."

"A TALKING OF THE LOVE OF GOD"

AH, MILD MARY! mother of mercy, succour of sorrowful and comfort of care, ne art thou lodestar to all those that in the sea of this world's anguish sail and fare? Thou art queen of angels, lady of all shafts [creatures], to whom is betaken the care and the comfort of them that them feel caitiff-wretches. Yea, that in their own eyes see themselves wretches and seek thine help with trust, hope of heart. In thine advocacy is put the cause of our sins, to stand at doomsday, our aller Judge's mother [mother of the judge of us all], in help and in maintenance of our soul-heal.

Think here on this wretch, mother and maiden, that falleth thee to foot in hope of thine help, crying ruthly after thy grace. Peace me, lady, for thy much mercy, to thy dearworthy son that I have with sin shamefully and lightly so fele [many] time aguilted. My sins be so ghastly, grisly, and great: *they* maketh me so wlatsome [disgusting] and stinking foul that I ne dare him nigh ne follow my need. I have with them will*fully* my soul forshaped, from the likeness of God to the devil of hell; wrathed have I willfully, through filth of my sin, my maker, my buyer that bought me so dear with his dearworthy death from thralldom of hell, that would rather suffer to die on rood than to thole [suffer] in his sight the wlating of sin. Himself sought my peace in mine own guilts, as *on* his head be the guilt many time and oft—with stirring of my conscience and preaching of *the* wise; with hard wrack that I saw of other men's sins; with behest of bliss and unmete [immeasurable] meed that holy writ us behights [promises] if we let [leave] sin; with gifts of grace bodily and ghostly anents [against] worldly

Rhetorical, half-metrical lang.

weal to do all my will and to shield me from mine enemy that I
have ay followed and given me to his will and to his luther [hate-
ful] lore and flowen fro the love of him, my dearworthy Lord, that
with his dearworthy blood bought me so dear. He washed me
with cristendom of Adam's sin, and I me fouled sith [afterwards]
manyfold worse. He healed my soul that wounded was then
through my elders' guilt of Adam and Eve, and I have slain it all
out that I have fele [many] times wrought and long lain therein.
Sith, through his grace, he printed in my soul the image of himself,
and I imprinted above the likeness of hell . . .

Jesu my dearworthy lord; Jesu mine own father; sweet Jesu,
heaven-king, my drury, my darling, my dearing, my loving, mine
honeybird, my sweeting, mine heal and mine honeyter, mine
honey-life, mine hallow, sweeter art thou than honey or milk in
mouth, mead, meath, or piement made with spices sweet or any
liking liquor that anywhere may be found. Who ne may love, Lord,
thy lief lovesome leer [face]? What heart is so over-hard that he
may not to-melt in the meaning [mention] of thee, lovely Lord,
and who may not love thee, sweet Jesu? For inwith thyself are all
things gathered that ever may make any man love-worth to other.
Fairness, lovesome leer, flesh white under shroud maketh many
man be beloved and the more dear. Some, freedom and largesse,
that liefer is—menskly [nobly] to give than quadly [foully] to
withhold. Some, wit and wisdom and hap of the world; some,
noblesse and hendelike [graciousness] and gentise of kind; some,
great courtesy and loathless leets [manners]; some, mildness and
meekness and debonair heart, with sweet, lordlike, and godly
deeds. And yet, over all these, Kind most *makes* sib-friends each
one love other. There is something much more profound than the earthly virtue

Now, my dearworthy love, my sweet life, my liking, my love-
liest lief, mine heart and mine hallow, my longing, my mourning,
my soul-sweetness, thou art lovesome of leer [face], my sweet
Jesu, thou art all so sheen [bright] that all angels' life is to behold
thy lovely face. For thy leer is so bright and unmete [immeasur-
ably] lovesome, that if the forwaried [damned] that wail in hell
might it *see* with eyes and look thereon, all that paining pitch that
they wail in ne would them-think but a soft bath-bathing. For if
it so might be, dearworthy Lord, liefer them were evermore in
woe for to dwell and on thy lovesome leer evermore to look than

in all bliss be evermore without end and of that bright blissful leer
forgo the sweet sight. Thou art so sheen and so bright that the sun
were dark if it to thy blissful leer might be evened [compared]. If
I will love any man for his fairness, forsooth, dearworthy Lord, I
will love thee—my lief blessed Lord, mother-son fairest, of all
thing sweetest found in taste. Ah! sweet Jesu, good lief! Let me be
thy servant and lear [teach] me for to love thee, loving Lord, that
only the love of thee be ever all my liking, my yearning, my longing, my thought, and all my working. *Amen.*

"THE CLOUD OF UNKNOWING"

THE THIRD CHAPTER. Lift up thine heart unto God with a meek
stirring of love; and mean himself and none of his goods. And
thereto look thee loathe to think on aught but himself, so that
nought work in thy wit nor in thy will but only himself. And do
that in thee is to forget all the creatures that ever God made and
the works of *t*hem, so that thy thought nor thy desire be not directed or stretched to any of them, neither in general nor in special. But let them be, and take no heed of them.

This is the work of the soul that most pleaseth God. All saints
and angels have joy of this work and hasten them to help it with
all their might. All fiends be wood [mad] when thou thus dost, and
prove [try] for to fell [defeat] it in all that they can. All men living
on earth be wonderfully helpen by this work, thou wost not how.
Yea, the souls in purgatory be eased of their pain by virtue of this
work. Thyself art cleansed and made virtuous by no work so much.
And yet it is the lightest work of all, when a soul is helpen with
grace in sensible list [desire], and soonest done. But else it is hard
and wonderful for thee to do.

Let [cease] not, therefore, but travail therein till thou feel list.
For at the first time when thou dost it, thou findest but a darkness,
and as it were a cloud of unknowing—thou wost never what, saving that thou feelest in thy will a naked intent unto God. This
darkness and this cloud is, howsoever thou dost, betwixt thee and
thy God and letteth [hinders] thee, that thou mayest not see him
clearly by light of understanding in thy reason, nor feel him in

sweetness of love in thine affection. And therefore shape thee to bide in this darkness as long as thou mayest, evermore crying after him that thou lovest. For if ever thou shalt feel him or see him, as it may be here, it behooveth always be in this cloud and in this darkness. And if thou wilt busily travail as I bid thee, I trust in his mercy that thou shalt come thereto.

THE FOURTH CHAPTER. But forthy [so] that thou shalt not err in this working, and ween that it be otherwise than it is, I shall tell thee a little more thereof, as me thinketh.

This work asketh no long time ere it be once truly done, as some men ween; for it is the shortest work of all that man may imagine. It is neither longer nor shorter than is an atom; the which atom, by the definition of true philosophers in the science of astronomy, is the least part of time. And it is so little that, for the littleness of it, it is indepartable and nighhand incomprehensible. This is that time of the which it is written, "All the time that is given to thee, it shall be asked of thee how thou hast dispended it." And skillful [reasonable] thing it is that thou give account of it. For it is neither longer nor shorter, but even according to one only [single] stirring that is within the principal working might [power] of thy soul, the which is thy will. For even so many willings or desirings —and no more nor no fewer—may be and are in one hour in thy will, as are atoms in one hour. And if thou were reformed by grace to the first state of man's soul, as it was before sin, then thou shouldst evermore, by help of that grace, be lord of that stirring or of those stirrings. So that none yede forby [should go wrong], but all they should stretch into the sovereign desirable and into the highest willable thing, the which is God.

For he is even mete to our soul by measuring of his Godhead; and our soul is even mete unto him by the worthiness of our creation to his image and likeness. And he by himself withouten more, and none but he, is sufficient at the full, and much more, to fulfill the will and the desire of our soul. And our soul, by virtue of this reforming grace, is made sufficient at the full to comprehend all him by love, the which is incomprehensible to all created knowable might [power], as is angel and man's soul—I mean, by their knowing and not by their loving: and therefore I clepe [call] them, in this case, "knowable mights."

But see! All reasonable creatures, angel and man, hath in them, each one by themself, one principal working might, the which is cleped a knowable might, and another principal working might, the which is called a loving might. Of the which two powers, to the first, the which is a knowing might, God, that is the maker of them, is evermore incomprehensible; and to the second, the which is the loving might, in each one diversely, he is all comprehensible at the full. Insomuch that *one* loving soul only [alone] in itself, by virtue of love, should comprehend in itself him that is sufficient at the full—and much more, without comparison—to fill all the souls and angels that may be. And this is the endless marvellous miracle of love, the which shall never take end, for ever shall he do it, and never shall he cease for to do it. See, whoso by grace see may; for the feeling of this is endless bliss, and the contrary is endless pain.

And therefore whoso were reformed by grace thus to continue in keeping of [heeding] the stirrings of the will, should never be in this life—as he may not be without these stirrings in Kind [nature]—without some taste of the endless sweetness; and in the bliss of heaven without the full food. And therefore have no wonder though I stir thee to this work. For this is the work, as thou shalt hear after, in the which man should have continued if he never had sinned. And to the which working man was made, and all thing for man, to help him and further him thereto. And by the which a man shall be reparelled [restored] again. And for the defailing [lack] in this working a man falleth deeper and deeper into sin, and further and further fro God. And by keeping and continual working in this work only, without more, a man evermore riseth higher and higher fro sin, and nearer and nearer unto God.

And therefore take good keep into time, how thou dispendest it; for nothing is more precious than time. In *one* little time, as little as it is, may heaven be won and lost. A token it is that time is precious: for God, that is giver of time, giveth never two times together, but each one after other. And this he doth for he will not reverse the order or the ordinal [ordered] course in the cause of his creation. For time is made for man, and not man for time. And therefore God, who is the ruler of Kind [nature], will not in his giving of time go before the stirring of Kind in man's soul; the which is even according to one time only. So that man shall have none excusation against God in the Doom, and at the giving account of the dispending of time, saying: "Thou givest two times at once, and I have but one stirring at once."

But sorrowfully thou sayest now: "How shall I do. And sith this is sooth that thou sayest, how shall I give account of each time diversely; I that into this day, now of four-and-twenty year *of* age, never took heed of time? If I would now amend it, thou wost well, by very reason of thy words written before, it may not be after the course of Kind nor of common grace, that I should mow [be able to] keep or else make asset [claim] to any more times than to those that be for to come. Yea, and moreover well I wot, by very proof [experience], that of those that be to come I shall on no wise, for abundance of frailty and slowness of spirit, mow [be able to] keep one of a hundred. So that I am verily conclude [stopped] in these reasons. Help me now, for the love of Jesu!"

Right well hast thou said "for the love of Jesu!" For in the love of Jesu there shall be thine help. Love is such a might that it maketh all thing common. Love, therefore, Jesu, and all thing that he hath it is thine. He by his Godhead is maker and giver of time. He by his Manhead is the very keeper of time. And he, by his Godhead and Manhead together, is the truest doomsman [judge] and the asker of account of the dispending of time. Knit thee therefore by him, by love and by belief; and then by virtue of that knot thou shalt be common parcener [sharer] with him and with all that by love so be knitted unto him; that is to say, with Our Lady, Saint Mary, that full was of all grace in keeping of time, with all the angels of heaven that never may lose time, and with all the saints in heaven and in earth, that by the grace of Jesus keep time full justly in virtue of love.

Lo here lieth comfort. Construe [understand] thou wisely and pick thee some profit! But of one thing I warn thee amongst all other: I cannot see who may truly challenge [claim] community thus with Jesu and his just Mother, his high angels and also with his saints, but-if [unless] it be such one that doth what in him is, with helping of grace, in keeping time. So that he be seen to be a profiter on his part, so little as is, unto the community; as each one of them doth on his.

And therefore take keep to this work and to the marvellous manner of it within thy soul. For if it be truly conceived, as it is but a sudden stirring, and as it were unadvised, speedily springing unto God as a sparkle fro the coal. And it is marvellous to number the stirrings that may be in one hour wrought in a soul that is disposed to this work. And yet, in one stirring of all these, it may have suddenly and perfectly forgotten all created things. But fast after each stirring, for corruption of the flesh, it falleth down again to some thought, or to some done or undone deed. But what thereof? For fast after, it riseth again as suddenly as it did before.

And here mowe men shortly conceive the manner of this working, and clearly know that it is far fro any fantasy, or any false imagination, or quaint [over-clever] opinion; the which be brought in, not by such a devout and a meek blind stirring of love, but by a proud, curious, and an imaginative wit. Such a proud, curious wit behooveth algates [always] be borne down and stiffly trodden under foot, if this work shall truly be conceived in purity of spirit. For whoso heareth this work either be read or spoken and weeneth that it may or should be come to by travail in their wits—and therefore sit and seek in their wits how it may be: in this curiosity they travail their imagination peradventure against course of Nature, and they feign a manner of working the which is neither bodily nor ghostly—truly this man, whatsoever he be, is perilously deceived. Insomuch that, but-if God of his great goodness show his merciful miracle and make him soon to leave work and meek him to the counsel of proved workers, he shall fall either into frenzies, or else into other great mischiefs of ghostly sins and devils' deceits—through the which he may lightly be lorn, both life and soul, without any end. And therefore for God's love beware in this work, and travail not in thy wits nor in thy imagination on nowise; for I tell thee truly, it may not be come to by travail in them. And therefore leave them and work not with them.

And ween not, because I call it a darkness or a cloud, that it is any cloud congealed of the humours that flee in the air, nor yet darkness such as is in thine house on nights, when thy candle is out. For such a darkness and such a cloud mayest thou imagine with curiosity of wit, for to bear before thine eyen in the lightest day of summer; and also against-ward [contrariwise], in the darkest night of winter thou mayest imagine a clear shining light. Let be such falsehood: I mean not thus. For when I say darkness, I mean a lacking of knowing: as all that thing that thou knowest not, or else that thou hast forgotten, it is dark to thee, for thou seest it not with thy ghostly eye. And for this skill [reason] it is not cleped a cloud of the air, but a cloud of unknowing that is betwixt thee and thy God.

THE FIFTH CHAPTER. And if ever thou shalt come to this cloud and wone [dwell] and work therein as I bid thee, thee behooveth, as this cloud of unknowing is above thee, betwixt thee and thy God, right so put a cloud of forgetting beneath thee, betwixt thee and all the creatures that ever be made. Thou thinketh, peradventure, that thou art full far fro God, forthy that this cloud of unknowing is betwixt thee and thy God; but sickerly [surely] an it be well conceived, thou art well further fro him when thou hast no cloud of forgetting betwixt thee and all the creatures that ever be made. As oft as I say "all the creatures that ever be made," so oft I mean, not only the self-creatures, but also all the works and the conditions of the same creatures. I outtake [except] not one creature, whether they be bodily creatures or ghostly; nor yet any condition or work of any creature, whether they be good or evil. But, shortly to say, all should be hid under the cloud of forgetting in this case.

For though it be full profitable sometime to think of certain conditions and deeds of some certain special creatures, nevertheless yet in this work it profiteth little or nought. Forwhy [because] mind or thinking of any creature that ever God made, or of any of their deeds either, it is a manner of ghostly light; for the eye of thy soul is opened on it and even fixed thereupon, as the eye of a shooter is upon the prick [target] that he shooteth to. And one thing I tell thee, that all thing that thou thinkest upon it is above thee for the time and betwixt thee and thy God. And insomuch thou art the further fro God, that aught is in thy mind but only God.

Yea—and if it be courteous and seemly to say—in this work it profiteth little or nought to think of the kindness or the worthiness of God, nor on Our Lady, nor on the saints or angels in heaven, nor yet on the joys in heaven; that is to say, with a special beholding to them, as though thou wouldst by that beholding feed and increase thy purpose. I trow that on nowise it should be so in this case and in this work. For though-all it be good to think upon the kindnesses of God and to love and praise him for them, yet it is far better to think upon the naked being of him, and to love him and praise him for himself.

Walter Hilton

"OF ANGELS' SONG"

THOU YEARNEST PERADVENTURE greatly for to have more knowing and witting than thou hast of angels' song and heavenly sound; what it is and on what wise it is perceived and felt in a man's soul, and how a man may be sicker [sure] that it is true and not feigned, and how it is made by the presence of the good angel and not by the in-putting of the ill angel. These things thou would wit of me. But soothly, I cannot tell thee for sicker soothness of this matter. Neverthelater, somewhat as me think, shall I shew thee in a short word . . .

Dear friend, wit thou well that the end and the sovereignty of perfection stands in a very onehood of God and of man's soul by perfect charity. This end then is verily made when the mights of the soul are reformed by grace to the dignity and the state of the first condition; that is, when the mind is stabled sadly [fully], without changing and vagation, in God and ghostly things, and when the reason is cleared fro all worldly and fleshly beholdings and imaginations, figures, and fantasies of creatures, and is illumined with grace for to behold God and ghostly things, and when the will and the affection is purified and cleansed fro all fleshly lusts, kindly and worldly love, and is inflamed with burning love of the Holy Ghost.

But this wonderful onehood may not be fulfilled perfectly, continually, nor wholly in this life, for corruption of the flesh; but only in the bliss of heaven. Neverthelater, the nearer that a soul in this present life may come to this onehood, the more perfect it is; for the more that it is reformed by grace till [to] the image and the likeness of his Creator here on this manner-wise, the more joy and bliss shall it have in heaven. Our Lord God is an endless being without changing, almighty without failing, sovereign wisdom, light, soothfastness without error or mirkness, sovereign goodness, love, peace, and sweetness. Then, the more that a soul is oned, fastened, conformed, and joined to our Lord God, the more stable

[handwritten margin note: One must strive for perf. by imitating Christ]

[handwritten margin note: attempt to describe God.]

[handwritten note at bottom: Aspiring to perfection the key to mystic experience;]

Note that. just virtue is true of the things to be achieved this is a greater deeper thing

it is and mighty, the more wise and clear, good, peaceable, loving, and more virtuous: and so it is more perfect. For a soul that has, by grace of Jesu and long travail of bodily and ghostly exercise, overcome and destroyed concupiscences and passions and unskillwise [irrational] stirrings within itself and without in the sensuality, is clad in virtues—as in meekness and mildness, in patience, in soothfastness, in ghostly strength and righteousness, in continence, in wisdom, in truth, hope, and charity—then is it made perfect as it may be in this life.

Mickle comfort it receives of our Lord, not only inwardly in his privy substance, by the virtue of the onehood to our Lord, that lies in knowing and loving of God, in light of ghostly burning of him, in transforming of the soul in the Godhead; but also in many other comforts, and savors, sweetness, and wonderful feelings on sere [various] manners. After our Lord vouches safe to visit his creatures here in earth, and after the soul profits and waxes in charity, some soul—by virtue of charity that God gives it—is so cleansed that all creatures, in all that he hears or sees or feels by any of his wits, turns him till [to] comfort and gladness, and the sensuality receives new savor and sweetness in all creatures. And right as before the likings in the sensuality were fleshly, vain, and vicious, for the pain of the original sin, right so now they are made ghostly and clean without bitterness and biting of conscience.

And this is the goodness of our Lord, that, since the soul is punished in the sensuality and the flesh is partner of the pain, that afterward the soul be comforted in her sensuality and the flesh be fellow of the joy and comfort with the soul, not fleshly but ghostly, as he was fellow in tribulation and pain. This is the freedom and the lordship, dignity and worship, that a man's soul has over all creatures. The which dignity he may receive by grace here, that ilka [each] creature savor to him as it is; and that is when by grace he sees or hears or he feels only God in all creatures. On this manner-wise a soul is made ghostly in the sensuality by abundance of charity that is in the substance of the soul.

Also our Lord comforts a soul by angels' song. But what that song is it may not be described by no bodily likeness, for it is ghostly and above all manner of imagination and man's reason. It may be perceived and felt in a soul, but it may not be spoken. Neverthelater, I speak thereof to thee as methinks. When a soul is purified by the love of God, illumined by wisdom, stabled by might of God, then is the eye of the soul opened to behold ghostly things, as virtues, angels, and holy souls, and heavenly things. Then is the soul able, because of cleanness, to feel the touching, the speaking of good angels. This touching and speaking is ghostly, not bodily; for when the soul is lifted and raised out of the sensuality and out of mind of any earthly things, then in great fervour of love and light of God, if our Lord vouchsafe, the soul may hear and feel heavenly sound made by the presence of angels in loving [praise] of God.

Not that this song of angels is sovereign joy of the soul; but for the difference that is betwixt a man's soul in flesh and an angel, because of uncleanness, a soul may not hear it but by ravishing in love, and needs for to be purified full clean and fulfilled of mickle charity, ere it were able for to hear heavenly sound. For the sovereign and the essential joy is in the love of God by himself and for himself, and the secondary is in communing and beholding of angels and ghostly creatures. For, right as a soul in understanding of ghostly things is oftsithes [often] touched and kenned [informed] through bodily imagination, by working of angels—as Ezekiel the prophet saw in bodily imagination the soothfastness of God's privities—right so, in the love of God, a soul by the presence of angels is ravished out of all mind of earthly and fleshly things into a heavenly joy, to hear angels' song and heavenly sound, after that the charity is more or less.

Now, then, thinks me, that there may no soul feel verily angels' song ne heavenly sound but it be in perfect charity. And not-for-thy [nevertheless], all that are in perfect charity ne has not felt it; but only that soul that is so pured in the fire of love of God, that all earthly savor is burnt out of it, and all means letting [hindering] betwixt the soul and the cleanness of angels is broken and put away fro it. Then soothly may he sing a new song, and soothly may he hear a blissful heavenly sound and angels' song, without deceit or feigning. Our Lord wot where that soul is that, for abundance of burning love, is worthy to hear angels' song. Whoso then will hear angels' song and not be deceived by feigning ne by imagination of himself ne by illusion of the Enemy, him behoves have perfect charity: and that is when all vain love and dread, vain joy and sorrow, is cast out of the heart, that he loves nothing but

God, ne dreads nothing but God, ne joys ne sorrows nothing but in God or of God. Whoso might, by the grace of God, go this way, he should not err.

Neverthelater, some men are deceived by their own imagination or by illusion of the Enemy in this matter. Some man, when he has long travailed bodily and ghostly in destroying of sins and getting of virtues, and peradventure has gotten by grace a somedeal rest and a clarity in conscience, anon he leaves prayers, readings of holy writ, and meditations of the passion of Christ and the mind of his wretchedness, and, ere he be called of God, he gathers his wits by violence to seek and to behold heavenly things, ere his eye be made ghostly by grace, and overtravails by imaginations his wits, and by undiscreet travailing turns the brains in his head, and forbreaks the mights and the wits of the soul and of the body. And then, for feebleness of the brain, him-thinks that he hears wonderful sounds and songs; and that is nothing else but a fantasy caused by troubling of the brain. As a man that is in a frenzy, him-thinks that he hears or sees *w*hat no other man does; and all is but vanity and fantasy of the head, or else by working of the Enemy, that feigns such sound in his hearing. For if a man has any presumption in his fantasies and in his working and thereby falls into undiscreet imagination, as it were a frenzy, and is not kenned ne ruled of grace ne comforted by ghostly strength, the devil enters then by false illuminations, and false sounds and sweetness, and deceives a man's soul. And of this false ground springs errors and heresies, false prophecies, presumptions and false reasonings, blasphemies and slanderings, and many other mischiefs. And, therefore, if thou see any man ghostly occupied fall in any of these sins and these deceits, or in frenzies, wit thou well that he heard never ne felt angels' song ne heavenly sound. For soothly, he that verily hears angels' song, he is made so wise that he shall never err by fantasy ne by indiscretion ne by no sleight of the devil.

Also, some men feel in their hearts as it were a ghostly sound and sweet songs of divers manners, and this is commonly good—and sometimes it may turn to deceit. This sound is felt on this wise: some man sets the thought of his heart only in the name of Jesu and steadfastly holds it thereto, and in short time him-thinks that the name turns him to great comfort and sweetness, and him thinks that the name sounds in his heart delightably, as it were a song, and the virtue of this liking is so mighty that it draws in all the wits of the soul thereto. Whoso may feel this sound and this sweetness verily in his heart, wit he well that it is of God, and as long as he is meek he shall not be deceived. But this is not angels' song; but it is a song of the soul, by virtue of the Name and by touching of the good angel. For when a soul offers it*self* to Jesu truly and meekly, putting all his trust and his desire in him, and busily keeps *him* in his mind, our Lord Jesu, when he will, pures the affection of the soul and fills it and feeds it with sweetness of Himself and makes his name in the feeling of the soul as honey and as song and as anything that is delightable. So that it likes the soul evermore for to cry, "Jesu! Jesu!" And not only he has comfort in this, but also in psalms and hymns and anthems of holy kirk, that the heart sings them sweetly, devoutly, and freely, without any travail of the soul or bitterness, in the same time and notes that holy kirk uses. This is good and of the gift of God, for the substance of this feeling lies in the love of Jesu, which is fed and lightened by such manner of songs.

Neverthelater, in this manner *of* feeling a soul may be deceived by vainglory, not in that time that the affection sings to Jesu and loves Jesu in sweetness of him, but afterward, when it ceases and the heart cools of love of Jesu, then enters in vainglory. Also, some man is deceived on this wise: he hears well say that it is good to have Jesu in his mind or any other good word of God, and then he strains his heart mightily to that name and by accustom he has it nearhand alway in his mind. Not-for-thy, he feels neither thereby, in his affection sweetness, ne light of knowing in his reason but only a naked mind of God or of Jesu or of Mary or of any other good words. Here may be deceit, not for it is ill to have Jesu in mind on this wise, but-if he, this feeling and this mind, that is only his own working by custom, hold it a special visitation of our Lord and think it more than it is. For, wit thou well that a naked mind or a naked imagination of Jesu or of any ghostly thing, without sweetness of love in the affection or without light of knowing in reason, is but a blindness and a way to deceit, if a man hold it in his own sight more that it is. Therefore, I hold it sicker [sure] that he be meek in his own feeling and hold this mind in regard nought, till he mowe, by custom and using of this mind, feel the fire of love in his affection and the light of knowing in his reason.

Lo! I have told thee in this matter a little as methink, not affirming that this suffices ne that this is the soothfastness in this matter. But if thee-think it otherwise or else any other man savour by grace the contrary hereto, I leave the saying and give stead to him. It sufficeth me for to live in truth principally and not in feeling.

Nicholas Love

"THE MIRROR OF THE BLESSED LIFE OF CHRIST"

BEFELL UPON A TIME that our Lord Jesu went with his disciples into Bethany, that was cleped the castle of Martha and Mary, and come into the house of them. And they, that loved him with all their hearts, were glad and joyful of his coming.

And Martha the elder sister, that had the cure [care] of the household, anon busied her and went fast about to ordain for the meat convenable to him and his disciples. But her sister Mary, forgetting all bodily meats and desiring sovereignly to be fed ghostly of our Lord Jesu, set her down on the ground at his feet, and, casting her eyen and her heart and her ears into him only, with more joy and liking than may be spoken, was fed ghostly and comforted in the blessed words of our Lord Jesu. For he would not be idle, but, as his common manner was, occupied him with speaking of edification and words of everlasting life.

Martha, that was so busily occupied about the ministration and the service of our Lord Jesu and his disciples, seeing her sister Mary so sitting, as it were in idleness, took it heavily and complained her to our Lord as he had taken no regard thereto, and prayed him that he would bid her sister rise and help her to serve. And then was Mary afeared lest she should have been taken fro that sweet rest and ghostly liking that she was in; and nought she said, but hung down her head, abiding what our Lord would say.

And then our Lord, answering for her, said to Martha that though she was busy and troubled about many things, nevertheless one thing was necessary, and that was the best Mary chose— the which should never be taken fro her. And then was Mary

greatly comforted and sat more sickerly [surely] in her purpose;
and Martha, without envy, held her paid and served forth with
good will. . .

By these twain sisters beforesaid, Martha and Mary, as holy
men and doctors write, be understood two manner lives of Christian men, that is to say, active life and contemplative life. Of the
which there beeth many treatises and great process made of divers
doctors; and specially, the foresaid Bonaventura in this book of
Christ's life maketh a long process, alleging many authorities of
Saint Bernard. The which process, though it so be that it is full
good and fructuous to men (as unto many ghostly livers), nevertheless, for it seemeth as impertinent [irrelevant] in great part to
many common persons and simple souls that this book in English
is written to, as it is said oft before, therefore we pass over
shortly, taking thereof what seemeth profitable and edificative to
our purpose at this time.

But first, it is to understand that the process of the foresaid
Bonaventura of these twain manner of lives, active and contemplative, belongeth specially to spiritual persons, as be prelates,
preachers, and religious. And so he saith at the beginning that active life, that is understood by Martha, hath two parts. And the
first part is that manner of living by the which a man's business
standeth principally in, that exercise that belongeth to his own
ghostly profit; that is to say, in amending of himself—as withdrawing fro vices and profiting in virtues; first as to profit of himself,
and afterward as to his neighbour, by works of righteousness and
pity, and deeds of mercy and charity, as it shall be said after
more plenerly [fully].

The second part of active life is when a man's occupation and
business standeth in that exercise that 'longeth to the profit of
other men principally, though it be also therewith to his own
meed: the more thereby as it is in governing of other men and
teaching and helping to the heal of soul, as do prelates and preachers and others that have cure of soul.

And betwixt these twain parts of active life beforesaid standeth
contemplative life. So that in this order: first, a man travail and
give him to good exercise in prayer and in study of holy scriptures
and other good workings in common conversation, amending his
life and withdrawing fro vices and profiting in getting of virtues;

and after then, secondly, resting in contemplation, that is to say in
solitude at the list [desire] of heart, forsaking all world's business,
with all his might being about continually to think on God and
heavenly things, only attempting to please God; and then hereafter, when he is perfectly in those two foresaid exercises taught
and stabled in very wisdom and virtues and lightened through
grace, desiring the ghostly profit of other men, then may he sickerly take upon him the cure and governail of other.

And so, after the foresaid process, first it behoveth that in the
first part of active life man's soul be purged of vices and
strengthed and comforted in virtues; after that, it be taught and
lightened and informed in contemplative life; and then, in the
third degree, he may sickerly go out to governail and profit of
others, as it is said.

Upon this foresaid process of Bonaventura, so shortly touched,
he allegeth, after many authorities of Saint Bernard, for to prove
all the parts thereof; that is to say, the first of active, the second
of contemplative, and the third that is the second of active. The
which we pass over with great process of contemplation and many
authorities of Saint Bernard, for few there be—the more harm is!—
either in state of contemplative life touching the second point
beforesaid or in the state of perfect active life touching the third
point that come to their estate by the true way that is declared
before. And that is the cause that in this time many there be, both
men and women, in the estate of contemplative life (as especially
anchors and recluses or hermits) that wit little, as in effect, truly
what contemplative life is, by default of exercise in active life as
it is beforesaid. And therefore it is full perilous and full dreadful
to be in estate of perfection and have a name of holiness, as have
specially these recluses, but [unless] the living and the ghostly
exercise of them be according thereto. For Saint Gregory saith
that there be many that flee occupation of the world and take
them to rest, but therewith they be not occupied with virtues. And
therefore oftsithes it falleth that the more sikerly [surely] that
they cease fro outward occupation, the more largely they gather
into them by idleness the noise of unclean thoughts. And so of
every such soul that spendeth her time in idleness and sloth speaketh the prophet Jeremiah in his *Lamentations* in this manner:
Viderunt illam hostes et deriserunt sabbata eius; that is to say,

"The wicked spirits, enemies of mankind, seeing and taking heed of the living of such a idle soul, laugh to scorn her days of rest." For, in that she is far fro outward occupation and thereby is trowed to serve God in holiness, in so much she serveth the tyrantry of those wicked spirits in idleness.

Also, the same holy clerk Gregory in the same book, after speaking of these twain lives, active and contemplative, saith that man's soul should first be wiped and made clean of the desire of temporal joy and vainglory and of all delectation or liking of fleshly lust and desire, and then may he be lifted up to the sight and degree of contemplation. In figure and token hereof, when God gave Moses the law, the common people was forbidden to nigh the hill, in token that they that be of weak will and desire earthly things should not presume to climb up to high things of contemplation. And furthermore, declaring how they shall prove themselves able that will go to contemplative life, sith [since] that first it behoveth they prove themselves by exercise of virtues in the field of working; that is to say, that they know themselves busily—if they do none harm to their neighbor, and if they bear patiently harms or wrongs done to them of other men; also if they have no gladness in heart or liking when temporal goods fall to them and againward [contrariwise] if they be not too heavy or sorry when they be withdrawn; also, if they feel in their mind the love of spiritual things so mighty that it overcometh or putteth out of their hearts the affection and the imagination of all earthly things; and so, in that they covet to come to that thing that is above their Kind [nature], they overcome what they be by Kind. All this saith Gregory.

Hereto accorden Saint Bernard and all other doctors generally, saying that whoso will go to contemplative life it behoveth that he be first proved in exercise of active life. In figure whereof is allegedly commonly the story of the two daughters of Laban the which Jacob took to his wives, that were cleped [named], the elder Leah (that was for-aged but plenteously bearing children), by whom is tokened active; the younger was Rachel, fair and lovely, but barren, by whom is tokened contemplative life. And though it so were that Jacob loved better Rachel than Leah, and coveted first to have had her to wife for his seven-year service, nevertheless he was made first to wed the elder, Leah, in token that active life should be before contemplative life, as it is said.

And this story is plainly treated in many places to this purpose, and therefore we pass over so shortly.

But for to speak of the manner of living in these two lives, active and contemplative; in special and namely of active life, that standeth in so many degrees (as of seculars and religious, and learned and lewd), it were hard and ask-long process. And also, as it seemeth, it needeth nought for the general exercise of active life, as it longeth first to a man himself; that is, in fighting against vices and busy in getting of virtues. And also after as it 'longeth to his even-Christian; that is, in the fulfilling of the deeds of mercy and almsdeeds-doing of them that have abundance of temporal goods. In every degree is written sufficiently, as I hope, and therefore I leave to speak more of this matter at this time, save to make an end according to the beginning of the matter beforesaid in the gospel of these two sisters, Martha and Mary, by the which be understood these two lives, active and contemplative, as it is said.

First, they that be in active life have example of Martha of that virtue that is sovereignly needful to them in all their deeds; that is, charity. And first, as to themselves, that they be without deadly sin, for else Jesu would not dwell in her house nor accept her service. Also, as to others, that they deem not ne despise others, the which peradventure do not so many virtuous deeds as to man's sight as they do, for they mow [may] not know the privy dooms [judgments] of our Lord Jesu, that accepted more pleasingly and preferred the privy contemplation of Mary that sat at his feet in silence as she had been idle, before all the great busy service of Martha. And that was for the fervent love that she had in contemplation of him; and yet was the service and business of Martha full pleasing to Jesu and meedful to her, as active is good but contemplative is better.

And so furthermore it is to note that, notwithstanding the great commendation of our Lord Jesu touching Mary and the preferring of her part, Martha grudged not of her part but continued forth in her manner of living, serving customably to Jesu and his disciples (as John witnesseth after in his gospel), in token that he that is called to God and standeth in the state of active life holdeth him paid and grudgeth not though contemplative life be commended before his estate. For howsoever it stand of these two estates and degrees of living, God wot all-only who shall be before other in the bliss of heaven of the persons in these estates. And thus much be said as touching the part of Martha and of active life tokened by her.

Furthermore touching contemplative life: he that is in that estate hath example in Mary of three things that needeth sovereignly to that estate: that be, meekness, patience, and silence. First, meekness is tokened in the low sitting of Mary at the feet of our Lord Jesu; and but this ground be truly set in the heart of him that is in this degree of contemplation—that is to say, that he presume not of his own holiness, but that he despise himself truly in his own sight, as it is said before in divers places what longeth to meekness—soothly, else all his building of contemplation, be it never so high, will not stand steadfast, but soon at a little wind of adversity fall to nought. The second virtue according hereto is patience in suffering false deemings, scorns, and reproofs of the world that he shall suffer that fully foresaketh and despiseth the world as it needeth to the true contemplative, committing all-way by patience in heart his cause to his advocate Jesu, without answer reproving again, as Mary did when the Pharisee deemed and reproved her. Also, her sister 'plained upon her and the disciples had indignation and grudged against her; but in all these she kept silence, that is the third virtue needful to the contemplative. And so furtherforth, she gave example of silence—that we find not in all the gospel that she spake before the resurrection of our Lord, save once by a short word at the raising of her brother Lazarus, notwithstanding the great love that our Lord Jesu shewed to her and the great liking that she had in the words and the holy doctrine of him, that should stir her by reason the more boldly to speak. And whoso coveteth to know the fruit of virtuous silence, if he have affection and will to true contemplative living, without doubt he shall be better taught by experience than by writing or teaching of man: and nevertheless, Saint Bernard and many other holy fathers and doctors commend highly this virtuous silence, as it is worthy.

Whereof, and other virtuous exercise that longeth to contemplative living and specially to a recluse, and also of meddled life (that is to say, sometime active and sometime contemplative) as it longeth to divers persons that in worldly estate have grace of ghostly love, whoso will more plainly be informed and taught in English

tongue let him look [examine] the treatise that the worthy clerk
and holy liver Master Walter Hilton, the canon of Thurgarton,
wrote in English by grace and high discretion, and he shall find
thereof, as I *be*lieve, a sufficient school and a true of all these.
Whose soul rested in everlasting bliss and peace, as I hope he be
full high in bliss, joined and knit without departing to his spouse
Jesu by perfect use of the best part that he chose here with Mary.
Of the which part he grant us fellowship, Jesu our Lord God.
Amen.

Religious Controversialists

THE DISPUTES OF churchmen on matters of doctrine, dogma, politics, and observance have always tended toward writing that is, to say the least, vigorous. This is no less true of pre-Reformation times than of Luther's and since: Tertullian, Augustine, and Jerome bow to none in the downrightness of their denunciations. In the period that is our present concern the religious disagreements that brought men to the gallows and the country to arms is accompanied by propaganda and pamphleteering that at times bear the stigma of doctrinal war.

The topics and disputants were many: actives, contemplatives, parish priests, monks, and friars all praised their own ways of life and deplored the ways of others. But one conflict stood out as an occasion for passion and for peril to both church and state: the clash of orthodox churchmen with Wycliffites and their Lollard successors. The three writers who have been selected to represent the controversy—Wycliffe, William Thorpe, and Reginald Pecock—were all men of high education and all moved by strong conviction. They were, however, men of different temperaments, and the fact is apparent in the striking contrasts between their ways of handling English prose.

John Wycliffe (c. 1320-1384), scholar of Oxford, politician as well as reformer, tends toward the violence of the scholarly disputing—a style that, shorn of Billingsgate, still flourishes in journals devoted to linguistics and other explosive subjects. He is represented here by his own justification for translating the Bible and his attack upon the contemplatives and monks. The writing is tense, suited to its unqualified assertions and hostility; the sentences short, bare, and energetic; the phraseology charged with ejaculations and the popular resources of insult. One-sided as his argument is, there is no doubting the effectiveness of the dour, vigorous writing.

The style of William Thorpe, one of his followers, is more cautious, as befits its occasion. His *Examination,* which was published in a slightly modernized form by Tyndale in 1530, might be included among autobiographies, for it is a detailed account of his trial for heresy before Thomas Arundel, archbishop of Canterbury, in 1407. An Oxford scholar and a Lollard preacher, he was imprisoned in 1397 and ten years later subjected to the trial that he relates. The report was written some thirty

151

years after the event and sets down several days of thrust and parry between the archbishop and himself—a hostile dialogue which covers most of the points at issue between the church and the Lollards and one that admirably portrays the frustration of the archbishop and the cautious firmness of Thorpe. We select the debate about pilgrimages, which has more than a chance relevance to Chaucer's Canterbury pilgrimage and which exemplifies the scholarly eloquence that Thorpe used to express his discreetly controlled passion. It affords splendid testimony why some men are made martyrs even by good men.

The third disputant, Reginald Pecock (*c.* 1395–*c.* 1460) was also an Oxonian: a fellow of Oriel and bishop of St. Asaph and later of Chichester, he was a theologian who undertook, *inter alia,* to controvert Lollard propaganda against the orders, institutions, and usages of the church—monks, friars, the hierarchy, land tenure, images, pilgrimages, restriction of the Bible to Latinists, and so on. The bulk of his work, *The Rule of Christian Religion,* the *Donet* and its *Follower,* are theological *summae* that are abnormal in nothing save their use of English. It is his longest and best-known work, *The Repressor of Overmuch Blaming the Clergy, c.* 1449, that carries his counterchallenge to the challengers.

Apart from its combativeness, Pecock's style is the result of training in Latin scholasticism and a passion for reason and fine points of meaning. Bennett's recent complaints that it is stuffed with hybrid words, technical terms, and half-assimilated loans, that it perverts the natural orders of English syntax, and that it is now nearly unreadable, are as excessive as Kellner's earlier opinion that Pecock was "the greatest prosaist of his time." Not every man's meat, the style is still one that some skilled exponents of English might warmly approve. Above all, it is a lawyer's prose. Its habit is to take one subdivision of an argument and to set it forth, with all its logical distinctions, within a single sentence. The long sentences with many qualifications and parentheses, the repetitions, the abundant doublets, the occasional technical and Latinate vocabulary, the summaries and rebuttals—all these traits stem from a legalistic yearning for comprehensive clarity.

Pecock's is not a comfortable style nor one for light reading, but it has its own virtues, firm construction not the least of them. In the matter of his importance for the development of English prose style, declares his latest critic: "Pecock remains a lonely phenomenon." Nothing could be further from the truth, and anyone can affirm who has worked with lawyers or fully read a lease. Pecock may not be a bellwether for belle-lettrists, but he is a forerunner of those serious worriers over the semantic and constructional perils of our language, the conveyancing lawyers of England. From the *Repressor* we choose a passage that forcefully justifies religious images and paintings.

John Wycliffe

"ON TRANSLATING THE BIBLE" ("DE OFFICIO PASTORALI")

(CHAPTER XV). AND HERE the friars with their fautors [adherents] say that it is heresy to write thus God's law in English and make it known to lewd men. And forty signs that they bring for to shew an heretic be not worthy to rehearse, for nought groundeth *t*hem but necromancy.

It seemeth first that the wit [meaning] of God's law should be taught in that tongue that is more known, for this wit is God's word. When Christ saith in the Gospel that both heaven and earth shall pass, but his words shall not pass, he understandeth by his words his wit. And thus God's wit is holy writ, that may on no manner be false. Also the Holy Ghost gave to apostles wit at Whit-Sunday for to know all manner *of* languages, to teach the people God's law thereby—and so God would that the people were taught God's law in divers tongues. But what man, on God's half [for God's sake], should reverse God's ordinance and his will?

And for this cause Saint Jerome travailed and translated the Bible fro divers tongues into Latin, that it might be after translated to other tongues. And thus Christ and his apostles taught the people in that tongue that was most known to the people. Why should not men do now so?

And herefore, authors of the New Law, that were apostles of Jesu Christ, wrote their gospels in divers tongues that were more known to the people.

Also the worthy realm of France, notwithstanding all lettings [obstacles], hath translated the Bible and the gospels, with other true sentences of doctors, out of Latin into French. Why should not Englishmen do so? As lords of England have the Bible in French, so it were not agains*t* reason that they had the same sentence [meaning] in English; for thus God's law would be better known and more trowed, for onehood of wit, and more accord be betwix*t* realms.

And herefore, friars have taught in England the paternoster in English tongue, as men say in the play of York and in many other countries. Sithen [since] the paternoster is part of Matthew's gospel, as clerks know, why may not all be turned to English truly, as is this part? Specially sithen all Christian men, learned and lewd, that shall be saved, must algates sue [follow] Christ and know his lore and his life. But the commons of Englishmen know it best in their mother tongue, and thus it were all one to let [hinder] such knowing of the gospel and to let Englishmen to sue Christ and come to heaven.

Well I wot default may be in untrue translating, as might have been many defaults in turning fro Hebrew into Greek, and fro Greek into Latin, and from one language into another. But, live men good life and study many persons God's law, and when changing of wit is found, amend they it as reason will.

Some men say that friars travail, and their fautors, in this cause for three chesons [causes]: that I will not affirm, but God wot whether they be sooth [true]. First, they would be seen so needful to the Englishmen of our realm, that singularly [only] in their wit lays the wit of God's law, to tell the people God's law on what manner ever they would. And the second cause hereof is said to stand in this sentence: friars would lead the people in teaching them God's law, and thus they would teach some, and some hide, and dock some. For then defaults in their life should be less known to the people, and God's law should be untrulier known both by clerks and by commons. The third cause that men espy standeth in this, as they say: all these new orders dreaden them that their sin should be known and how they be not grounded in God to come into the church. And thus they would not, for dread, that God's law were known in English; but they might put heresy on men if English told not what they said.

God move lords and bishops to stand for knowing of his law!

"OF FEIGNED CONTEMPLATIVE LIFE"

FIRST, WHEN TRUE MEN teach by God's law wit and reason, that each priest ought to do his might, his wit, and his will to preach

Christ's gospel, the fiend blindeth hypocrites to excuse *t*hem by feigned contemplative life, and to say that, sith [since] it is the best and they may not do both together, they be needed [forced] for charity [love] of God to leave the preaching of the gospel and live in contemplation.

See now the hypocrisy of this false saying. Christ taught and did the best life for priests, as our faith teacheth, sith he was God and might not err. But Christ preached the gospel, and charged all his apostles and disciples to go and preach the gospel to all men. Then it is the best life for priests in this world to preach and teach the gospel.

Also, God in the Old Law teacheth that the office of a prophet is to shew to the people *t*heir foul sins. But each priest is a prophet by his order, as Gregory saith upon the gospels. Then it is the office of each priest to preach and tell the sins of the people, and in this manner shall each priest be an angel of God, as holy writ saith.

Also, Christ and John Baptist left *the* desert and preached the gospel to *t*heir death therefor. And this was most charity, for else they were out of charity or *im*paired in charity, that might not be in *t*hem both, sith that one was God and no man after Christ was holier than Baptist—and he sinned not for this preaching.

Also, the holy prophet Jeremiah, hallowed in his mother'*s* womb, might not be excused fro preaching by his contemplation, but *was* charged of God to preach the sins of the people and suffer pain therefor—and so were all the prophets of God.

Ah Lord! Sith Christ and John Baptist and all the prophets of God were needed by charity to come out of *the* desert to preach to the people and leave *t*heir solitary prayer, how dare we fond [foolish] heretics say that it is better to be still and pray our own fond ordinance than to preach Christ's gospel?

Lord! What cursed spirit of lesings [lies] stirreth priests to close *t*hem in stones or walls for all *t*heir life, sith Christ commandeth to all his apostles and priests to go into all the world and preach the gospel. Certes, they be open fools and do plainly against Christ's gospel. And, if they maintain this error, they be cursed of *God* and be perilous hypocrites, and heretics also. And sith men be holden heretics that do against the pope's law, and the best part of the pope's law saith plainly that each that cometh to priest-

hood taketh the office of a beadle, or crier, to go before Doomsday to cry to the people *their* sins and vengeance of God, why be
not tho*se* priests heretics that leave to preach Christ's gospel and
compel other true men to leave preaching of the gospel?—Sith
this law is Saint Gregory's law, grounded openly in God's law and
reason and charity, and other laws of the people be contrary to
holy writ and reason and charity, for to maintain pride and
covetise of Antichrist's worldly clerks.

But hypocrites allege the Gospel—that Magdalene chose to
herself the best part when she sat beside Christ's feet and heard
his word. Sooth it is that this meek sitting and devout hearing of
Christ's word was best to Magdalene, for she had not office of
preaching as priests have, sith she was a woman that had not
authority of God's law to teach and preach openly. But what is
this deed to priests, that have express the commandment of God
and men to preach the gospel? *I ask* whether they will all be
women in idleness and sue not Jesu Christ in life and preaching
the Gospel, that he commandeth himself, both in the Old Law
and New.

Also, this peaceable hearing of Christ's word and burning love
that Magdalene had was the best part, for it shall be ende*d* in
heaven of good life in this world. But in this world the best life
for priests is holy life in keeping God's *be*hests and true preaching
of the gospel, as Christ did and charged all his priests to do the
same. And these hypocrites ween that *t*heir dreams and fantasies
of *t*hemself be contemplation, and that preaching of the gospel be
active life. And so they mean tha*t* Christ took the worse life for
this world and needed [forced] all his priests to leave the better
and take the worse life. And thus these fond hypocrites put error
in Jesu Christ. But who be more heretics?

Also, these blind hypocrites allege that Christ biddeth us pray
evermore, and Paul biddeth that we pray without letting [cease]
—and then we may not preach, as they feign falsely. But here
these hypocrites shall wit that Christ and Paul understand of
prayer "of holy life," that each man doth as long as he dwelleth in
charity—and not of babbling of lips, that no man may ever do
without ceasing. For else no man in this world might fulfil the
commandment of God. And this teacheth Augustine and other
saints.

And sith men that fulfil not God's law and be out of charity, be not accepted in their praying of lips—for their prayer in lips is abominable, as holy writ saith by Solomon—these priests that preach not the gospel, as Christ biddeth, be not able to pray God for mercy, but deceive themselves and the people and despise God and stir him to wrath and vengeance, as Augustine and Gregory and other saints teach.

And principally, these hypocrites that have rents and worldly lordships and parish churches appropriated to them, against holy writ both old and new, by simony and lesings on Christ and his apostles, for stinking groanings and habit of holiness, and for destroying of God's ordinance, and for singular profession made to fools and, in case [perchance], to fiends of hell—these fools shall learn what is active life and contemplative by God's law. And then they might wit that they have neither the one ne the tother, sith they charge [enjoin] more vain statutes of sinful men and, in case, of devils than they charge the behest of God and works of mercy and points of charity. And the fiend blindeth them so much that they say, indeed, that they mote [must] never pray to pleasing of God, sith they unable themselves to do the office of priests by God's law, and purpose to end in their feigned devotion that is blasphemy to God.

William Thorpe

"EXAMINATION"

AND THEN [the archbishop] said to me, "What sayest thou to the third point that is certified against thee; preaching openly in Shrewsbury that pilgrimage is not lawful? And, over this, thou saidest that those men and women that go on pilgrimages to Canterbury, to Beverley, to Carlington, to Walsingham, and to any such other places, are accursed and made foolish, spending their goods in waste."

And I said, "Sir by this certification, I am accused to you, that I should teach that no pilgrimage is lawful. But I never said thus. For I know that there be true pilgrimages, and lawful and full pleasant to God. And, therefore, Sir, howsoever mine enemies have certified you of me, I told at Shrewsbury of two manner of pilgrimages."

And the archbishop said to me, "Whom callest thou true pilgrims?"

And I said, "Sir, with my protestation, I call them true pilgrims travelling towards the bliss of heaven which, in the state, degree, or order that God calleth them, do busy them faithfully for to occupy all their wits bodily and ghostly, to know truly and keep faithfully the biddings of God; hating and fleeting all the seven deadly sins and every branch of them; ruling them virtuously, as it is said before; with all their wits doing discreetly, wilfully, and gladly all the works of mercy, bodily and ghostly; after their cunning and power enabling them to the gifts of the Holy Ghost; disposing them to receive in their souls and to hold therein the right blessings of Christ; busying them to know and to keep the seven principal virtues. And so then they shall obtain here-through grace for to use thankfully to God all the conditions of charity; and then they shall be moved with the good spirit of God for to examine oft and diligently their conscience, that neither wilfully nor witingly they err in any article of belief, having continually (as frailty will suffer) all their business to dread and to flee the offence of God, and to love over all things and to seek ever to do his pleasant will.

"Of these pilgrims, I said, 'Whatsoever good thought that they any time think, what virtuous word that they speak, and what fruitful work that they work; every such thought, word, and work is a step numbered of God towards him into heaven.' These foresaid pilgrims of God delight sore, when they hear of saints or of virtuous men and women, how they forsook wilfully the prosperity of this life, how they withstood the suggestion of the Fiend, how they restrained their fleshly lusts, how discreet they were in their penance-doing, how patient they were in all their adversities, how prudent they were in counselling of men and women, moving them to hate all sin and to flee them and to shame ever greatly thereof, and to love all virtues and to draw them, imagining how Christ and his followers, by example of him, suffered scorns and slanders, and how patiently they abode and took the wrongful menacing of tyrants, how homely they were and serviceable to poor men to relieve and comfort them bodily and ghostly after their power and cunning, and how devout they were in prayers, how fervent they were in heavenly desires, and how they absented them from spectacles of vain seeings and hearings, and how stable they were to let [hinder] and to destroy all vices, and how laborious and joyful they were to sow and plant virtues. These heavenly conditions and such others, have the pilgrims, or endeavour them for to have, whose pilgrimage God accepteth.'

"And again I said, 'As their works shew, the most part of men or women that go now on pilgrimages have not these forsaid conditions; nor loveth to busy them faithfully for to have.' For—as I well know, since I have fully oft assayed—examine, whosoever will, twenty of these pilgrims! and he shall not find three men or women that know surely a commandment of God, nor can say their Paternoster and Ave Maria nor their Credo readily, in any manner of language. And, as I have learned and also know somewhat by experience of these same pilgrims, telling the cause why that many men and women go hither and thither now on pilgrimages—it is more for the health of their bodies than of their souls, more for to have richesse and prosperity of this world than for to be enriched with virtues in their souls, more to have here worldly and fleshly friendship than for to have friendship of God and of his saints in heaven! For whatsoever thing a man or woman doth, the friendship of God, nor of any other saint, cannot be had without keeping of God's commandments.

"For with my protestation, I say now, as I said at Shrewsbury, 'Though they that have fleshly wills travel for their bodies and spend mickle [much] money to seek and to visit the bones and images, as they say they do, of this saint and of that, such pilgrimage-going is neither praisable nor thankful to God, nor to any saint of God, since, in effect, all such pilgrims despise God and all his commandments and saints. For the commandments of God they will neither know nor keep, nor conform them to live virtuously by example of Christ and of his saints.'

"Wherefore, Sir, I have preached and taught openly, and so I purpose all my lifetime to do, with God's help, saying that 'such fond people waste blamefully God's goods in their vain pilgrimages, spending their goods upon vicious hostelers, which are oft unclean women of their bodies, and, at the least, those goods

with the which they should do works of mercy, after God's bidding, to poor needy men and women.'

"These poor men's goods and their livelihood, these runners-
about offer to rich priests which have mickle more livelihood than
they need! And thus those goods they waste wilfully, and spend
them unjustly, against God's bidding, upon strangers—with which
they should help and relieve, after God's will, their poor needy
neighbors at home. Yea, and over this folly, ofttimes divers men
and women of these runners-thus-madly-hither-and-thither-into-
pilgrimage borrow hereto other men's goods—yea, and sometimes
they steal men's goods hereto—and they pay them never again.

"Also, Sir, I know well that when divers men and women will
go thus after their own wills, and finding out one pilgrimage, they
will ordain with them before*hand* to have with them both men
and women that can well sing wanton songs, and some other pilgrims will have with them bagpipes—so that every town that they
come through, what with the noise of their singing and with the
sound of their piping and with the jangling of their Canterbury
bells and with the barking out of dogs after them—they make more
noise than if the king came there-away with all his clarions and
many other minstrels. And if these men and women be a month
out in their pilgrimage, many of them shall be, a half year after,
great janglers, tale-tellers, and liars."

And the archbishop said to me, "Lewd losell! Thou seest not
far enough in this matter, for thou considerest not the great travail
of pilgrims; therefore thou blamest that thing that is praisable! I
say to thee, that it is right well done that pilgrims have with
them both singers and also pipes, that when one of them that
goeth barefoot striketh his toe upon a stone and hurteth him
sore and maketh him to bleed, it is well done that he or his fellow
begin then a song or else take out of his bosom a bagpipe for to
drive away with such mirth the hurt of his fellow. For with such
solace the travail and weariness of pilgrims is lightly and merrily
brought forth."

And I said, "Sir, Saint Paul teacheth men to weep with them
that weep."

And the archbishop said, "What janglest thou against men's
devotion? Whatsoever thou or such other say, I say that the pilgrimage that now is used is to them that do it a praisable and a

good means to come the rather [sooner] to grace. But I hold thee unable to know this grace, for thou enforcest thee to let [hinder] the devotion of the people, since by authority of holy scripture men may lawfully have and use such solace as thou re-provest. For David in his last psalm teacheth men to have divers instruments of music for to praise therewith God."

And I said, "Sir, by the sentence [opinion] of divers doctors ex-pounding the psalms of David, the music and minstrelsy that David and other saints of the Old Law spake of owe [ought], now, neither to be taken nor used by the letter. But these instru-ments with their music ought to be interpreted ghostly; for all those figures are called virtues and grace, with which virtues men should please God and praise his name. For Saint Paul saith, 'All such things befell to them in figure.' Therefore, Sir, I understand that the letter of this psalm of David, and of such other psalms and sentences, doth slay them that taken them now literally. This sentence, I understand, Sir, Christ approveth himself, putting out the minstrels ere that he would quicken the dead damsel."

And the archbishop said to me, "Lewd losell! Is it not lawful for us to have organs in the church, for to worship therewithal God?"

And I said, "Yea, Sir, by man's ordinance. But, by the ordinance of God, a good sermon to the people's understanding were mickle more pleasant to God."

And the archbishop said that organs and good delectable songs quickened and sharpened more men's wits than should any sermon.

But I said, "Sir, lusty men and worldly lovers delight and covet and travail to have all their wits quickened and sharpened with divers sensible solace; but all the faithful lovers and followers of Christ have all their delight to hear God's word, and to under-stand it truly and to work thereafter faithfully and continually. For, no doubt, to dread to offend God and to love to please him in all things quickeneth and sharpeneth all the wits of Christ's chosen people and enableth them so to grace that they joy greatly to withdraw their ears and all their wits and members from all worldly delight and from all fleshly solace. For Saint Jerome, as I think, saith 'Nobody may joy with this world and reign with Christ.'"

And the archbishop, as if he had been displeased with mine answer, said to his clerks, "What guess ye this idiot will speak there where he hath none dread, since he speaketh thus now here in my presence? Well, well, by God, thou shalt be ordained for!"

Reginald Pecock
not one of the more beautiful writers; much misunderstood at his day; somewhat apart from ordinary ways of things.

"THE REPRESSOR OF OVERMUCH BLAMING THE CLERGY"

ON IMAGES AND ICONS. That right singular advantages of remembering come by images and pilgrimages which not come or not so well and so soon come by writings, I prove thus:—If a man would be remembered on the passion of Saint Peter or of Saint Paul or of the holy life of Saint Nicholas, certes, though he could read in a book the story thereof, yet he should read six or seven or more leaves in the book ere he should bring into knowing or into remembrance so much as he may know and remember thereof in a little and much less while by sight of the eye in beholding an image carven with *ap*purtenances set about him, or in beholding a story openly thereof portrayed or painted in the wall or in a cloth. As that this is true, I commit me to the doom [judgment] of experience and of assay and to the experience of this point—that the eyesight sheweth and bringeth into the imagination and into the mind within in the head of a man much matter and long matter sooner, and with less labor and travail and pain, than the hearing of the ear doth. And if this now said is true of a man which can read in books stories written, that much sooner and in shorter time and with less labor and pain in his brain he shall come into remembrance of a long story by sight than by the hearing of other men's reading or by hearing of his own reading, much rather this is true of all tho*se* persons which cannot read in books, namely [especially] since they shall not find men so ready for to read a dozen leaves of a book to *t*hem as they shall find ready the walls of a church painted or a cloth stained or images spread abroad in divers places of the church.

Also, in beholding by sight of eye upon many divers stories or images in the church, a man shall in a little while be remembered, now upon the passion of Saint Laurence, and now anon after upon the passion of Saint Stephen, now anon after upon the passion of Peter, and so forth of many changes. And if in thilk [that] while in the church were not images and pictures, he should not by reading in a book in twenty sithes [times] longer time come into so much remembrance, and namely of so many divers passions to be read; namely since the reader shall not find writings of all tho*se* passions save in divers books—or at the least in divers places of one book; and ere one of tho*se* writings should be overread perfectly, a greater time should be spent than in the perfect overseeing of all tho*se* said passions.

Also full oft, when a man cometh to church and will be remembered upon such now-said things, his head is feeble for labor or study before had, or for sickness or for age. And, certes, if he should be about for to remember him upon such said things, and that by calling into mind what he hath before thilk [that] day read or heard read in book or heard preached or seen painted, it shall be to him much greater labor for to labor so in his brain by taking mind and for to withinforth call into mind, without sight of the eye withoutforth upon images, what he before knew and thought upon, than it should be to him if he behold by eyesight upon images or other painting according to his labor. And againward, by beholding upon images or upon such painting, his wit shall be dressed and led forth evener and more stably and with much less pain and labor than for to wrestle within-forth in his own imaginations, without leading without-forth had by beholding upon images—as experience undoubtably will shew and as men wont for to haunt daily contemplation will bear witness hereto, upon peril of *t*heir soul. Wherefore, though for none other commodity than for this now said, the use of images were so profitable, certes the use of *t*hem were well worthy to be maintained.

Also herewithal into the open sight of images in open churches all people, men and women and children, mowe [may] come whenever they will, in each time of the day, but so mowe they not come into the use of books to be delivered to *t*hem, neither to be read before them. And therefore, as for *t*o soon and oft come into remembrance of a long matter by each person, and also as for to make that the more persons come into remembrance of a matter, images and pictures serve in a specialer manner than books do, though in another manner full substantially books serve better into remembrancing of those same matters than images and pictures do. And therefore, though writings serve well into remembrancing upon the before-said things, yet not at the full, for-why [because] the books have not the avail of remembrancing now-said which images have.

Confirmation into this purpose may be this:—When the day of Saint Katherine shall be come, mark whoso will in his mind all the books which be in London written upon Saint Katherine's life and passions, and I dare well say that though there were ten thousand more books written in London in thilk day of the same saint's life and passion, they should not so much turn the city into mind of the holy, famous life of Saint Katherine and of her dignity in which she now is, as doth in each year the going of people in pilgrimage to the college of Saint Katherine besides London, as I dare put this into judgment of whomever hath seen the pilgrimage done in the vigil of Saint Katherine by persons of London to the said college. Wherefore, right great special commodities and profits into remembrance-making images have and do which writings not so have and do.

Another confirmation into this same purpose is this. In London sometime was a bishop whose name was Gravesend and which lieth now buried in the church of Saint Paul at London, in the plain pavement of the church well beneath the midst of the church. This bishop, when he was Chancellor of England did great benefits to the city of London and ordained therefore that the mayor and the aldermen of London, with many more notable persons of crafts in London, should at divers times in the year come openly to the church of Paul's and stand in every-either side of his sepulchre by two long rows, and say "De profundis" for his soul. Now, though it so had been that this bishop had not intended this to be done for him into this end, that his great benefiting which he did to London should be had and continued in mind of the citizens, but that he intended only this, that prayers thereby should yearly be made the securer for his soul—as doubt is to me whether he intended these both effects or the one of them only—yet truth is, that if the said bishop would have ordained twenty thousand books to be written of his said benefitting and would have ordained *t*hem to be spread abroad in divers places of the city and for to have b*een* chained in tho*se* divers places of the city, that of the people who so would might read therein the said benefitting, thilk [that] multitude of books should not have continued so much and so well into this day the mind of that bishop's benefitting as the said solemn yearly going by two times each year (done by the mayor and aldermen of London) hath d*one* and shall do in each year to come. Wherefore, needs is it true that writing may not contain and comprehend in him all the avail which the sight and the beholding of the eyes may give and is ready for to give.

Political Philosophers

THE FUNCTION OF the English treatises on political philosophy that appear in the fifteenth century is not to be judged entirely by their dedications. Many are advices to rulers, who, it must be supposed, had counsellors accomplished enough to read the Latin and French originals. Possibly they are part of the general movement toward using English, even for documents of policy: in 1418, Henry V broke long tradition by addressing letters to the mayor and council of London in their mother tongue. But the truth may be simply that the audience for these works was wider than royalty, that they were really directed toward politically-minded members of the middle and noble classes who were literate only in their own language. The normal style of these works might support this opinion. Only rarely do they follow the *florida verborum venustas*, the recondite and magniloquent style that Latin secretarial practice favored for matters of state. Their normal manner is either pennyplain or elequent in moderation.

Our selections begin with two pieces that deal with the way of the gentleman. The first concerns chivalry, the code by which the medieval aristocrat would hope to be vindicated. The most famous formalization of these aspirations is that set down in the thirteenth century by Ramon Lull, a Spanish Dominican, and it might be held to confirm the dictum that in origin chivalry was an attempt to harness feudal aggressiveness to the church's dominion. From a French version, two belated English translations were made; one by Caxton, the other—in Malory's days—by Sir Gilbert Hay, one of the rare Scotsmen who employed English prose. From Hay's text, *The Book of the Order of Knighthood,* we have taken a large part of the rules that follow an account of the origin of chivalry in Old Testament times. Its style, even when freed of Scotticisms, is heavy-footed, and it is also excessively balanced and over-copious: Hay was a literal, timid translator, and his source followed the preciosity of the new *rhétoriqueurs.*

The second piece represents a revolt from the blue-blooded concept of social merit. It is part of a translation made by John Tiptoft, Earl of Worcester, from the *Controversia de Nobilitate,* 1428, written by Buonaccorso da Montemagno, famous as a jurist and an exemplar of the

Florentine Renaissance. Like many Elizabethan works of the kind, this is a social debate embodied in a romantic fiction. Lucresse is wooed by two suitors, the nobleman Scipio and the noble-hearted commoner Flammineus. Scipio argues the case for family and blood in a lengthy speech before the Roman Senate and the lady. At still greater length Flammineus exhorts them with the claims of the gentle heart and the defects of inherited nobility. There is little that is new in the matter save in its concern with symbols of fame and its adulation of Greek example, little that would have surprised Chaucer for example; but the emphasis and the manner is Renaissance-classical. All the voices, the author's as well as the debaters', are carefully adjusted to the tones of Ciceronic eloquence. Our sample comes from Flammineus' oration, and it reveals how competently Tiptoft, one of the few fifteenth-century Englishmen to study in Italy, transferred into English the neo-Ciceronic Italian of his source.

The third selection comes from an original treatise (though it owes much to the *Secreta Secretorum,* a spurious letter from Aristotle to Alexander that was highly popular in the Middle Ages) that was written for the guidance of the young Scottish king, James IV, by John of Ireland, his tutor. One of the very few examples of Scottish prose at the time, it is nevertheless a mature and able piece of writing, one that proves that even in the fifteenth century it was possible to write a firm periodic style in original composition.

The fourth extract deals with a theme that was a major concern of late medieval writers, the problem of war. The original work from which this translation was made, Alain Chartier's *Le Quadrilogue Invéctif,* 1422, was a bitter attack by the French royal secretary upon the forces of Orleans and Burgundy who were reducing France to ruin by civil war. In form it is a debate between the author and representatives of the nobility, the clergy, and the people, and its burden is the bitter need to cease civil war and to join forces against the threat from England. Possibly because of its relevance to the Wars of the Roses, this heartfelt treatise was translated at least twice in the later fifteenth century, and from one of these unpublished texts we take a speech of the People, which in the author's view was also the voice of God. Chartier was a great prose stylist, eloquent and controlled in his rhetoric; and although the English translation, a good part of it word for word, is marred by occasional Gallicisms, most of it competently matches the calculated structures and rhythms of the original.

The last piece in this section is taken from the earliest constitutional treatise to be composed in English, Sir **John** Fortescue's *On the Governance of England,* which was written shortly after 1470, addressed, in all probability, to Edward IV. Its first three chapters, which form our selection, discuss the differences between an absolute and a limited monarchy, and they are adapted from one of Fortescue's Latin works on political theory. The remaining seventeen chapters deal with the political evils of the time, and suggest remedies. A lawyer, chief justice, and royal adviser, Fortescue was Lancastrian in bias, but practical patriotism directs his treatise. Constitutional, limited monarchy is for him not only English but also ancient and best: it needed only to be strengthened by endowments, limitation of the power and influence of the nobility, sound finance, and the maintenance of firm justice.

Better than any other single work possibly, this treatise indicates that by the late fifteenth century English prose had been established as a respected medium for serious writing aimed at an educated general public. Its vigorous and most English common sense is embodied in a style that is becoming to both subject and writer, the argumentation and selection of evidence adroitly directed toward an English bias, the manner, though learned and logical, adapted to men of all professions, the sentences firm and varied, with a syntax and idiom that is unfailingly native, the vocabulary judiciously poised between familiar English and an impressive quotation of Latin authorities. Shunning any obvious eloquence, it is masculine and effective English prose.

Sir Gilbert Hay

"THE BOOK OF THE ORDER OF KNIGHTHOOD"

Now, since the doctor has declared in some part the points of the Order with the proprieties and conditions, now likes it him to speak of the office that follows the said order. That is to say, to what purpose it was ordained, to what fine [end], and what intention, and how if knights use not their office, they are contrarious to their Order and to the beginning of their own making; for the which cause he is not very knight indeed, suppose he bear the name; for such knights are more villainous na [than] is either smith, wright, or mason, that do their craft as they are taught. And therefore to show the points of the Order is great merit to them that wot it not, the which he declares hereafterwards.

And first and foremost, knighthood was ordained to maintain and defend holy church and the faith . . . And therefore knights that have faith and baptism in them and use not the virtues and proprieties of the faith are contrarious till [to] others that keep the faith, even as a man that God has given till reason and discretion, and he does even the contrary. Thus, he that has faith and keeps it not is contrarious to himself, for he would be saved and goes not the high gate [way] to his salvation: forwhy [because] his will discords with his wit and leads it the way of mistruth that is against his salvation, and leads him to the way of eternal damnation. And such men take the office and Order more to be prized and honoured in this world na for any profit that they think to do to God, na to their prince that gave them the office. But the most noble officers and orders in this earth are office and order of clerks and of knights, and the best love in this earth is ay betwixt them. And therefore, right as clergy was not ordained to be against the order of knighthood, but to honour it and them that worthily bears it; so should knights not be against the holy order and office of clergy, to maintain worship and defend it against the rebellers and evil-willers of the kirk, that are called sons of iniquity, as they are obliged in taking of the said order of knighthood. . .

The office also of knighthood ought to defend his natural lord and maintain him, for a king is but a man alone but [without] his men; and but them there may no king govern, na defend his people, na yet none other lord, for they are but singular persons. And thus, if any man be against the majesty or other lords of the temporality, the knights should help him to defend and maintain his rights. . . . For the knights are indebted to maintain and defend justice; for right as a judge has power by his office to judge and give a sentence, right so has he power to keep his judgments fro force and fro wrong and violence in exercision and in execution of his judgment and sentence. And because that till [to] judgment of cause pertains well wisdom and discretion of clergy to know the laws, it is a noble thing when knighthood and clergy is assembled together, so that knights were clerks and well-lettered men, so that they were the more sufficient to be judges by the knowledge of the science of laws, for then were there no man more worthy na able to be a judge na a knight-clerk. For but [without] science of clergy to know the laws there is no man worthy to bear office of justice.

Knights should be well-ridden and in youthhead learn to be

well-ridden on destrels and coursers, to haunt jousts and tournaments, to hold Table Round, to hunt and hawk at hart and hind, doe and roe, bear and boar, lupe [wolf] and lion, and all such honourable pleasaunces, and so maintaining the office and order of knighthood worthily. And as all these proprieties beforesaid pertain to a knight as to the ableness of his corps [body], right so is there other proprieties pertaining to the soul: as justice, force, prudence, and temperance, charity and verity, loyalty and humility, faith, esperance, subtlety, agility, and with all other virtues touching to wisdom, appertain to him, as to the soul. And forthy [so], when a knight has all strengths and abilities that appertain to the corps and has not them that appertain to the soul, he is not very knight, but is contrarious to the Order and enemy of knighthood. For then it were like that knighthood were contrarious to the soul's behoof: the which is false, for the principal cause of the order is to the maintenance of the Christian faith and of all virtues, and enemy to vices.

Office of knights is to maintain and govern lands and policy and to defend them. For the radour [fear] and dread that the people have of the knights, they bide upon [continue in] their crafts and labours and grathe [make] living for the lords, for doubt [fear] to be undone, destroyed, and deserted; and thus are the kings dreaded for the knights. And there, says the doctor, that a false knight, that will not help to defend his king and his lord natural, is like faith but [without] good charitable works, or knighthood tume [empty] and idle but office, or heretic against the faith. And thus, a false knight that is untrue, that does not the bidding of his prince and is contrarious to his biddings and opinions, does great wrong to the knights that fight to the death for justice and for the faith and for his prince and his natural lord, and is worthy to be punished utterly. . . .

The order of knighthood stands in the courage [heart] and not the corsage [body], for else were the Order little worth. Forwhy? A little person may whilom through ability of corps overcome a mickle, and take him and imprison him. But a thousand men, suppose they be never so stark [strong] may not overcome na vanquish a good knight's courage. And thus, is the order of knighthood more worthily in the courage na in the corsage, for else were not that the knighthood accorded better to the body na to the soul. And by that, the unworthy cowardice-knights that flee in battles fro their lords are not worthy to be called knights na to bear the honour *that* to worthy knights efferes [belongs], for they dread more the disturbance and malaise of their corsage na the honour and worship of their courage that appertains to the Order of knighthood of right. . . .

Office of knighthood is to maintain and defend widows, maidens, fatherless and motherless bairns, and poor miserable persons and piteable, and to help the weak again*st* the stark and the poor again*st* the rich. For ofttimes such folk are, by more stark na they, pilled and robbed and their goods taken and put to destruction and poverty for *de*fault of power and defence. And because all such deeds is wickedness, cruelty, and tyranny, therefore is the order of knighthood ordained, as in that point among the lave [rest] to gainstand. And if a knight himself be the maintainer or doer of these things, he is unworthy to bear the Order for his wickedness. And right as God has given to the knight pity, hardiness, and great courage, right so has he given him pity in heart, to have mercy of the poor that greets [weeps] on him, asking help and comfort for trust that they have in them of help. And thus should a knight have good sight to the miserable persons, good ears to hear them, and good mind to think on them that piteously cries upon him for help and comfort. . . .

For the office of knighthood should have stark place in governance, and he should be well-horsed and have power of men to keep the country and the king's ways, all pilgrims, travelers, merchants, labourers, and should have the jurisdiction of justice in cities and towns; and, when need were, to assemble the folk for the profit of the community; and when perils were appearing in the land, to burn measle-[leper]-houses and destroy perilous passages, ger [to order to] hedge woods and big [build] and make reparation of evil-bigged places, castles, and walled towns, and fortresses; and keep and defend all goodly persons; chastise and punish all misdoers and wicked cruel persons. . . .

Another point of the order of the knighthood is to accuse traitors against his prince, or others that it efferes, and to appel [challenge] them of battle and fight with them. And office of traitor is to deny his treason, and hide it and cover it while he may, and eschew all proofs thereof. And thus are the two courages well

contrarious together, that never courage of traitor might overcome a noble courage of a true knight but-if it be through pride
or surquidy [arrogance], that is called over-presumptuous in himself; the which God tholes [permits] whilom be punished in
battle-place. But the courage of a loyal knight, that for a loyal
cause debates [fights], may not be overcome, but-if it be for some
sin against the order of knighthood. . . .

Another point of the office of knighthood is to hold his armours
clean and fair and well-at-point, and to see well to the governance
of his horse, and not to play them at plays of dice and of tables
[backgammon] and other light plays, which are not contained in
the points of the Orders. For it is forbidden in the laws to make
any oath contrary to the order of knighthood na to the office; and
he that puts down the principal things wherewith the order and
office is holden at honour and worship, through light plays or
other ways, he honours not well his Order. For knight in wars but
[without] horse and harness is little prized. And since it is so, that
God and man accord in the points of the order of knighthood, that
no false oaths should be therein nor in them that governs the said
order, should then none be.

Lords nor knights should not break the oath of marriage
through misordinate lechery, for that is a point that discords with
the points of the Order. For there is three degrees of chastity, the
which all honourable persons are beholden to. That is: one in
marriage, one in widowhood, and one in maidenhead that is called
virginity. Of which the holy writ bids them that may not live
chaste, marry them and syne [afterwards] keep their marriage.
For if they do not and they break marriage, that breaks their oath
to-god-ward, the which is against the order and office of knighthood, for chastity is virtue and misordinate lechery is vice. And
thus, since all virtue follows the Order and all vice discords with
it, it sits well that princes, lords, and knights keep honour in that
point, and namely [particularly] not to forfeit to their marriage. . . .

Another point of knighthood is that a knight should be meek
and full of clemency, and not pridey na presumptuous na orguil-
lous [arrogant], for ofttimes of pride and orguille and presumption come injury and dissension. For orguille is contrary to justice
and enemy to concord. And therefore, there should no knight be

hautain na fier na prideful na presumptuous, but ever with meekness, and clemency and humility be simple as a maid among people, and in his enemies' presence be as lion-rampant. For whatever he be that be full of pride and presumptuousness, among virtuous men *he* is reputed nought, for they are contrarious to peace and concord, and peace and concord are contrarious to justice. And so is pride against the points of the Order, and humility is the root of the steadfastness of knighthood. For, shortly to say, knighthood accords to all virtue and justice, and all things that are contrarious to virtue and justice are contrarious to the order and office of knighthood. For knighthood should defend all injuries and wrongs, all pilleries, wrong wars, and tribulations, and should hold the people in all justice, equity, verity, and loyalty, peace and debonairty.

John Tiptoft

"CONTROVERSIA DE NOBILITATE"

NE LET NO MAN trow but that a poor man which hath worshipful manners and virtuous deeds should mowe [be able to] well be called noble, and namely these which I have rehearsed, that acquited them so manly and assuredly for their estate public, friends, and kin, when they had greatest need of comfort and succour. Were not these folks liberal and worthy to be praised in the highest degree of liberality, when they left all their own pleasure and profits to do their service for the common weal? I trow it was a greater liberality to give to their city the freedom which was taken fro it, and delivered their kinsmen and friends from all peril, wrong, and jeopardy, than if they had departed all their whole patrimony to their city, kinsmen, and friends. And whosoever paineth him, be it in things public or private, to be called liberal, so much the more he is proved every day more liberal when he useth his diligence and devoir to promote his city, kin, or friends.

Then, Cornelius, the liberality of a worshipful poor man may be right great, and such that poverty may not despoil the virtue of noblesse. Honest poverty may take away no part of virtue. Was it not the fairest gift and richest liberality of Nature to give every man power and ability to be virtuous? And therefore she hath set it in the inward places of the spirit and not in the foolhardiness of Fortune. And there is no hap so hardy and so cumbrous that may take virtue from him which is well willed to keep it, ne there is no hap so marvellous or pleasant that may bring worship to him that is a reckless man or a coward. For sooth it is, if Fortune had sovereignty above virtue, within a while there should be no virtue or any merit of virtue, for the choice of things to be worshipfully perfected should much rather rest in fortune than in the dispositions of our free wills.

And therefore, Cornelius, cease of that opinion: that is to say, to trow that virtue, liberality, and noblesse should have their first course or beginning in the abundance of richesse, for then it should follow that how worshipful a person were, whensoever he failed richesse his name of worship should cease. And the contrary is true, for that which is very [true] worship or noblesse is neither subject to fortune or hap; and those men which I have rehearsed afore, their poverty attended, should never have ascended so high in honour, ne have merited such fame of worship as they did.

And therefore, ye fathers conscript, if worshipful progenitors have had children worshipful, and if poor progenitors have had worshipful children, and if marvellous and great virtue have rested in such as have been right poor, the sequel is to your wisdoms manifest, which is this: that noblesse resteth neither in richesse ne in blood, but in a free and noble courage which is neither servant to vice ne uncleanness, but is exercised in cunning and virtue. And he that is endued with such a courage deserveth best to be called noble, worshipful, and excellent. Therefore, in this controversy of noblesse, having between me and my fellow, meseemeth he should best deserve the palm of victory that may prove himself most virtuous and worshipful.

Fathers conscript, I have liefer in that behalf to have one other to speak for me than to speak myself, lest I speak anything sounding unto my own laud and be boasted with the vice of boast. Nevertheless, it is to me inly joyous when I behold your most rightwise courages and most benign humanities, for I wot well I shall mowe [be able to] say nothing in praising of myself untruly but that ye will understand it well enough, and this that I shall say of myself truly shall not mowe hurt me in your conceits. I trust ye know the life and the manners of us both well enough. Howbeit, I shall remember your wisdoms and accustomed benignities what my life hath been sith my first years.

Forsooth, when I was right young, I was set to school, and when I waxed more ripe of years I took great pleasure to spend my time in the study of philosophy, and meseemeth I could not have spent it better ne more worshipfully. And to my masters I had them that understood both Greek and Latin, and certain years I abode in Athens to hear the Greeks, the princes of eloquence and philosophy. And how greatly I profited there, I report me to the judgment of them which be perfect in that tongue; yet I may say thus much of myself, that there was no day which passed me idle, ne no night without study and learning of somewhat. The which high desire to have knowledge of cunning was granted to me, I deem, of Nature, for meseemed my mind was never appeased but when it had knowledge of something that I knew not afore and of the very truth of things.

I had plenty of masters and teachers and many learners with me, and among the wisdom of so many there might no man be left an idiot. I was so used in my youth to the doctrine of virtue that there is left no place in my courage [spirit] of vicious desires, for, in good faith, vices be to me as noyous, displeasant, and grievous as they may be, and virtues as pleasant, joyous, and acceptable as they may be.

But after that, when I remembered me how every man which hath virtue or cunning is bound to serve therewith the estate public, I gave myself wholly and fully to the weal public of this city. And when I had done so, I never stinted to think upon the weal and the increase of the same, dreading therefor no peril or labour. I never spared myself in that which should cause it to flower in worship and surety, for few years passed when our seas were occupied and encumbered with pirates, and Gaius Flammineus Publius, a man of great worship, had taken upon him the charge of your navy and ships and had delivered to my governance ten ships of forestage for to fight against one of the rovers, called Horantes. It fortuned me to meet with him and to board the same ship in which he was himself; and howbeit he resisted manly and with great force, trusting upon the multitude of his ships and people, I overcame him and brought him and all his navy to my captain. And in the battle against Metridates I was a knight and in the service of the same emperor. And how oft I had for my guerdons [rewards] the round crown accustomed to be given to that knight which advanced himself most farforthly and manly in the battle I report me to mine emperor and fellowship.

And where is that worship that may be gotten in the office or dignity of consul by the merits of knightly discipline that I have not had? And I trust to our gods that I have acquitted me in the years of my force and lustiness that in mine age I shall not be reckoned among them which have done nothing for our weal public.

How well I am befriended, ye my best beloved friends which be here now present can bear sufficient witness, and whether I have been ready in every place to assethe [satisfy] your desires, as well in things public as things private. For I trow I was never strange to do for you what lay in my power, and of what faith, pity, and love I have been to you ye all know well.

Great grace and fortune I have received of our gods to have so great benevolence and friendlihood of all folks, for there is no man in this city ne in all the world hath cause to hate me, if he be not an enemy to our common weal. Nevertheless, the sum of all my labours hath rested in this—to be a curious searcher for our weal public, merry at home, laborious outward, busy to attain science, piteous of them which had necessity (namely [especially] to my father, mother, and kin), wellbeloved of my neighbours, true to my friends, obeisant and devout in things religious. By the which means I have judged myself to attain best noblesse, and I have trowed by these virtues to polish my courage and to make it more worshipful.

John of Ireland

TREATISE FOR THE GUIDANCE
OF JAMES IV

AND, SOVEREIGN LORD, since thy highness is of tender age, rising
to strength and wisdom, I will in this last chapter give part of
doctrine how thy highness should proceed in taking of counsel,
and of what persons, and what persons thy highness should eschew to ask counsel fro, and how thou should examine the counsel
given to thee, and when thou should by wisdom and prudence
change thy counsel.

And as to the first, Sovereign Lord, thy highness should in all
thy works and operations ask at the high God of Wisdom that he
will direct thee to work in all thing after his pleasaunce and will,
for so taught Tobias his son. And after this, thy highness should
consider in thyself what is most expedient for thy person, thy
realm and people. And, in consideration of the things that thy
highness pretends, let not crabbedness, nor covetise, nor hastiness,
nor such passions have domination in thy mind or person, for
these things, as I have said before, put impediment against wisdom and virtuous counsel.

And when thy highness has found by wise and sad [full] de-
liberation what thing is best and most convenient in the matter
that propones to do, then should it be secretly kept in thy mind,
for, an it were told ofttimes, the intention and purpose of the wise
prince might be lightly broken. And when a person reveals his
secret counsel to another, then puts he him in his danger of reveal-
ing of it. And if thou prays him to hold it secret, it were better
that thyself held it secret, for if that thyself cannot do, how should
thou trust in another person? And if thou will always speak of that
matter, thou may propone the matter in such a manner to thy
friend, saying, "What think ye most expedient, that I have war or
peace?" or of any such thing that thou propone to do. And what
part that thy counsellor answers, to speer [ask] his reason and
cause thereof, for, an the king or prince show his mind and pur-

pose, he that hears him incontinent is able for pleasance of him to condescend to the same, whether it be right or wrong, and, as the secret mind and purpose of the king, it is able to be revealed.

And after this, the prince should consider his friends and which of them loves him best, and who are loyalest, who wisest, and who oldest and have most experience in governing and in counsel. And at such men should the prince ask counsel, as the matter requires; *quia in senibus viget sapiencia et in longo tempore addicitur prudencia,* as says noble philosophers and also the holy scripture. And thus the counsellors of the king and prince should be true, wise, and old, for they should have experience in the matters that they should counsel of; for Solomon says, *Ibi salus ubi consilia multa.* And the great poet of Greece, Homer, says that Ulysses, that had great experience, was one of the wisest among all the Greeks in the winning of Troy—Aristotle and syne [later] Horace the poet allege Homer in that and say, *Dic michi, musa, virum capte post menia troie, qui mores hominum nouit cognovit et urbes.* And therefore, though Ajax was more of strength and hardiness, yet the Greeks preferred Ulysses to him for his great wisdom and prudence: *Et dabant ei arma Achillis,* as declares Ovid the poet *in maiore opera,* where he induces the great contention betwixt Ajax and Ulysses.

But now will I declare what persons the prince should not admit to his counsel.

In the first, fools and men of no knowledge should not be counsellors to princes: this is in the self manifest, for they have neither wisdom nor prudence. The prince should not thole [suffer] flatterers be of his counsel. Tully the orator says, *quod nulla capitalior pestis in amicitia quam adulacio.* And so it is in counsel the flatterer shows to the prince nothing but it that may please him: but the holy and wise king, St. David the prophet, asked of God counsellors to argue him and tell him the verity and not to flatter or deceive him: *Corripiat me justus in misericordia; oleum autem peccatoris et adulacio non inpinguet capud meum.* Also, the noble king or prince should not take his old enemy that is reconciled to him of his tender and secret counsel, for there remains yet an evil root in his mind and many things that he does to the prince he does by dissimulation; but, an he might see his time, the prince should beware with him. The prince should have none of his counsel that are soon charged with ale or wine, nor to them should no secret counsel be revealed, for no secret is kept with him, as Solomon says and it is manifest by experience, and the counsel of the prince should be secret. Also, the noble prince should not take of his counsel the persons that counsel him a thing secretly, and openly they counsel the contrary, for these persons use neither in virtue nor verity. Also, the king should not use the counsel of sinners and evil-livers or wicked men, for commonly their persons are full of fraud and deception, and so is their counsel. And of the good virtuous king says the prophet, *beatus vir qui non abiit in consilio impiorum.*

And to the third point, the king and prince should wisely examine his counsel that is given to him. In the first, he should consider if very truth be said to him of the thing that he desired counsel of, for the person that desires counsel should propone his matter in writ without any dissimulation or fiction, and the good counsellors should answer by verity. And after this, the prince should consider if reason inclines to use and do all thing that is counselled to him, and if his power extends thereto. And if the counsel stand in division, the prince should consider what part hold they that are loyalest, wisest, and of most experience. And he should consider of which counsel is able to follow most surety, honour, and profit, and with less peril or danger. And of all these the prince should ever choose the best and principally, if he can, come to the end and perfection thereof. But, an the prince see apparently that there is great doubt or peril in the matter, or that he cannot come to the end and perfection of the work that he propones or that the counsel ordains, or that there would follow more lack or damage *than* profit or honour, then were better leave and not begin than to forthink greatly afterward. And then were expedient and profitable to change the counsel without any lack or reproof. For when a man sees that he cannot come to the honour nor profit that he pretended, but great lack and scathe he would incur by very necessity following that purpose, then should he change his purpose, *quia sapientis est mutare propositum.* Or, if he knows a great error or deception in the counsel, then he may change it for and he know great dishonour in it: for the laws says, *In male promissis prescinde fidem: in turpi voto muta decretum.* Or, if the thing that thou propones to do be impossible or may not goodly be done, then thou *should* change the purpose and proceed by better purpose and wiser counsel, for the counsel that is taken and concluded so starkly that it shall not be changed for no condition or thing that may be or hap, that counsel is wrongous and unprofitable.

And Sovereign Lord, these rules and doctrines are led fro the fountain and well of the noble lady and moral virtue, Dame Prudence, and they may help thy highness in thy tender age and also when thy highness increases to more knowledge, prudence, virtue, and wisdom. And this labour I have taken for love and service of thy highness and profit of thy people and realm. And, high and mighty prince and sovereign lord, I pray humbly thy highness to consider and understand this great work that I have taken: to put in this tongue and language the great matters of theology profitable to all thy people to their salvacion, after six years' preaching in thy father's realm and thine, that thy nobility and people may in their own tongue know the law of God and keep it, that stands ever stark in the self, though the people ofttimes fail in transgression and breaking of it—and hap [perhaps] for the fault of the kirkmen, that should be of good life and give example of good life to the people and syne after preach the word of God, for the evangel says, *Incepit Jesus facere et docere.* And if thy highness accepts this labour and work, (that has been great to me considering that I was thirty years nourished in France and in the noble study of Paris in Latin tongue and knew not the great eloquence of Chaucer nor colours that men use in this English metre that great clerks make no count of) and if thy highness accepts and approves this work, thy people of good mind will have merit and profit through it, and a work made with such travail for thy highness and eternal salvation of the people should not be refused without cause, or-if [unless] there were errors in it.

Alain Chartier

"LE QUADRILOGUE INVÉCTIF"

SCANTLY HAD THE Knight concluded his reason when he that first spake took the language, full of impatience for to hear reproved his defaults, saying in this wise.

THE PEOPLE. Now I see well that as violence giveth itself forced right there as it ought not to be, in semblable manner will presumption put down and destroy truth through high and great words and himself discharge of his own shameful deeds upon them that may not redress it. O God, how much is worldly affection vain and changeable when Fortune hath set so untrue a way in his variable operation that, as soon as a mischief falleth to the caitiff, men put upon them that *it* is through their deserving, like as he that will slay his dog and, for to colour his own misdeeds, putteth on him that he is wood [mad].

Thou sayest that I am cause of this cursed war and that I have purchased it through the impatience of the high prosperity of peace. Thou sayest that my mad error and the parties that I have holden be causers of this confusion and unhappy mischief. Wherefore I answer thee, that the folly of the poor people is founded upon the outrage of the great men and that the sins and disordinate governance be descended from the greatest to the lowest. For, as the princes and high men maintain themselves in their living and estate, the people taketh of them rule and example, be it good or ill, of peace or of slander. And, therefore, I tell thee that of the great plenty of goods and richesse in the time of peace, the mighty and noblemen have them used in waste and dissolution of life, and also in disknowing and in-gratitude of God, which hath caused the murmur of the people against them. And so is your unmeasurable life and disordinate governance the causer of our impatience and beginning of mischief. For at such time as the goods and riches were multiplying in the realm and the treasures were abundant, like a spring of quick water, your unreasonable pomps, tender idleness, annointed with delices and unknowing of yourself, hath already misturned your wits, so that ambition of estates, covetise of goods, and envy to govern hath brought *you* into the confusion wherein ye be now. And by these three mischiefs is the royal money consumed and the treasures of the seignorie wasted in time of abundance. Nor then the multiplication of goods coming and growing in every part, nor the consideration of the need ensuing, might not move your courages [moods] to understand that it was expedient some of the goods to reserve for the prince at his need, nor to make any purveyance ere it be rather spent than received. And, like as dryness of thirst, to them that be in the dropsy, in drinking increaseth and augmenteth, so he that had most riches more coveted for to have.

Thus was the voice of the people as the sea-mews, which by their cry denounceth the floods of the sea: for our words, that thou callest murmur, betokened then the mischief which for these causes was for to come. Then it is so that through outrage and disordinate rule cometh murmur, of murmur rumour, of rumour division, of division desolation and slander. And whosoever is causer of such beginnings ought not to be guiltless of the sequels following. Therefore, if thou blame me that in so hard adversity I may keep no patience, and in thine high prosperity thou mightest not keep temperance ne moderation, thine inconstancy ought to be called less than mine and thine excuse less reasonable for so much as thy wit and authority is greater than mine.

Come we to speak of the mad error and of the parties whereof thou accusest me that I should sustain. If it were as needful to declare as it is honesty to keep it, of such opprobrious vice as therein, maybe some of thine might no more clear them nor excuse than I may. And sith that the operation of deeds goeth before the affections and light words of the common people, I report me to thee to conclude who is most charged. So much may I say: that I have believed what by letters, by renown, by predications and exhorting of presumptuous clerks it hath been put in mine ears. Therefore, *an* I have erred, let them bear the blame and upon them be it the vengeance, sith that under colour to declare us truth they have brought us in this obscure darkness.

Of another thing I am by thee constrained to answer, when thou noticed me suspect of default of help and refuge or doubt of receiving thee and thine, and also that thou affirmest that some of the people, which under colour of thee set up themselves, do thee harms whereof thou bearest the slander. At few words, I dare well say that thy deeds, which all men know, give me more cause of defiance against thee than they give confidence to the prince. And if it must needs be shewed, I shall lay examples instead of reasons and rehearse the places and towns where many of thine have inhabited as long as the victuals and rape [supply] of goods might sustain them. But they have left the places when their prey and rape and felony was failed, and they have taken of the friends *w*hat they durst not challenge on the enemies, for to leave the places to the enemies which they had taken in charge to keep for the friends. And of all this, language shall suffice me. But whereas thou sayest that some of mine do and commit the faults under colour of thee, such as they be thou hast made them and for their misdeeds thou oughtest to bear the burden. Thou art to them colour to perform their iniquities and they make thee member to multiply thy vices and to increase thy company of thieves for to have the more sous and wages and for to arett name [achieve fame], whereby thou destroyest the people and thy worship. And so they yield thee thy sin and the horrible cruelties of thy fellow-ship, unworthy to have the grace of good-deeds-doing, defied and discouraged to have victory upon thine enemies. And in the end they will bring thee to confusion but-if [unless] by a better ad-vice thou seek some good and nigh remedy.

Sir John Fortescue
Written shortly after 1470.

"ON THE GOVERNANCE OF ENGLAND"

CHAPTER I. There be two kinds of kingdoms, of the which that one is a lordship called in Latin *dominium regale,* and that other is called *dominium politicum et regale.* And they diversen [differ] in that the first king may rule his people by such laws as he maketh himself; and therefore he may set upon them tails [taxes] and other impositions, such as he will himself, without their as-sent. The second king may not rule his people by other laws than such as they assent unto; and therefore he may set upon them none impositions without their own assent. This diversity is well taught by Saint Thomas, in his book which he wrote *Ad regem Cipri de regimine principum.* But yet it is more openly treated in a book called *Compendium moralis philosophiæ* and somewhat by Giles in his book *De regimine principum.*

The children of Israel, as saith Saint Thomas, after that God had chosen them *in populum peculiarem & regnum sacerdotale,* were ruled by him under judges *regaliter & politice,* into the time that they desired to have a king, as then had all the gentiles (which we call paynims), that had no king but a man that reigned upon them *regaliter tantum*. With which desire God was greatly offended, as well for their folly as for their unkindness; that sith [since] they had a king, which was God, that reigned upon them politically and royally, and yet would change him for a king, a very man, that would reign upon *t*hem only royally. And therefore God, menacing them, made them to be *a*feared by thunders and other ghastful things from the heaven. And when they would not thereby leave their foolish desire, he charged the prophet Samuel to declare unto them the law of such a king as they asked; which among other things said that he would take from them their land and give it to his servants, and set their children in his carts, and do to them such other many harmful things, as in the 8th chapter of the first book of Kings it may appear. Whereas before that time, while they were ruled by God royally and politically under Judges, it was not lawful to any man for to take from them any of their goods, or to grieve their children that had not offended.

Whereby it may appear that in tho*s*e days *regimen politicum & regale* was distinguished *a regimine tantum regale*, and that it was better to the people to be ruled politically and royally than to be ruled only royally. Saint Thomas also in his said book praiseth *dominium politicum & regale*, because the prince that reigneth by such lordship may not freely fall into tyranny, as may the prince that reigneth *regaliter tantum*. And yet they both be equal in estate and in power, as it may lightly be shewed and proved by infallible reason.

Chapter II. It may peradventure be marvelled by some men, why one realm is a lordship only royal, and the prince thereof ruleth it by his law called *Jus regale;* and another kingdom is a lordship royal and politic, and the prince thereof ruleth it by a law called *Jus politicum et regale*, sith these two princes be of equal estate. To this doubt it may be answered in this manner.

The first institution of these two realms upon the incorporation of them is cause of this diversity. When Nimrod by might, for his own glory, made and incorporate*d* the first realm and subdued it to himself by tyranny, he would not have it governed by any other rule or law but by his own will, by which and for the accomplishment thereof he made it. And, therefore, though he had thus made him a realm, holy scripture disdained to call him **a** king, *quia rex* *dicitur a regendo;* which thing he did not but oppressed all the people by might, and therefore he was a tyrant and called *primus tyrannorum.* But holy writ calleth him *robustus venator coram Domino;* for, as the hunter taketh the wild beast for to slay and eat him, so Nimrod subdued to him the people with might, to have their service and their goods, using upon them the lordship that is called *dominium regale tantum.*

After him, Belus, that was first called a king; after him his son Ninus; and after him other paynims, that by example of Nimrod made *them* realms, would not have them ruled by other laws than by their own wills. Which laws be right good under good princes, and their kingdoms be then most resembled to the kingdom of God, which reigneth upon man, ruling him by his own will. Wherefore, many Christian princes use the same law, and therefore it is that the laws say, *quod principi placuit, legis habet vigorem.* And thus I suppose first began in realms *dominium tantum regale.*

But afterward, when mankind was more mansuete [civilized] and better disposed to virtue, great commonalties, as was the fellowship that came into this land with Brutus, willing to be united and made a body politic called a realm, having a head to govern it—as after the saying of the philosopher, every commonalty united of many parts must needs have a head—then they chose the same Brutus to be their head and king. And they and he upon this incorporation, institution, and one-ing of *t*hemself into a realm, ordained the same realm to be ruled and justified by such laws as they all would assent unto. Which law, therefore, is called *politicum,* and because it is ministered by a king it is called *regale.*

Policia dicitur a "poles", quod est plures, et "ycos", scientia; quo regimen politicum dicitur "regimen plurium scientia sive consilio ministrarum." The king of Scots reigneth upon his people by this law, *videlicet, regimine politico et regali.* And as Diodorus Siculus saith in his book *de priscis historiis,* the realm of Egypt is ruled by the same law, and therefore the king thereof changeth not his laws without the assent of his people. And in like form, as he saith, is ruled the kingdom of Saba in *Felici Arabia,* and the land of Lybia, and also the more part of all the realms of Africa. Which manner *of* rule and lordship the said Diodorus in that book praiseth greatly; for it is not only good for the prince, that may thereby the more surely do justice than by his own arbitrement, but it is also good for his people, that receive thereby such justice as they desire themself.

Now, as me-seemeth, it is shewed openly enough why one king reigneth upon his people *dominio tantum regali* and that other reigneth *dominio politico et regali,* for that one kingdom began of and by the might of the prince, and that other began by the desire and institution of the people of the same prince.

CHAPTER III. And howsobeit that the French king reigneth upon his people *dominio regalia,* yet Saint Louis, sometime king there, nor any of his progenitors set never *en*tails or other imposition upon the people of that land without the assent of the three estates, which when they be assembled be like to the court of the parliament in England. And this order kept many of his successors into late days, that [when] England-men made such war in France that the three estates durst not come together. And then for that cause and for great necessity which the French king had of goods for the defence of that land, he took upon him to set *en*tails and other impositions upon the commons without the assent of the three estates; but yet he would not set any such charges, nor hath set, upon the nobles, for fear of rebellion.

And because the commons there, though they have grouched, have not rebelled or been hardy to rebel, the French kings have yearly sith [since] set such charges upon them, and so augmented the same charges, as the same commons be so impoverished and destroyed that they may unneth [scarcely] live. They drink water, they eat apples, with bread right brown made of rye, they eat no flesh but-if it be right seldom a little lard [bacon] or of the entrails and heads of beasts slain for the nobles and merchants of the land. They wear no wool, but-if it be a poor coat under their outermost garment, made of great canvas and called a frock. Their hose be of like canvas and pass not their knee; wherefore they be gartered and their thighs bare. Their wives and children go barefoot; they may in none other wise live. For some of them that were wont to pay to his lord for his tenement, which he hireth by the year, a scute [crown], payeth now to the king over that scute five scutes; wherethrough they be arted [forced] by necessity so to watch, labor, and grub in the ground for their sustenance that their nature is wasted and the kind [nature] of them brought to nought.

They go crooked and be feeble, not able to fight nor to defend the realm; nor they have weapons nor money to buy them weapons withal. But verily, they live in the most extreme poverty and misery—and yet dwell they in one *of* the most fertile realms of the world. Wherethrough the French king hath not men of his own realm able to defend it, except his nobles, which bear none such impositions and therefore they be right likely of their bodies; by which cause the said king is compelled to make his armies and retinues for the defence of his land of strangers, as Scots, Spaniards, Arragoners, men of Almaigne, and of other nations, or else all his enemies might overrun him, for he hath no defence of his own except his castles and fortresses. Lo, this is the fruit of his *Jus regale!*

If the realm of England, which is an isle and therefore may not lightly get succour of other lands, were ruled under such a law and under such a prince, it would be then a prey to all other nations that would conquer, rob, or devour it. Which was well proved in the time of the Britons, when the Scots and the Picts so beat and oppressed this land that the people thereof sought help of the Romans, to whom they had been tributary. And when they could not be defended by them, they sought help of the duke of Brittany, then called Little Britain, and granted therefore to make his brother Constantine their king. And so he was made king here and reigned many years, and his children after him, of which great Arthur was one of their issue. But, blessed be God!, this land is ruled under a better law, and therefore the people thereof be not in such penury nor thereby hurt in their persons, but they be wealthy and have all things necessary to the sustenance of nature. Wherefore they be mighty and able to resist the adversaries of this realm and to beat other realms that do or would do them wrong. Lo, this is the fruit of *Jus politicum et regale* under which we live.

Somewhat now I have shewed the fruits of both laws, *ut ex fructibus eorum cognoscatis eos, &c.*

Moral Philosophers

❧⊰§⊱❧

MORE WAS WRITTEN on philosophy in the Middle Ages, very likely, than on any other subject, but being theological in nature it was composed in the holy language, the common medium of western scholars—Latin—and was almost never translated. The exceptions belong to antiquity. One was a popular collection, *The Dicts and Sayings of the Philosophers*, which summarizes classical doctrines and makes them palatable with a wealth of familiar anecdotes about the philosophers. Compiled about 1050 by an Arab, the work inspired three separate "Englishings" in the mid-fifteenth century, their immediate source being Guillaume de Tignonville's French version. Our short selection is taken from the anonymous translation of the Helmingham *MS.*, done about 1450. At times, when the summaries and anecdotes are brief, its style is akin to Mandeville's, an innocent aggregation of tumbling short sentences, with no obvious projection into larger logical units; in longer anecdotes, however, the prose is plain and mature.

More significant were the translations of Boethius's *De Consolatione Philosophiae*. Boethius' work may not stand high as a monument of original thought, but in the Middle Ages it far outranked in popularity any other work of its kind. Its Stoic and Platonic doctrine and its underlying Christianity, a form which combined vision, autobiography, and dialogue, and its mood of moral earnestness were gloves fitted to medieval hands. Copies of the Latin text, commentaries upon it, translations into the vernaculars were all abundant, and the substance and form of the treatise may be traced in a large part of the thoughtful writings of the medieval centuries. Chaucer, who constantly quarried its learning, was only one of several English translators; among the rest were King Alfred and Queen Elizabeth. From Chaucer's version we select the discussion on free-will and necessity that provided the substance for the hero's monologue in *Troilus and Criseyde*, Book IV. The style, as is usual with Chaucer's always-serious prose, lacks the ease of his verse. He drew from a French translation and a commentary as well as from the Latin, and this attempt to ride three horses at once partly explains the paired synonyms, parenthetical notes, heavy-footed periods, and gallic constructions that mar the writing, despite a logical firmness in the construction of the units and the work as a whole.

188

"THE DICTS AND SAYINGS OF THE PHILOSOPHERS"

DIOGENES WAS CALLED of some folk *chien,* that is to say, "he having a condition of a hound," and was the wisest man that was in his time, and dispraised greatly the world, and lay always in a tun which had not but one bottom, the which he would always turn about when him list to save him from the great heat of the sun and fro the wind. And he would have none other house, and wherever that he went he had this tun with him; and alway where that the night fell upon him, there would he rest in his tun. And ate and drank at all times when he had any hunger, were it night or day, were it in the street or in any other place, without having any shame. And so he lived, and he held him well content with two gowns of woollen cloth. And in such wise was he governed unto the time that he deceased. And some asked him a question: why his surname was called *chien.* And he answered and said: for he abayed [barked] to fools and worshipped [honored] and pleased wise men.

And the great Alexander came to this Diogenes upon a time for to speak with him, and Diogenes set but little by him. And so King Alexander asked him why he set so little by him, seeing that he was a mighty king and nothing withstood him. To whom he answered and said, "What have I to do with my servant's servant?"

Then said Alexander, "How may I be servant to thy servant?"

Diogenes said, "Yes, for I am lord above all covetise and hold him under my feet as my servant, but covetise is thy master and thou art his servant; wherefore, thou servest him that is my servant."

Then said Alexander, "If there be anything that thou wilt ask me that may help thee in this world, I will give it thee."

Diogenes answered, "It were no reason that I should ask thee anything, where that I am richer than thou art; for that good that I have sufficeth better unto me than all the great quantity of riches that thou hast."

Then Alexander asked him a question: who should put him into the earth when he was dead.

"Forsooth," quoth he, "He that would not savor the stink of my carrion."

And then said Diogenes, "He is not good that keepeth himself fro evil deeds, but he is good that doth good deeds." He saw a young man that was of right good manners, to whom he said, "The great goodness that is in thee hath made right fair thy visage." And some asked him when it was time to eat, and he answered, "What time that a man hath his appetite and hath meat; and also he that hath not whereof, whensoever he may have it." Then it was asked him what manner of men should be called friends. He answered and said, "They that have but one soul in divers bodies." And then he saw a young man which should be married, to whom he said that a little rest engendered great labor. And it was asked him a question: from what manner thing a man should keep him fro. And he answered and said that a man should keep him fro the enmity of his friend and fro the beguiling of his enemy. And men asked him why that he dispraised so the people, and he answered, "I dispraise the evil people for their evil living, and the good people for they live among the evil people."

And he saw a child which was led to be buried, to whom he said, "Thou are delivered of great pain." And saith, "In likewise as the body impaireth in the cold winter when it is frost and snow, in like wise the error appeareth in a man when he is angry and wroth." And as he stood he saw a man that pursued a thief for to have taken him, to the which he said, "I have great marvel how the privy thief pursueth the open thief." And then it was asked him why he would not buy him an house for to rest him in, and he answered again and said, "I rest me for that I have none house."

And said to Alexander, "Look thou think not thyself the better for thy great beauty, for thy fair clothings, nor for thy fair riding, but only for thy goodness and thy freedom. And when that thou takest for evil that that thou seest in other men, look thou beware that thou have not that same evil in thee. And when thou seest a hound that hath forsaken his master for to sue [follow] thee, cast stones at him and chase him away, for in like wise he will forsake thee for to go with another."

And it was asked him why he ate so in the street, and he answered and said: for he was hungry in the street. And he saw a man which prayed God for to send him wisdom, to whom he answered and said, "His prayers sufficed not unless than he would labor himself for to learn first." And saith, "The most profitable thing that longeth unto man is for to speak but little." And saith, "It is dishonesty and lewdness to give laud to a man of a thing that he never did."

And in the time of Diogenes there was a painter which had left his craft and was become a physician. To whom he said, "Thou knowest well that a man might see at [with] his eye clearly thy faults when thou were a painter, but now they may not be known, for they be hid under earth."

Geoffrey Chaucer

BOETHIUS' "DE CONSOLATIONE PHILOSOPHIAE"

Boethius. "This [the non-existence of chance] understand I well," quoth I, "and I accord me that it is right as thou sayest. But I ask if there be any liberty of free will in this order of causes that cleave thus together in *themselves*. Or else I would wit if that the destinal chain constraineth the moving of the courages [dispositions] of men?"

Philosophy. "Yes," quoth she, "There is liberty of free will. Ne there ne was never no nature of reason that it ne had liberty of free will. For everything that may naturally use reason, it hath doom [judgment] by which it discerneth and deemeth everything. Then knoweth it, by itself, things that be to flee and things that be to desire. And that thing that any wight deemeth to be desired, that asketh or desireth he; and fleeth that thing that he troweth be to flee. Wherefore, in all things that reason is, in *t*hem also is liberty of willing and of nilling.

"But I ne ordain not (as who saith, I ne grant not) that this liberty be even-like in all things. Forwhy [because], in the sovereign divine substances (that is to say, in spirits), Judgment is more clear, and Will not corrupted, and Might ready to speed things that be desired. But the souls of men moten [must] needs be more free when they lock them in the speculation or locking of the divine thought, and less free when they slide into the bodies, and yet less free when they be gathered together and comprehended in earthly members. But the last servage [slavery] is when they be given to vices and have fallen fro the possession of their proper reason. For after that they have cast away their eyes fro the light of the sovereign soothfastness to low things and dark, anon they darken by the cloud of ignorance and be troubled by felonous talents [wishes]. To the which talents when they approach and assent, they heap and increase the servage which they have joined to themselves, and in this manner they be caitiffs [captives] fro their proper liberty. The which things, nevertheless, the looking of the divine purveyance [providence] seeth, that all things beholdeth and seeth fro eternity, and ordaineth them everich in their merits as they be predestinate (and it is said in Greek that all things he seeth and all things he heareth)."

BOETHIUS. Then said I, "Now am I confounded by a more hard doubt than I was."

PHILOSOPHY. "What doubt is that?" quoth she. "For certes, I conjecture now by which things thou are troubled."

BOETHIUS. "It seemeth," quoth I, "to repugn and to contrary greatly that God knoweth before all things and that there is any freedom of liberty. For if it so be that God looketh [sees] all things before, ne God ne may not be deceived in no manner, then mote [must] it needs be that all things betide [happen] the which that the purveyance of God hath seen before to come. For which, if that God knoweth before not only the works of men but also their counsels and their wills, then ne shall there be no liberty of arbitrement. Ne, certes, there ne may be none other deed, ne no will, but thilk which that the divine purveyance, that ne may not be deceived, hath felt before. For if that they might writhe away in other manner than they be purveyed, then ne should there be no steadfast prescience of thing to come, but rather an uncertain opinion. The which thing to trow of God I deem it felony and unleaveful.

"Ne I ne approve not thilk [that] same reason (as who saith, I ne allow not, or I ne praise not, thilk same reason), by which that some men ween that they may assoil [resolve] and unknit the knot of this question. For certes, they say that thing nis not to come for that the purveyance of God hath seen before that it is to come, but rather the contrary; and that is this: that, for that the thing is to come, therefore ne may it not be hid fro the purveyance of God. And in this manner this necessity slideth again into the contrary party. Ne it ne behoveth, not needs [necessarily], that things betide that be unpurveyed [unforeseen]; but it behoveth needs that things that be to come be purveyed but as it were travailed (as who saith, that thilk answer proceedeth right as though me [one] travailed or were busy) to inquire, the which thing is cause of the which thing: as, whether the prescience is cause of the necessity of things to come or else that the necessity of things to come is cause of the purveyance.

"But I ne enforce me not now to shew it, that the betiding of things wist [known] before is necessary, how so or in what manner that the order of causes hath itself; although that it ne seem not that the prescience bring in necessity of betiding to things to come. For certes, if that any wight sitteth, it behoveth by necessity that the opinion be sooth [true] of him that conjectureth that he sitteth. And again-ward also is it of the contrary: if the opinion be sooth of any wight for that he sitteth, it behoveth by necessity that he sit. Then is here necessity in the one and in the other: for in the one is necessity of sitting and, certes, in the other is necessity of sooth. But therefore ne sitteth not a wight for that the opinion of the sitting is sooth; but the opinion is rather sooth for that a wight sitteth before.

"And thus, although that the cause of the sooth cometh of the other side (as who saith, that although the cause of sooth cometh of the sitting and not of the true opinion), algates [always] yet is there common necessity in the one and in the other. Thus sheweth it that I may make semblable skills [similar reasons] of the purveyance of God and of things to come. For although that for that things be to come therefore be they purveyed; and not, certes, for that they be purveyed therefore ne betide they not: nonetheless, behoveth it by necessity that either the things to come be purveyed of God or else that the things that be purveyed of God betide. And this thing only sufficeth enough to destroy the freedom of our arbitrement (that is to say, of our free will).

"But now, certes, sheweth it well how far fro the sooth and how upsodown is this thing that we say: that the betiding of temporal things is because of the eternal prescience. But for to ween that

God purveyeth the things to come for they be to come, what other thing is it but for to ween that thilk things that betide whilom [sometimes] be causes of thilk sovereign purveyance that is in God?

"And hereto I add yet this thing: that, right as when that I wot that a thing is, it behoveth by necessity that that self thing be; and eke [also], when I have known that anything shall betide, so behoveth it by necessity that thilk same thing betide: so followeth it then that the betiding of the thing that I wist before ne may not be eschewed. And at the last, if that any wight ween [expect] a thing to be otherways than it is, it nis not only unscience but it is deceivable opinion, full diverse and far fro the sooth of science [knowledge].

"Wherefore, if anything be so to come, that the betiding of it ne be not certain ne necessary, who may wit before that thilk thing is to come? For, right as science ne may not be meddled with falseness (as who saith, that if I wot a thing it ne may not be false that I ne wot it), right so thilk [that] thing that is conceived by science may not be none otherways than as it is conceived. For that is the cause why that science wanteth lesing [lacks deceit] (as who saith, why that witting ne receiveth not lesing of that it wot), for it behoveth by necessity that everything be right as science comprehendeth it to be.

"What shall I then say? In which manner knoweth God before the things to come, if they ne be not certain? For if that he deem that they be to come uneschewably, and so may be that it is possible that they ne shall not come, God is deceived. But not only to trow that God is deceived, but for to speak it with mouth, it is a felonous sin. But if that God wot that right so as things be to come, so shall they come—so that he wit [know] equally (as who saith, indifferently) that things mow be done or else not done— what is thilk prescience that ne comprehendeth no certain thing ne stable. Or else, what difference is there betwixt the prescience and that japeworthy divining of Tiresias the diviner, that said, 'All that I say,' quoth he, 'either it shall be or else it ne shall not be'? Or else, how much is worth the divine prescience more than the opinion of mankind, if so be that it deemeth the things uncertain, as men do: of the which dooms of men the betiding nis not certain?

"But if so be that none uncertain thing ne may be in him that is right certain well of all things, then is the betiding certain of thilk [those] things which he hath wist before firmly to come. For which it followeth that the freedom of the counsels and the works of mankind nis none, since that the thought of God, that seeth all things without error of falseness, bindeth and constraineth them to a betiding by necessity.

"And if this thing be once granted and received (that is to say, that there nis no free will), then sheweth it well how great destruction and how great damages there follow of things of mankind. For in idle be there then purposed and behight meeds [rewards] to good folk and pains to bad folk, since that no moving of free courage voluntary ne hath not deserved them (that is to say, neither meed ne pain). And it should seem then that thilk thing is altherworst which that is now deemed for althermost just and most rightful; that is to say, that shrews be punished or else that good folk be guerdoned [rewarded]. The which folk, since that their proper will ne sent them not to the one ne to the other (that is to say, neither to good ne to harm), but there constraineth them certain necessity of things to come; then ne shall there never be, ne never were, vice ne virtue, but it should rather be confusion of all deserts, meddled without discretion.

"And yet there followeth another inconvenience of the which there ne may be thought no more felonous ne more wicked, and that is this. That, so as the order of things is led and cometh of the purveyance of God ne that nothing is leaveful [permissible] to the counsels of mankind (as who saith that men have no power to do nothing ne will nothing), then followeth it that our vices be referred to the Maker of all good (as who saith, then followeth it that God ought to have the blame of our vices, since he constraineth us by necessity to do vices).

"Then nis there no reason to have hope in God ne for to pray to God. For what should any wight hope to God or why should he pray to God, since that the ordinance of destiny, the which that may not be inclined, knitteth and straineth all things that men may desire? Then should there be done away thilk only alliance betwixt God and men; that is to say, to hope and to pray. But by the price of righteousness and of very meekness, we deserve the guerdon of the divine grace which that is inestimable (that is to

say, that it is so great that it ne may not be full *ap*praised). And
this is only the manner (that is to say, hope and prayers) for
which it seemeth that men mow speak with God, and by reason of
supplication be conjoined to thilk clearness that nis not approached no rather [sooner] ere that men beseech it and impetren
[request] it. And if men ne ween not that hope ne prayers ne have
no strengths by the necessity of things to come *be* received, what
thing is there then by which we mow be conjoined and cleave to
thilk sovereign Prince of things? For which, it behoveth by necessity that the lineage of mankind, as thou sang a little here-before,
be departed and unjoined from his well [service] and fail of his
beginning (that is to say, God)."

PHILOSOPHY. Then said she, "This is," quoth she, "the old question of the purveyance of God. And Marcus Tullius, when he
divided the divinations (that is to say, in his book that he wrote
of divinations), he moved greatly this question, and thou thyself
hast sought it much, and utterly and long. But yet ne hath it not
been determined, ne sped firmly ne diligently of any of you.

"And the cause of this darkness and of this difficulty is for that
the moving of the reason of mankind ne may not move to (that is
to say, apply or join to) the simplicity of the divine prescience.
The which simplicity of the divine prescience, if that men might
think it in any manner (that is to say, that if men might think and
comprehend the things as God seeth *t*hem), then ne should there
dwell utterly no doubt. The which reason and cause of difficulty
I shall essay at the last to shew and to speed, when I have first
spended [responded] and answered to the reasons by which thou
art moved.

"For I ask why thou weenest that thilk reasons of *t*hem that
assoil [resolve] this question ne be not speedful enough ne sufficient?—the which solution or the which reason, for that it deemeth
that the prescience nis not cause of necessity to things to come,
then weeneth it not that freedom of will be disturbed or let
[hindered] by prescience. For ne drawest thou not arguments fro
elsewhere of the necessity of things to come (as who saith, any
other way than thus) but that thilk things that the prescience wot
before ne mow not unbetide? (That is to say, that they mote
[may] betide).

"But then, if that prescience ne putteth no necessity to things to come, as thou thyself hast confessed it and beknown [witnessed] a little herebefore, what cause or what is it (as who saith, there may no cause be) by which that the ends voluntary of things might be constrained to certain betiding? For by grace of position, so that thou mow the better understand this that followeth, I *suppose* that there ne be no prescience. Then ask I," quoth she, "inasmuch as appertaineth to that, should then things that come of free will be constrained to betide by necessity?"

Boethius. "Nay," quoth I.

Philosophy. "Then againward," quoth she, "I suppose that there be prescience but that it ne putteth no necessity to things. Then trow I that thilk self freedom of will shall dwell all whole and absolute and unbound. But thou wilt say, albeit so that prescience nis not cause of the necessity of betiding to things to come, algates [always] yet it is a sign that the things be to betide by necessity. By this manner then, although the prescience ne had never been, yet algate, or at the least way, it is certain thing that the ends and betidings of things to come should be necessary. For every sign sheweth and signifieth only what the thing is, but it ne maketh not the thing that it signifieth.

"For which it behoveth first to shew that nothing ne betideth that it ne betideth by necessity, so that it may appear that the prescience is sign of this necessity. Or else, if there ne were no necessity, certes thilk prescience ne might not be sign of thing that nis not. But certes, it is now certain that the proof of this, sustained by steadfast reason, ne shall not be led ne proved by signs, ne by arguments taken fro without, but by causes convenable [suitable] and necessary.

"But thou mayest say, 'How may it be that the things ne betide not that be purveyed to come?' But certes, right as we trow that tho*se* things which that the purveyance wot before to come, ne be not to betide. But that ne should we not deem; but rather, although that they shall betide, yet ne have they no necessity of *t*heir kind to betide. And this mayest thou lightly apperceive by this that I shall say. For we see many things when they be done before our eyes, right as men see the carter work in the turning or in attempering or addressing of his carts or chariots—and by this manner (as who saith, mayest thou understand) of all other workmen. Is there then any necessity (as who saith, in our looking)

that constraineth or compelleth any of thilk things to be done so?"
BOETHIUS. "Nay," quoth I, "for in idle and in vain were all the
effect of craft if that all things were moved by constraining (that
is to say, by constraining of our eyes or of our sight)."

PHILOSOPHY. "The things then," quoth she, "that, when men do
them, ne have no necessity that men do them, eke those same
things, first ere they be done, they be to come without necessity.
Forwhy [because] there be some things to betide, of which the
ends and the betidings of them be absolute and quit of all necessity. For certes, I ne trow not that any man would say this: that
those things that men do now, that they ne were to betide first or
[ere] they were done; and thilk same things, although that men
had wist them before, yet they have free betidings. For right as
science of things present ne bringeth in no necessity to things that
men do, right so the prescience of things to come ne bringeth in
no necessity to things to betide.

"But thou mayest say that of thilk same it is doubted, as whether
that of thilk things that ne have none issues and betidings necessary, if thereof may be any prescience: for certes, they seem to
discord. For thou weenest that, if that things be seen before, that
necessity followeth them; and if necessity faileth them, they ne
might not be wist before; and that nothing ne may be comprehended by science but certain; and if those things that ne have no
certain betidings be purveyed as certain it should be darkness of
opinion, not soothfastness of science. And thou weenest that it be
diverse fro the wholeness of science that any man should deem a
thing to be otherways than it is itself.

"And the cause of this error is, that of all the things that every
wight hath known, they ween that those things be known all-only
by the strength and by the nature of the things that be wist or
known: and it is all the contrary. For all that ever is known, it is
rather comprehended and known, not after his strength and his
nature, but after the faculty (that is to say, the power and the
nature) of them that know. And, for that this thing shall mow [be
able to be] shewn by a short example: the same roundness of a
body, otherways the sight of the eye knoweth it and otherways
the touching. The looking, by casting of his beams, waiteth
[watches] and seeth fro afar all the body together, without
moving of itself; but the touching cleaveth and conjoineth to the

round body, and moveth about the environing, and comprehendeth by parts the roundness. And the man himself, otherways
wit beholdeth him, and otherways imagination, and otherways
reason, and otherways intelligence. For the wit comprehendeth
without-forth [outwardly] the figure of the body of the man that
is established in the matter-subject; but the imagination comprehendeth only the figure without the matter. Reason surmounteth
imagination, and comprehendeth by universal looking the common species that is in the singular pieces. But the eye of intelligence is higher, for it surmounteth the environing of the universal
and looketh over that, by pure subtlety of thought, thilk same
simple form of man that is perdurably in the divine thought.

"In which this ought greatly to be considered, that the highest
strength to comprehend things embraceth and containeth the
lower strength; but the lower strength ne ariseth not in no measure
to the higher strength. For wit ne may nothing comprehend out of
matter, ne the imagination ne looketh [sees] not the universal
species, ne reason ne taketh not the simple form so as intelligence
taketh it; but intelligence, that looketh all above, when it hath
comprehended the form, it knoweth and deemeth all the things
that be under that form. But she knoweth them in thilk manner
in the which it comprehendeth thilk same simple form that ne
may never be known to none of that other (that is to say, to none
of those foresaid strengths of the soul). For it knoweth the uni-
versality of reason and the figure of imagination and the sensible
material conceived by wit. Ne it ne useth not nor of reason ne of
imagination ne of wit without-forth; but it beholdeth all things, so
as I shall say, by a stroke of thought formally, without discourse
or collation. Certes, reason, when it looketh anything universal, it
ne useth not of imagination nor of wit, and algates yet it comprehendeth the things imaginable and sensible; for reason is she that
defineth the universal of her conceit right thus: man is a reasonable two-footed beast. And how so that this knowing is universal,
yet is there no wight that ne wot well that a man is a thing imaginable and sensible. And this same considereth well reason; but that
nis not by imagination nor by wit, but it looketh it by reasonable
conception. Also imagination, albeit so that it taketh of wit the
beginnings to see and to form the figures, algates, although that
wit ne were not present, yet it environeth and comprehendeth all

things sensible; not by reason sensible of deeming, but by reason imaginative.

"Seest thou not then, that all the things, in knowing, use more of *t*heir faculty or of *t*heir power than they do of the faculty or power of things that be known? Ne that nis not wrong: for so as every judgment is the deed or the doing of him that deemeth, it behoveth that every wight perform the work and his intention, not of foreign power, but of his proper power."

Natural Scientists

❧❦❧

BACONIAN PROPAGANDA and latter-day achievement have joined to create a notion that medieval science was entirely and deliciously absurd. In some ways it was. Small reading is needed in its authorities to realize that it was less clear than ours in discriminating between the "inexacter" and "exacter" sciences, between report, speculation, fact, and probability. Nor did it have the benefit of either the preciser methods, instruments and concepts, or the status and funds that have facilitated the achievements of recent centuries. As a result it often filled the vacuums of ignorance with old wives' tales. Nevertheless, western science in the centuries between Galen and Galileo was not a wholly green and yellow melancholy: from Greeks and Arabs it inherited concepts and techniques that are still interesting; speculatively and even by experiment and direct observation, it made contributions of its own, particularly in technology.

This farrago of fact and fancy appears in books of many kinds: encyclopoedic surveys of Nature's dominion, small-range treatises for scientific specialists, works on government, philosophy, or morals. Their form and linguistic media vary with their time and audience, the tendency being for the more serious and weighty works to be written in Latin prose. As early as the fourteenth century, however, begins the practice of turning these works, even the learned ones, into the vernaculars. In English there is an abundance of such translations, many still unprinted; our selections represent a few of the types and levels of these works, their various styles, and the topics with which they deal.

An encyclopedic survey which was authoritative for nearly three centuries is the *De Proprietatibus Rerum* that was written about 1260 by Bartholomew de Glanville, an English Franciscan. Often copied and printed, it was excruciatingly translated in 1398 by John Trevisa, a version that was edited and printed by Wynkyn de Worde in 1491.

A briefer work, also originally written about 1250, that covers the general principles of natural science and was extremely popular in its day is Gossouin's *L'Image du Monde*. In 1480, Caxton translated it (*The Mirror of the World*) at the request of Hugh Brice, a fellow-member of the Mercers' Gild. The matter is organized geographically, in reports on the universe and the continents, and is preceded by a summary and defense of the seven branches of knowledge. Our selection consists of this defense and some dispersed passages that summarize medieval ideas concerning the universe.

Besides these over-all studies, there was an abundance of treatises on surgery and medicine, mineralogy, herbs, arithmetic and astronomical calculations, alchemy, physiognomy, the meanings of dreams, astrology, chiromancy, and so on. Nearly all are translations from Latin, and they are witness that although professional men may have been reared on *mensa, mensam, mensae,* many were comfortable only in English.

Most of these "Englishings" of scientific treatises have never been printed. Elsewhere in this book a sampling of John Arderne's treatise on fistula has been reproduced; in this section are included specimens from some other scientific works in English. Medicine is represented by two pieces. The first comes from a fifteenth-century text of *Agnus Castus,* a herbal that was popular enough to be still represented by some thirty manuscripts. Clearly and directly it sets out botanical descriptions of a large number of plants and an account of their medical virtues (both scientific and folkloristic). The second piece is part of an engaging pamphlet on Quintessence, a remarkable specific (brandy, despite the label) that was good for almost anything that ailed medieval man and which is described bravely, with the mystery and the lingo that have long been the potent stock-in-trade of vendors of quack medicines.

The medieval science of physiognomy and the related doctrines of natural marks and the humors are represented by a chapter from James Yonge's version of the *Secreta Secretorum.* This social science was in vogue as a guide to human character and it appears in Aristotle's purported letter to Alexander as a principal means by which a ruler should make decisions as to which men to trust and which to avoid.

The doctrine and the methodology of these late medieval works on science would have found little regard among the Baconians who established the Royal Society. But about the medieval way of writing there might have been quite another opinion. Here (with such licensed exceptions as the *Book of Quint-Essence*) is often an unconsidered form of that "primitive purity and shortness," that "close, naked, natural way of speaking, positive expressions, clear senses, a native easiness, bringing all things as near the mathematical plainness as they can, and preferring the language of Artizans, Countrymen, and Merchants before that of Wits or Scholars" which it was the resolution of the Royal Society to promote among its own members.

William Caxton

"THE MIRROR OF THE WORLD"

THE SEVEN ARTS. The first of the seven sciences is grammar, of which (for the time that is now) is not known the fourth part. Without which science sickerly [truly] all other sciences in especial be of little recommendation, because without grammar there may none profit, for grammar is the fundament and the beginning of clergy [learning], and it is the gate by the which in the infancy is begun and in continuing men come and attain to sapience of clergy. This is the science to form the speech, be it in Latin, French, or English, or in any other language that men speak with. And who that could [knew] all grammar, he could make and construe every word and pronounce it by example. God made the world by word, and the word is to the world sentence [meaning].

The second science is logic, which is called dialectic. This science proveth the *pro* and the *contra;* that is to say, the verity or truth, and otherwise. And it proveth whereby shall be known the true fro the false and the good fro the evil, so verily that for the good was created heaven and made, and on the contrariwise for the evil was hell made and established, which is horrible, stinking, and redoubtable.

The third of the seven sciences is called rhetoric, which containeth in substance righteousness, reason, and ordinance of words, and ought not to be holden for folly—for the droits [rights] and laws by which the judgments be made and that by reason and after right be kept and maintained in the court of kings, of princes, and of barons, come and proceed of rhetoric. Of this science were extrac*ted* and drawn the laws and decrees which by need serve in all causes and in all rights and droits. Who well knew the science of rhetoric, he should know the right and the wrong. For to do wrong to another, whoso doth it is lost and damned; and for to do right and reason to every man, he is saved and getteth the love of God his creator.

The fourth science is called art-metric. This science cometh
after rhetoric and is set in the middle of the seven sciences. And
without her may none of the seven sciences perfectly ne well and
entirely be known. Wherefore it is expedient that it be well known
and conned, for all the sciences take of it their substance, in such
wise that without her they may not be. And for this reason was she
set in the middle of the seven sciences and there holdeth her
number, for fro her proceed all manners of numbers, and in all
things run, come, and go. And nothing is without number. But
few perceive how this may be but if he have been master of the
seven arts so long that he can truly say the truth. But we may not
now recount ne declare all the causes wherefor, for who that
would dispute upon such works, him behoved dispute and know
many things and much of the gloss. Whoso knew well the science
of art-metric he might see the ordinance of all things. By ordinance was the world made and created, and by ordinance of the
Sovereign it shall be defaited [unmade].

The fifth is called geometry, the which more availeth to astronomy than any of the seven other, for by her is compassed and
measured astronomy. Thus is by geometry measured all things
where there is measure; by geometry may be known the course of
the stars, which always go and move, and the greatness of the
firmament, of the sun, of the moon, and of the earth; by geometry
may be known all things and also the quantity: they may not be
so far (if they may be seen or espied with eye) but it may be
known. Who well understood geometry, he might measure in all
masteries, for by measure was the world made and all things high,
low, and deep.

The sixth of the seven sciences is called music, the which
formeth him of art-metric. Of this science of music cometh all at-
temperance and of this art proceedeth some physic, for like as
music accordeth all things that discord in themselves and remain
them to concordance, right so in like wise travaileth physic to
bring Nature to the point that disnatureth in man's body, when
any malady or sickness encumbereth it. But physic is not of the
number of the seven sciences of philosophy; but it is a mystery
or a craft that intendeth to the health of man's body and for to
preserve it fro all maladies and sicknesses as long as the life is in
the body; and therefore it is not liberal, for it serveth to heal

man's body, which else oftentimes might lightly perish, and there is nothing liberal ne free that groweth of the earth. And forasmuch as science that serveth to man's body loseth his franchise [freedom], but science that serveth to the soul deserveth in the world to have name liberal, for the soul ought to be liberal, as thing that is of noble being, as she that cometh of God and to God will and ought return. And therefore be the seven sciences liberal, for they make the soul all free. And on the other part, they teach and enseign [instruct] all that in everything ought properly to be done. And this is the very reason why these arts all seven be called seven sciences liberal, for they make the soul liberal and deliver it fro all evil.

Of this art is music thus common, that she accordeth her to everyone so well that by her the seven sciences were set in concord that they yet endure. By this science of music be extracted and drawn all the songs that be sung in holy church and all the accordances of all the instruments that have divers accords and divers sounds. And where there is reason and intendment [understanding] of some things, certes, who can [knows] well the science of music he knoweth the accordance of all things. And all the creatures that pain them to do well remain them to concordance.

The seventh and last of the seven sciences liberal is astronomy, which is of all clergy the end. By this science may and ought to be enquired of things of heaven and of the earth, and in especial of them that be made by Nature, how far that they be. And who knoweth well and understandeth astronomy, he can set reason in all things, for our Creator made all things by reason and gave his name to everything. By this art and science were first emprised and gotten all other sciences of decrees and of divinity, by which all Christianity is converted to the right faith of our Lord God to love him and to serve the King Almighty, fro whom all goods come and to whom they return, which made all astronomy and heaven and earth, the sun, the moon, and the stars, as he that is the very ruler and governor of all the world and he that is the very refuge of all creatures, for without his pleasure nothing may endure. Certes, he is the very Astronomer, for he knoweth all, the good and the bad, as he himself that composed astronomy, that sometime was so strongly frequented and was holden for a right high work, for it is a science of so noble being that, who that

might have the perfect science thereof he might well know how
the world was compassed and plenty of other partial-sciences, for
it is the science above all others by which all manner of things be
known the better. . . .

THE UNIVERSE. This clearness of which we have spoken, which is
called air-spiritual and where the angels take their array and at-
tourement, environeth all about the world the four elements which
God created and set, that one within that other. Of which that one
is the fire, the second is the air, the third is the water, and the fourth
is the earth; of which that one is fastened in that other, and that
one sustaineth that other in such manner as the earth holdeth
him in the middle. The fire, which is the first, encloseth this air in
which we be; and this air encloseth the water after, the which
holdeth him all about the earth—all in like wise as is seen of an
egg, and as the white encloseth the yolk and in the middle of the
yolk is also as it were a drop of grease which holdeth on no part;
and the drop of grease, which is in the middle, holdeth on neither
part.

By such and semblable regard is the earth set in the middle of
heaven so just and so equally that as far is the earth fro heaven
fro above as fro beneath. For, wheresomever thou be upon the
earth, thou art alike far fro heaven, like as ye may see the point
of a compass which is set in the middle of the circle; that is to say,
that it is set in the lowest place; for, of all forms that be made in
the compass, always the point is lowest in the middle. And thus
be the four elements set, the one within the other, so that the
earth is always in the middle, for as much space is always the
heaven from under the earth as it appeareth from above. . .

All the earth that is in the world inhabited is divided into three
parts, and therefore it behoveth by this reason to make another division. Of which, the part toward orient is called Asia the Great,
and taketh the name of a queen that sometime was lady of this
region and was called Asia. This part named Asia holdeth and
containeth as much space as do the other twain, and therefore it
is called Asia the Great. . . . The other part is called Europe and
taketh his name of a king called Europes, the which was lord of
this country, and therefore it was so called; and it endureth fro
the west unto the north and marcheth unto Asia the Great. The

other part is Africa, which stretcheth fro the south unto the west. And Africa hath his name of hell, and is as much *as* to say, *borne-away*. . . .

Ye ought to know that above *the air* is *the fire*. This is an air which is of much great resplendure and shining and of much great noblesse. And by his right great subtlety he hath no moisture in him and is much more clear than the fire that we use and of more subtle nature than the air *that* is against the water or also the water against the earth. This air in which is no manner of moisture, it stretcheth unto the moon. . .

The *pure air* is above the fire, which pourpriseth and taketh his place unto the heaven. In this air is no obscurity ne darkness, for it was made of clean purity, and it resplendisheth and shineth so clearly that it may to nothing be compared. In this air be seven stars which make their course all about the earth, the which be much clean and clear and be named *the seven planets*. Of whom that one is set above that other and in such wise ordained that there is more space from that one to that other than there is fro the earth to the moon, which is further fifteen times than all the earth is great. And every *one* runneth by miracle on the firmament and maketh his circle, the one great and the other little, after that it is and sitteth more low. . . These seven planets be such that they have power on things that grow on the earth and abound their virtues more than all the others that be on the firmament, and more apertly work, like as the ancient sage philosophers have ensearched by their wits. . .

Above Saturn, which is the last planet and highest from us of all the seven planets, is the heaven that men see so full of stars, as it were sown, when it is clear time and weather. This heaven that is so starred is the firmament which meveth and goeth round. Of which meving is so great joy, so great melody and so sweet, that there is no man that, if he might hear it, the never after should have talent ne will to do thing that were contrary unto Our Lord in anything that might be, so much should he desire to come thither where he might alway hear so sweet melodies and be alway with them. Whereof some were sometime that said that little young children heard this melody when they laughed in their sleep; for it is said that then they hear the angels of Our Lord in heaven sing, whereof they have such joy in their sleep. . . .

As ye may understond, the seven sciences liberal were founden by auncient wise men, out of which all other sciences proceed. The first that applied him and entermeted for to enquire and search these sciences after the Flood was Shem, one of the sons of Noah, which had given his courage thereto. And in such wise he did therein such diligence and so continued that, by his wit, he founded a great part of Astronomy. After him was Abraham, which also founded a great part. . . . And after came Plato the sage, and right sovereign in philosophy, and his clerk named Aristotle, the wise clerk. This Plato was the man above all them of the world in clergy, the most expert of them that were tofore or after him. He preved first that there was but One, that was only sovereign, which all made and of whom all good thing cometh; yet his books approve highly that there ne is but one sovereign good, that is Our Lord God, which made all things. And in this only verity he preved the right truth; for he preved his power, his wisdom, and his goodness. These three bounties reclaim all Christian men, that is, the Fader, the Son, and the Holy Ghost. Of the Father, he said the power and the puissance; of the Son, the sapience; and of the Holy Ghost, the benevolence.

And Aristotle, which came after him, holdeth plenty of things nigh to him and knew the things that he had said, and ordained right well the science of logic, for he knew more thereof than of other sciences.

These two notable clerks found by their wisdom and cunning three persons in one essence, and preved it; but they put it not in Latin, for both two were paynims, as they that were more than three hundred year tofore the coming of Our Lord, Jesu Christ; and all their books were in Greekish letters. After came Boethius, which was a great philosopher and right-wise clerk, the which could behelp him with diverse languages and loved much righteousness. This Boethius translated of their books the most part, and set them in Latin. But he died ere he had all translated them; whereof was great domage to us all. Sith have other clerks translated; but this Boethius translated more than any other, the which we have yet in usage; and compiled in his life plenty of fair volumes anourned [adorned] of high and noble philosophy, of which we have yet great need for to address us toward Our Lord God.

"AGNUS CASTUS"

ABSINTHIUM is an herb men clepe [call] wormwood. This herb hath leaves like to mugwort, and the leaf is sumdeal whiter under and it hath a great root, and of the root come many branches, and this herb brancheth as mugwort. The virtue of this herb is to comfort the stomach and cleanse the heart. For Galen saith that if this herb be given to a man that hath an evil, of the which evil the matter is not fully defied [digested], it shall hard the stomach and lithe [ease] the digestion; and if the evil be riped, then the herb shall make a laxative and easily put away the matter and that evil, and deliver him. This herb is good for drunkenness, for if a man be drunken let him chewen on this herb and it shall put away all his drunkenness. Also, if this herb be drunken with spikenard it assuageth the aching of the stomach and of the womb that is 'gendered of wicked winds. Also, if this herb be tempered with honey and drunken, it healeth the swelling in man's mouth and putteth away the blackness about the sore teeth and clarifieth them. Also, if the juice of this herb be 'stilled into a man's nostrils it driveth out the moisture that renneth fro him. Also, if this herb be meddled with gall of a bull and put to a man's ears, it putteth away all manner hossings [buzzings] of hearings in man's head. Also, Dioscurides saith that if this herb be put in an hutch or in a press among clothes it will keep the clothes that no moths shall fret [devour] them. Also the same doctor saith that if the same herb be laid by books or charters it shall keep the books fro worms. Also, strew this herb in a chamber among fleas and it shall 'stroy them. This herb is dry and hot.

MANDRAGORA is an herb men clepe mandrake and there be two species thereof: one is mandrake the male; and mandrake the female. Mandrake the male hath leaves like beets and mandrake the female hath leaves like to lettuce. And the leaves of this herb spreadeth about on the earth; and this herb hath two stocks or three growing together. And the stocks are black withouten and white within; and the mandrake-male hath a long leaf and a small and thin, and the root of this herb is shaped after a man or

woman, and the virtue of this herb accordeth to Isidore in a book
that he made of herbs. Also, this herb beareth apples in time of
year, and the apples growen in the leaves right as oak-apples
growen in oak's leaves; and the apples are yellow, and sweet in
smelling, and in taste they are bitter. And the virtue of this herb
is that if the rind thereof be sodden in wine it will make a man to
sleep so fast that though a man cut him he should not wake ne
unnethe [hardly] feel no pain for the strong sleep. And this experiment have these physicians and surgeons that use to cut men
sleeping. Also the juice of this herb, tempered with woman's milk
and drunken, maketh a man to sleep fast and yet never-the-latter
it is forbode that no man take thereto much in his medicines, for it
might be cause of his death, for this herb hath great strength of
cooling and destroying of kind. For this herb is wonder-cold.
This herb quencheth and destroyeth wild fire; also, it quencheth
and destroyeth the great heat of brenning choler. Also, it will
heal a man of the flux. Also, these virtues and properties of this
herb telleth Placens in the same book, and saith that by kind
there is found no manner shape of man ne woman in this herb;
but this is a common tale among lewd men, that it should be like
to a man. But it is not so. But the root hath a shape. Also Dioscurides saith, and Placens both, and allege that if this herb be taken
in due time or in reasonable manner it will cool a woman that is
too hot to conceive a child: it will make her disposed well enough
to conceive, and make her cold; but if a woman that is disposed
well enow to conceive and cold enow use it, it will destroy her if
she will use it, for it shall make her so cold that it shall destroy
her. And therefore, women, beth ware how ye take it, and that
ye know in what degree that ye be, whether too hot or too cold. If
ye be too hot, take it; if ye be too cold, leave it, in saving of your
life. Also this herb is good to 'sauge all swellings in man's body;
also, it is good for biting of venomous beasts and worms. Also, it
is good for aching in the head: take leaves of this herb and bind
them to thine temples, or else take the oil of this mandrake or the
juice, and meddle it with cummin, and then let it boil a little
while, and then strain it through a cloth, and then clepe it oil of
mandrake. Also, if a man have a fester that is 'gendered of heat, it
is good to annoint his pounse [pulse] therewith; also, it is good to
annoint a man therewith that hath a hot posteme [abscess] in the

beginning. Also, the powder of this herb is good to all these medicines if it be meddled with the juice of any cold herb. This herb is cold and dry, and it shall be gathered in the sun going down and it must be kept in shadow.

James Yonge

"SECRETA SECRETORUM"

PHYSIOGNOMY IS A science to deem the conditions or virtues and manners of people after the tokens or signs that appeareth in fashion or making of body, and namely [especially] of visage and of the voice and of the color. One light manner and general of physiognomy is to deem virtues and manners of men after the complexion.

Complexions be four, for a man is sanguine or phlegmatic or choleric or melancholy, and right up [govern] these four complexions of four humours of the body, which answereth to the four elements and to the four times of the year. The blood is hot and moist, to the likeness of the air; phlegm is cold and moist after the kind of the water; choler, hot and dry, after kind of fire; melancholy, cold and dry after kind of earth.

The sanguine by kind should love joy and laughing and company of women and much sleep and singing. He shall be hardy enough, of good will and without malice. He shall be fleshy, his complexion shall be light to hurt and to impair for his tenderness, he shall have a good stomach, good digestion, and good deliverance; and if he be wounded, he shall soon be whole. He shall be free and liberal, of fair semblance, and deliver [nimble] enough of body.

The phlegmatic by kind, he should be slow, sad, full still, and slow of answer; feeble of body; lightly fall in palsy. He shall be great and fat. He shall have a feeble stomach, feeble digestion, and good deliverance. And, as touching manners, he shall be piteous, chaste, and little desire company of women.

The choleric by kind, he should be lean of body. His body is hot and dry, and he shall be somewhat rough and light to wrath and light to *ap*pease, of sharp wit, wise, and of good memory, a great

intermetter [busybody], full large [generous], and foolhardy, deliver of body, hasty of word and of answer. He loveth hasty vengeance. Desirous of company of women more than him needeth.
He should have a stomach good enough, namely in cold time.

The melancholy man should be lean of body and dry. He
should have good appetite of meat, and commonly he is a glutton
and good deliverance hath of his belly. And, as touching manners,
he should be pensive and slow, and of still will, still and dreadful,
and a small intermetter. More later is he wroth than a choleric
man, but he holdeth longer wrath. He is of subtle imagination as
of handiworks, and well are wont the melancholic men to be
subtle workmen.

The sanguine men should be ruddy of color, the phlegmatic
white and pale, the choleric should have yellow color somewhat
meddled with red, the melancholic should be somewhat black and
pale. . . .

Those that have fully black eyes tokeneth that they be faint, for
black color approacheth nigh to darkness and in darkness a man
lightly is a-dread more than in light. And those that have eyes not
well black but declining to yellow be of good courage. Speckled
eyes and white eyes tokeneth dreadfulness, for white color tokeneth dread. Those that have eyes of the color of a camelhair be
courageous, likened to the lion and the eagle. And those that have
eyes colored like red wine be disposed to woodness [madness],
likened to beasts which may not be daunted. And those that have
eyes like lie [flame] of fire, branding and sparkling, be angry and
shameless, likened to hounds. Those that have eyes discoloured
and troubled tokeneth dread, for he that is a-dread waxeth pale.
And they that have eyes shining be lechers, likened to rooks and
cocks. . . .

He that hath a sharp nose and small, he is wrathful. And he
that hath a long nose and somewhat stooping and stretching toward the mouth he is worthy and hardy. He that hath a crooked
nose, he is hasty, malicious, and angry. Whoso hath the nostrils
much open, he is strongly angry. Whoso hath a low and plat nose
amid, stooping toward the butt, he is a juggler [trickster] and a
liar. And that nose is best to praise that is meanly [middling] long
and meanly broad and the butt not over-coped ne over-plat ne
stooping and the nostrils meanly great.

"THE BOOK OF QUINT-ESSENCE"

IT IS NOT moist ne cold as common water, for it burneth, and so doth not common water. Ne it is not hot and moist as air, for air corrumpeth [corrupts] a thing anon, as it sheweth well by generation of flies and arains [spiders] and such other, but sickerly [surely] this is always incorruptible, if it be kept close fro flight. Also it is not cold and dry as earth, for sovereignly it worketh and changeth. And it is not hot and dry as fire, as it sheweth by experience, for hot things it cooleth and hot sicknesses it doth away. Also that it giveth incorruptibility and keepeth a thing from corruptibility and rotting, it is proved thus: for-why, what piece of flesh, fish, or dead bird, be put therein, it shall not corrump ne rot whiles it is therein; much more, then, it will keep quick [living] flesh of man's body from all manner corruptibility and rotting.

This is our *quintessentia,* that is to say, man's heaven, that God made to the conservation of the four qualities of man's body, right as he made his heaven to the conservation of all the world. And wit ye for certain, that many philosophers and leeches that be now know not this quintessentia ne the truth thereof. For-why: God will not that they know it, for their great burning covetise and vicious living. . .

Take the best wine that ye may find, if ye be of power; and if ye be right poor, then take corrupt wine, that is, rotten, of a watery humour, but not aigre, that is, sour, for the quintessentia thereof is naturally incorruptible, the which ye shall draw out by sublimation. And then shall there leave in the ground of the vessel the four elements, as it were, rotten faeces of wine. But first ye must distill this wine seven times and then have ye good burning water. Forsooth, this is the watery matter fro which is drawn our quintessentia. Then must ye do make, in the furnace of ashes, a distillatory of glass, all whole of *one* piece, with a hole above in the head, where the water shall be put in and be take*n* out. And this is a wonderful instrument, that that thing that by virtues of fire ascendeth and distilleth within the vessel *per canales brachiales,* that is, by pipes like to arms, be borne again [back] and eftsoons ascendeth, and eft [again] descendeth continually, night and day, till the burning water heavenly be turned into *quintam essentiam*. And so, by continual ascensions and descensions, the quintessentia is departed fro the corruptible composition of the four elements. For, before that thing that is twice sublimed is more glorified and is more subtle and far from the corruption of the four elements, more separate than when it ascendeth but once, and so unto a thousand times, so that by continual ascending and descending, by the which it is sublimed to so much highness of glorification, it shall come that it shall be a medicine incorruptible almost as heaven above, and of the nature of heaven. And, therefore, our quintessentia worthily is cleped "man's heaven." And, after many days that it hath been in this subtle vessel of glass distilled, ye shall open the hole of the vessel in the head, that was sealed with the seal of lute [cement] of wisdom, made of the subtlest flour and of white of eggs and of moist paper, y-mingled, so that nothing respire out. And when ye open the hole, if there come out a passing heavenly sweet flavor, that all men that come in naturally draw thereto, then ye have our quintessentia. And, else, seal the vessel and put it to the fire again till ye have it. . .

The first medicine is to reduce an old, feeble, evangelic man to the first strength of youth. Also, to restore again his nature that is lost and to length his life in great gladness and perfect health, unto the last term of his life that is set of God. Ye shall take our quintessence aforesaid, that is to say, man's heaven, and therein put a little quantity of quintessentia of gold and of pearl, and the old feeble man shall use this divine drink at morn and at even, each time a walnut-shell full. And, within a few days, he shall *be* so whole that he shall feel himself of the state and the strength of forty years, and he shall have great joy that he is come to the state of youth. And, when his youth is recovered and his nature restored and health had, it is needful that little and seldom he use quintessence. Also it is needful that he use oft good wine at his meat and at the supper, in the which be fixed the quintessence of gold as I taught you afore. . .

The fifteenth medicine, to make a man that is a coward hardy and strong, and put away all manner of cowardice and dread. I say you, forsooth, that nothing may tell all the miracles-virtues that God hath made in our quintessence, and not only in him but also into his mother, that is to say, fine burning water. For to cure this sickness, take a little quantity of our quintessence and put thereto double so much of burning water and a little quantity of the juice of herb-peony and of saffron, distilled together, and a little of quintessence of gold and of pearl, and give it to him to drink. And after, suddenly, as it were by miracle, the coward man shall lose all manner dread and faintness of heart, and he shall recover strength that is lost by dread and take to him hardiness, and he shall despise death. He shall dread no perils, and passingly he shall be made hardy. This is true, for it hath ofttimes by old philosophers *been* proved. Therefore, it were a great wisdom that Christian princes in battles again*st* heathen men had with them, in tuns, burning water, that they might take to every fighting man half a right little cupful thereof, to drink in the beginning of the battle. And this privity ought to be hid from all enemies of the church, and also princes and lords ministering these things should not tell what it is.

Travelers

❦

ALTHOUGH MEDIEVAL MEN were not so incontinent in travel as we are, they had their own spurs to visiting far places: trade, administration, war, fishing, pilgrimages. In consequence, travel guides and travel descriptions form a substantial part of medieval literature, increased notably in the later centuries, when they were sometimes set down in the vernaculars.

Of all these travel books, the most popular was one that declared itself to be a first-person account of the travels that Sir John Mandeville, of St. Albans in England, made into the Holy Land, the near East, and the lands of Gog and Magog, the Great Cham, and Prester John. Originally written in French—Anglo-French it now appears—the work survives in over three hundred manuscripts in many languages (a number surpassed only by copies of Holy Writ), and the numerous English copies represent no fewer than three separate translations.

The old debate as to the authorship has now been settled: recent investigations by Mr. Letts and Mrs. Bennett have proved that the book's own statement is the truth. As much cannot be claimed for the contents. Sir John, a soldier and physician, may very well have been in the Holy Land in the mid-fourteenth century; that he served with the Great Cham and Prester John or had seen the Valley of Diamonds is hardly likely. But in works of this nature truth is no great matter: as Mandeville says himself, he who wishes to believe it let him believe it. Like Henry Vizetelly's fine, though London-bound, version of the California goldrush, the virtue of this book lies in its telling: in amplifying his own travels from Boldensele or in taking to himself the far journeys of Friar Odoric, Mandeville was graced by a literary zest beyond theirs. Their reports, true to experience though they be, contrive to make marvels dull. Mandeville's own wonder and curiosity—like Pepys, he seems ever with child to see new things—suffuse his retelling with the voice of a born romantic. His style is like his mood. Abstractly, little could be said for it, but in the context of his matter its disorderliness and its childlike sentences, similar in length, similar in formula, schoolboyish in vocabulary, reiterating words of wonder, strung together with "and's", ring-around-the-roses style, have a fitness beyond art. From the earliest English translation, late-fourteenth century and done soon after the original, we select some passages relating to the courts of the Great Cham and Prester John.

Our second piece is no fashion-plate either, but it is still an interesting piece. Each age finds its own rationale for wanderlust: ours justifies its pleasure with the sanctions of culture and the open mind; medieval tourists had more religious objectives. But although pilgrimages were the basis of a large tourist trade, the everyday experience of pilgrims was not dissimilar to ours. Among many witnesses is William Wey, who in his fifties made the same major pilgrimages as Dame Alison, Chaucer's Wife of Bath: to Santiago in 1456 and to Jerusalem in 1458 and 1462. Wey, a Devonshire man, was an original Fellow of Eton College and later a monk in Wiltshire. So as not to lose his fellowship through too prolonged absence, he obtained special permission for these trips from the king himself. Unfortunately, his travelogues are in Latin. But, for the benefit of the unlearned, he also wrote in English a doggerel travel-poem, a detailed explanation of the many coinages with which pilgrims needed to grapple, and the practical vade-mecum which is here reproduced. The style has the note-like associationalism of the average letter home. But the matter is fascinating, if only as a reminder of matters that still plague secular pilgrims despite all the insulations of Thomas Cook or American Express.

Sir John Mandeville

TRAVELS

Late 14c. Translation — done soon after the original which was in Fr. or Anglo-French

CATHAY IS A great country and a fair, noble and rich and full of merchants. Thither go merchants all years, for to seek spices and all manner of merchandises, more commonly than in any other part. And ye shall understand that merchants that come fro Genoa or fro Venice or fro Romagna, or other parts of Lombardy, they go by sea and by land, eleven months or twelve, or more sometime, ere they may come to the isle of Cathay that is the principal region of all parts beyond. And it is of the Great Cham.

Fro Cathay go men toward the east by many journeys [stages], and then men find a good city between these others, that men clepe Sugarmago. That city is one of the best-stored of silk and other merchandises that is in the world. After, go men yet to another old city, toward the east; and it is in the province of Cathay.

And beside that city the men of Tartary have let make another
city, that is clept Caydon, and it hath twelve gates and between
the two gates there is always a great mile, so that the two cities,
that is to say the old and the new, have in circuit more than
twenty mile.

In this city is the siege [throne] of the Great Cham, in a full
great palace and the most passing fair in all the world. Of the
which the walls be in circuit more than two mile, and within the
walls it is all full of other palaces. And in the garden of the great
palace there is a great hill, upon the which is another palace, and
it is the most fair and the most rich that any man may devise. And
all about the palace and the hill be many trees bearing many
divers fruits. And all about that hill be ditches, great and deep,
and beside *t*hem be great vivaries on that *one* part and on that
other, and there is a full fair bridge to pass over the ditches. And
in these vivaries be so many wild geese and ganders and wild
ducks and swans and herons that it is without number. And all
about these ditches and vivaries is the great garden, full of wild
beasts, so that when the Great Cham will have any disport, either
to take any of the wild beasts or of the fowls, he will let chase
*t*hem and take *t*hem at the windows, without going out of his
chamber.

This palace where his siege is is both great and passing fair.
And within the palace, in the hall, there be twenty-four pillars of
fine gold and all the walls be covered within of red skins of
beasts that men call panthers, that be fair beasts and well-
smelling, so that for the sweet odour of tho*se* skins none evil air
may enter into the palace. Tho*se* skins be as red as blood, and
they shine so bright again*st* the sun that unethes [scarcely] no
man may behold *t*hem. And many folk worship tho*se* beasts when
they meet *t*hem first at morrow, for their great virtue and for the
good smell that they have, and tho*se* skins they *ap*praise more
than though they were plate of fine gold.

And in the mid*st* of this palace is the monture [stairs] for the
Great Cham, that is all wrought of gold and of precious stones
and great pearls, and at the four corners of the monture be four
serpents of gold, and all about there is made large nets of silk
and gold and great pearls hanging all about the monture. And
under the monture be conduits of beverage that they drink in the

emperor's court, and beside the conduits be many vessels of gold, by the which they that be of *the* household drink at the conduit.

And the hall of the palace is full nobly arrayed and full marvelously attired on all parts, in all things that men apparel with any hall. And first, at the chief [head] of the hall, is the emperor's throne, full high, where he sitteth at the meat, and that is of fine precious stones, bordered all about with pured gold and precious stones and great pearls; and the grees [steps] that he goeth up to the table be of precious stones, meddled with gold. And at the left side of the emperor's siege is the siege of his first wife, one gree lower than the emperor; and it is of jasper bordered with gold and precious stones. And the siege of his second wife is also another *gree* more lower than his first wife; and it is also of jasper bordered with gold, as that other is. And the siege of the third wife is also more low, by a gree, than the second wife. For he hath always three wives with him where that ever he be. . . .

And at great solemn feasts before the emperor's table, men bring great tables of gold, and thereon be peacocks of gold and many other manner of divers fowls, all of gold and richly wrought and enameled; and men make *t*hem dance and sing, clapping their wings together, and make great noise. And whether it be by craft [skill] or by necromancy, I wot never, but it is a good sight to behold, and a fair, and it is great marvel how it may be. But I have the less marvel, because that they be the most subtle men in all sciences and in all crafts that be in the world, for of subtlety and of malice and of forecasting they pass all men under heaven. And, therefore, they say *t*hemselves that they see with two eyes and the Christian men see but with one, because that they be more subtle than they; for all other nations, they say, be but blind in cunning and working in comparison to *t*hem. I did great business for to have learned that craft, but the master told me that he had made avow to his god to teach it to no creature but only to his eldest son. . . .

And ye shall understand that my fellows and I with our yeomen, we served this emperor and were his soldiers fifteen months against the King of Mancy, that held war against him. And the cause was for we had great lust to see his noblesse and the estate of his court and all his governance, to wit if it were such as we heard say that it was. And, truly, we found it more noble and

more excellent and richer and more marvelous than ever we heard
speak of, in so much that we would never have believed it had we
not a-seen it. For I trow that no man would believe the noblesse,
the richesse, ne the multitude of folk that be in his court but he
had seen it. For it is not there as it is here: for the lords here have
folk of certain number, as they may suffice; but the Great Cham
hath every day folk at his costages and expense as without number. But the ordinance ne the expenses in meat and drink, ne the
honesty, ne the cleanness, is not so arrayed there as it is here; for
all the commons there eat without cloth upon their knees, and
they eat all manner of flesh and little of bread, and after meat
they wipe their hands upon their skirts, and they eat not but once
a day. But the estate of lords is full great and rich and noble. And
albeit that some men will not trow me, but hold it for fable, to
tell them the noblesse of his person and of his estate and of his
court and of the great multitude of folk that he holdeth, nonetheless I shall say you a part of him and of his folk, after that I have
seen the manner and the ordinance, full many a time. And whoso
that will may believe me if he will; and whoso will not may leave
also. . .

From thence [Persia], go men by many journeys through the
land of Prester John, the great Emperor of Inde. And men clepe
[call] his realm the Isle of Pentexoire.

This emperor, Prester John, holdeth full great land and hath
many full noble cities and good towns in his realm, and many
great divers isles and large. For all the country of Inde is devised
in isles, for the great floods that come from Paradise, that depart
all the land in many parts. And the best city in the Isle of Pentexoire is Nysa, that is a full royal city and a noble and full rich.

This Prester John hath under him many kings and many isles
and many divers folk of divers conditions. And this land is full
good and rich, but not so rich as is the land of the Great Cham,
for the merchants come not thither so commonly for to buy merchandises as they do in the land of the Great Cham, for it is too
far to travel to. And, on the other part, in the isle of Cathay men
find all manner of thing that is need to man, cloths of gold and
of silk, spicery, and all manner avoirdupois. And, therefore, albeit
that men have greater cheap in the Isle of Prester John, nonetheless men dread the long way and the great perils in the sea in those

parts. . . . And the merchants pass by the kingdom of Persia and go to a city that is clept Hermes [Ormuz], for Hermes the philosopher founded it; and, after that, they pass an arm of the sea and then they go to another city, that is clept Golbach [Cambaye?], and there they find merchandises—and of popinjays as great plenty as men find here of geese. And if they will pass further they may go securely enough.

In that country is but little wheat or barley, and therefore they eat rice and honey and milk and cheese and fruit. This Emperor Prester John taketh always to his wife the daughter of the Great Cham, and the Great Cham also, in the same wise, the daughter of Prester John, for these two be the greatest lords under the firmament. In the land of Prester John be many divers things and many precious stones, so great and so large that men make of them vessels, as platters, dishes, and cups. And many other marvels be there, that it were cumbrous and too long to put in scripture of books. But of the principal isles and of his estate and of his law I shall tell you some part.

This Emperor Prester John is Christian, and a great part of his country also, but yet they have not all the articles of our faith as we have. They believe well in the Father, in the Son, and in the Holy Ghost, and they be full devout and right true one to another, and they set not by no barrats [frauds], ne by cautels [tricks] ne of no deceits. And he hath under him seventy-two provinces, and in every province is a king, and these kings have kings under them, and all be tributaries to Prester John.

And he hath in his lordships many great marvels. For in his country is the sea that men clepe the Gravelly Sea, that is all gravel and sand, without any drop of water; and it ebbeth and floweth in great waves, as other seas do, and is never still ne in peace in no manner of season. And no man may pass that sea by navy ne by no manner of craft, and therefore may no man know what land is beyond that sea. And albeit that it have no water, yet men find therein and on the banks full great fish, of other manner of kind and shape than men find in any other sea, and they be of right good taste and delicious to man's meat. And, a four journeys long fro that sea be great mountains, out of the which goeth out a great flood that cometh out of Paradise, and it is full of precious stones, without any drop of water, and it runneth through the desert on the one side, so that it maketh the sea gravelly. And it beareth into that sea, and there it endeth. And that flume [river] runneth also three days in the week, and bringeth with him great stones and the rocks also therewith—and that great plenty. And anon as they be entered into the Gravelly Sea they be seen no more, but lost for evermore; and in tho*se* three days that that river runneth no man dare enter into it, but in the other days men dare enter well enough.

Also, beyond that flume, more upward to the deserts, is a great plain, all gravelly, between the mountains. And in that plain, every day at the sun-rising, begin to grow small trees. And they grow till midday, bearing fruit—but no man dare take of that fruit, for it is a thing of Faerie. And after midday they decrease and enter again into the earth, so that at the going down of the sun they appear no more. And so they do every day; and that is a great marvel.

In that desert be many wild men that be hideous to look on, for they be horned and they speak not, but they grunt as pigs. And there is also great plenty of wild hounds; and there be many popinjays that they clepe "psittacus" in *t*heir language—and they speak, of *t*heir proper nature, and salute men that go through the deserts, and speak to *t*hem as *a*pertly as though it were a man. And they that speak well have a large tongue and have five toes upon a foot. And there be also of other manner, that have but three toes upon a foot; and they speak not—or but little—for they cannot but cry.

This Emperor Prester John, when he goeth into battle against any other lord, he hath no banners born before him, but he hath three crosses of gold, fine, great, and high, full of precious stones. And every of tho*se* cros*se*s be set in a chariot full richly arrayed, and for to keep every cross be ordained ten thousand men-of-arms and mo*re* than 100,000 men on foot, in manner as men would keep a standard in our countries when that we be in land of war. . . And when he hath no war, but rideth with a privy meinie, he hath bor*n*e before him but one cross of tree [wood], without painture and without gold or silver or precious stones, in remembrance that Jesu Christ suffered death upon a cross of tree. And he hath borne before him also, a platter of gold, full of earth, in token that his noblesse and his might and his flesh shall turn to earth. . . .

Beside the isle of Pentexoire, that is the land of Prester John, is a great isle, long and broad, that men clepe Milstorak, and it is in the lordship of Prester John. In that isle is great plenty of goods. There, was dwelling sometime a rich man—and it is not long sith [since]—and men clept him Gatholonabes, and he was full of cautels and of subtle deceits. And he had a full fair castle and a strong in a mountain, so strong and so noble that no man could devise a fairer ne a stronger. And he had let muren [wall] all the mountain about, with a strong wall and a fair. And within those walls he had the fairest garden that any man might behold; and therein were trees bearing all manner of fruits that any man could devise; and therein were also all manner of virtuous herbs of good smell, and all other herbs also that bear fair flowers. And he had also in that garden many fair wells, and beside those wells he had let make fair halls and fair chambers, depainted all with gold and azure. And there were in that place many a divers things and many divers stories, and of beasts and of birds that sung full delectably and moved by craft, that it seemed that they were quick [alive]. And he had also in his garden all manner of fowls and of beasts that any man might think on, for to have play or disport to behold them. And he had also in that place the fairest damsels that might be found under the age of fifteen year and the fairest young striplings that men might get of that same age; and all they were clothed in cloths of gold, full richly; and he said that those were angels. And he had also let make three wells, fair and noble and all environed with stone of jasper, of crystal, diapered with gold, and set with precious stones and great Orient pearls. And he had made a conduit under earth, so that the three wells, at his list [pleasure], one should run milk, another wine, and another honey. And that place he clept Paradise.

And when that any good knight that was hardy and noble came to see this royalty, he would lead him into his Paradise and shew him these wonderful things to his disport—and the marvelous and delicious song of divers birds, and the fair damsels, and the fair wells of milk, of wine, and of honey, plenteously running. And he would let make divers instruments of music to sound in an high tower, so merrily that it was joy for to hear; and no man should see the craft thereof; and those, he said, were angels of God and that place was Paradise, that God had behight [promised] to his friends, saying, "Dabo vobis terram fluentem lacte et melle." And then would he make *t*hem to drink of a certain drink, whereof anon they should be drunken—and then would them think [seem] greater delight than they had before.

And then would he say to them: that if they would die for him and for his love, that after *t*heir death they should come to his Paradise and they should be of the age of tho*se* damsels and they should play with them, and yet be maidens. And after that, yet should he put *t*hem in a fairer paradise, where that they should see God of Nature, visibly in his majesty and in his bliss.

And then would he shew *t*hem his intent, and say *to t*hem: that if they would go slay such a lord or such a man, that was his enemy or contrarious to his list, that they should not dread to do it and for to be slain therefor *t*hemselves— for after *t*heir death he would put *t*hem into another paradise that was an hundred fold fairer than any of the other*s*, and there should they dwell with the most fairest damsels that might be, and play with them evermore.

And thus went many divers lusty bachelors for to slay great lords in divers countries, that were his enemies, and made *t*hemselves to be slain, in hope to have that paradise. And thus oftentime he was revenged of his enemies, by his subtle deceits and false cautels.

And when the worthy men of the country had perceived this subtle falsehood of this Gatholonabes, they assembled *t*hem with force; and assailed his castle and slew him, and destroyed all the fair palaces and all the nobleties of that paradise. The place of the wells and of the walls and of many other things be yet apertly seen; but the richesse is voided clean. And it is not long gone sith that place was destroyed.

William Wey

TRAVELS

A GOOD PROVISION when a man is at Venice and purposeth, by the grace of God, to pass by the sea unto Port Jaffa in the Holy Land

and so to the sepulchre of our Lord Christ Jesu in Jerusalem. He must dispose him in this wise:

First, if ye go in a galley, make your covenant with the patron betimes and choose you a place in the said galley in the overest stage [top deck], for in the lowest under it is right smouldering hot and stinking. And ye shall pay for your galley and for your meat and drink to Port Jaffa and again to Venice forty ducats for to be in a good honest place and to have your ease in the galley and also to be cherished.

Also, when ye shall your covenant take, take good heed that the patron be bound unto you, afore the duke or lords of Venice, in an hundred ducats, to keep all manner covenants with you. That is to say, that he shall conduct you to certain havens by the way to refresh you and to get you fresh water and fresh bread and flesh. Also, that he shall not tarry longer at none haven than three days at the most, without consent of you all. And that he shall not take into the vessel, neither going nor coming, no manner of merchandise without your will, to distress you in your places and also for tarrying of passage by the sea. And by the havens he shall lead you, if you will: first, to Polo, one hundred mile from Venice by water; from Polo to Corfu, six hundred mile; from Corfu to Modin, three hundred mile; from Modin to Candia, three hundred mile; from Candia to Rhodes, three hundred mile; from Rhodes to Bagga in Cyprus, four hundred mile; from Bagga to Port Jaffa, three hundred mile, without more. But make covenant that ye come not at Famagusta in Cyprus for no thing, for many Englishmen, and others also, have died, for that air is so corrupt thereabout, and in the water also. Also, that your patron give you every day hot meat twice, at two meals: in the morning at dinner and after noon at supper, and the wine that ye shall drink be good and your water fresh (if ye may come thereto) and also biscuit.

Also, ye must ordain for yourself and your fellow, if ye have any, three barrels, each of a quarter, which quarter holdeth ten gallons: two of these barrels shall serve for wine and the third for water. In the one barrel take red wine and keep it ever in store, and tame [broach] it not if ye may till ye come homeward again—without sickness cause it or any other need. For ye shall this in special note: an ye had the flux, if ye would give twenty ducats for a barrel ye shall none have after ye pass much Venice. And that other barrel shall serve when ye have drunk up your drinking wine, to fill again at the haven where ye next come unto.

Also, ye must buy you a chest to put in your things; and if ye may have a fellow with you, two or three. I would then buy a chest that were as broad as the barrel were long. In the one end I would have lock and key and a little door, and lay that same barrel, that I would spend [use] first at the same door-end—for if the galleymen or pilgrims may come there, too many will tame and drink thereof and steal your water, which ye would not miss ofttimes for your wine. And in the other part of the chest ye may lay your bread, cheese, spices, and all other things.

Also, ye must ordain you biscuit to have with you, for though ye shall be at the table with your patron, notwithstanding, ye shall ofttime have need to your victuals, bread, cheese, eggs, fruit, and bacon, wine, and other, to make your collation. For sometimes ye shall have feeble bread, wine, and stinking water: many times ye shall be full fain to eat of your own. Also, I counsel you to have with you out of Venice confections, comfortatives, laxatives, restoratives, ginger, rice, figs, raisins great and small (which shall do you great ease by the way), pepper, saffron, cloves, maces (a few as ye think need) and powder-duke. Also, take with you a little cauldron and fryingpan, dishes, platters, saucers of tree [wood], cups of glass, a grater for bread, and such necessaries.

Also, when ye come to Venice, ye shall buy a bed by St. Mark's church: ye shall have a feather bed, a mattress, two pillows, two pair sheets, and a quilt, and ye shall pay three ducats: and when ye come again, bring the same bed to the man that ye bought it of and ye shall have a ducat and half again, though it be broke and worn.

Also, make your change at Venice, and take with you at the least thirty ducats of groats and grossines: ye shall have at Venice twenty-eight of new grossets and a dime—for when ye pass Venice ye shall have in some places twenty-six grossets or twenty-four. And also take with you three or four ducats of sous, that be galley-halfpence of Venice—for every grosset four sous. Take also with you fro Venice a ducat or two of Tournois: it is brass money of Candia—it will go by all the way—ye shall have eight for a sou at Venice: at Modin (and Candia oftentime) but four, five, or six at the most for a sou.

Also, buy you a cage for half a dozen of hens or chicken to have with you in the galley, for ye shall have need unto them many times: and buy you half a bushel of millet seed of Venice for them. Also, take a barrel with you, closed, for a siege [commode] for your chamber in the galley: it is full necessary if ye be sick that ye come not in the air. Also, when ye come to haven-towns, if ye will, ye may buy eggs if ye come betimes to land, for then ye may have good cheap; for they be full necessary in the galley, sometimes fried with oil-olive and sometimes for a caudel [mixed drink].

Also, when ye come to haven-towns, if ye shall tarry there three days, go betimes to land, for then ye may have lodging before others, for it will be taken up anon; and if any good victual be, be ye sped afore others. Also, when ye come to divers havens, be well ware of divers fruits, for they be not according to your complexion and they gender a bloody flux: and if an Englishman have that sickness, it is a marvel and scape-it but he die thereof. Also, when ye shall come to Port Jaffa, take with you out of the galley into the land two gourds, one with wine, another with water, each of a pottle at the least, for ye shall none have till ye come to Ramleh, and that is right feeble and dear: and at Jerusalem it is good wine—and dear. Also, see that the patron of the galley take charge of your harness [baggage] within the galley till ye come again to the galley.

Ye shall tarry in the Holy Land thirteen or fourteen days. Also, take good heed of your knives and other small things that ye bear upon you, for the Saracens will go talking with you and make good cheer but they will steal fro you what ye have, an they may. Also, when ye shall take your ass at Port Jaffa, be not too long behind your fellows; for, an ye come betimes, ye may choose the best mule or ass, for ye shall pay no more for the best than for the worst. And ye must give your *asman* [guide] a courtesy [tip], a groat or a grosset of Venice. And be not too much before, neither too far behind, your fellows, for dread of screws.

Also when ye shall ride to flume Jordan, take with you out of Jerusalem bread, wine, water, hard cheese, and hard eggs, and such victuals as ye may have for two days, for there neither by the way is none to sell. Also keep one of your bottles or gourds with wine, and ye may when ye come from flume Jordan to Monte Quarentine. And if ye go up to the place where our Lord

Jesu Christ fasted forty days and forty nights, it is passing hot and right high: when ye come down again, for nothing drink no water, but rest you a little, and then eat bread and drink clean wine without water—after that great heat, water gendereth a great flux or a fever, or both; then a man may haply lose his life thereby.

Keep all these things afore-writ and ye shall, with the grace of God, well speed in your journey to go and come, to the pleasure of God and increase of your bliss—the which Jesus grant you. Amen.

Literary Critics

❦

LITERARY CRITICISM was not one of the genres that the Middle Ages recognized—unless the term be stretched to include books of rhetoric or model-letters. But, criticism being an inescapable concomitant of both oral and written literature, it must certainly have existed. Most of it, one must suppose, was conversational or private, but vestiges of its criteria and evaluations may be traced in the prologues and epilogues to poems, incidental comments, imitations, quotations, and the like. Now and then, however, as with Dante, it attained to independent form, as the matter of treatise or preface. Caxton's prefaces—many adapted from the prologues of his French books—are of this kind, justifications for his printings or translations that turn on the moral, historical, or linguistic value of the work or author with whom he was dealing. In his comments there is obvious the same concern with puritan attacks upon the arts that is familiar through Sir Philip Sidney's defence of poetry against Gosson and others. Caxton's rebuttal is the traditional one: that, despite its fictions and catering to pleasure, literature makes its own important contribution to morality. He does not go so far as to assert that his authors were better teachers than Scotus or Aquinas, but he does claim that, after their own fashion, they helped men to a love of Christ and so to salvation. Other men, however, disputed the claim, and their views find expression in sermons and treatises.

Four pieces have been chosen to represent the late-medieval turn in this ceaseless debate. First, the essential parts of the *Treatise against Miracles-Playing*, a Wycliffite piece that presents the pros and cons about play-acting in an energetic, logical, and seeming-judicious statement of the puritan view. Second, Chaucer's retraction to the *Canterbury Tales*, which elegantly voices contrition for a lifetime of literary self-indulgence. Third, the proem to Caxton's second edition of the *Canterbury Tales*, 1484, which cautiously defends Chaucer from his own ayenbite of inwit [remorse] and which is notable for its use of a criterion that was to become highly important later—the contribution that a good writer makes to the improvement of the language—and also for its evidence of Caxton's scrupulosity in editorial matters. Fourth, Caxton's preface to his edition of Malory's *Le Morte Darthur*, 1485, which states

the occasion of the edition and justifies it by the prime medieval criteria: truth, morality, entertainment. *Ex parte* though it be, it is still the
best short critique of Malory's work.

A further topic for occasional literary comment is translation—so
much might be expected of a time when the extension of literacy beyond the groves of academe had produced so many necessary "Englishings." These discussions of translating turn on two main points: justification and technique. Unfortunately, they seldom go into detail about
the basic problem, that of substituting the structural patterns, idioms,
and lexicon of one language for those of another; but they do offer
some interesting generalizations. To represent them we select the
pleasantly anecdotal prologue to the *Eneydos*, 1490, in which Caxton,
most prolific of translators, reports on his linguistic problem and the
critical views of members of his public on the respective merits of the
plain and the ornate styles. Apart from its content, the passage is interesting as evidence of the comparative ease in writing that the printer
had attained near the close of his fifteen years of incessant Englishing.

"A TREATISE AGAINST MIRACLES-PLAYING"

THEN, SITH [since] these miracles-players take in bourde [jest]
the earnestful works of God, no doubt that they scornen God, as
did the Jews that bobbed [mocked] Christ, for they laughed at his
passion as these laugh and jape at the miracles of God! Therefore,
as they scorned Christ, so these scorn God. And, right as Pharaoh,
wroth to do that that God bade him, despised God, so these miracles-players and maintainers, believing pleasingly to do *w*hat God
biddeth *t*hem, scornen God. He, forsooth, hath bidden us all to
hallow His name, giving dread and reverence in all mind [recol-
lection] of his works, without any playing or japing, as all holiness
is in full earnest men. Then, playing the name of God's miracles,
as pleasingly they *b*elieve to do *w*hat God biddeth *t*hem, so they
scorn his name and so scorn him.

But hereagainst they say that they play these miracles in the
worship of God, and so did not these Jews that bobbed Christ.
Also, oftsithes [often] by such miracles-playing be men converted
to good living: as men and women, seeing in miracles-playing
that the devil by their array—by the which they move each on

other to lechery and to pride—maketh them his servants to bring themselves and many others to hell and to have far more villainy hereafter by their proud array here than they have worship [honor] here; and seeing, furthermore, that all this worldly being here is but vanity for a while—as is miracles-playing!—they leave their pride and take to them afterward the meek conversation of Christ and of his saints. And so miracles-playing turneth men to the belief, and not perverteth. Also, oftsithes by such miracles-playing men and women, seeing the passion of Christ and of his saints, be moved to compassion and devotion, weeping bitter tears: then they be not scorning of God, but worshipping. Also, profitable to men and to the worship of God it is to fulfil and seek all the means by the which men may flee sin and draw them to virtues. And sith as there be men that only by earnestful doing will be converted to God, so there be other men that will not be converted to God but by game and play—and nowadays men be not converted by the earnestful doing of God ne of men. Then now it is time and skilful [reasonable] to essay to convert the people by play and game, as by miracles-playing and other manner of mirths. Also, some recreation men must have, and better it is—or less evil—that they have their recreation by playing of miracles than by playing of other japes. Also, sith it is leaveful to have the miracles of God painted, why is it not as well leaveful to have the miracles of God played, sith men may better read the will of God and his marvelous works in the playing of them than in the painting; and better they be held in men's mind and often rehearsed by the playing of them than by the painting, for this is a dead book, the other a quick.

To the first reason we answer, saying that such miracles-playing is not to the worship of God, for they be done more to be seen of the world and to please to the world than to be seen of God or to please to him. As Christ never exampled them, but only heathen men that evermore dishonor God, saying that to the worship of God what is to the most villainy of him; therefore, as the wickedness of the misbelief of heathen men lieth to themselves when they say that the worshiping of their Mahometry [idols] is to the worship of God, so men's lechery nowadays to have their own lusts lieth to themselves when they say that such miracles-playing is to the worship of God. . . .

The same wise [similarly], miracles-playing, albeit that it be sin, is otherwhiles occasion of converting men. But, as it is sin, it is far more occasion of perverting of men, not only of one singular person but of all a whole community—as it maketh all a people to be occupied in vain against this behest of the Psalter Book, that saith to all men, and namely to priests that each day read it in their service: "Turn away mine eyes that they see not vanities." And eft [again], "Lord, thou hatest all waiting [lying] vanities." How then may a priest play in interludes or give himself to the sight of them? . . .

Miracles-playing, sith it is against the behest of God, that biddeth that thou shalt not taken God's name in idle, it is against our belief, and so it may not give occasion of turning men to the belief, but of perverting. And, therefore, many men ween that there is no hell of everlasting pain, but that God doth but threaten us and not to do it in deed—as is playing of miracles in sign [symbol] and not in deed. . . .

These men that say, "Play we a play of Antichrist and of the Day of Doom, that some man may be converted thereby," fall into the heresy of them that, reversing the apostle, said, "Do we evil things, that there come good things." "Of whom," as saith the apostle Paul, "damning is righteous."

By this we answer to the third reason, saying: that such miracles-playing giveth no occasion of very [sincere] weeping and meedful [profitable]. But the weeping that befalleth to men and women by the sight of such miracles-playing, as it is not principally for their own sins, ne of their good faith withinforth [inwardly], but more of their sight withoutforth, is not allowable before God, but more reprovable. For, sith Christ himself reproved the women that wept upon him in his passion, much more they be reprovable that weep for the play of Christ's passion, leaving to weep for the sins of themselves and of their children, as Christ bade the women that wept on him.

And by this we answer to the fourth reason, saying: that no man may be converted to God but only by the earnestful doing of God, and by no vain playing. For that that the word of God worketh not, nor his sacraments, how should playing work, that is of no virtue, but full of default? . . .

And hereby we answer to the fifth reason, saying: that very

recreation is leaveful occupying in less [smaller] works, to more ardently work greater works. And, therefore, such miracles-playing, ne the sight of them, is no very recreation, but false and worldly, as prove the deeds of the fautors [attendants] of such plays . . . And, if men ask what recreation men should have on the holiday, after their holy contemplation in the church, we say to them two things. One, that if he had verily occupied him in contemplation before, neither he would ask that question nor have will to see vanity. Another, we say that his recreation should be in the works of mercy to his neighbour and in delighting him in all good communication with his neighbour, as before he delighted him in God—and in all other needful works that reason and kind [nature] ask.

And to the last reason we say: that painture, if it be very [true] without mingling of lesings [lies] and not too curious to much feeding men's wits and not occasion of Mahometry to the people, they be but as naked letters to a clerk to read the truth. But so be not miracles-playing, that be made more to delight men bodily than to be books to lewd [unlearned] men. And, therefore, if they be quick [living] books, they be quick books to shrewdness [wickedness] more than to goodness.

Good men, therefore, seeing their time too short to occupy them in good works, and seeing the day of their reckoning nigh fast, and unknowing when they shall go hence, flee all such idleness, hieing [hurrying] that they were [be] with their spouse Christ, in the bliss of heaven.

Geoffrey Chaucer

RETRACTION TO THE "CANTERBURY TALES"

Now PRAY I to them all that hearken this little treatise or read, that if there be anything in it that liketh them, that thereof they thanken our Lord Jesu Christ, of whom proceedeth all wit and all goodness. And if there be anything that displease them, I pray them also that they arrette [ascribe] it to the default of mine uncunning [ignorance] and not to my will—that would full fain have said better if I had had cunning. For our book saith, "All that is written is written for our doctrine," and that is mine intent.

Wherefore, I beseech you meekly, for the mercy of God, that ye pray for me that Christ have mercy on me and forgive me my guilts. And namely [especially] of my translations and enditings of worldly vanities, the which I revoke in my retractions: as is the book of *Troilus*, the book also of *Fame*, the book of the *Twenty-five Ladies*, the book of the *Duchess*, the book of Saint Valentine's day of the *Parliament of Birds*, the *Tales of Canterbury*—thilk [those] that sounden into [make for] sin—the book of the *Lion*, and many another book, if they were in my remembrance, and many a song and many a lecherous lay—that Christ for his great mercy forgive me the sin.

But of the translation of Boethius' *De Consolatione* and other books, of legends of saints and homilies and morality and devotion, that thank I our Lord Jesu Christ and his blissful Mother and all the saints of heaven, beseeching them that they from henceforth unto my life's end send me grace to bewail my guilts and to study to the salvation of my soul, and grant me grace of very penitence, confession, and satisfaction, to do in this present life, through the benign grace of him that is King of Kings and priest over all priests, that bought us with the precious blood of his heart, so that I may be one of them at the day of doom that shall be saved. *Qui cum patre et spiritu sancto vivit et regnat Deus per omnia secula. Amen.*

William Caxton

PROEM TO THE "CANTERBURY TALES," 1484

GREAT THANKS, laud, and honour ought to be given unto the clerks, poets, and historiographs that have written many noble books of wisdom of the lives, passions, and miracles of holy saints, of histories of noble and famous acts and faits [deeds] and of the chronicles sith the beginning of the creation of the world unto this present time, by which we be daily informed and have knowledge of many things of whom we should not have known if they had not left to us their monuments written.

Among whom and in especial tofore all others, we ought to give a singular laud unto that noble and great philosopher Geoffrey Chaucer, the which for his ornate writing in our tongue may well have the name of a laureate poet. For to-fore that he by his labour embellished, ornated, and made fair our English, in this realm was had rude speech and incongru*ous*, as yet appeareth by old books, which at this day ought not to have place ne be compared among, ne to, his beauteous volumes and ornate writings. Of whom he made many books and treatises of many a noble history, as well in metre as in rhyme and prose; and them so craftily made that he comprehended his matters in short, quick, and high sentences, eschewing prolixity, casting away the chaff of superfluity, and shewing the picked grain of sentence [meaning] uttered by crafty and sugared eloquence.

Of whom, among all other of his books, I purpose to emprint, by the grace of God, the book of the Tales of Canterbury, in which I find many a noble history of every estate and degree: first rehearsing the conditions and the array of each of them as properly as possible is to be said, and after, their tales, which be of noblesse, wisdom, gentilesse, mirth, and also of very [true] holiness and virtue—wherein he finisheth this said book.

Which book I have diligently overseen and duly examined, to the end that it be made according unto his own making. For I find many of the said books which writers have abridged it, and many things left out; and in some places have set certain verses that he never made ne set in his book. Of which books, so incorrect, was one brought to me six years past, which I supposed had been very true and correct, and according to the same I did do emprint a certain number of them, which anon were sold to many and divers gentlemen, of whom one gentleman came to me and said that this book was not according in many places unto the book that Geoffrey Chaucer had made.

To whom I answered that I had made it according to my copy, and by me was nothing added ne *di*minished. Then he said he knew a book which his father had and much loved, that was very true and according unto his own first book by him made. And said more, if I would emprint it again he would get me the same book for a copy, howbeit he wist well that his father would not gladly depart fro it. To whom I said, in case that he could get me such a book, true and correct, yet I would once endeavour me to emprint it again for to satisfy the author, whereas tofore by ignorance I erred in hurting and defaming his book in divers places, in setting in some things that he never said ne made, and leaving out many things that he made which be requisite to be set in it.

And thus we fell at accord, and he full genteely got of his father the said book and delivered it to me. By which I have corrected my book, as hereafter, all along by the aid of almighty God, shall follow; whom I humbly beseech to give me grace and aid to achieve and accomplish to his laud, honour, and glory; and that all ye that shall in this book read or hear, will of your charity among your deeds of mercy remember the soul of the said Geoffrey Chaucer, first author and maker of this book. And also that all we that shall see and read therein may so take and understand the good and virtuous tales, that it may so profit unto the health of our souls that after this short and transitory life we may come to everlasting life in heaven. Amen.

William Caxton

PREFACE TO MALORY'S "LE MORTE DARTHUR"

AFTER THAT I had accomplished and finished divers histories, as well of contemplation as of other historical and worldly acts of great conquerors and princes, and also certain books of examples and doctrine, many noble and divers gentlemen of this realm of England came and demanded me, many and oft times, wherefore that I have not do made and imprint the noble history of the Saint Grail and of the most renoméed Christian king, first and chief of the three best Christian and worthy, King Arthur, which ought most to be remembered among us English to-fore all other Christian kings. . . .

The said noble gentlemen instantly required me to imprint the history of the said noble king and conqueror King Arthur, and of his knights, with the history of the Saint Grail, and of the death and ending of the said Arthur—affirming that I ought rather to imprint his acts and noble feats than *those* of Godfrey of Bouillon or any of the other eight *worthies,* considering that he was a man born within this realm, and king and emperor of the same, and that there be in French divers and many noble volumes of his acts and also of his knights!

To whom I answered: that divers men hold opinion that there was no such Arthur, and that all such books as been made of him be but feigned [false] and fables, because that some chronicles make of him no mention nor remember him nothing, nor of his knights.

Whereto they answered and one in special said: that in him that should say or think that there was never such a king called Arthur might be aretted [charged] great folly and blindness. For he said that there were many evidences of the contrary. First, ye may see his sepulchre in the monastery of Glastonbury. And, also, in [Higden's] *Polychronicon,* in the fifth book the sixth chapter and in the seventh book the twenty-third chapter, where his body was buried and after found and translated into the said monastery. Ye shall see also in the history of Boccaccio, in his book *De Casu Principum,* part of his noble acts and also of his fall. And Geoffrey in his British book recounteth his life. And in divers places of England many remembrances be yet of him, and shall remain perpetually, and also of his knights. First: in the abbey of Westminster, at St. Edward's shrine, remaineth the print of his seal in red wax closed in beryl, in which is written *Patricius Arthurus Britannie, Gallie, Germanie, Dacie, Imperator.* Item [similarly], in the castle of Dover ye may see Gawain's skull and Cradock's mantle; at Winchester, the Round Table; in other places, Lancelot's sword and many other things. Then, all these things considered, there can no man reasonably gainsay but here was a king of this land named Arthur. For in all places, Christian and heathen, he is reputed and taken for one of the nine worthy and the first of the three Christian men. And also, he is more spoken of beyond the sea, more books made of his noble acts, than there be in England, as well in Dutch, Italian, Spanish, and Greekish, as in French. And yet of record remain in witness of him in Wales in the town of Camelot—the great stones, and the marvellous works of iron lying under the ground, and royal vaults—which divers now living have seen. Wherefore, it is a marvel why he is no more renowned in his own country, save only it accordeth to the word of God which saith that no man is accepted for a prophet in his own country.

Then, all these things aforesaid alleged, I could not well deny but that there was such a noble king named Arthur, and reputed one of the nine worthy, and first and chief of the Christian men. And many noble volumes be made of him and of his noble knights in French, which I have seen and read beyond the sea, which be not had in our maternal tongue. But in Welsh be many, and also in French, and some in English—but nowhere nigh all. Wherefore, such as have late been drawn out briefly into English I have, after the simple cunning that God hath sent to me, under the favour and correction of all noble lords and gentlemen, emprised [undertaken] to imprint a book of the noble histories of the said King Arthur and of certain of his knights, after a copy unto me delivered. Which copy Sir Thomas Malory did take out of certain books of French and reduced it into English.

And I, according to my copy, have done set it in imprint, to the intent that noble men may see and learn the noble acts of chivalry, the gentle and virtuous deeds that some knights used in those days, by which they came to honour, and how they that were vicious were punished and oft put to shame and rebuke—humbly beseeching all noble lords and ladies, and all other estates of what estate or degree they be of, that shall see and read in this said book and work, that they take the good and honest acts in their remembrance, and to follow the same. Wherein they shall find many joyous and pleasant histories, and noble and renomée acts of humanity, gentleness, and chivalries. For herein may be seen noble chivalry, courtesy, humanity, friendliness, hardiness, love, friendship, cowardice, murder, hate, virtue, and sin. Do after the good and leave the evil, and it shall bring you to good fame and renomée.

And for to pass the time, this book shall be pleasant to read in. But for to give faith and belief that all is true that is contained herein, ye be at your liberty. But all is written for our doctrine, and for to beware that we fall not to vice nor sin, but to exercise and follow virtue, by which we may come and attain to good fame

and renomée in this life, and after this short and transitory life
to come unto everlasting bliss in heaven. The which he grant us
that reigneth in heaven, the blessed Trinity. Amen.

William Caxton

PREFACE TO "ENEYDOS," 1490

AFTER DIVERS WORKS made, translated, and achieved, having no
work in hand, I sitting in my study, where as lay many divers
pamphlets and books, happened that to my hand came a little
book in French which late was translated out of Latin by some
noble clerk of France, which book is named *Eneydos*, made in
Latin by that noble poet and great clerk Virgil. Which book I saw
over and read therein: how after the general destruction of the
great Troy, Aeneas departed, bearing his old father Anchises upon
his shoulders, his little son Yolus [Ascanius] in his hands, his wife
with much other people following; and how he shipped and departed, with all the history of his adventures that he had ere he
came to the achievement of his conquest of Italy, as all along
shall be shewed in this present book. In which book I had great
pleasure because of the fair and honest terms and words in
French, which I never saw to-fore like, ne none so pleasant ne so
well ordered. Which book, as it me-seemed be much requisite to
noble men to see, as well for the eloquence as the histories, how
well that many hundred years past was the said book of *Eneydos*,
with other works, made and learned daily in schools, especially in
Italy and other places—which history the said Virgil made in
metre.

And when I had advised me in this said book, I deliber*a*ted and
concluded to translate it into English, and forthwith took a pen
and ink and wrote a leaf or twain. Which I oversaw again to correct it; and when I saw the fair and strange terms therein, I
doubted that it should not please some gentlemen which late
blamed me, saying that in my translations I had over-curious
terms which could not be understood of common people, and desired me to use old and homely terms in my translations. And

fain would I satisfy every man and so to do took an old book and read therein: and certainly the English was so rude and broad that I could not well understand it. And also, my lord abbot of Westminster did do shew to me late certain evidences written in old English, for to reduce it into our English now used: and certainly it was written in such wise that it was more like to Dutch than English—I could not reduce ne bring it to be understood.

And certainly, our language now used varieth far from that which was used and spoken when I was born. For we Englishmen be born under the domination of the moon, which is never steadfast, but ever wavering, waxing one season and waneth and decreaseth another season. And that common English that is spoken in one shire varieth from another. Insomuch, that in my days happened that certain merchants were in a ship in Thames for to have sailed over the sea into Zealand. And for lack of wind they tarried at Foreland and went to land for to refresh them. And one of them, named Sheffield, a mercer, came into an house and asked for meat, and specially he asked after "eggs." And the good wife answered that she could speak no French. And the merchant was angry, for he also could speak no French, but would have had eggs, and she understood him not. And then at last, another said that he would have "eyren." Then the good wife said that she understood him well. Lo, what should a man in these days now write, "eggs" or "eyren"?

Certainly, it is hard to please every man because of diversity and change of language, for in these days every man that is in any reputation in his country will utter his communication and matters in such manners and terms that few men shall understand them. And some honest and great clerks have been with me and desired me to write the most curious terms that I could find. And thus, between plain, rude, and curious terms I stand abashed. But in my judgment, the common terms that be daily used be lighter to be understood than the old and ancient English.

And forasmuch as this present book is not for a rude uplandish man to labour therein ne read it, but only for a clerk and a noble gentleman that feeleth and understandeth in faits of arms, in love, and in noble chivalry, therefore, in a mean between both I have reduced and translated this said book into our English: not over-rude ne curious but in such terms as shall be understood, by

God's grace, according to my copy. And if any many will enter-
mete [meddle] in reading of it and findeth such terms that he cannot understand, let him go read and learn Virgil or the epistles of
Ovid, and there he shall see and understand lightly all, if he have a
good reader and informer. For this book is not for every rude and
uncunning man to see, but to clerks and very gentlemen that understand gentleness and science.

Then I pray all them that shall read in this little treatise to hold
me for excused for the translating of it. For I acknowledge myself
ignorant of cunning to emprise on me so high and noble a work.
But I pray Master John Skelton, late created poet-laureate in the
University of Oxford, to oversee and correct this said book, and
to address and expound whereas shall be found fault to them that
shall require it. For him I know for sufficient to expound and English every difficulty that is therein, for he hath late translated the
epistles of Tully and the book of Diodorus Siculus, and divers
other works out of Latin, into English, not in rude and old language but in polished and ornate terms craftily, as he that hath
read Virgil, Ovid, Tully, and all the other noble poets and orators
to me unknown. And also he hath read the nine muses and understood their musical sciences and to whom of them each science is
appropered—I suppose he hath drunk of Helicon's well! Then I
pray him and such others to correct, add, or diminish whereas he
or they shall find fault, for I have but followed my copy in French
as nigh as me is possible. And if any words be said therein well, I
am glad; and if otherwise, I submit my said book to their correction.

Allegorists

❦

MEDIEVAL ALLEGORY was usually composed in verse, a medium that may have been considered more appropriate than prose to the fictional framework of extended allegory. Nevertheless, the later medieval tendency to enlarge the dominion of prose beyond fact, history, and truth, applied to this genre too. Guillaume de Deguileville's three long verse-allegories were turned into French prose and soon after, early in the fifteenth century, two of them were translated into English. A generation before, Thomas Usk even wrote an original allegory, *The Testament of Love*, in prose—although in his case the choice was determined by a reading of Chaucer's version of Boethius. And still earlier, under the influence of Richard Rolle, the same medium was used for an interesting spiritual allegory, *The Abbey of the Holy Ghost*.

The Abbey was written about 1350 and is sometimes, though wrongly, ascribed to Rolle. Everyday occupations were favorite bases for spiritual allegories, and this one, written in direct and shapely prose, draws on the craft of building to make familiar to lay-contemplatives the regimen of spiritual life. Unlike many similar treatises it has the virtue of not running the analogies into the ground. Our selection follows the story to the point where the abbey is staffed. The allegory then goes on to describe the rest of the officers one by one, Discretion the treasurer, Pity the despenser, Meditation the garnerer, and so on, and also the damsel-enemies of the new abbey, Jealousy and Envy.

Thomas Usk's work, like many medieval allegories, is autobiographical. In 1384 he was imprisoned, to compel him to bear witness against a mayor of London to whom he was secretary. He gave the required testimony, but still spent the first six months of 1385 in prison. Later, he joined the party of another London mayor, Nicholas Brembre, Richard II's adviser during his minority. Usk shared the fate of Richard's advisers in 1387, when the king failed to overthrow the regency: accused of treason, he was drawn, hanged, decapitated, and his head set up over Newgate on March 4, 1388. His *Testament,* which is both political and pious, refers to his imprisonment in 1385, although it must have been written somewhat later. Despite the autobiographical form and content, the work is highly derivative. Its model is Chaucer's translation of Boethius's *Consolations*, and it is heavily embroidered with quotation, reminiscence, and paraphrase of *Troilus and Criseyde*, *Hous of Fame*, *Legend of Good Women*, *Piers Plowman*, a treatise on predestination by St. Anselm, and possibly the French allegories of Gower and Deguileville.

Usk in his prison prays to Margaret, the grace of God. Heavenly Love appears to aid him, and he recounts—the chapters selected here—how he was attacked by wild animals, escaped in a boat manned by abstractly-named seamen, landed on an island, and there found Margaret, his pearl without price. The rest of the three books form a Boethian debate with an autobiographical thread, Usk complaining of his misfortunes, Love instructing and consoling him on fame, providence, free will and predestination, the role of women, God's mercy and grace, and so on.

The prose-style of this Christian Boethius is unusual for its time: self-conscious, extravagant, sugared, and obscure, it calls to mind some of the Elizabethan mannerists. Chaucer's *Boethius* is the inspiration for its Latinate tinge in syntax and vocabulary and its balanced structures. But the metrical form of its rhythms, the literary reminiscences, imagery drawn from natural history and classical myth, its oxymoron, symbolism, rhymes and alliterative formulae—even some of the tense forms—betray Usk's heavy debt to rhetorics and poetry and his intention to be reckoned a man of letters.

Interesting as it is historically, Usk's prose is too narcissistic, too incongruent with the matter, to be anything but irritating. It is very different with the English versions of Deguileville's two *Pilgrimages*, whose originals are written in the more Latinate and rhetorical form of the narrative style that developed in France in the later fourteenth century. The translator, a man of considerable resource in English, usually matches this style excellently, so that although he suffers from the loquaciousness of his source and every now and then is over-literal or commits a syntactical blunder, most of his work is firm and well-shaped, a highly competent example of mature English prose, and one which benefits greatly from the ordered clarity of Deguileville's narrative.

Our selection comes from *The Pilgrimage of the Lyf of Manhode*, translated about 1430 from Jean de Gallopes' French prosing. The original poem was written in 1331 at the Cistercian abbey at Chaalis. Goaded by the enormity of the *Roman de la Rose*, Deguileville describes a dream in which he saw his moral pilgrimage from birth to death: his arming by Grace-Dieu, his journey and the many perils he suffered from sins and errors in the guise of savage beasts and monsters, his escape aboard the ship of religion and his life there in Cistercian quarters up to the time that Death called for him. Despite its close relation to the moral handbooks and its tendency to load the story with too heavy a burden of exegesis, the work remains reasonably entertaining by virtue of its autobiographical mode and a narrative of marvelous adventures that may owe something to the legends of the Irish saints. It is no *Pilgrim's Progress,* despite the opinion that it may have influenced Bunyan's work, but that it is far from being so tedious as critics commonly say may be judged by the present specimen, which deals with the unpromising topic of the dangers of over-literal dependence upon Biblical texts on the part of laymen.

"THE ABBEY OF THE HOLY GHOST"

AH, DEAR BROTHERS and sisters! I see that many would be in religion but they may not, either for poverty or for dread of their kin or for bond of marriage, and forthy [so], I make here a book of the religion of the heart; that is, of the Abbey of the Holy Ghost, that all tho*se* that ne may not be bodily in religion, that they may be ghostly.

Ah, Jesu mercy! where may this abbey best be founded, and this religion? Now certes, nowhere so well as in a place that is called Conscience. And whoso will, be busy to found this holy religion—and that may each good Christian man and woman do that will be busy thereabout. And at the beginning it is behovely that the place of thy Conscience be cleansed clean of sin. To the which cleansing the Holy Ghost shall send two maidens that are cunning: the one is called Righteousness and the tother is called Love of Cleanness. These two shall cast fro the Conscience and fro the heart all manner of filth of foul thoughts and desires. When the place of the Conscience is well cleansed, then shall the ground be made large and deep, and these two maidens shall make: the one is called Meekness, that shall make the ground deep through lowliness of herself; the tother is called Poverty, that makes it large and wide above, that casts over each half [side] the earth out—that is to say, all earthly lusts and worldly thoughts far fro the heart, that if they have earthly goods with love they forget them for the time and casts no love to them nor has not ne sets not for that time their hearts nothing on them—and these are called poor in spirit, of whom God speaks in the gospel and says that theirs is the kingdom of heaven, by these words: *Beati pauperes spiritu, quoniam ipsorum est regnum celorum.* Blessed is then that religion that is founded in poverty and in meekness. This is against many religious that are covetous and proud.

This abbey also shall be set on a good river, and that shall be the river of tears. For such abbeys that are set on such good rivers, they are well at ease and the more delicious dwelling is there. On such a river was Mary Magdalene founded, for-thy [so] grace and richesse came all to her will. And for-thy said David thus: *Fluminis impetus laetificat civitatem;* that is to say, "the good river makes the city liking," for it is clean, secure, and rich of all good merchandise. And so the river of tears cleanses God's city; that is, man's soul that is God's city: and also the holy man says of filth of sin that it brings out the riches of virtues and of all good thews [customs].

And when this ground is made, then shall come a damsel, Buxomness [obedience], on the one half, and Damsel Misericord on the tother half, for to raise the walls on height and to make them stalwart, with a free heart largely giving to the poor and to them that myster [a trade] have. For when we do any good works of charity through the grace of God, also oftsithes [as often] as we them do in the love and the loving [praising] of God and in good intent, as many good stones we lay on our housing in the bliss of heaven, fastening together with the love of God and our even-Christians. We read that Solomon made his housing of great precious stones: these precious stones are alms-deeds and works of mercy and holy works, that shall be bound together with quicklime of love and steadfast belief. And for-thy says David, *Omnia opera eius in fide;* that is to say, "all his works be done in steadfast belief." And, as a wall may not last without cement or mortar, also no works that we work are nought worth to God nor speedful to our souls but they be done in the love of God and in true belief, for all that the sinful does, all is lost.

Sithen [afterwards], Damsel Sufferance and Damsel Fortitude shall raise the pillars and underset them so strongly that no wind of words, anger or strife, fleshly nor ghostly, sour ne sweet, cast them down. Ah, dear brothers and sisters! yet behoves the cloister be made, on four corners; and it is called "cloister" for it closes and sticks and warely [cautiously] shall be locked. My dear brothers and sisters, which of you as will hold this ghostly religion and be in rest of soul and in sweetness of heart, hold thee within the cloister, and so spar [shut] thou the gates and so warely keep thou the wards of thy cloister, that no other fandings [temptations] nor evil stirrings have ingate in thee and make thee thy silence for to break or stir thee to sin. Stick thine eyes fro foul sights, thine ears fro foul hearings, thy mouth fro foul speech, and thine heart fro foul thoughts. Shrift [confession] shall make thy chapter, Predication [preaching] shall make thy fratour [dining-hall], Oracion [prayer] shall make thy chapel, Contemplation shall make thy dortour [dormitory], that shall be raised on height with high yearning and with love-quickening to God and that shall be out of worldly noise and of worldly angers and busyness, as far forth as thou may for the time through grace, for the time of prayer.

Contemplation is a devout rising of heart with burning love to God to do well, and in his delights *rejoices* his soul and somedeal receives of that sweetness that God's chosen childer shall have in heaven.

Devotion shall make the cellar; Meditation shall make the garner. And when all the houses be made, then behoves the Holy Ghost ordain the convent of grace and of virtue; and then shall the Holy Ghost, that this religion is of, be warden and visitor. The which God the Father founded through his power, for thus says David, *Fundavit eam altissimus;* and this is to say, "the high God the Father founded this religion." The Son through his wisdom then ordained it, as St. Paul witnesses it, *Que sunt, a deo ordinata sunt;* that is to say, "all that is of God, the Son it rules and ordains." The Holy Ghost yemes [cares for] it and visits it; and that say we in holy kirk when we say this, *Veni creator Spiritus,* with *Qui paraclitus diceris;* that is for to say, "Come thou God, the Holy Ghost, and thine thou visit and fulfill them with grace."

And then the good lady Charity, as she that is most worthy before all other, shall be abbess of this selly [blessed] abbey. And also, as they that are in religion shall do nothing, ne say *nothing,* ne gang [go] into no stead, ne take no gift withouten leave of the abbess, all-so ghostly shall none of such things be done withouten leave of charity. For thus commands St. Paul, *Omnia vestra in caritate fiant;* that is, "What so ye do or say or think with heart, all ye mon [must] do in charity." Ah, dear brothers and sisters, what

here is *a* hard commandment! But it is notfull [useful] to our souls
that our thoughts and our words and our works be only done for
love. Welaway, if I durst say! For many are in religion, but too
few religious that they ne do the commandment of St. Paul or the
counsel of the good lady Charity that is abbess of this selly religion; and for that they lose mickle time, and lose their meed,
and eke [increase] their pain greatly, but-if they amend them.
Wherefore, lief brothers and sisters, be evermore wak*ing* and
ware, and in all your works think deeply, that whatso ye do be it
done in the love of God and for the love of God.

The lady Wisdom shall be prioress, for she is worthy—*Nam
prior omnium creaturarum est sapiencia;* that is, "alderfirst is wisdom made." And through the lore and the counsel of this prioress
shall we do all that we do: and this says David, *Omnia in sapientia
fecisti;* that is to say, "all that thou has*t* made thou has*t* made
wisely." The good lady Meekness, that ay alike makes herself
lowly and under all other*s*, shall be sub-prioress. Her shall ye honour and worship with buxomness [obedience].

Ah Jesu! blessed is that abbey and selly is that religion that has
so holy an abbess as Charity, a prioress as Wisdom, a sub-prioress
as Meekness.

Thomas Usk

"THE TESTAMENT OF LOVE"

GREATLY WAS I the*n* gladded of these words and—as who saith—
waxen somedeal light in heart, both for the authority of witness
and also for sickerness [sureness] of help of the foresaid behest,
and said:

"Truly, lady, now am I well gladded through comfort of your
words. Be it now liking unto your nobil*ity* to shew which folk de-
fame your servants, sith your service ought above all other things
to be commended."

"Yet," quoth she, "I see well thy soul is not all out of the amazed
cloud. Thee were better to hear thing that thee might light out of
thy heavy charge and after knowing of thine own help, than to stir

sweet words and such reasons to hear. For in a thoughtful soul—
and namely [especially] such *a* one as thou art—will not yet such
things sink. Come off, therefore, and let me see thy heavy charge,
that I may the lightlier for thy comfort purvey."

"Now, certes, lady," quoth I, "the most comfort I might have
were utterly to wit me be sure in heart of that Margaret I serve;
and so I think to do with all mights while my life dureth."

"Then," quoth she, "mayest thou thereafter, in such wise that
mispleasance ne enter?"

"In good faith," quoth I, "there shall no mispleasance be caused
through trespass on my side."

"And I do thee to wit," quoth she, "I set never yet person to
serve in no place—but-if he caused the contrary in defaults and
trespasses—that he ne sped of his service."

"Mine own earthly lady," quoth I tho [then], "and yet remember to your worthiness how long sithen, by many revolving of
years, in time when October his leave ginneth take and November
sheweth him to sight, when barns be full of goods as is the nut on
every halk [corner], and then good land-tillers gin shape for the
earth with great travail, to bring forth more corn to man's sustenance against the next year's following, in such time of plenty
he that hath an home and is wise list not to wander marvels to
seek, but he be constrained or excited. Oft the loath thing is done
by excitation of other man's opinion which would fain have mine
abiding. Tho gan I take in heart of lust to travel and see the wind-
ing of the earth in that time of winter. By woods that large streets
were in, by small paths that swine and hogs had made, as lanes
with ladels [cross-paths] their mast [acorns] to seek, I walked
thinking alone a wonder great while. And the great beasts, that the
wood haunt and adorn all manner *of* forests, and the herds gan to
wild. Then, ere I was *a*ware, I nighed to a sea-bank, and for fear
of the beasts, 'Shipcraft!' I cried. For, lady, I trow ye wit well
yourself, nothing is worse than the beasts that should be tame if
they catch *t*heir wildness and gin again *to* wax ramage [wild].
Thus, forsooth, was I afeared and to ship me hied.

"Then were there enough to latch mine hands and draw me to
ship, of which many I knew well the names. Sight was the first,
Lust was another, Thought was the third, and Will eke was there
a master. These brought me within-board of this ship of Travail.

So when the sail was spread and this ship gan to move, the wind waves seemed as they kissed together, but often under colour of and water gan for to rise and overthwartly to turn the welkin. The kissing is muckle old hate privily closed and kept. The storm so strangely and in a devouring manner gan so fast us assail that I supposed the date of my death should have made there his *be-ginning*. Now up, now down, now under the wave and now above was my ship a great while.

"And so, by muckle duress of weathers and of storms, and with great avowing of pilgrimages, I was driven to an isle, where utterly I weened first to have been rescued. But truly, at the first 'ginning it seemed me so perilous the haven to catch, that but through grace I had been comforted, of life I was full despaired. Truly, lady, if ye remember aright of all manner things, yourself came hastily to see us sea-driven and to wit what we were. But first ye were deignous [disdainful] of cheer; after which, ye gan better alight. And ever, as me thought, ye lived in great dread dis-ease, it seemed so by your cheer [face]. And when I was certified of your name, the longer I looked on you the more I you goodly dreade*d* and ever mine heart on you opened the more: and so in a little time my ship was out of mind.

"But, lady, as ye me led, I was *a*ware both of beasts and of fishes, a great number thronging together. Among which, a mussell in a blue shell had enclosed a Margaret-pearl, the most precious and best that ever tofore came in my sight. And ye told yourself that ilke [same] jewel in his kind was so good and so virtuous that her better should I never find, al*though* sought I thereafter to the world's end. And with that I held my peace a great while, and ever sithen I have me bethought on the man that sought the precious margarets [pearls] and, when he had found one to his liking, he sold all his goods to buy that jewel. Ywis, thought I—and yet so I think—now have I found the jewel that mine heart desireth, whereto should I seek further? Truly, now will I stint, and on this Margaret I set me for ever: now then also sith I wist well it was your will that I should to such a service me take and so to desire that thing of which I never have bliss. There liveth none but he hath dis-ease; your might then that brought me to such service, that to me is cause of sorrow and of joy. I wonder of your words that ye say, "to bring men into joy"; and, pardee, ye wit well that default ne trespass may not reasonably be put to-me-wards, as far as my conscience knoweth.

"But of my dis-ease me list now a while to speak and to inform you in what manner of bliss ye have me thronged. For truly, I ween that all gladness, all joy, and all mirth is beshut under lock and the key thrown in such place that it may not be found. My burning woe hath altered all my hue: when I should sleep, I wallow and I think and me disport [bear ill]. Thus cumbered, I seem that all folk had me amazed. Also, lady mine, desire hath long dured some speaking to have—or else at the least have been amused with sight—and for wanting of these things my mouth would, and he durst, 'plain right sore, sith evils for my goodnesses are manifold to me yolden [given]. I wonder, lady, truly—save evermore your reverence—how ye owe [may] for shame such things suffer on your servant to be so multiplied.

"Wherefore, kneeling with a low heart, I pray you to rue on this caitiff, that of nothing now may serve. Good lady, if ye list, now your help to me shew, that am of your priviest servants at all assays in this time, and under your wings of protection. No help to me-wards is shapen: how shall then strangers in any wise after succour look when I, that am so privy, yet of help I do fail? Further may I not, but thus in this prison abide. What bonds and chains me holden, lady, ye see well yourself: a renyant [renegade] forjudged hath not half the care! But thus, sighing and sobbing, I wail here alone, and ne were it for comfort of your presence, right here would I starve [die]. And yet a little am I gladded that so goodly such grace and none hap have I hent, graciously to find the precious Margaret that—all others left—men should buy, if they should therefor sell all their substance. Woe is me that so many let-games and purpose-breakers be made waiters [watchers], such prisoners as I am to overlook and to hinder. And, for such letters [hinderers], it is hard any such jewel to win.

"Is this, lady, an honour to thy deity? Me thinketh, by right, such people should have no mastery ne be overlookers over none of thy servants. Truly, were it lawful unto you, to all the gods would I 'plain, that ye rule your divine purveyance amongst your servants nothing as ye should. Also, lady, my meuble [property] is insufficient to countervail the price of this jewel or else to make th'exchange. Eke, no wight is worthy such pearls to wear but kings or princes or else their peers. This jewel for virtue would adorn and make fair all a realm: the nobility of virtue is so much that her goodness overall is commended. Who is it that would not wail, but he might such richesse have at his will? The virtue thereof out of this prison may me deliver, and nought else. And if I be not therethrough helpen, I see myself without recovery. Although I might hence void [escape], yet would I not: I would abide the day that destiny hath me ordained, which I suppose is without amendment. So sore is my heart bounden, that I may think none other.

"Thus strait, lady, hath Sir Danger laced me in stocks. I believe it be not your will, and for I see you take so little heed, as me thinketh, and will not make by your might the virtue in mercy of the Margaret on me for to stretch, so as ye mow well in case that you list, my bliss and my mirth are felled, sickness and sorrow be always ready. The cope of teen [vexation] is wound about all my body, that standing is me best—unnethes [hardy] may I lie for pure mis-easy sorrow.

"And yet all this is little enough to be the earnest-silver in forward of this bargain, for treblefold so muckle must I suffer ere time come of mine ease. For he is worthy no wealth that may no woe suffer. And certes, I am heavy to think on these things. But who shall give me water enough to drink, lest mine eyes dry for running streams of tears? Who shall wail with me mine own happy heaviness? Who shall counsel me now in my liking tene [trouble] and in my goodly harm? I ne wot! For ever the more I burn, the more I covet; the more that I sorrow, the more thirst I in gladness. Who shall then give me a contrarious drink to staunch the thirst of my blissful bitterness? Lo, thus I burn and I drench [drown]; I shiver and I sweat. To this reversed evil was never yet ordained salve. Forsooth, all leeches [doctors] be uncunning—save the Margaret alone—any such remedy to purvey."

Guillaume De Deguileville

"THE PILGRIMAGE OF
THE LYF OF MANHODE"

As I HAD ORDAINED me at all points to go my way, I began mickle
to think why it was that I might not thus bear mine armours or
why that I had not as great power as thilk [that] wench had that
bare them after me. "Now I am a man," quoth I, "that seemeth
a champion; for maim wot I none in me, but am whole of all limbs
and that am made enough to bear both this wench and her burden. Whence cometh it that I am thus failed of might, that I may
not endure an hour that that I see her bear? Shame and confusion
it is to me when she is strenger than I."

As on this I thought and that alway thinking went, I met in my
way a great churl, evil-shapen, great brows and frounced, that
bare a staff of crabtree and seemed to be a well evil-myster man
and an evil-pilgrim. "What is this?" quoth he. "Whither goeth
this pilgrim? Lord, whither goeth he? He weeneth he be now full
well-arrayed and quaintised [adorned]. But anon with me he shall
let [stop] and to questions he shall answer."

When thus I heard him speak, I became wonder sore-abashed,
for I weened he would have run upon me without more abiding.
Algates [always], courteously I spake to him and humbly. "Sire,"
quoth I, "I require you that ye will not annoy me ne impeach me
of my voyage, for I go far in pilgrimage and a little letting would
grieve me greatly."

"Certain," quoth he, "the disturblance cometh of thine over-
trowing. Whence cometh it thee, so God save thee, and why art
thou such and such that thou darest pass the law that the king
hath well ordained? A while ago the king made a defence [pro-
hibition] that none took scrip ne that none bare it with him ne
handled burdon. And thou, against his ordinance, by thy foolish
surquidry hast undertaken to bear both that one and that other as
methinketh. Whence cometh it thee and how hast thou dared be
so hardy? Evil thou come and evil thou wentest and evil hither

thou broughtest them. Never day in thy life ne didst thou a greater folly."

When these words I understood more than before, I was abashed. For what to answer I ne wist, ne answerer had I none. Gladly an advocate I would have hired me if I might have founden him, for great need I had of one if I had wist where to have purchased him. Algates I studied how I might escape. As I lifted up mine eyen, I saw come that after which I had great desire. That was Dame Reason the wise, which men mown [may] well know by the language, for she will nothing say but sittingly [suitably] and well-ordained. Before I had seen her: wherefore she was the more known to me. I was right joyful when I saw her, for well I thought that by her should that crooked churl be mate [checked] which hard had grouched me: and so he was at the last, and I pray you understandeth how.

Reason came even to him and said to him, "Churl, say me now, so God keep thee, whereof thou servest and why thou seemeth so divers. Art thou a reaper or a mower or an espier of wayfarers? How hightest thou, and where gatheredest and took thy great staff? The staff is not avenant ne sitting [proper] to a good man."

And then the churl leaned him on his staff and said to her, "What is this? Art thou a mayoress or a new enquiress? Shew thy commission, and at the least thy name I shall wit and the great power that thou hast that by semblant thou shewest me. For if I were not sure thereof I would to thee answer nothing."

And then Reason put her hand into her bosom by a spayer [opening] and took out a box, of which she drew a letter, and sith said to him, "Certain, my power I will do thee to wit. Hold! See here my commission. Read it, and thou shalt well wit my name and my power and who I am and why I am come hither."

"Certain," quoth he, "I am no clerk ne I can [know] nothing in thy leaves. Read them as thou wilt, for wit well I appraise them little!"

"Beau sire," quoth she, "All men be not of thine opinion. Of mickle folk they be well praised and loved and authorised. And naught-for-then [yet] thou shalt hear them. But [unless] my clerks fail me all, I will put thee out of suspicion and shew thee what power I have. Come forth, clerk!" quoth she to me, "Undo these letters out of plight [folds]; read them before this bachelor that weeneth he be a lord! When he heareth them read, if God will, he shall answer me."

And then I took *them* and read *them*. Whereof the churl was nothing well-apaid [pleased]. For alway he grummed and alway shook his chin, and at every word I read I saw his teeth grind.

If ye will wit the tenor of the letter, hereafter ye shall hear it:

"Grace-Dieu, by whom govern *them* (as they say) the kings and reign to reason, our good loved friend and in all good deeds well-proved—greeting! And of that we send, doeth plain execution!

"Of new we have understood, whereof us is not fain, that a churl—shrewd, proud, and dangerous—that by his name maketh clepe him and name him *Rude Intendment* hath made him an espier of ways and a waiter [waylayer] of pilgrims and will benim [rob] *them* *their* burdons and unscrip *them* of *their* scrips, beguiling *them* with lying words. And for he would be the more dread, he hath borrowed of *Orgeuille* [pride] his wicked and cruel staff, that men clepe *Obstination*—the which mickle more displeaseth me than doth the frounced churl. For the which thing, *com*mandment we give you, nought in commanding, that ye go thitherward and admonish that musard that his staff he lay adown and that he cease of the surplus. And if anything he withstand or will not obey, giveth him day competent at the assizes of judgment. Of this, plain power we give you and make you commissary. Given in our year that each wight clepeth 1331."

When all was read, Reason took again her letters and put them in safety and sith arraigned the churl and said him such words, "Beau sire," quoth she, "Now thou hast heard my power and why I come here. Wilt thou more answer to me of that I have asked thee?"

"Who art thou?" quoth the churl.

"Who am I?" quoth Reason. "For Saint Germain, hast thou not heard right now what men have read here? Thinkest thou on thy loves, or to take towers or castles?"

Quoth he, "I have well heard, by Saint Simeon, that thou hightest Reason. But for it is a name defamed, therefore I have asked who thou art, and with good right."

"Not defamed, by Saint Benedict!" quoth Reason. "But where hast thou found that?"

"At the mill," quoth he, "there I have bee*n*! There thou measurest falsely and stealest folks' corn."

"Beau sire," quoth she. "Hear now twain [two] little words, and understand! Missaying is no worthiness, ne thou speakest not as the wise. At the mill peradventure ye have seen a measure that is clept Reason; but therefore it is not Reason, but it is fraud and deceit. Betwixt name and being I will well make difference. One thing is to be Reason; and another to have his name. Of the name men mown [may] make coverture for to hele with [hide] their filth: this thing is fallen many a time in many a street, that who that is not fair makes him quaint and who that is not good makes him simple. All vices gladly do it and ofttimes make them covering with the name of the virtue-contrary, for to less displease the folk. And yet is not the virtue the less worth by a straw. But it is sign that it is good when the vice appareleth him and clotheth him therewith. So that if with my name that measure will quaintise him and hele him, therefore am I not defamed, but worshipped should be thereby of all folk of good understanding."

"What is this," quoth he, "that God have part? Thou wilt be praised of that that others should be blamed? If I knew not a fly in milk when thou toldest it me, I had great wrong. Ween not that when I hear named a cat or a hound that I ne wot well it is no ox ne cow, but that it is a hound and a cat. By their names I know well each of them, for their names and they be all one. So that if thou hightest Reason, I say also thou art Reason. And if Reason steal the corn, I say that of thee it is stolen. All the water that maketh the mill turn ne might wash thee thereof. For all thine sly words and fallacies, ween not that ever otherways thou make me understand."

And then Reason, smiling and all turning it into jape, said to him, "Now I see well that of Art thou hast learned and subtly canst argue and bring forth fair examples. And if thou hadst a greater belly thou wouldst well seem worthy!"

"Oh!" quoth he, "thou scornest me."

"That I do certain," quoth Reason. "Wit it well! And yet more I will scorn thee, for to I wit thy name as thou wost mine. And wit well thou hast no worship of the helling [hiding]: I ne wot what thou shalt have of the telling."

"Worship?" quoth he, "What sayest thou? The unworship is thine. Thou hast my name in thy leaves, and askest it! Thou art like him that sitteth on his ass and yet seeketh it overall. I ne wot what it tokeneth but if it be scorning."

"Ah!" quoth Reason. "Art thou that that art set in my leaves? The name within well I wist; but thee knew I not. I held an opinion that I and my name is not one. For with my name may apparel him each thief that goeth to steal, and therefore I weened so of thee, for had I not yet learned that thou and Rude Intendment were one joiningly. But now I see well, without suspicion, that ye be one without distinction. Thine examples have taught it me and thine sayings that be so subtle. I wot by thy words that thou properly art Rude Intendment. More might thou not argue but only so be thou named, for by existence thou art it without difference. Wherefore I forgive thee the villainy that thou hast said to me by felony, for I see well thou weendest that of me it were as it is of thee. But Rudeness taught thee so to ween, for rude thou art, as each wight seeth well, and evil-willed. And therefore set thee was this name."

With these words the churl was attaint to the heart. Naught he said, for he could not but only grind with his teeth. Reason stinted not but sang him of another song. "Now," quoth she, "I wot thy name, great need have I not to ask more of the remnant: in my letters it is all clear. For an espier thou art of ways and an assailer of pilgrims: thou wilt benim [rob] them their burdons and unscrip their scrips. Why dost thou it, by thy soul, against the will of my Lady?"

"For that they" quoth he, "wittingly pass the gospel that I have heard said in our town and keep it shrewdly. There it is defended to all, as I have understood, that no man bear out of his home neither scrip ne burdon. So, when that I see them *bear* them against the defence of the king, gladly for to keep the law I do pain to make them to leave them."

"Oh!" quoth Reason. "Otherways it goeth. That defence was long ago all otherways turned and removed to the contrary. Well it is sooth that it was defended, but afterward it was recommanded. Cause reasonable there was for which there needed well change. It is not unworship to the king though he change his law for cause honest. The cause of the changing again shortly I will tell thee, if thou wilt. Whoso is at the end of his way hath no need to be pilgrim, and he that were no pilgrim should little do with scrip or with burdon. Jesu the king is the end to which all good pilgrims think: that is the end of good voyage and of good pilgrimage. To that term and to that end were come his good pilgrims by his cleping. When he defended them that no more they bear scrip ne burdon, but left them and laid them down, sufficient he was and mighty to deliver them plenteously all that them needed, without being in any other's danger. On the other side, he would that when he sent them to preach that their hearkeners administered to them and found them their victuals, for every worker is worthy to have and receive hire. And each wight did thereof so mickle that at the turning-again no wight plained him. Whereof thou hast heard that he asked them once, when him thought good: 'Have you,' quoth he, 'anything lacked when I have thus sent you without scrip to preach to the folk and to shew the word of God?' And then they answered him: 'Certainly, sire, nay. Sufficiently we have had and nothing ne failed us.'

"Lo, here the cause for why was defended that they bare no scrip and that they used not of the burdon. But when he should afterward go and pass by the bridge of death, when he saw that he that was the end of their way departed from them, then would he change his law as a soft and treatable king, and said to them that they took again their scrips and did them on again. 'Whoso hath,' he said, 'any sack, take it, and a scrip therewith.' As though he said apertly and clearly: 'Though I (for ye were come to the end of your way) defended you that ye had ne bare no scrip, now I must aloign [remove] me from you and leave you, I will that ye take again all as ye had before, for I wot well that when ye have lost the sight of me a scrip shall be needful to you and a burdon to lean you to. Pilgrims ye must be again and set you to your way again: else should ye not mowe [be able to] follow me ne come to me. On the other side, when I am gone ye shall find none that gladly shall do you good ne that with good heart *shall* speak anything to you. To your scrip ye shall hold you till ye come again to me. Now taketh it, for I grant it you for the need I see thereof.' So see here, all in apert, the cause which is sufficient to bear scrip and burdon! Wherefore, thou shouldest not meddle thee to arrest those that have it ne that bear it where they go. Leave they have: and cause there is, into the time that each cometh to the end of his voyage and his pilgrimage."

"What is this?" quoth the walker. "What goest thou thus jangling me? Wilt thou hold the gospel at fable and lesing [lie]?

Thou sayest it uncommanded that that God had ordained. Which thing, if it so were right, so all his ordinances should be put out of the book and defaced and scraped."

"Not so," quoth Reason. "For it is right to wit the time past, how men did, how men said; why that was, what cause there lieth, why there were mutations of doings. And therefor is not the gospel reproved ne defaced; but to good understanders it is the more gracious and the more pleasant. The more diverse flowers be in the meadow, the more is the place gracious; and the more that their fashion is diverse the more gladly men behold them."

And then blessed him the churl with his rude crooked hand. "What is this?" quoth he. "Thou wilt amaze me and enchant me. All that I say thou turnest and stirrest all to the contrary. Falseness thou clepest fairness, and of fairness thou sayest falseness. That that was of the king defended [forbidden] thou sayest was commanded, turning the gospel all upsodown by disguisy words and lying. Thou ne art but a beguileress of folk. Let me stand, for I praise not thy words ne thy deeds at three beans! In my purpose I will hold me and of nothing beseech thee."

"At the least," quoth Reason, "that staff thou shalt lay down, for thou wost well Grace-Dieu hath commanded it and ordained it."

"To Grace-Dieu," quoth he, "of what it may grieve, I see not. On the other side, necessary it is to me to that that I have to do: I lean me thereto and I defend me therewith, and set the less by all folk. And methinketh I am mickle the more dread. And, therefore, if I laid it down a great fool I were and a great cockard."

"Oh!" quoth Reason. "Thou sayest not well. Thou hast need to have other friends. Grace-Dieu should never love thilk [that one] that bare such a staff: it was never lief to her, she hateth it more than the goat the knife, so that if thou laidest it not down thou wert not wise."

"Oh!" quoth the churl. "How thou art a fool to say such words. If the staff grieved her not, why should it displease her?"

"I will say thee," quoth Reason, "rudely, for other meat I see well thy rude throat asketh not. If thou hadst a friend to which any wight did dis-ease, it should of nothing grieve thee but of as mickle as it should displease thee. Grace-Dieu loveth all folk and willeth the advancement of all. And, therefore, when any man hath mischief, or that men do him any dis-ease, albeit she hath no grievance yet hath she displeasance. This staff is enemy to those that she would have friends. Ne were it, the Jews would come to her and convert them; all heretics would also leave their error and amend them. By it were put to confusion Nabal and Pharaoh, for to it they leaned, so that they purchased their death. If it ne were, Obedience should reign over all, and command; each should do that that he were commanded, and of nothing disobey. If it ne were, all rude wits would be inclined and humble them. Thyself, that hightest Rude Intendment, if thou ne leanedest so fast to it, would believe me and amend thee. And, therefore, I rede [advise] thee, lay it down and lean thee no more thereto."

"Ha, God," quoth he, "what I praise little words that be of this manner! I will to thee of nothing obey, ne I will not leave the staff: I will lean thereto, wilt thou or wilt thou not. Wit it well!"

"Now," quoth Reason, "I see well that there is no more to speak with thee, but only to cite thee to assizes of judgment. I summon thee without more tarrying. Come thither without sending any other!"

Then Reason turned her again to me-ward and clept me. "Go," quoth she, "hardily, without dreading Rude Intendment. Say him nothing ne answer him not, for the teaching of Solomon is that men answer no word to him that men see and find a fool."

Short-Story Writers

❧🙙❧

SHORT STORIES as we now know them owe much to our way of publishing them as items in magazines of miscellaneous reading. Medieval occasions for their telling were mostly oral, and whenever they were put into script a more serious justification than simple entertainment was usually thought necessary. Only rarely did the form appear in its butterfly nature; normally it was a prisoner to moral disquisition, pinned to a framework of pedagogy. The exceptions are not many. In France, Marie de France gathered together the simple novellas that she called Breton lais; the broad tales known as fabliaux were sometimes published in collections, as also were the similar yarns about Reynard the Fox and the more moral fables of Aesop, and the fifteenth century produced anthologies like *Les Cent Nouvelles nouvels*. Italy has collections only lightly touched by seriousness, Sacchetti's anecdotes, the *Cento Novelle Anitche,* and the *Decameron,* for example; and in England there is the *Canterbury Tales*, a gathering so surprising in objective and content—and so alarming to its author—that one critic thinks it must have been inspired by some naughty French manuscript. Far more numerous than these, however, and more representative of the literary way with the short story, are the treatises on vices and virtues which haul in anecdotes from every corner of the universe to bear witness to moral truths.

In this guise there is an infinity of medieval short stories. But their technique is conditioned by their use. The originality in matter and the sophistication in manner that have developed as the anecdote has subtilized into an art-form, are almost entirely absent. Although contemporary and local stories—even bawdy ones—are not lacking, the vast majority are simple retellings of time-tried moral yarns, chronological in narrative arrangement, unadventurous in language and style, driving straight to their moral or humorous point with no dawdling over settings or subtleties of mood or characterization. Simple as they are and innocent of the stylistic interplay between narrator and audience that characterizes good oral anecdote—such matters may have been left to the oral retelling that most collections assume—they are not necessarily naïve, nor are they devoid of merit: their common virtues are clarity, concentration upon plot and, therefore, upon good plot, and neat brevity. And every now and then such a yarn is blessed by falling into the hands of a more literary raconteur, Marie de France, Chaucer, Boccaccio, and many another, who can bridle its precipitateness, time its climax, touch it with grace, complicate its appeal.

Many of these collections were translated into English prose. Among the most popular was *Gesta Romanorum,* which was compiled in Latin about 1300, possibly in England and possibly in connection with the democratization of preaching that is often credited to the Franciscans. Its tales, each concluded with a point-by-point moral of allegorical kind, were meant for pious reading or for use in sermons. The collection is superficially tied together by setting all the tales in the time of various Roman emperors; but the individual items came from many sources, and medieval editors varied the contents at will. Three times it was translated into English, and from the version done about 1450 we have selected a tale made famous by Shakespeare. Somewhat more spicy than Shakespeare's, it is also nicely told in its simple way, the narrative well disposed betwen exposition and dialogue, the language native but varied in syntactical structure. The caudal morality (slightly docked here) is a good example of the resource in allegory and symbolism that fifteen centuries of Christian exegesis had conferred upon medieval explicators. Simpler still are the anecdotes of the *Alphabet of Tales,* compiled in Latin by Arnold of Liège, and translated in the early fifteenth century. For the convenience of preachers, the stories— culled from all the best-known medieval anthologies—were thinned to the narrative bones and arranged alphabetically according to their subjects: *abbas, abbatissa, abscondere, absolucio,* and so on. The utilitarian objective prompted not only a naked narrative, but also a naked style, one with no grace but the basic ones, directness, economy, and conformity to familiar English. Our examples, average in length, are chosen to represent the chief types of story in the collection and a few of the many sources.

The use to which such stories were put is exemplified by *Jacob's Well, c.* 1400, a huge moral treatise which is similar in form, content, and provenance to *Vices and Virtues,* but which is provided with an elaborate (and wearisome) allegorical framework—a moral counterpart to Chaucer's Canterbury pilgrimage—which recounts every operation in the cleansing of a well. Into each unit of this allegory is fitted one or more exemplary tales. The whole work, it would seem, was set up for pulpit use. From it we select two stories that are notably more independent and English than the rest—possibly because of the narrator's obvious delight in them.

Less clerical, but otherwise similar in objective, is the book of anecdotes and commentary compiled by Geoffrey de la Tour-Landry. Formally, the work is a treatise on social ethics illustrated with anecdotes,
most of them taken from clerical collections. Where it differs, and
differs so delightfully, from the usual treatise is in the amused good
sense of the writer, his easy autobiographical mode—he was a widower
writing for his three young daughters—and the contemporaneity of
several of his anecdotes. From an anonymous translation of about
1450 we select the introduction, one of the tales, and an engaging
domestic debate on a subject vital to medieval life and literature. Far
more than Caxton, who printed his own translation in 1484, this translator had a pretty command of the nuances of English speech, and his
moderately free translation—the prologue is based upon French verse—
is an excellent anglicizing of the well-bred, conversational style of the
French original.

Of the collections which emphasize delight rather more than teaching, a few found their way into English prose. Caxton translated
Aesop's Fables and there is a painfully literal translation of the Arabic
and Classical tales that Petrus Alfonsis assembled in the eleventh century as *Disciplina Clericalis*. More interesting than these, however, is
the *Reynard the Fox* that Caxton published in 1481: for one thing, it
is translated from Flemish; for another it represents the major attempt
of the Middle Ages to fuse a collection of tales into a larger unity—it
is common to speak of it now as a beast-epic. First told separately and
then gathered together, the tales of rascality that clustered around
Reynard became highly popular among satirists and no less popular
among the European multitudes who had a weakness for what is called,
somewhat parochially, *l'esprit gaulois*—an amused, amoral interest in
mankind's peccadillos and sins. Caxton's translation, partly because of its
Flemish original and the tradition of simple narrative behind it, is clean-
cut and native, and from it we select the episode of Reynard's ingenious
escape from hanging.

"GESTA ROMANORUM"

THE LOVER'S BOND. Celestinus reigned, a wise emperor in Rome,
and he had a fair daughter.

And in his time there was a knight that loved this daughter,
but he thought in himself that he did all in vain, for he thought,
as for sooth, that the emperor would not let him to have her, for

he was unworthy thereto. Nevertheless, he thought, if he might by any way have love of the damsel, "it were enough to me."

He yede [went] ofttime to the damsel and espied her will, and she said to him again that he travailed all in vain: "For trowest thou," quoth she, "with thy deceivable and fair words to beguile me? Nay, sir, by my soul, it shall not be so!"

Then said the knight, "What shall I give to thee, and let me lie by thee a night?"

"Not though [unless] thou woldest give me an hundred mark of florins," quoth she, "thou shalt not lie by me a night."

"Then it shall be as thou wilt," quoth he.

What did he but purveyed him of so much money, *scilicet,* an hundred mark of florins, and gave her.

When night came, the knight entered into the bed of the maid, and anon he was asleep. And she did off her harness and come and lay down by him. So the knight lay sleeping all the night.

On the morrow, she rose and did on her clothes and washed her hands. And the knight awoke of his sleep and then he said, "Come hither to me, that I may do my will with thee."

"Nay, by the health of my father, that will I not," quoth she, "For, friend, I do thee no wrong. Thou accordest with me that I should lie with thee all night, and so it is y-done, for I lay by thee all night and thou sleptest and profferdest me no solace. And, therefore, blame thyself and not me."

And the knight was heavy and said, "What shall I give to thee and let me lie by thee another night?"

"As much," quoth she, "as thou did afore, and no less."

"I assent," said he.

And the knight yede and sold all his movable goods and made ready an hundred mark of florins. But see now a marvelous case! For, right as it was the first night, so it was in the second.

Then the knight marvelled more than man may suppose, and heavy he was, and said, "Alas! for now have I spent all my goods without speed [success], and therefore, though I shall die therefore, I will make another end. How much shall I give thee and let us be together the third night? quoth the knight to the damsel. "Soothly," she said, "If thou have me, as thou paid afore, *fiat voluntas tua.*" "I assent," quoth he, "Thou shalt have thine asking and thy will."

The knight yede into far country till he come to a great city, in the which were many merchants and many philosophers, among the which was Master Virgil the philosopher. Then the knight yede to a great merchant and said, "I have *need* of money, and if thou wilt lend me an hundred mark unto a certain day I will lay to thee all my lands, under this condition, that if I hold not my day thou shalt have my lands for ever."

Then said the merchant, "Dear friend, I set not so much by thy lands, but if thou wilt make this covenant that I shall say to thee, I will fulfill thy will."

"Yes," said he, "I am ready to do thy will if thou wilt do my petition."

"Then," said he, "When this covenant is made that I shall say unto thee, then I shall fulfil thine asking. And the covenant shall be this, that thou make to me a charter of thine own blood, in condition that if thou keep not thy day of payment it shall be lawful to me for to draw away all the flesh of thy body fro the bone with a sharp sword. And if thou wilt assent hereto I shall fulfil thy will."

The knight loved the damsel so much that he granted all this, and made a charter of his own blood and sealed it. And after the sealing this merchant took him the money that he asked.

When he had the money, he thought to himself, "If I get not my will by this money, I am but dead. Nay, nay, it may not be so!"

When he heard tell of the great name of Master Virgil, he yede to him and said, "Good sir, I have privy council to speak atween us two, and I beseech you of your wise counsel in this case."

"Say on," quoth Virgil, "and I shall tell thee after my discretion."

"Sir, I love the daughter of the emperor more than ye will trow, and I accorded with her for a certain sum of money. I have been deceived two nights in such manner"—and told all the case as well as he could—"and, sir, now I have borrowed of a merchant so much money for the same case to be fulfilled, and under this conclusion, that if I hold not my day of payment, it shall then be lawful to him to heeld off all the skin of my body with his sword, and then I am but dead. And, therefore, sir, I am come to you to have counsel and wit how I may both have help against such a peril and also to have the love of that lovely lady."

"Thou hast made a lewd covenant," said Virgil, "For as a man bindeth him with his own will, right so he shall be served, by the law of the emperor. And, therefore, thou shalt do wisely for to

keep the day of thy payment, all things left. And touching the
damsel, I shall give thee a tale of truth. Between her sheet and her
coverlet of her bed is a letter of such virtue that whosoever goeth
with her to bed, he shall anon fall into a dead sleep and he shall
not wake till time that it be put away. And, therefore, when thou
comest to her bed, seek atween the sheet and the coverlet and
thou shalt find the letter. And when thou hast found it, cast it far
from the bed and then enter into the bed, for thou shalt not sleep
till time that thou hast done thy will with the damsel, and that
shall turn to thee great honor and joy."

The knight took his leave of Virgil and thanked him much of his
counsel, and yede to the damsel and gave her the money. When
night came, the knight entered the chamber and privily put his
hand between the coverlet and the sheet, and there he found the
letter. And when he had it, he cast it far fro the bed and lay down
and feigned as he had slept.

And then the damsel, trowing that he had slept, as he did
afore, she cast off her clothes and went to bed. Anon the knight
set hand to her, as is the manner of bed, and she perceived that
and prayed him of grace, and to save her maidenhood—"and I
shall double all the money that thou hast given to me, and give it
to thee."

Then said he, "Thou lookest at a wrong hole. Thy words be in
waste. I shall now do indeed *w*hat I have long laboured for"—
and occupied him with her body as course is of kind.

And, after, he loved her so much that he drew so much to her
company that he forgot the merchant, and the day of payment
was past by the space of fourteen days. And, as he lay in a certain
night in his bed, it came to his mind the day that he made to the
merchant, and all his bowels were stirred therewith. And then *he*
said to her, "Alas, woman, that ever I saw thee, for I am but dead.
I borrowed for thy love such a sum of money for to pay at a certain day, by this condition, that if I pay not at my day he shall
have full power for to heeld off the flesh of my body without con-
tradiction. And now my day is past fortnight ago, so highly I set
mine heart in thee."

Then said she, "Sorroweth not so much. Goeth to him and
doubleth the money to him, and, if he will not, ask how much he
will have, and I shall pay it."

Then was the knight comforted. He yede to the city and there he met with the merchant in the street, and lowly he saluted him.

Then said the merchant, "So say I not to thee."

Then said the knight, "Sir, for the trespass that I have made against your convention, I will double the payment."

"Nay," said the merchant, "That spake we not of. I will have right as thou didst bind thee to me."

"Ask of me," quoth the knight, "as much money as thou wilt and thou shalt be paid for my trespass."

"It is vain that thou speakest," quoth the merchant, "for though thou give to me all the goods of thy city, I will have the covenant holden, and none other will I have of thee than as the charter asealed maketh mention of." And anon he made the knight to be taken and led to the castle, and set him in a safe ward, abiding the justice.

When the judge was come and sat in the doom, the knight came to bar among other prisoners, and the merchant shewed his letter afore the judge.

Anon, as the judge saw there his own deed, he said to all that stood about, "Sirs, ye know well it is the law of the emperor that if any man bind him by his own free will he shall receive as he serveth. And, therefore, this merchant shall have covenant as law will."

Now, in all this time, the damsel, his love, had sent knights for to espy and enquire how the law was pursued against him. And when she heard tell that the law passed against him, she cut off all the long hair of her head and clad her in precious clothing like to a man and yede to the palace there as her lemman [lover] was to be deemed, and saluted the justice. And all they trowed that she had been a knight. And the judge enquired of what country she was and what she had to do there.

She said, "I am a knight and come of far country and hear tidings that there is a knight among you that should be deemed to death for an obligation that he made to a merchant. And therefore, I am come to deliver him."

Then the judge said, "It is law of the emperor that whosoever bindeth him with his own proper will and consent, without any constraining, he should be served so again."

When the damsel heard this, she turned to the merchant and said, "Dear friend, what profit is it to thee that this knight, that standeth here ready to the doom, be slain? It were *better* to thee to have money than to have him slain."

"Thou speakest all in vain," quoth the merchant, "for without doubt, I will have the law, sith he bound him so freely. And, therefore, he shall have none other grace than law will. For he came to me and I not to him. I desired him not thereto against his will."

Then said she, "I pray thee, how much shall I give to have my petition? I shall give thee thy money double, and, if that be not pleasing to thee, ask of me what thou wilt and thou shalt have."

Then said he, "Thou heard me never say but that I would have my covenant kept."

"Soothly," said she, "and thou shalt, trow me. Afore you, sir judge, and afore you all, I say now, sir judge, giveth a right wisdom of that that I shall say to you.

"Ye have heard how much I have proferred this merchant for the life of this knight. And he forsaketh all and asketh the law. And that liketh me much. And, therefore, lordings that be here, heareth me what I shall say. Ye knoweth well that the knight bound him never by letter but [except] that the merchant should have power to cut his flesh fro the bones. But there was no covenant made of shedding of blood: thereof was nothing spoken. And, therefore, let him set hand on him anon, and, if he shed any blood with his shaving of the flesh, forsooth, then shall the king have good law upon him."

And when the merchant heard this, he said, "Give me my money and I forgive my action."

"Forsooth," quoth she, "Thou shalt not have one penny, for, afore all this company, I proferred to thee all that I might, and thou forsook it and saidest with a loud voice, 'I shall have my covenant.' And, therefore, do thy best with him, but look that thou shed no blood, I charge thee, for it is not thine, ne no covenant was thereof."

Then the merchant, seeing this, yede away confused. And so was the knight's life saved and no penny paid. And she yede home again and did off that clothing and clothed her as she was afore, like to a woman. And the knight yede home again. And the damsel turned and met him and asked how he had sped, as though she had not known thereof.

"Ah, lady!" quoth he, "This day was I in point to be dead for thy love, but as I was in point to be con*demned*, there came in suddenly a knight, a fair and well shap*ed*, the which I saw never afore, and he delivered me by his excellent wisdom both from death and eke from payment of money."

"Then were thou," quoth she, "unkind, that wouldest not bid that knight to meat, that so far had saved thee."

He answered thereto and said that he came suddenly and suddenly yede. Then said she, "Knowest thou him if thou saw him?"

"Yea," quoth he, "right well!"

She yede up, and clad her as she did afore. And then she yede forth, and the knight knew her then well, and for joy fell down upon her and said, "Blessed be thou, and the hour in the which I first knew thee!" And he wept. And after he wedded her and lived and died in the service of god. And *they* yielded to god good souls.

MORALITY. Dear friends, this emperor is the father of heaven, our lord Jesu Christ. The daughter that is so fair is the soul made to the similitude of god. The knight that stirreth her to sin is every worldly man, the which is about both night and day to foul his soul, and, therefore, he proffereth many great gifts, *scilicet,* vain worldly goods. *But as long* as the letter lieth in the bed, *scilicet,* virtues which the soul received in baptism, so long he may not foul the soul. . . Then the knight, *scilicet,* the fleshly man, goeth to the merchant, *scilicet* to the devil, as oft as he delighteth in deadly sin, and he writeth the charter when he consenteth to sin; he sealeth it when he doth the sin. . . Virgil, that moved him to move the letter, is pride of life, the which suffereth not that a soul liveth not in cleanness. For as soon as virtues be removed by assenting to sin, as soon the soul faileth and a man is delighted in sin, that he forgeteth the everlasting life which he lost for sin, till time that sickness come of feebleness, by poverty, or tribulation. And then such men be ofttime attached by the merchant, *scilicet* the devil, in so much that the wretched man shall have no power to make satisfaction or sorrow for his sins, but utterly standeth in perils of death. Then the damsel seeing this, she clotheth herself like to a knight. Right so we should do. We should cast fro us the old life and clothe us with a new, *scilicet,* good virtues, and ascend upon the palfrey of reason, and so go forth to holy church, and there pray god with a full heart and allege against the devil, that he slay us not because that god bought us. But then us must take away the flesh, *scilicet,* fleshly affections, so that no blood fall, *scilicet,* no sin be in us, for if we do not so, *scilicet,* take away fleshly affections, that there be no sin, else the emperor of heaven will have an action against us. And if we will thus allege against the devil, as the damsel did against the merchant, withouten doubt then shall the flesh and the spirit be married, to live in bliss.

"AN ALPHABET OF TALES"

ADULTERIUM. We read how that one that hight Gingolph in France bought a well. And he was a wed man and he was a holy man. And when he came home into Burgundy *w*here he dwelt, he found the same well sprung in his garden. So on a day, this Gingolph and his wife walked samen [together] in their garden and set them down by the well. And he reproved her for avoutery [adultery], and said it was told him that another man held her beside him. And she denied it and said nay.

Then he said unto her, "Bare thine arm and take up a little stone in the bottom of this well, and if thine arm come up unhurt I shall trow that thou art innocent of this that is put on thee."

And she trowed that she had been secure enough, and shoved in her arm into the well. And when she drew it out, it was as it had been scalded with the fire.

And then this holy man said unto her, "Lo! Now appears the truth of thy falsehood, and, therefore, fro henceforth thou shall never be my fellow." And he divided his goods in two and gave her the one half and let her dwell by her own.

And within a little while, a clerk that held [served] this Gingolph came to him on a night when he lay sleeping in his bed, and slew him. And when he was buried he did miracles. And when his wife heard tell that he did miracles, she scorned him and said on this manner of wise, "It is as true that Gingolph does miracles as it is that mine arse sings!"

And anon her arse made an ugly noise, and would not leave for naught she could do. And ever after, upon the Friday that her husband suffered martyrdom on, weekly when she spake any word, her arse began to sing and make an ugly noise. And would never leave it on the Friday whilst that she lived.

LEO. On a day when Saint Jerome sat with his brethren, suddenly there came a halting lion and went into the abbey. And anon as the brethren saw him they fled all, and Saint Jerome rose and met him, as he had been a guest. And this lion lifted up his sore foot and let him see it. And he called his brethren and gart [made] one of them wash it; and laid salves and medicines thereto, made of herbs, and anon this lion was hale and was as meek as a horse.

And Saint Jerome charged him that he should every day take charge of and keep an ass that brought him and his brethren fuel fro the wood. And he would every day, at due time, have this ass of the field and bring it home, and kept her surely.

So on a day, as this ass was pasturing, this lion list well sleep, and laid him down and fell upon a sad [full] sleep. And there came merchants with camels by this ass's way: and saw that no-body was stirring, and they took this ass with them. And when they were gone, this lion wakened and missed his fellow, and sought here and there, roming [roaring], and could not find it. And when he saw he could not find it, he went home all heavily unto the abbey and stood at the gate overom [away from] and durst come no nearer because he brought not home the ass, and he durst not come in as he was wont to do.

And the monks, when they saw him, that he came home and brought not the ass with him as he was wont to do, they trowed he had eaten her; and herefor they withdrew his meat fro him that they were wont to give him, and would not give him it, but bade him go and eat the hinder-end of the ass, as he had eaten the fore-end. And then Saint Jerome charged this lion to do the ass's office, and to bring home wood on his back daily to the kitchen as it was wont to do. And meekly he did it as he was commanded, and grouched nothing therewith.

So on a day, as this lion was walking by his own, he was ware of these merchants come of ferrom [far off] with their camels laden and this lion's ass that they kept among them. And with a great roming he ran upon them, and all the men fled and were passing *a*feared. And all these camels and this ass—both with merchants as they were laden—he brought unto the abbey.

And when Saint Jerome saw, he commanded his brethren to give these cattle meat and then to abide the will of God.

And then this lion came into the abbey as he was wont to do, and went to Saint Jerome and syne [afterwards] from monk to monk, and fawned *on* them and louted [bowed] unto the earth, even as he had asked them forgiveness. And then the merchants came and knew their fault, and asked Saint Jerome forgiveness. And he forgave them when they confessed how they did, and let them have all their goods again. And they gave the abbey, to amends, a measure of oil and bound them and their successors for evermore yearly to give unto that abbey the same measure—and so they do yearly unto this day.

MARIA. We read in "Our Lady's Miracles" how some time there was a noble knight of Kirkby that was devout unto our Lady, and on a time, as he went unto the war, he went into an abbey that was founded of our Lady and was in his way, and there he heard mass. And when each mass was done after other, and he for worship of our Lady would not go ere he had heard them all, at the last he went forth of this abbey and hasted him unto this tournament.

He met many coming fro the tournament, and all was done. They said that he had fought manlily in the battle and borne him passing well. And they stood still unto all came about, and each man with a hale voice commended and said he had fought worthily. And there came some and offered them unto him, and said that he had taken them prisoners in the battle.

So the man was discreet and perceived how our Lady had rewarded him, and he gave up all worldly things and served her Son and her ever after whilst he lived.

MULIER. Petrus Alphonsis tells how sometime there was a young wed man, and through counsel of an old wise man he closed his wife in a high chamber that had no door but one and a window, and ever as he came either in or out he sparred [locked] the door fast, and on the night he would hide the keys at his bed-head. And thus he did a long time.

So on a time, when her husband was away, she looked forth at the window and she was ware of a fresh young man, and anon she waxed jolious on him. And to the intent that she mote [might] get out unto him three nights or four, by and by she made her husband drunken. And on a night privily, when he was asleep, she stole the keys fro his head and opened the doors, and privily she went unto this young man.

So her husband wakened and missed her, and compassed [deduced] that without a cause she would not have desired *him* to drink so fast on evens as she did—and said nothing, but lay still and slept. So when she had had her lust, she came in again and he let as he missed her not.

So, on a night afterward, he feigned himself drunken, and the same night she rose up as she did afore and went unto her love. And anon as she was gone he rose privily and followed her and came unto the door and sparred it fast, and went up again and stood in the window watching. And at the last he was ware of her coming in her sark [shirt]. And she knocked, and he asked who was there. And she besought him forgive her that she went forth, and to let her come in.

And he said she should not come in, but she should stand still there and he should show her unto her father and her mother in the array that she was in—and the use was that they that were found thereout at midnight, watchmen should take them and on the morn set them on the pillory, that all men might wonder on them.

And when she saw that on no wise he would let her in, she said she should leap into a draw-well that was but a little fro the door, and drown herself rather or [than] she were taken and shamed. And when she saw for all that that he would not let her in, she took up a great stone and cast *it* into the draw-well, and bade farewell for evermore. And when he heard it fall into the well he weened it had been she had leapen into the well, and he was somewhat astonished. And opened the door fast and ran unto the well to look if he mote get her out. And she had hid her by the well, and saw the door was open and whipped in and locked the door fast and got her up into the window.

And when he heard she was gotten in, he said, "O thou false woman, and full of devils' craft! Let me come in!"

And she said, "Nay!"—he should not. And there she held him out until watchmen came and took him and had him unto prison. And on the morn she went unto her father and her mother and told them how that he went out on the night to his strumpets and forsook her, and there they came unto the prison all-samen [all together] and made plaint on him. And there in his sark and his breek he was set on the pillory, that all folk wondered on him. And thus maliciously she put her blame upon him.

POTENCIA. Esopus tells in his fables how the lamb and the wolf were both thirsty, and they came both unto the water to drink. And the wolf drank above and the lamb beneath. Then the wolf said unto the lamb, "Why hast thou troubled the water unto me?" And the lamb answered him again and said, "How should I make the water drovy when it came fro thee unto me?" And then the wolf said, "Why banst [curse] thou me?" And the lamb said, "Nay, I ban thee not." And then the wolf said, "Thy father did unto me mickle ill, and now I shall venge me of thee." And with that he ran on the silly lamb and worried it. And this had the lamb that did no trespass.

RELIGIOSUS. Jacob de Vitry tells how sometime there was a knight that left all his possessions and his worships and his welfares and made him a monk.

And the abbot saw that he was a wise man, and sent him unto the market to sell asses of the abbey that was old, and that he should buy young. Though-all he were displeased therewith, nevertheless he went, and would not break his obedience. And when men asked him if the asses were good and young, he answered ever again and said, "Trow ye that our abbey is fallen unto such poverty that we should sell our good asses and our profitable?"

So one came and asked him why their tails were so pilled and no hair left on them. He answered again and said, "Because they fall oftsithes [often] under the load, and we lift them ever up by the tails. And that is cause their tails are bare." And thus he would not lain [belie] the truth. So him happened sell none of them, and came home unto his cloister.

Another lewd monk that was with him at the market accused him even openly in their chapter-house, and the abbot displeased him—as it had been for a great trespass. And he answered unto the abbot again and said, "I left many asses and mickle other good thing in the world; and I came hither to serve God and because I should not lie—but that I should save my soul."

And thus fro thenceforth he was never sent out forward [bargainer].

"JACOB'S WELL"

THE CANON AND THE JEW'S DAUGHTER. In England was a young canon of a great minster, cousin to the bishop of that same diocese, and he loved a Jew's daughter of that city, dwelling with her father and mother. And she loved him again [back]. But she was kept so straight in with father and mother that her love and she might not come together but it were on Good Friday night, for then all Jews bleed beneath for wreak [injury] of Christ's death. For, when Pilate said to the Jews, "I am unguilty of the blood of Christ," the Jews said again to Pilate, "His blood be on us and on all our children." Therefore, on Good Friday night, all the Jews lie and bleed beneath.

And that night the canon lay by the Jew's daughter.

On the Saturday, by the morn, the father rose betimes when his blood was staunched, and saw the canon in his daughter's bed with her. The Jew durst not slay him, for he was the bishop's nephew, but the Jew cried loud and said, "What dost thou here, thou false Christian man? Where is thy faith?"

The canon ran out to his church, all ashamed. That day, he should read the bishop's epistle. He durst not for shame be shriven. He stood in his vestment before the bishop afore the epistle.

The Jew, with all neighbours, cometh into the church to accuse the canon to his bishop—how he lay by his daughter that night. Then that young canon was adread to have been shamed, and was full in heart sorry for his lechery—and that *in* holy time done—and said in his heart, "Lord God, help me this hour, and I behote [promise] thee that I shall be shriven and do penance, and never do this cursed deed more."

The bishop weened the Jews had come to the church to have been converted, and asked them why they came thither. The Jews opened their mouths to accuse the canon of his lechery, and they might speak never a word. The bishop weened they had scorned him and holy church, and did them be put out at the doors.

The canon, after, shrove him to the bishop of that sin, and entered into a straighter religion. And the Jew's daughter was baptized and was a nun.

BEATRIX. A nun that hight Beatrix—sexton of her house, fair in body, fairer in soul, meek, mild, benign, and obedient to God, to holy church, to her abbess, and lowly to all her sistren, devout in prayers and in her service, and she loved specially Our Lady—often and long she was wooed of a clerk to be his love.

At the last, after compline, she, so sore tempted, accorded to go away with the clerk. But first, afore an image of Our Lady kneeling, she said, "Lady, this temptation may I no longer withstand. Have here the keys of mine office if thou wilt. I go my way." She laid her keys by the image, and went her way with the clerk.

Long after, he was weary of her and put her away fro him. She wept sore, she could [knew] no craft to live thereby, she durst not go again to her cloister for shame, but she was common to all that would have her, fifteen years during.

After those fifteen years, in a beggar's weeds she went home to the gates of her house, with a full sorrow in heart for her sin, purposing to be shriven and to leave her sin, and to obey to the correction of her abbess for her default. And said to the porter, "Knowest thou aught such a nun that hight Beatrix, that was sexton of this house fifteen year gone and more?"

The porter said, "I know her well for a blessed woman; she is yet here in her office—most meek, mild, and obedient of all her sisters."

This Beatrix said it was not so, for she was out of this house fifteen year afore.

The porter said, "Nay, for she is here yet. She went never out sith she was professed."

Beatrix, knowing that it was not so, turning fro her house purposed to go on begging, weeping, and sorrowing.

Our Lady met with her and said, "Beatrix, in thy likeness and thy clothing I have done thine office sith thou cast to me thy keys of thine office, because thou were meek, mild, and obedient. Therefore, go now thou and do forth thine office as I have done for thee. For no man knoweth thy sin here but thyself, for all thy sistren weened of me that it had been you."

Our Lady brought her to her cell, and took her again her keys, and vanished away fro her. Beatrix, without shaming of her sisters, was shriven privily and did penance, and kept meekness, mildness, and benignity, and obedience, unto her end.

Geoffrey de la Tour-Landry

"THE BOOK OF THE KNIGHT OF TOUR-LANDRY"

THE PROLOGUE. In the year of the incarnation of Our Lord 1371, as I was in a garden, all heavy and full of thought, in the shadow, about the end of the month of April, but a little I rejoiced me of the melody and song of the wild birds. They sang there in their languages, as the throstle, the thrush, the nightingale, and other birds, the which were full of mirth and joy.

And their sweet song made my heart to lighten and made me to think of the time that is passed of my youth—how Love in great distress had held me and how I was in her service many times full of sorrow and gladness, as many lovers be. But my sorrow was healed and my service well set and quit, for he gave me a wife that was both fair and good, and of all good she was bell and the flower, and I delighted me so much in her that I made for her love songs, ballades, roundels, virelais, and diverse new things, in the best wise that I could.

But Death, that on all maketh war, took her from me, the which hath made me have many a sorrowful thought and great heaviness. And so it is more than twenty year that I have been for her full of great sorrow, for a true lover's heart forgetteth never the woman that once he hath truly loved.

And as I was in the said garden, thinking of these thoughts, I saw come towards me my three daughters, of the which I was joyful and had great desire that they should turn to good and worship above all earthly things, for they were young and had but tender wit. And so at the beginning, a man ought to learn his daughters with good example-giving . . . And, therefore, I purposed to make a little book, in the which I would write the good conditions and deeds of ladies and gentlewomen that for their goodness were worshipped, honored, praised, and renowned, the time past and ever shall be, for their well-doing and goodness, to that intent that my daughters should take example of fair continuance and good manner. . . . I parted and yede [went] out of the garden, and found in my way two priests and two clerks that I had. And I said to them that I would make a book of examples for to teach my daughters, that they might understand how they should govern *them* and know good from evil.

And so I made *t*hem extract me examples of the Bible and other books that I had, as the gests of kings, the chronicles of France, Greece, of England, and of many other strange lands. And I made them read me every book, and there that I found a good example, I made extract it out, and then I made this book. But I would not set it in rhyme but in prose, for to abridge it and that it might be better and more plainly to be unders*t*ood.

And I made this book for the great love that I had to my said daughters, the which I loved as father ought to love his child, having heartily joy to find ways to steer and turn *t*hem to goodness and worship and to love and serve their Creator and to have love of *t*heir neighbours and of the world. And, therefore, all fathers and mothers, after good nature, ought to teach their children to leave all wrong and evil ways and shew *t*hem the true right way, as well for the salvation of the soul as for the worship of the worldly body.

THE MARSHAL OF FRANCE AND THE LADIES. Yet I will tell you more on this matter [of reproving a man openly in company]—how Boucicaut was among three ladies that cast for to have made him ashamed. And he, that was a wise knight amongs*t* all other knights, help*ed* him as ye shall hear.

These three ladies sat together in a privy chamber and talked of their adventures, unto the time that one said, "Much maugre [ill-will] have she of us that will not tell, of good fellowship here among us three, of that she shall be asked, that is, if any of us was this year prayed of love.

"Truly," said the first, "I have been prayed."

The second and the third said the same.

"Now," said the boldest lady, "Sorry love have she that telleth not the name of him that last prayed her." And there they were accorded they should tell.

"Forsooth," said the first, "It was Boucicaut that prayed me."

"And in good sooth," said the second, "So did he me."

"By my troth," quoth the third, "And he prayed me also."

"In good faith," said the three ladies, "He nis not so true a knight as we weened, for he is but a trumper and a japer, no force. Let us send for him."

And when he came, he said, "My ladies, what would ye?"

And they bade him sit down on the ground by them. And he said, "Since I am come and must sit, let me have some cushion or a stool, for I might, an I sat low, break some of my points, and ye would say, peradventure, it were somewhat else."

And so they got him a stool, and, when he was set, as they that were full of ire and wrath, said, "Boucicaut, we are foul deceived in you the time past, for we weened that ye had be a true knight, and ye are but a mocker and a japer of ladies, and that is a foul tache [blot]."

And he answered, "Ladies, how know ye that?"

"For, sire, ye have here prayed my cousin of love, and so have ye me, and ye said ye loved us and each of us had your heart—the which was false leesing [lying], for ye might *not* love us all three best, for ye are not three persons, nor ye have not three hearts, and therefore ye are false and deceivable, and ye ought not to be set in the number of true knights."

And he said, "Ladies, ye have wrong, and that will I shew you, an ye will give me leave to speak—and I will tell you why. For at that time I spake with each of you I loved her best that I spake with and thought truly the same, and methinketh, therefore, ye be in the wrong to have such language on me—but I must suffer."

And when they saw him no more abashed, they said they would draw cut among them there, to wit to whom he should abide.

"In good faith," said the first lady, "I will draw no cut for him, for I quit my part of him."

And that other two ladies said, "So do we our part, for we will not of him."

"Ah!" said the knight, "Ye need not strive, for she nis not here that shall have part of me."

And, with that, he rose and yede [went] his way and let the three ladies be there, all abashed and shamed.

And, therefore, it is a great peril to begin to have language with such men that can [know] skill of the world.

ON LOVE PARAMOURS. My dear daughters, as for to love par amours, I shall tell you all the debate and strife of me and of your mother . . .

Thus, then, I said to your mother, "Lady, why shall not the ladies and damsels love par amours? For, in certain, meseemeth that in good love and true may be but wealth and honor, and also the lover is the better therefor, and more gay and jolly, and also the more encouraged to exercise himself more oft in arms. And taketh therefore better manner in all estates, for to please unto his lady or love. And in like wise doth she of whom he is enamoured, for to please him the better, as far as she loveth him. And also I tell you that great alms [well-doing] it is when a lady or damsel maketh a good knight or a good squire." These be my reasons.

Then answered to me your mother, "Sire, I marvel me not if, among you, men sustain and hold this reason that all women ought to love par amours. But sith this debate and strife is come before our own daughters, I will answer after mine advice and intention [understanding], for unto our children we must hide nothing.

"Ye say, and so do all other men, that a lady or damsel is the better worth when she loveth par amours, and that she shall be the more gay and of fair manner and countenance, and how she shall do great alms to make a good knight. These words are but sport and esbatement [play] of lords and of fellows, in a language much common. For they that say that all the honor and worship which they get and have is coming to them by their paramours, and that their love encourageth them to go in viages [travel] and for to please to them by estate of arms.

"But these words cost to them but little to say for to get the better and sooner the grace and good will of their paramours. For of such words, and others much marvellous, many *a* one useth full oft. But, howbeit that they say that 'For them and for their love they do it,' in good faith, they do it only for to enhance themself and for to draw unto them the grace and vainglory of the world.

"Therefore, I charge you, my fair daughters, that in this matter ye believe not your father. But I pray you that ye hold yourself cleanly and without blame, and that ye be not amorous, for many reasons which I shall rehearse unto you.

"First, I say not but that every good woman of age may love well and better the one than the other, that is to wit, folk of worship and honor and them also that shall counsel her for her own health and worship. And thus men ought to love, by this manner, the one more than the other. But, as for to be so far forth enamoured, in so much that this love be master of her and maketh them to fall in some foul and shameful delight, sometimes with right and sometimes with wrong . . . all women which be not wedded may keep and hold themself fro it. And that for many reasons. The first reason is because that a woman which is enamoured of a man may not serve God of no good heart ne true as she did before. . . . Whereof I shall tell you an example.

"Two queens were at this side of the sea, which in Lent, upon the Holy Thursday in the Passion week, took their foul delights and pleasaunce within the church during the service divine and rested not of their folly till it was all done. Wherefore, God, which was displeased with them for their enorm and foul sin, made their foul deed and feat to be openly known among the folk, in such wise that they were taken and put under a great and heavy cope of lead. And there they died of an evil death. And the two knights, their putiers [whoremasters], died also, as they that were flayed, being yet alive.

"The other reason is because of many gentlemen which be so false and deceivable that they require every gentlewoman that they may find. And to them they swear that they shall keep to them their faith and be true to them, and shall love them without falsehood or deceivance, and that rather they should die than to think any villainy or dishonor, and that they shall be the better praised for the love of them, and that if they have any good and worship it shall come by them. And thus they shall shew and say to them so many reasons and abusions that a great marvel is to hear *them* speak. And yet more, they give out of their breasts great and feigned sighs, and make as they were thinking and melancholious, and, after, they cast a false look. And then the good and debonair women that see them suppose that they be esprised [seized] of true and faithful love.

"But all such manner of folk which usen to make such semblant be but deceivers or beguilers of the ladies and damsels. For there is no lady ne damsel that would hear them but that they should be deceived of them by their false reasons, which they should not hear. These be contrary to the faithful and true lovers. For he that loveth with good and true love, as he cometh before his paramours, he is fearing and dreadful lest he do anything that may displease her."

William Caxton

"REYNARD THE FOX"

REYNARD'S PILGRIMAGE. Isegrim *the wolf* came proudly over the field before the king, and he thanked the queen, and spake with a fell mood ill words on the fox, in such wise that the king heard it and was wroth, and made the wolf and the bear anon to be arrested. Ye saw never wood [mad] dogs do more harm than was done to them. They were both fast bound, so sore that all that night they might not stir hand ne foot. They might scarcely roar ne move any joint.

Now hear how the fox forth did. He hated them. He laboured so to the queen that he got leave for to have as much of the bear's skin upon his ridge [back] as a foot long and a foot broad, for to make him thereof a scrip. Then was the fox ready, if he had four strong shoon [shoes]. Now hear how he did for to get these shoon.

He said to the queen, "Madam, I am your pilgrim. Here is mine eme [uncle], Sir Isegrim, that hath four strong shoon which were good for me. If he would let me have two of them I would on the way busily think on your soul, for it is right that a pilgrim should

alway think and pray for them that do him good. Thus may ye do
your soul good if ye will. And also if ye might get of mine aunt,
Dame Arsewind, also two of her shoon to give me, she may well
do it, for she goeth but little out but abideth alway at home."

Then said the queen, "Reynart, you behooveth well such shoon.
Ye may not be without them. They shall be good for you to keep
your feet whole for to pass with them many a sharp mountain and
stony rocks. Ye can find no better shoes for you than such as
Isegrim and his wife have and wear. They be good and strong.
Though it should touch their life, each of them shall give you two
shoes for to accomplish with your high pilgrimage.

Thus hath this false pilgrim gotten from Isegrim two shoes fro
his feet, which were haled off, the claws to the sinews. Ye saw
never fowl that men roasted lie so still as Isegrim did when his
shoes were haled off. He stirred not, and yet his feet bled. Then,
when Isegrim was unshod, then must Dame Arsewind his wife lie
down in the grass with an heavy cheer. And she lost there her
hinder shoes.

Then was the fox glad, and said to his aunt in scorn, "My dear
aunt, how much sorrow have ye suffered for my sake!—which me
sore repenteth, save this: hereof I am glad, for ye are the liefest of
all my kin. Therefore I will gladly wear your shoon. Ye shall be
partner of my pilgrimage, and deal [share] of the pardon that I
shall with your shoon fetch over the sea."

Dame Arsewind was so woe that she unnethe might speak.
Nevertheless, this she said, "Ah, Reynart, that ye now all thus have
your will, I pray God to wreke [avenge] it!"

Isegrim and his fellow the bear held their peace and were all
still. They were evil at ease, for they were bound and sore
wounded. Had Tibert the cat have been there, he should also somewhat have suffered, in such wise as he should not escaped thence
without hurt and shame.

The next day, when the sun arose, Reynard then did grease his
shoes which he had of Isegrim and Arsewind his wife, and did
them on, and bound them to his feet, and went to the king and to
the queen and said to them with a glad cheer, "Noble lord and
lady, God give you good morrow, and I desire of your grace that
I may have male [wallet] and staff blessed, as belongeth to a
pilgrim."

Then the king anon sent for Bellin the ram, and when he came, he said, "Sir Bellin, ye shall do mass tofore Reynart, for he shall go on pilgrimage. And give to him male and staff."

The ram answered again and said, "My lord, I dare not do that, for he hath said that he is in the Pope's curse."

The king said: "What thereof? Master Gelys hath said to us, If a man had do as many sins as all the world and he would those sins foresake, shrive them and receive penance, and do by the priest's counsel, God will forgive them and be merciful unto him. Now will Reynard go over the sea into the Holy Land, and make him clear of all his sins."

Then answered Bellin to the king, "I will not do little ne much herein but-if ye save me harmless in the spiritual court before the bishop Prendelor and tofore his archdeacon Loosewind and tofore Sir Rapiamus his official."

The king began to wax wroth, and said, "I shall not bid you so much in half a year! I had liefer hang you than I should so much pray you for it!"

When the ram saw that the king was angry, he was so afeared that he quoke for fear, and went to the altar and sang in his books, and read such as him thought good over Reynart, which little set thereby, save that he would have the worship [honor] thereof.

When Bellin the ram had all said his service devoutly, then he hung on the fox's neck a male covered with the skin of Bruin the bear and a little palster [pilgrim's staff] thereby. Then was Reynard ready toward his journey. Then looked he toward the king as if he had been sorrowful to depart, and feigned as he had wept, right as he had yammered in his heart. But, if he had any sorrow, it was because all the others that were there were not in the same plight as the wolf and bear were brought in by him. Nevertheless, he stood and prayed them all to pray for him, like as he would pray for them. The fox thought that he tarried long, and would fain have departed—for he knew himself guilty.

The king said, "Reynart, I am sorry ye be so hasty and will no longer tarry."

"Nay, my lord, it is time, for we ought not spare to do well. I pray you to give me leave to depart. I must do my pilgrimage."

The king said, "God be with you!" and commanded all them of the court to go and convey Reynard on his way—save the wolf and

the bear, which fast lay bound. There was none that durst be
sorry therefor, and if ye had seen Reynard, how parson-ably he
went with his male and palster on his shoulder and the shoes on
his feet, ye should have laughed. He went and showed him outward wisely, but laughed in his heart that all they brought him
forth which had a little before been with him so wroth. And also
the king which so much hated him—he had made him such a fool
that he brought him to his own intent. He was a pilgrim of
deuce-ace.

"My lord the king," said the fox, "I pray you to return again. I
will not that ye go any further with me. Ye might have harm
thereby. Ye have there two murderers arrested. If they escape
you, ye might be hurt by them. I pray God keep you from misadventure!" With these words, he stood up on his after-feet and
prayed all the beasts, great and small, that would be partners of
his pardon, that they should pray for him. They said that they all
would remember him. Then departed he from the king so heavily
that many of them ermed [grieved].

Then said he to Coward the hare and to Bellin the ram, merrily,
"Dear friends, shall we now depart? Ye will, an God will, accom-
pany me further. Ye two made me never angry. Ye be good for to
walk with, courteous, friendly, and not complained on of any
beast. Ye be of good conditions and ghostly of your living. Ye live
both as I did when I was a recluse. If ye have leaves and grass,
ye be pleased—ye reck not of bread, of flesh, ne such manner
meat." With such flattering words hath Reynard these two flat-
tered, that they went with him till they came tofore his house,
Malpertuis.

Romancers

FROM THE FIRST DECADE of the thirteenth century it became common in France to adapt the more popular romances and chansons de geste into prose and sometimes to assemble them into cycles, loosely connected by genealogical details or by inserted cross-allusions. In this way the heroic legends of Greece and Rome, Britain, and France, and a number of other less familiar topics, most of them legendary or historical, made their appearance in French prose and provided occasions for the development of that unemphatic, unhurried, and well-mannered language and those well-ordered narrative techniques which were the social inheritance of such writers as De Joinville, Froissart, Geoffrey de la Tour-Landry, or Antoine de la Salle. In similar fashion, though for a scholarly audience, the more serious of these stories were sometimes turned into Latin prose.

When English came into its own in the mid-fourteenth century, therefore, extended narratives equivalent to our novels were available in both verse and prose and in French and Latin. As the writings of Chaucer, Lydgate, and the northwestern alliterative poets indicate, the English inclination was toward verse—witness the several poetic treatments of the story of Troy based upon the Latin prose of Guido delle Colonne. But now and then the fifteenth-century English translators followed their sources in adopting prose. Most of the examples are Caxton's translations of popular books on the chief subjects, *The History of Troy, Jason, Aeneid, Charles the Great, The Four Sons of Aymon,* and *Godfrey of Bologne,* and his versions of two minor recent romances, *Paris and Vienne* and *Blanchardyn and Eglantine.* Caxton was not alone, however; Malory's *Le Morte Darthur,* an earlier *Merlin,* prose epitomes of the stories of Troy and Thebes, *Ponthus and Sidone,* several versions of the *Life of Alexander, Melusine, Ipomedon,* and *The Three Kings of Cologne* are others. The style of these translations varies with the sources; except for Malory's none of them is a masterpiece but several are written in competent prose of a simple kind and since they recount stories that are still interesting and also represent the milieu of narrative prose to which Malory's must be related we represent them by some characteristic episodes.

The first heroic stories to be turned into French verse recounted the activities of Charlemagne and his peers and the feudal conflicts between French kings and their vassals. Despite the renown of the *Chanson de Roland*, the most popular of these stories were those gathered together as the cycle of Doon de Mayence, which related the conflicts of Charlemagne with his barons—among them Ogier the Dane, Huon of Bordeaux, and the four sons of Aymon. The story of the last-named is a medieval "western," recounting Aymon's rise in favor at Charlemagne's court, a quarrel that leads Renaud de Montauban, Aymon's son, into killing the emperor's nephew, Renaud's flight to the Ardennes with his brothers and the emperor's pursuit, further attacks and resistance in Gascony and later on the Rhine, the settlement of the feud, Renaud's pilgrimage to the Holy Land, his conversion, and his martyr-death in Cologne while working as a mason on the new cathedral. Originally written in epic verse in the late twelfth century, this poem about the four sons of Aymon was soon turned into prose, and it was from a late prose-version that Caxton translated his, *The Four Sons of Aymon*, in 1489. The story is lengthy, and from it we choose the episode that sets off the long feud. The style, even at this late remove, preserves some of the oral formulae and rhetoric of the original poem, and it is marred by many a French word and syntactical construction. But, following the French closely, it is also largely free from the stretched-out sentences and wandering syntax that characterizes Caxton's original work, and it has the great advantage of a source that is lively in action and conflict.

When in the mid-twelfth century, French poets began to look beyond their own history for heroic subjects, they turned first to classical story; and it was the turning of these into a romance vernacular that first gave the name romance to the long quasi-historical narrative. The procedure determines many of the characteristics of the form; historical in its sources, fictional in its development, it vacillates between fact and fancy, instruction and entertainment, classical and medieval interests.

This is particularly true of the romances that describe the campaigns, triumphs, and ultimate tragedy of that nonpareil of supermen, the medieval Alexander. The core of this career—his birth, education by Aristotle, campaigns in Africa, Greece, Persia, India, his founding of cities, his early death—is firm in the classical facts. The emphasis and elaboration—his supernatural birth, adventures with strange monsters and still stranger men, travels toward the Earthly Paradise, love for Candace, even the colloquies with Brahmin-hermits—these are the reflex of medieval wonder at an oriental and phantasmagorical world, the rich, strange lands of Prester John and the Grand Cham. Of all classical heroes, Alexander was the most popular in England and Scotland in the latter Middle Ages. There are several full-scale treatments, most of them poetical but some in prose. From a competent prose version of about 1400, an abridged translation of the archpriest Leo's *Historia de Preliis,* we have selected the episode of Alexander's campaign against Porus of India, after his victories over Darius and the Amazons.

The success of these first classical romances soon stimulated Thomas, Béroul, Chrétien de Troyes, and other northern French poets to draw into the treasury of heroic narrative the matter of Britain, the stories of Tristan, Arthur, Lancelot, Gawain, and the Table Round, and to salt them with relevance to the moral and social problems of their own time. It is from the prosings of their work, made in the first half of the thirteenth century, that Malory derives the matter and some elements of the style of his great cycle. But he was not the first to do so. A few years before, about 1450, another Englishman translated the prose *Merlin,* a long French romance that deals mainly with Arthur's accession to the throne and his early wars. Unlike Malory, this writer was content to translate word for word, without kindly abbreviation, so that his style is seamed with French locutions and retains the unhurried loquaciousness that Malory avoided.

The passage that has been selected from this anonymous version is the sword-in-the-stone episode by which Arthur is miraculously shown to be Uther Pendragon's true successor: it begins just after the discovery of the stone outside the cathedral—"A great stone, four square . . . and above, in the middle place of this stone, there stood a stith [block] of iron that was largely half a foot of height, and through the stith was a sword fixed into the stone . . . and letters of gold in the steel . . . that said, 'Who taketh this sword out of this stone should be king by the election of Jesu Christ.' " The style of the episode and of the translation as a whole is easy, clear, and well-ordered but it is twice as long as Malory's version, and comparison will show readily the directness and energy that Malory achieved by his own method of selective translation.

Few would enter a rival against the claim that Malory was the best writer of narrative prose among the Englishmen of his time. But that his style was completely *sui generis,* as has been claimed, is unlikely. The basic elements—a markedly native vocabulary of familiar sort, varied by occasional dialectal, colloquial, or French terms; reiteration of favored words and phrases, almost as formulae; a steady, though subtly varied, rhythm that flows from the use of a few syntactical structures, arranged as compound and compound-complex sentences with units of similar length; a nice balance of exposition, dialogue, description, and comment; supremacy of verbs and nouns over adjectives and adverbs; the thinning down of the original material toward its most vivid and dramatic elements; gusto and bright energy; a high sense of chivalry; and an accompanying touch of romantic nostalgia—all these, together with linguistic and intellectual traits that are not nearly so obvious, fuse into a manner of translation that bears Sir Thomas' own clear hallmark.

It is rash, however, to assert that Malory owes nothing to the style of his French book—some prose collection as yet unidentified, but one close to the Vulgate Cycle and the Tristan—which he translated and abbreviated, skipping from one key-phrase to another, and paraphrasing when necessary. Except for the abbreviation and paraphrase, his method is essentially the same as that of the other translators of the time and as a result his prose commonly matches French versions word for word, phrase for phrase, rhythm for rhythm, and his grammar and diction are sprinkled with Gallicisms.

To represent the matter and manner of *Le Morte Darthur*, we select one of the basic episodes of Arthurian romance, the Knight of the Cart story that was first set down by Chrétien de Troyes. The basis is Caxton's text, which is of no less authority than the Winchester text that Vinaver has edited.

Our concluding specimen of prose-romance is taken from *Melusine,* one of the last products of medieval aristocratic romance: it was composed in 1387 by Jean d'Arras at the direction of the great bibliophile, Jean, Duc de Berry, and for the pleasure of the Duchesse de Bar. Two English translations were made late in the fifteenth century, one in verse, the other a prose version of the French text that was printed at Geneva in 1478. The story, a form of the Lamia legend but here associated with the great French family of Lusignan, revolves around the lamentable history of Melusine and her two sisters, daughters of a fairy-mother who had been made vengeful by the default of her mortal husband. Every Saturday, Melusine is transformed partly into a serpent; she marries, keeping her nature secret from Raymondin, her husband, but the secret is discovered and tragedy follows. Our selection is the episode in which Raymondin learns the secret. The anonymous prose translation is a competent one, closely following the flowing, compound-complex sentences, the unaccentuated rhythm, the ornate eloquence, and the unsparing detail of the French original.

William Caxton

"THE FOUR SONS OF AYMON"

YE SHALL NOW hear and understand from this henceforth a terrible and piteous song, if ye thereafter list to hearken.

This was at the feast of Pentecost, after the Holy Thursday, that the King Charlemagne held a great court in Paris, after that he had accorded with the brethren of the Duke Benes of Aigremont. And to the said feast came William the English, Galleron of Boulogne, fifteen kings and thirty dukes. And well sixty earls were there at that day, for to crown Charlemagne. And also was come there the Duke Aymon of Dordogne with his four sons, that is to wit, Renaud, Alard, Richard, and Guichard.

To the which Aymon, the king said, "Aymon," said he, "I love you and your children well. And wit that I will make of the fair Renaud my steward, and the others shall serve me for to bear my falcons and go with me."

"Sire," said the good Aymon, "I thank you much of the great worship that ye do to me and to my children. And wit that they shall serve you truly as your liegemen. But well I tell you, good king, that ye misprised [misjudged] sore when my brother, the Duke Benes of Aigremont, under your safe-conduct and in treason, ye made thus shamefully die. And believe that it grieveth me full sore at heart. And if we doubted not you so much, certes, vengeance we should take thereof. But sith that my brother Gerard hath pardoned it to you, I forgive it you also."

"Aymon," sid the king, "Ye know better than that ye say. For ye know well the offence that your brother had done to me, for to have slain so cruelly Lohier, my eldest son, that I loved so much. Now set the one against the other, and let be spoken no more thereof."

"No more we shall," said Duke Aymon. "But well I pray God to have mercy of his soul, for he was a right worthy knight."

Then came forth Renaud, Alard, Guichard, and Richard, which reasoned with the king, saying in this manner. "Sir," said Renaud, the fairest of all knights and most expert in feats of knighthood, "ye have made me and my brethren that be now here afore you, knights. But, wit it for very certain that we love you not, and that we have toward you a great and a mortal hate for the death of our uncle, the Duke Benes of Aigremont, of the which death ye have not accorded with us."

When the king understood Renaud, he looked grimly and fiercely in his visage for great wrath, and became black as a coal, and smote his forehead for anger. And after said to Renaud, "Thou young boy, void out of my presence! For I swear thee, by Saint Simon, and-if it were not the company of the barons that be here, I should make ye to be put in such a prison that thou shouldest not see neither hand nor foot that thou hast."

"Sire," said Renaud, "It were not reason. But sith that it is so far come that ye will not hear us, we shall keep our peace."

Thus left the four sons of Aymon the debate, and spake nomore to the King Charlemagne for that time of this matter. Fair was the court, and the day was full fair and bright. And fair was the company, as of fifteen kings, thirty dukes, and sixty earls. They went to the church for to hear the fair mass that was sung, and much rich was the offering. And when they had heard the mass, they came again to the palace, and asked after water for to wash their hands. And the dinner was ready, so they washed and set them down to dinner. And the fifteen kings were all set, except the King Solomon, that served that day with the Duke Godfrey.

But Renaud at this dinner might not eat, because that the King Charlemagne had rebuked him so shamefully. "Ha!" said Renaud to himself. "Alas, how shall I con [be able to] do so much that I may avenge myself of Charlemagne for the death of my uncle that so much was beloved, which traitorously and shamefully hath he slain. And if I take no vengeance of it, I shall wax mad." In this wise sorrowed the good Renaud, and his brethren re-comforted him.

The barons came out after dinner for to play and sport themselves; and Berthelot, the nephew of Charlemagne, called Renaud for to play with him. Whereof grew a great mischief, for afterward many a good knight died therefor and many a fair child was fatherless, as hereafter ye shall hear if ye hearken well.

Now was set Berthelot and the worthy Renaud for to play at

the chess, which were of ivory, whereof the board was of gold-massive. And so long they played that debate fell between them two, by such manner that Berthelot called Renaud "Whoreson" and took up his hand and smote Renaud in the visage, so that the blood fell to the ground.

And when Renaud saw himself thus shamefully outraged, he was right wroth and sore angered, and swore, "By God, him should ill betide!" Therefore, then took Renaud the chess-board and smote Berthelot upon his head so hard, that he clove him to the teeth. And thus Berthelot fell down dead to the ground afore him.

So began the cry at that hour sore strong in the palace, that Renaud, the son of Aymon, had slaid Berthelot, the nephew of King Charlemagne. When the king understood this, he went nigh out of his wit and called on high, "Barons! Keep well that Renaud scape not, for, by St. Denis of France, he shall not escape quick [alive] if we may hold him. For he hath slain our nephew Berthelot."

Then ran soon the knights upon Renaud, and his kinsmen defended him nobly. And thus was there great strife, and many hairs pulled and many gowns torn. For such affray was there never seen as that day was in the palace of Paris. Many strokes gave there Maugis, the cousin of Renaud and son to the Duke Benes of Aigremont. And while that this fray was in the palace, Renaud and his three brethren and their cousin Maugis escaped readily out of the palace and came to their horses, that soon were made ready. So lighted they on horseback, and rode soon out of Paris, and fled straight to Dordogne, toward their lady-mother.

And when the Emperor Charlemagne wist that Renaud and his brethren were gone out of Paris, he made to be ready well two thousand knights for to follow them. Now keep them, Our Lord that on the cross suffered passion! For if the king hold them, they shall die without remission.

But Renaud, on him is no care, for he was upon his horse Bayard, that goeth as the wind. So tarried not the four brethren and their cousin, till that they came to Saumur and they baited [fed] their horses of Alard, Richard, and Guichard.

Then began Renaud to make sorrow, saying, "Fair God that suffered death and passion, keep this day my brethren and my cousin from the death and from cumbrance and from falling in the hands of Charlemagne the cruel!"

And of the other part, chased them the Frenchmen, broaching with the spur as fast as their horses might run—so much that a knight, that was better horsed than the others were, overtook Renaud and said to him, "Ye shall abide, ye untrue knight, and I shall bring you to King Charlemagne."

And when Renaud heard him, he turned Bayard against him, and smote the knight with his spear in his shield, and reached him with so great a might that stark-dead he overthrew him. So scaped [set free] Renaud the knight's horse, and took him to his brother Alard, that lighted anon upon the back of him. And after that he was upon this good horse, he went and smote another knight with his sword, so that he made him fall all dead afore him. And so betook this knight's horse to his brother Guichard, that thanked him much for it. And another knight of the King Charlemagne came to them.

"Gluttons!" said the knight, "Ye shall come to the king, that shall make you all to be hanged."

"Ha, by my faith!" said Renaud, "Thou shalt lie." And with this, Renaud took up his sword and give him such a stroke that he overthrew him, dead at the ground. Then took Renaud the horse by the rein, and gave him to his brother Richard, that great need had of it.

Now be the three brethren new-horsed, and Renaud is upon Bayard, and his cousin Maugis, that he loved so well, behind him. Now they go! God will lead them and keep them from evil. And Charlemagne pursued after them, but for naught he travailed, for they were never the rather [sooner] taken for him. Then was the sun gone under and the night began to come. And the four brethren and their cousin were come into the town of Soissons.

So much rode Renaud by night and by day upon Bayard, that bore him and Maugis his cousin, that they came to Dordogne. There they met with the Duchess, their mother, that ran for to kiss them and coll [embrace] them, and sin [after] asked what they had done of their father, and if they were departed from the court with wrath.

"Lady," said Renaud, "Yea! For I have slain Berthelot, the

nephew of King Charlemagne. The reason why I did so was because he called me 'whore-son' and gave me with his fist upon my visage, so that the blood run out of it."

And when the lady understood him, she fell down all in a swoon, and Renaud took her up readily.

And when the good lady was come again to herself, she said to Renaud, "Fair Son, how durst ye do this that ye have done, for I promise you ye shall only repent for it. And your father shall be destroyed therefor and cast out of his lands. And if ye scape alive, it shall be great marvel. So pray I you, all my children, that ye flee away. But take afore all my treasure, for if your father come again from the court, he shall will [wish to] yield you to the King Charlemagne."

"Lady," said Renaud, "Ween ye that our father is so cruel and so wroth with us that he would take and deliver us into the hands of the King Charlemagne, that is our great enemy mortal?"

Renaud, his three brethren, and Maugis would make none other sojourning, but took so much of the avoir [possessions] and treasure of their father and mother that they had enough of it. And then took they their leave of their lady-mother. Whereof there was great pity at the departing, for the children wept tenderly, and the mother also of the other side, when she saw that her children thus went fro her, and wist not if she should ever see them again.

So departed the new knights with their cousin Maugis, and issued out of the town and entered into the great forest of Arden, straight through the valley of Faerie. And rode so much that they came upon the river of Meuse. And there they chose a fair ground, where they made to be builded a fair castle upon a fair rock, much strong, and at the foot of it passed the said river of Meuse. And when that the castle was made up, they called it Mountainford, and, as I trow, there was not such another of strength fro the said place unto Montpélier, for it was closed with great walls and environed round about with ditches sore deep, and well garnished with all manner of victuals and of all things be needful to be had in a fortress. Now doubt the new knights nothing of Charlemagne —if he wrought not by treason.

THE LIFE OF ALEXANDER

TRANS. FROM LEO'S "HISTORIA DE PRELIIS"

IN THE MEANTIME, it was told Alexander that Porus, the king of
India, was in Bactria and assembled a great host for to fight eftsoons with him. And when Alexander heard this, he removed his
host, and chose out 150 of divers that knew the country for to have
the governance of his host and to lead them surely through that
strange country.

In the month of August, when the sun is most hot, they began
for to take their journey. And they went through a dry country,
sandy and withouten water. And needlings [perforce], them behoved *to* wend armed, there was so great plenty of adders and
cruel wild beasts. For these foresaid guides were more favorable
to Porus than to Alexander and his host, and therefore they led
them through such barren and perilous countries.

And when Alexander saw it shaped thus, and *w*hat his counsel
before had said the truth; that is *to* say, both his own friends and
men of Caspia, that counselled him that he should not hie him
overfast ne trust too much to strangers, then he commanded that
all men should wend armed. And so they did. And then all the
host shone right as it had been stars, for some of their armours
were of gold, some of silver, and some of precious stones.

And when Alexander saw the array of his host, and their banners before them, shining so fair, he was right glad. Nevertheless,
great dis-ease he had that neither he ne his men might find no
water.

So it fell that a knight of Macedonia that hight Zephilus found
water standing in an hollow stone, that was gathered there of the
dew of the heaven. The which this foresaid knight put in his
basnet [helmet], and brought it to Alexander for to drink. And
Alexander said unto him, "I suppose," quoth he, "that I drink this
water. Shall the Macedonians and the Persians be anything refreshed thereby? Or I shall have all the refreshing by myself?"

And he answered and said, "Thou alone, lord," quoth he, "shall be comforted thereby."

Quoth Alexander then, "And if ye shall all perish, trowest thou that it should be liking to me for to live in sorrow and dis-ease, seeing the dead of the Macedonians and the Persians?" And belive [quickly] he gart hell down [caused to be thrown down] the water on the earth before all his men. And when his knights saw that, they were hugely comforted thereby, right as each one of them had drunken a great draught of water. And then went forth their way.

And on the morn they came to a river, whose banks was growing full of great reeds, and they were as high as pine-trees; yea, for the most part, of forty foot long. Then bade *he* that they draw of the water and bring to the host. But all that drank thereof, it cast them into a flux and slew a great heap of them. For that water was wonder sharp, and as bitter as any great grass.[1]

But then was Alexander greatly dis-eased and all his host, not only of themselves but also for their horses and their beasts that they led with them, the which began for to fail for thirst. Alexander had with him a thousand elephants that bore his gold, and four hundred carts of war, and 1200 wains. He had also in his host 300,000 horsemen, and mules and camels withouten number, that bore their victuals and other things that was necessary to the host. Also oxen and *kine*, sheep and swine withouten number, the which perished for default of drink.

Some of Alexander's knights licked iron, some drank oil, and some were at so great mischief that they drank their own staling [urine]. And there was so great abundance of adders and other venomous beasts that them behoved needs travel armed. And that was a great *annoy* to them and an high dis-ease. Then was Alexander wonder sorry and namely for the dis-ease that his host suffered.

And as they went along this river, about the eigh*th* hour of the day, they came to a castle that stood in a little isle in this foresaid river. And this castle was made of the foresaid reeds. The breadth of this river was four furlong length. And in that castle they saw a few men. And then Alexander bade his man speer [ask] them that were in the castle, in the language of India, where they might

[1] *hellbore* in the Latin.

find any sweet water, able for to drink. And as soon as they spake
to them, they withdrew them and hid. And Alexander gart shoot
[caused to be shot] arrows into the castle; and then they hid them
well the more. And when Alexander saw that they would in no
wise speak with him, he had a certain [few] of his knights naked
them and swim over the water to the castle. And then thirty-seven
bold knights and hardy of Macedonia naked them, and took each
one of them a sword in his hand, and went into the water and
swam it till they were past the fourth part thereof. And, suddenly,
there rose out of the water a great multitude of beasts, that are
called hippopotami, greater of body than an elephant, and devoured these knights every one. And then was Alexander right
sore grieved, and belive [quickly] gart take the foresaid guides
(150) and cast them into the water. And anon the hippopotami
devoured them.

And Alexander thought it was not speedful [profitable] longer
to strive with those monsters, and gart trump up, and removed
his host fro thence, and went so all that day, wonder weary for
thirst. And also they had great dis-ease and *an*noy of wild beasts
that came upon them, that is to say, of lions, bears, unicorns,
tigers, and pards, with the which they fought and great travail
had.

And, as they went on this wise, with great anger and dis-ease,
about the eleventh hour they saw a little boat in the river, made
of reeds, and men rowing therein. And Alexander gart speer
[asked] them in the language of India, where they might find any
fresh water. And they told where, and shewed them a place a
little thence, wherein they said they should find a great stang
[pond] of sweet water and good. And then Alexander and his
host went all about that river, and came to this foresaid stang
and lodged them about it. And Alexander commanded that they
should fell a wood that growed fast thereby, three mile on length
and as much on breadth. That wood was all of the reeds that I
spake of before, and the stang was a mile on length. Then Alexander commanded that they should make many fires in the host,
and gart trump to the meat.

And as soon as the moon began to shine, there came a great
multitude of scorpions toward the stang, for to take them a drink.
And then there came other manner of adders, and dragons wonder

great, of diverse colors. And all that country resounded of the noise and the hissings that they made. These dragons came down fro the high mountains for to drink of the stang, and they had crests on their heads, and their breasts were bright like gold, and their mouths open. Their onde [breath] slew any quick thing that it smote upon, and out of their eyen there came flames of fire.

And when Alexander and his host saw them, they were right afeared for them, for they weened they should have weried [attacked] them each one. And then Alexander comforted them, and said unto them, "My worshipful knights," quoth he, "Be not aghast of them, but do each as ye see me do." And then he took a net and set it betwixt him and them, and took his shield and his spear, and fought with them manfully. And when his knights saw that, they were greatly comforted, and belive [quickly] took their weapons and did as they saw Alexander do. And slew of them a great multitude, what through divers weapons, what in their fires. And of Alexander's knights, the dragons slew twenty, and thirty footmen.

After them, there came out of the foresaid wood of reeds, crabs of a wonderful greatness, and their backs were harder than cockadrils. And when the knights smote them on the backs with their spears, they might not pierce them, ne no harm do them. Nevertheless, they slew many of them in their fires, and the remnant of them got into the stang. And about the sixth hour of the night, there came upon them white lions greater than bulls, and they shook their heads at them, and great menace made in their manner. Then the knights keped [captured] them in their nets, and slew them. After this, there came upon them then a great multitude of swine that were all of a wonderful mickleness, with tusks of a cubit-length. And with them there came wild men and women, of the which each one had six hands. But Alexander and his knights keped them in their nets, and slew many of them. And in this wise, Alexander and his host was greatly dis-eased. Then commanded Alexander that they should make many fires withouten the host, about the stang.

After this, there came upon them a wonder great beast, greater and stronger than an elephant, and he had in his front three long horns. And he was shapen like a horse, and he was all black. And this beast was called in the language of India, 'Ondontotiranus.'

And ere he went to the water *to* drink, he assailed the host. But Alexander went here and there amongs*t* the host and comforted them. This same beast slew of his knights twenty-eight and bore down fifty-two, and at the last it fell in the nets and was slain.

After this, there came out of the reeds a great multitude of mice as great as foxes, and ate up the dead bodies. There was no quick things that they bit that ne all so soon it died. But harm they did none to the host. Then came there flying amongs*t* them bats greater than wild doves, and their teeth were like men-teeth, and they did men much dis-ease and hurt many men. Of some they bit off the noses, of some the ears. In the morning early, there came many fowls as great as vultures, red of color and their feet and their beaks all black. But they did no dis-ease to the host, but went to the stang-side and drew fishes and eels out of the water and ate them.

Then left Alexander these perilous places, and came with his host into the country of Bactria, the which was full of gold and other riches. And the men of the country received him benignly and worshipfully, and gave him and his host great gifts. And there he abode twenty days. In that country they saw trees that, instead of leaves, bore wool—the which folks of the country gathered and made cloth thereof. The knights of Alexander wax*ed* wonder bold and strong of heart because of the victories they had won of the wild beasts before named.

Fro thence Alexander removed his host, and came to the place where Porus lay with the folk that he had assembled. And on the morn both Alexander and Porus took their ground, and array*ed* their battles [divisions] for to fight. And then Alexander leapt upon his horse Bucephalus and went before his host. And then they trumped up, and the battles joined samen [together] and fought together right sore. But the Indians fell thickfold in the battle, as corn does in the field before the scythe.

And when Porus saw that, he went and stood before all his men, and cried unto Alexander and said on this wise; "It suits not to an emperor," quoth he, "to lose his men thus in vain. But it suits to him for to determine his cause with his own hands. And, therefore, let thy folk stand still on the one side and mine of the tother, and let thee and me fight together, hand for hand. And if it happen that thou overcome me, my folk and I shall be sub-

jects unto thee. And if I overcome thee, then thou and thy folks
be subjects unto me."

These words said Porus, despising Alexander because that he
was a man of little stature—for he was but three cubits high and
Porus was five cubits high and more. And, therefore, he trusted
him all in strength of his body, not knowing the virtue and the
hardness that was hid in Alexander.

And then both the hosts stood still and let the two kings fight
samen. Porus gave Alexander a great stroke on the head, and was
in point to have felled him. And then Porus's knights set up a great
shout, and Porus turned him to themward, for to 'prove them for
their shouting. And Alexander went to him manfully, and took his
sword in both his hands and let fly at him, and hit him full-butt
on the head and slew him. And when the Indians saw that, they
began sharply for to fight with Alexander and his host.

Unto whom, Alexander spake and said, "Wretches!" quoth he,
"Whereto fight ye, since your king is dead. Wot ye not well that
where no governor is the folk are sparpled [scattered] belive, as
sheep that are withouten an herd?"

The Indians answered and said, "Us is liefer," quoth they, "fight
manfully and die in the field, than for to see the desolation of our
folk and our land be destroyed and wasted."

"Leave your fighting," quoth Alexander, "And wend home to
your houses peaceably and surely. For I swear you by our gods,
if ye will do so ye shall have no harm, ne your land shall not be
destroyed ne spoiled, because that ye have foughten so manfully
for your king."

And when the Indians heard these words, they cast fro them
their weapons, and thanked Alexander, and worshipped him right
as he had been a god. Then King Alexander lodged him there, and
his host with him, and he commanded to bury the dead corpses
that were slain in the battle, and offered sacrifice to his gods. Also
he gart inter Porus the king of India worshipfully.

"MERLIN"

THEN THE GOOD MAN sang forth the mass, and when it was finished, they assembled about the stone, both one and other who that might take out this sword first. And then they said, and accorded all, that they should essay it as the ministers of holy church would assign. To this there was great discord among the highest men and most puissant; and they that had force said they would essay first. So there were many words that ought not to be rehearsed.

The archbishop spake that all might hear, and said, "Sirs, ye ne be not so wise, ne so well-advised men as I weened. And I will well that ye all wit that our Lord hath one chosen, but I know not whom. And thus much may I say to you, that gentleness [aristocracy] ne richesse shall have no power against the will of Jesu Christ. But trust so much in him that, if he that is thereto chosen were yet unborn, it shall never be taken out of the stone till he come that is ordained the honor."

Then accorded all the noble men and wise, and said that he had said sooth. And the wise men and the high barons took their counsel and accorded to stand the ordinance of the archbishop, and came again and said, hearing all the people.

And then made the bishop great joy and did weep for pity, and said. "This humility that is in your hearts is of God, and, I will that ye know after mine intent, shall be to the volunté of God and profit of Christian faith, so that I shall have no blame if God will."

This parliament was before high mass of the essay of the sword, till that high mass was said. Then said the archbishop to the people and shewed them the great miracle that God had done for them at this election, "and when our Lord set justice in earth, he set it in the stith [anvil] and in the sword, and the justice over the lay-people ought to be the sword, for the sword at the beginning was taken to the three orders to defend holy church and maintain righteousness. And our Lord hath now made election by the sword, and, wit it well, all that this have seen and beholden, to whom he will the justice give! And let no man be too hasty for to essay, for it shall never be drawn out for richesse ne for pride; ne the poor people be not displeased, though the lords and the high estates essay before, for it is right and reason that the lords essay first. For there ne is none of you but he ought to have his king and his lord the best and most worthy man that he could know by his reason."

Then they accorded to the archbishop with good heart and without evil will, that he should choose them that he would to essay first. Thus they granted all to hold him for their king to whom God would show his grace. Then the archbishop chose out one hundred and fifty of the highest and most worthy lords, and made them go to the essay. And when they had all essayed, then he commanded all others to essay. And then they essayed, all they, one after another, that essay would; but there was none that might it take out. And so it was commanded to be kept with ten noblemen, and they were charged to take good heed who came to essay, and if any there were that might draw out of the stone.

Thus was the sword essayed all the eight days, and all the barons were at high mass, and the archbishop them preached and shewed as him seemed best. And then he said, "I told you well that all by leisure might he come that was furthest fro the essay of this sword. Now may ye verily know that never none, save he that our Lord will, ne shall it not out take."

And then they said all, that they would not out of the town till they wist to whom God would grant that honor. In that manner they abode out the mass, and after they went to their hostels to meat; and after meat, as they were used that time, yede [went] the barons and the knights to bourd [sport] in a fair plain, and the ten men that were ordained to keep this sword yede also to see this bourdise.

And when the knights had tourneyed a while, they took their shields to their squires, so that the people of the town yede [should go] to arm them. And Antor [Hector] had made his eldest son knight at the hallowtide before Yule. And when the melée was begun, Kay called his brother Arthur, and said, "Go fast to our host and fetch my sword."

And Arthur was good and serviceable, and said, "With good will!" and then smote the horse with the spurs and rode forth to his hostel for to fetch his brother's sword, or else some other, if he might any find. And he found none, for the hostess had set it in her chamber. And so he turned to them again, and when he saw he might none find he gan to weep for great anger.

And as he came before the minster where the stone was, he saw the sword which he had never essayed, and thought, if he might it get, to bear it to his brother. And as he came thereby on horseback, he hent the sword by the hilts and drew it out, and covered it with his lap. And his brother that abode after without the town, saw him come and rode against him, and asked his sword. And Arthur said he might not have it—"but I have brought here another"—and drew it out from under his coat and took it to his brother.

And anon as Kay saw this sword, he knew it well that it was the sword of the stone, and thought he would be king, and said he would seek his father till he found him. And then he said, "Sire, I shall be king. Lo, here is the sword of the stone!"

When the father it saw, he had marvel how he it got. And he said he took it out of the stone.

When Antor heard that, he believed it not, but said he did lie. Then they yede to the minster where the stone was, and the tother squire after. When Antor saw the stone, and the sword not therein, he said, "Fair son, how had ye this sword? Look ye, do not lie! An thou do lie, I shall it know well, and never shall I thee love."

And he answered, as he that was sore ashamed, "I shall you lie no lesing [falsehood], for my brother Arthur it me brought when I bade him to go fetch mine. But I wot never how he it had."

When Antor heard this, he said, "Son, give it me, for ye have thereto no right."

And Kay it delivered to his father. And he looked behind him and saw Arthur, and cleped [called] him and said, "Come hither, fair son, and take this sword, and put it where as ye it took."

And he took the sword and put it in the stith, and it held as well or better than it did before. And Antor commanded his son Kay to take it out, and he essayed but it would not be. Then Antor cleped them both, and said to Kay, "I wist well that thou hadst not taken the sword out!" Then he took Arthur in his arms, and said, "Fair dear son, if I might purchase [arrange] that ye be king, what good should I have therefor?"

"Father," quoth he, "I may neither have that honor, ne none other good, but that ye be thereof lord, as my lord and my father."

And he said, "Sir, your father I am as in nurture, but certes I did you never engender, ne I wot never who did you engender."

When Arthur saw that Antor him denied to be his father, he wept tenderly and had great dole [sorrow] and said, "Fair sir, how should I have this dignity, or any other, when I have failed to have a father?"

"A father must ye need have; but, fair dear sir, if our Lord will that ye have this grace and I help you it to purchase, tell me what I shall be the better."

And Arthur said, "Sir, so as ye will yourself."

Then Antor told him what bounty he had him done, and how he had him nourished, and how he put away his son Kay and made him to be nourished of a strange woman—"wherefore, ye ought to give my son and me guerdon [reward], for there was never man more tenderly nourished than I have you. Wherefore, I pray you, if God give you this grace and I may help you thereto, that ye guerdon me and my son."

And Arthur said, "I pray you that ye deny not me to be my father, for then I should not wit whither that I should go; and if ye may help to purchase this grace and God will that I have it, ye can nothing say ne command but I shall it do."

And Antor said, "I shall not ask thy land; but this much I will pray you: that if ye be king, that ye make my son Kay your steward in such manner that for no forfeit that he do to you, ne to man of your land, that he lose not his office. And if he be fool, or fell, or villainous, ye ought better to suffer him than any other. And, therefore, I pray you to grant him *w*hat I you demand."

And Arthur said he would it do with good will, and then he led him to the altar and swore that he should this truly perform. And when he had sworn, he came before the minster—and the tournament was ended and the barons come to their evensong.

Then Antor cleped all his friends and came to the archbishop, and said, "Sir, lo! Here is a child of mine that is no knight, that prayeth me that I would help that he might essay the adventure of the sword, and that it please you to clepe the barons."

And so he did. And they assembled about the stone. Then Antor bade Arthur take out the sword and deliver it to the archbishop. And Arthur took the sword by the hilts and, without more tarrying, gave it to the archbishop. And anon he took Arthur in his arms, and said, "Te deum laudamus," and so brought him into the minster.

And the barons and high men that this had seen and heard were angry and sorrowful for this, and said it might not be that such a simple man of so low degree should be lord of them all. Therewith was the archbishop displeased, and said, "Sirs, our Lord knoweth best what every man is."

And Antor and his friends abode by Arthur, and all the common people. And all the barons were against them and against Arthur. And then said the archbishop words of great hardiness: "I do you to wit, though all they that be in the world would be against this election, an our Lord will that this man be king, he shall be it without fail. And I shall shew you how, and what affiance I have in our Lord Jesu Christ! Now, fair brother Arthur, go put the sword again in the same place that ye took it fro!" And Arthur put the sword again in the same place, and it held as fast as before. And then said the archbishop, "So fair election was never seen. Now go ye, rich barons and lords, and essay if ye may take out the sword."

Then yede all for to essay, but none it might remove from the place that it was in. Then said the archbishop, "Great folly do ye that be against our Lord's will, for now ye see well how it is."

And they said, "Sir, we ne be not against our Lord's will. But it is a grievous thing to us to have a garcion [boy] to be lord over us all."

And the archbishop said, "He that hath him chosen knoweth best what he is."

Then the barons prayed the bishop to let the sword be still in the stone till Candlemas, and by that time men of further countries might come to essay the adventure. And the archbishop them granted. Then came out of every country and essayed who that would. And when they had essayed, the archbishop said, "Arthur, if it be pleasure to our Lord Jesu Christ that thou be king, go forth and bring that sword." And Arthur yede to the sword and took it out as lightly as nothing had it holden.

When the prelates and the common people saw this, they gan to weep for joy and pity, and said, "Sirs, is there yet any man that saith against this election?" And the barons said, "Sir, we pray you that the sword be suffered yet in the stone to Pasch [Easter] but [unless] any man come by that term that may take it thence, and else we will obey to this. And if ye will not suffer so long time, every man do the best he may."

And the archbishop said, "If so be he abide to Pasch, and none other come that may perform this adventure, will ye then obey you to this election?" And they said all, "Yea."

Then the archbishop said to Arthur, "Set the sword again in the stone, for if God will, thou shalt not fail of the dignity that he hath thee promised." And Arthur did as he commanded, and there was ordained to keep the stone ten men and five clerks, and in this manner they abode to Pasch. And the archbishop that had taken Arthur in ward, said, "Wit ye right well ye shall be king and lord of this people. Now look that ye be a good man, and fro henceforth chooseth such men as shall be of your counsel, and officers for your household, even as ye were now king, for so ye shall be with the help of God."

And Arthur said, "I put me wholly in God and in holy church and in your good counsel. Therefore, choose ye as ye seem [consider] to be most to the pleasance of Jesu Christ, and, I pray you, clepe to you my lord my father." Then the archbishop cleped Antor and shewed him the answer of Arthur. Then chose they such counsellors as they would; and, by counsel of the archbishop and certain of the barons, Kay was made steward. And of all other things they abode to Pasch and then they assembled all at Logres.

When they were all assembled on the Easter-even, the archbishop drew them all to his palace, and rehearsed them the great wisdom and the good conditions that he found in Arthur.

And the barons said, "We will not be against God's ordinance, but it is unto us a marvelous thing that so young a man, and of so base lineage, should be lord and governor of us all."

The archbishop said, "Ye do not as Christian men, thus to be against Christ's election."

And they said, "We be not there-against; but ye have seen his conditions and we ne have not done so, and therefore we pray you to suffer us to know his conditions, and the manner of his governance that he will be of hereafter."

The archbishop said, "Will ye thus delay his coronation?" And

they said, "We would that his sacring [consecration] and coronation be respited to Pentecost. Thus we all pray and require." And
the archbishop it granted.

Thus departed all the council, and on the morrow, when high
mass was said, Arthur yede to the sword and took it out as lightly
as he had done before. Then they said all that they would have
him to their lord and governor, and they prayed him to set there
the sword again. And Arthur answered to the barons full debon-
airly and said he would do their request or anything that they
would of him desire. Then they led him into the minster to speak
with him and to essay his conditions, and said, "Sir, we see well
that God will that ye be our king and lord over us; wherefore we
will do to you our homage and of you hold our honors. And we
beseech you to respite your sacring unto Pentecost; ne therefore
shall ye nothing be interrupted, but that ye shall be our lord and
our king. But to this we pray you to say us what is your volunté."

Quoth Arthur, "Of that ye say ye will do to me your homages
and hold your honors of me, I may it not receive, ne I ne ought
not to do, for I may not to you ne to none other give no honors
till I have received mine. And there ye say ye will that I be lord
of you and of the realm, that may not be before that I be sacred
and received the honor of the empire. But the respite that ye
desire, I it grant you with good will, for I will not be sacred ne
nothing that thereto appertaineth, ne I may not, without god's
will and your volunté."

Then said the barons among themselves, "If this child live he
shall be right wise, and well he hath us answered." And then they
said, "Sir, us seemeth with your advice that ye be crowned and
sacred at Pentecost, and by that term we shall obey to you at the
commandment of this archbishop."

Then they made be brought jewels and all other richesse, and
gave it to him to see whether he would be covetous and catching.
And when he had all these gifts received, the book saith he departed [shared] it: to knights, the steeds and coursers and fresh
robes; and to them that were jolly and annoyous, he gave the
jewels; and to them that were avaricious, gold and silver; and to
sad wise men, he gave such things as him thought should them
please; and with them all he held company, and enquired in the
country what might them best please.

Thus departed he the gifts that were given him for to know of what condition that he would be of. And when they saw him thus demeaned there was none but that him greatly praised in their hearts, and said that he should be of high renown, and that they could not in him espy no point of covetise. But as soon as he had the great avoirs [possessions], he beset them in such manner that every man said that none could have done better, every estate and degree.

Thus they essayed Arthur, and nought could find in him but high virtue and great discretion. And so they abode to the Whitsuntide. And then all the baronage assembled at Logres, and there they essayed again at the sword, all that essay would, but never was there found man that it might remove from the stone. And the archbishop had ordained ready the crown and scepter and all that longed to the sacring. On Whitsun-even, by common counsel of all the barons, the archbishop made Arthur knight. All that night did he watch in the chief minster, till on the morrow day. And when it was day, all the barony came to the minster.

The archbishop said, "Sirs, lo, here is the man that God hath chosen to be your king, like as ye have seen and know. And, lo, here is the crown and the vestments royal, ordained by your advice and all the common assent. And if there be any of you that to this election will not assent, let him now say."

And they answered and said, "We accord that in God's name he be sacred and annointed with this, that if there be any of us that he be with displeased, of that we have been against his coronation, that he pardon us all into this day." And therewith they kneeled all at once to Arthur, asking him mercy.

And Arthur, for pity, gan weep, and said to them, "That Lord which hath granted me to have this honor may you pardon, and as much as is in me I make you quit." And therewith they risen up and took him between their arms and led him to the vestments royal.

And when he was arrayed, the archbishop was made ready to sing mass, and said to Arthur, "Now go fetch the sword, wherewith ye shall keep justice to defend holy church and maintain right and the Christian faith to your power." And so they yede in procession to the stone.

Then said the archbishop to Arthur, "If thou wilt swear to God

and to our Lady Saint Mary and to our mother holy church and
to Saint Peter and to all saints, to save and to hold truth and peace
in the land, and to thy power keep true justice, come forth and
take this sword, whereby God hath made the election upon thee."

When Arthur heard this, of pity he gan weep, and so did many
other. And he said, "As verily as God is lord over all things, so he
of his great mercy grant me grace and power this to maintain like
as ye have rehearsed, and I have it well understood." And then he
set him on his knees, holding up his hands. And then took out the
sword lightly, without grievance, and so bore it upright. And they
led him to the altar, and there he laid the sword. And then they
him sacred and annointed and did *w*hat longed to a king.

And after all the service was ended, they yede out of the minster
and came by the place there as was the stone. And no man could
know where it was become.

Thus was Arthur chosen to king, and held the realm of Logres
long in peace.

Sir Thomas Malory

"LE MORTE DARTHUR"

So IT BEFELL in the month of May, Queen Guenevere called unto
her knights of the Table Round, and she gave them warning that
early upon the morrow she would ride a-Maying into the woods
and fields beside Westminster.

"And I warn you that there be none of you but that he be well
horsed, and that ye all be clothed in green, *ei*ther in silk *ei*ther in
cloth. And I shall bring with me ten ladies, and every knight shall
have a lady behind him, and every knight shall have a squire and
two yeomen. And I will that ye all be well horsed."

So they made them ready in the freshest manner. And these
were the names of the knights: Sir Kay le Seneschal, Sir Agravaine, Sir Brandiles, Sir Sagramore le Desirous, Sir Dodinas le
Savage, Sir Ozanna le Cure Hardy, Sir Ladinas of the Forest Savage, Sir Persant of Inde, Sir Ironside, that was called the Knight
of the Red Launds, and Sir Pelleas the lover. And these ten

knights made them ready in the freshest manner to ride with the queen.

And so upon the morn they took their horses with the queen, and rode a-Maying in woods and meadows as it pleased them, in great joy and delights. For the queen had cast to have been again with King Arthur at the furthest by ten of the clock, and so was that time her purpose.

Then there was a knight that hight Meliagrance, and he was son unto King Bagdemagus. And this knight had at that time a castle of the gift of King Arthur, within seven mile of Westminster. And this knight, Sir Meliagrance, loved passing well Queen Guenevere, and so had he done long and many years. And the book saith he had lain in a wait for to steal away the queen, but evermore he forbare for because of Sir Lancelot, for in no wise he would meddle with the queen an Sir Lancelot were in her company, or else an he were near-hand her.

And, that time, was such a custom: the queen rode never without a great fellowship of men-of-arms about her. And they were many good knights and the most part were young men that would have worship. And they were called the Queen's Knights, and never in no battle, tournament, nor jousts, they bare none of them no manner of *ac*knowledging of their own arms, but plain white shields, and thereby they were called the Queen's Knights. And then when it happed any of them to be of great worship by his noble deeds, then at the next Feast of Pentecost, if there were any slain or dead, as there was none year that there failed but some were dead, then was there chosen in his stead that was dead the most men of worship that were called the Queen's Knights. And thus they came up all first, ere they were renowned men of worship, both Sir Lancelot and all the remnant of them.

But this knight, Sir Meliagrance, had espied the queen well and her purpose, and how Sir Lancelot was not with her, and how she had no men-of-arms with her but the ten noble knights, all arrayed in green for Maying. Then he purveyed him a twenty men-of-arms and an hundred archers for to destroy the queen and her knights, for he thought that time was best season to take the queen.

So, as the queen had Mayed and all her knights, all were bedashed with herbs, mosses, and flowers, in the best manner and freshest. Right so, came out of a wood Sir Meliagrance with an eight score men well harnessed, as they should fight in a battle of arrest, and bade the queen and her knights abide, for maugre their heads they should abide.

"Traitor knight," said Queen Guenevere, "What cast thou for to do? Wilt thou shame thyself? Bethink thee how thou art a king's son, and knight of the Table Round. An thou to be about to dishonor the noble king that made thee knight, thou shamest all knighthood and thyself. And me, I let thee wit, shalt thou never shame, for I had liefer cut mine own throat in twain rather than thou shouldest dishonor me."

"As for all this language," said Sir Meliagrance, "be it as it may. For, wit you well, madam, I have loved you many a year, and never ere now could I get you at such an advantage as I do now. And, therefore, I will take you as I find you."

Then spake all the ten noble knights at once, and said, "Sir Meliagrance, wit thou well ye are about to jeopard your worship to dishonor, and also ye cast to jeopard our persons howbeit we be unarmed. Ye have us at a great avail, for it seemeth by you that you have laid watch upon us. But, rather than we should put the queen to a shame and us all, we had as lief to depart from our lives, for an if we otherways did, we were shamed for ever."

Then said Sir Meliagrance, "Dress you as well as ye can and keep the queen!"

Then the ten knights of the Table Round drew their swords, and the other let run at them with their spears. And the ten knights manly abode them, and smote away their spears, that no spear did them none harm. Then they lashed together with swords, and anon Sir Kay, Sir Sagramore, Sir Agravaine, Sir Dodinas, Sir Ladinas, and Sir Ozanna were smitten to the earth with grimly wounds. Then Sir Brandiles and Sir Persant, Sir Ironside, Sir Pelleas, fought long. And they were sore wounded, for these ten knights, ere ever they were laid to the ground, slew forth men of the boldest and the best of them.

So, when the queen saw her knights thus dolefully wounded and needs must be slain at the last, then for pity and sorrow she cried Sir Meliagrance, "Slay not my noble knights and I will go with thee, upon this covenant—that thou save them and suffer them not to be no more hurt: with this—that they be led with me wheresoever thou leadest me, for I will rather slay myself than

I will go with thee unless that these my noble knights may be in my presence."

"Madam," said Meliagrance, "For your sake they shall be led with you into mine own castle, with-that ye will be ruled and ride with me."

Then the queen prayed the four knights to leave their fighting, and she and they would not depart.

"Madam," said Sir Pelleas, "We will do as ye do, for as for me I take no force of my life nor death." For, as the French book saith, Sir Pelleas gave such buffets there that none armour might hold him.

Then, by the queen's commandment, they left battle and dressed the wounded knights on horseback, some sitting, some overthwart their horses, that it was pity to behold them. And then Sir Meliagrance charged the queen and all her knights that none of all her fellowship should depart from her, for full sore he dread Sir Lancelot du Lac, lest he should have any knowledging.

All this espied the queen, and privily she called unto her a child of her chamber that was swiftly horsed, to whom she said, "Go thou, when thou seest thy time, and bear this ring unto Sir Lancelot du Lac, and pray him as he loveth me that he will see me and rescue me, if ever he will have joy of me. And spare not thy horse," said the queen, "neither for water, neither for land."

So the child espied his time, and lightly he took his horse with the spurs, and departed as fast as he might. And when Sir Meliagrance saw him so flee, he understood that it was by the queen's commandment for to warn Sir Lancelot. Then they that were best horsed chased him and shot at him. But from them all the child went suddenly.

And then Sir Meliagrance said to the queen, "Madam, ye are about to betray me. But I shall ordain for Sir Lancelot that he shall not come lightly at you!"

And then he rode with her, and they all, to his castle, in all the haste that they might. And by the way Sir Meliagrance laid in an ambushment the best archers that he might get in his country, to the number of thirty, to await upon Sir Lancelot, charging them that if they saw such a manner of knight come by the way upon a white horse, that in any wise they slay his horse, but in no manner of wise have not ado with him bodily, "for he is over-hardy to be overcome."

So this was done, and they were come to his castle. But in no wise the queen would never let none of the ten knights and her ladies out of her sight, but always they were in her presence. For the book saith Sir Meliagrance durst make no masteries, for dread of Sir Lancelot, insomuch he deemed that he had warning.

So when the child was departed from the fellowship of Sir Meliagrance, within a while he came to Westminster, and anon he found Sir Lancelot. And when he had told his message and delivered him the queen's ring, "Alas!" said Sir Lancelot, "Now I am shamed for ever unless that I may rescue that noble lady from dishonor."

Then eagerly he asked his armour. And ever the child told Sir Lancelot how the ten knights fought marvellously, and how Sir Pelleas, and Sir Ironside, and Sir Brandiles, and Sir Persant of Inde fought strongly, but namely Sir Pelleas—there might none withstand him. And how they all fought, till at the last they were laid to the earth, and then the queen made appointment for to save their lives and go with Sir Meliagrance.

"Alas!" said Sir Lancelot, "That most noble lady! That she should be so destroyed! I had liefer," said Sir Lancelot, "than all France that I had been there well armed."

So when Sir Lancelot was armed and upon his horse, he prayed the child of the queen's chamber to warn Sir Lavaine how suddenly he was departed, and for what cause. "And pray him, as he loveth me, that he will hie him after me, and that he stint not until he come to the castle where Sir Meliagrance abideth or dwelleth. For there," said Sir Lancelot, "He shall hear of me, an I am a man living, and rescue the queen and the ten knights the which he traitorously hath taken. And that shall I prove upon his head, and all them that hold with him."

Then Sir Lancelot rode as fast as he might. And the book saith he took the water at Westminster Bridge and made his horse to swim over Thames unto Lambeth. And then within a while he came to the same place thereas the ten noble knights fought with Sir Meliagrance. And then Sir Lancelot followed the track until that he came to a wood, and there was a straight way. And there the thirty archers bade Sir Lancelot turn again, and follow no longer that track.

"What commandment have ye thereto," said Sir Lancelot, "to cause me, that am a knight of the Round Table, to leave my right way?"

"This way shalt thou leave, other-else thou shall go it on thy foot. For, wit thou well, thy horse shall be slain."

"That is little mastery," said Sir Lancelot, "To slay mine horse! But, as for myself, when my horse is slain, I give right naught for you, not an ye were five hundred more."

So then they shot Sir Lancelot's horse, and smote him with many arrows. And then Sir Lancelot avoided his horse and went on foot. But there were so many ditches and hedges betwixt them and him that he might not meddle with none of them.

"Alas, for shame!" said Lancelot, "That ever one knight should betray another knight. But it is an old saw, 'A good man is never in danger but when he is in the danger of a coward.'"

Then Sir Lancelot went a while, and then he was foul cumbered of his armour, his shield, and his spear, and all that longed unto him. Wit ye well, he was full sore annoyed, and full loath he was for to leave anything that longed unto him, for he dread sore the treason of Sir Meliagrance.

Then by fortune there came by him a chariot that came thither for to fetch wood. "Say me, carter," said Sir Lancelot, "What shall I give thee to suffer me to leap into thy chariot, and that thou bring me unto a castle within this two mile?"

"Thou shalt not come within my chariot," said the carter, "for I am sent for to fetch wood for my lord, Sir Meliagrance."

"With him would I speak!"

"Thou shalt not go with me," said the carter.

Then Sir Lancelot leapt to him, and gave him such a buffet that he fell to the earth, stark dead. Then the other carter, his fellow, was afeared, and weened to have gone the same way. And then he cried, "Fair lord, save my life and I shall bring you where ye will."

"Then I charge thee," said Sir Lancelot, "That thou drive me and this chariot even unto Sir Meliagrance's gate."

"Leap up into the chariot," said the carter, "And ye shall be there anon."

So the carter drove on a great wallop [gallop], and Sir Lancelot's horse followed the chariot, with more than a forty arrows broad and rough in him.

And, more than an hour and a half, Dame Guenevere was await-
ing in a bay window with her ladies, and espied an armed knight
standing in a chariot.

"See, madam!" said a lady, "where rideth in a chariot a goodly
armed knight. I suppose he rideth unto hanging."

"Where?" said the queen.

Then she espied by his shield that he was there himself, Sir
Lancelot du Lac. And then she was ware where came his horse
ever after that chariot, and ever he trod his guts and his paunch
under his feet. "Alas!" said the queen, "Now I see well and prove
that well is him that hath a trusty friend. Ha, ha, most noble
knight!" said Queen Guenevere, "I see well thou art hard bestead, when thou ridest in a chariot."

Then she rebuked that lady that likened Sir Lancelot to ride in
a chariot to hanging. "It was foul-mouthed," said the queen, "and
evil-likened, so for to liken the most noble knight of the world
unto such a shameful death! O Jesu defend him and keep him,"
said the queen, "from all mischievous end."

By this was Sir Lancelot come to the gates of that castle. And
there he descended down and cried, that all the castle rang of it,
"Where art thou, false traitor, Sir Meliagrance, and knight of the
Table Round? Now come forth here, thou traitor knight—thou
and thy fellowship with thee. For here I am, Sir Lancelot du Lac,
that shall fight with you!"

And therewithall he bare the gate wide open upon the porter,
and smote him under his ear with his gauntlet, that his neck brast
asunder.

When Sir Meliagrance heard that Sir Lancelot was there, he
ran unto Queen Guenevere and fell upon his knee, and said,
"Mercy, madam, now I put me wholly into your grace."

"What aileth you now?" said Queen Guenevere. "Forsooth, I
might well wit some good knight would revenge me, though my
lord Arthur wist not of this your work."

"Madam," said Sir Meliagrance, "All this that is amiss on my
part shall be amended right as yourself will devise. And wholly
I put me in your grace."

"What would ye that I did?" said the queen.

"I would no more," said Meliagrance, "but that ye would take
all in your own hands and that ye will rule my lord Sir Lancelot.

And such cheer as may be made him in this poor castle, ye and he shall have until to-morn. And then may ye and all they return unto Westminster. And my body and all that I have I shall put in your rule."

"Ye say well," said the queen, "and better is peace than ever war, and the less noise [rumor] the more is my worship."

Then the queen and her ladies went down unto the knight Sir Lancelot, that stood wroth out of measure in the inner court to abide battle. And ever he bade, "Thou traitor-knight, come forth!"

Then the queen came to him and said, "Sir Lancelot, why be ye so moved?"

"Ha, Madam!" said Sir Lancelot, "Why ask ye me that question? Meseemeth," said Sir Lancelot, "Ye ought to be more wroth than I am, for ye have the hurt and the dishonor. For, wit ye well, madam, my hurt is but little for the killing of a mare's son; but the despite grieveth me much more than all my hurt."

"Truly," said the queen, "Ye say truth. But heartily I thank you," said the queen. "But ye must come in with me peaceably, for all thing is put in my hand. And all that is evil shall be for the best, for the knight full sore repenteth him of the misadventure that is befallen him."

"Madam," said Sir Lancelot, "Sith it is so that ye be accorded with him, as for me, I may not be against it, howbeit Sir Meliagrance hath done full shamefully to me, and cowardly. Ah, madam!" said Sir Lancelot, "An I had wist ye would have been so soon accorded with him, I would not have made such haste unto you."

"Why say ye so?" said the queen, "Do you forthink yourself of your good deeds? Wit you well," said the queen, "I accorded never unto him for favor nor love that I had unto him, but for to lay down every shameful noise."

"Madam," said Sir Lancelot, "Ye understand full well I was never willing nor glad of shameful slander nor noise. And there is neither king, queen, nor knight that beareth the life—except my lord King Arthur and you, madam—should let me, but I should make Sir Meliagrance's heart full cold ere ever I departed from hence."

"That wot I well," said the queen, "But what will ye more? Ye shall have all thing ruled as ye list to have it."

"Madam," said Sir Lancelot, "So ye be pleased, I care not. As for my part, ye shall soon please."

Right so, the queen took Sir Lancelot by the bare hand—for he had put off his gauntlet—and so she went with him till [to] her chamber. And then she commanded him to be unarmed.

And then Sir Lancelot asked where were the ten knights that were wounded sore. So she showed them unto Sir Lancelot, and there they made great joy of the coming of him, and Sir Lancelot made great dole of their hurts and bewailed them greatly. And there Sir Lancelot told them how cowardly and traitorly Meliagrance set archers to slay his horse, and how he was fain to put himself in a chariot. Thus they complained every-each to other, and full fain they would have been revenged. But they peaced themselves because of the queen. Then, as the French book saith, Sir Lancelot was called many a day after, "Le Chevalier du Chariot," and did many deeds, and great adventures he had.

And so leave we off this tale—"Le Chevalier du Chariot"—and turn we to this tale.

So Sir Lancelot had great cheer with the queen. And then Sir Lancelot made a promise with the queen that, the same night, Sir Lancelot should come to a window outward toward a garden. And that window was y-barred with iron. And there Sir Lancelot promised to meet her when all folks were asleep.

So then came Sir Lavaine, driving to the gates, crying "Where is my lord, Sir Lancelot du Lac?"

Then was he sent for. And when Sir Lavaine saw Sir Lancelot, he said, "My lord, I found well how ye were hard bestead, for I have found your horse that was slain with arrows."

"As for that," said Sir Lancelot, "I pray you, Sir Lavaine, speak ye of other matters and let this pass, and we shall right it another time, when we best may."

Then the knights that were hurt were searched [examined], and soft salves were laid to their wounds. And so it passed on till supper-time, and all the cheer that might be made them there was done unto the queen and all her knights. Then, when season was, they went unto their chambers. But in no wise the queen would not suffer the wounded knights to be fro her, but that they were laid within draughts [rows] by her chamber, upon beds and pillows, that she herself might see to them that they wanted nothing.

So when Sir Lancelot was in his chamber that was assigned unto him, he called unto him Sir Lavaine and told him that night he must go speak with his lady, Dame Guenevere.

"Sir," said Sir Lavaine, "Let me go with you an it please you, for I dread me sore of the treason of Sir Meliagrance."

"Nay," said Sir Lancelot, "I thank you, but I will have nobody with me."

Then Sir Lancelot took his sword in his hand and privily went to a place where he had espied a ladder toforehand. And that he took under his arm, and bare it through the garden, and set it up to the window. And there anon the queen was ready to meet him. And then they made either to other their complaints of many divers things, and then Sir Lancelot wished that he might have come into her.

"Wit ye well," said the queen, "I would as fain as ye that ye might come into me."

"Would ye, madam," said Sir Lancelot, "with your heart that I were with you?"

"Yea, truly," said the queen.

"Now shall I prove my might," said Sir Lancelot, "for your love." And then he set his hands upon the bars of iron. And he pulled at them with such a might that he brast them clean out of the stone walls, and therewithal one of the bars of iron cut the brawn of his hands throughout to the bone. And then he leapt into the chamber to the queen.

"Make ye no noise," said the queen, "For my wounded knights lie here fast by me."

So, to pass upon this tale, Sir Lancelot went unto bed with the queen. And he took no force of his hurt hand, but took his pleasaunce and his liking until it was in the dawning of the day. And, wit ye well, he slept not but watched. And when he saw his time that he might tarry no longer, he took his leave and departed at the window, and put it together as well as he might again, and so departed unto his own chamber. And there he told Sir Lavaine how he was hurt. Then Sir Lavaine dressed his hand and staunched it, and put upon it a glove, that it should not be espied.

And so the queen lay long in her bed until it was nine of the clock. Then Sir Meliagrance went to the queen's chamber and found her ladies there, ready clothed. "Jesu mercy," said Sir

Meliagrance, "What aileth you, madam, that ye sleep thus long?"
And right therewithal he opened the curtain for to behold her.
And then was he ware where she lay—and all the sheet and pillow
was be-bled with the blood of Sir Lancelot and of his hurt hand.

When Sir Meliagrance espied that blood, then he deemed in her
that she was false to the king, and that some of the wounded
knights had lain by her all that night. "Ah, madam," said Sir
Meliagrance, "Now I have found you a false traitress unto my
lord Arthur, for now I prove well it was not for naught that ye
laid these wounded knights within the bounds of your chamber.
Therefore, I will call you of treason before my lord, King Arthur.
And now I have proved you, madam, with a shameful deed. And
that they be all false, or some of them, I will make good, for a
wounded knight this night hath lain by you."

"That is false," said the queen, "And that I will report me unto
them all."

Then when the ten knights heard Sir Meliagrance's words, they
spake all in one voice and said to Sir Meliagrance, "Thou sayest
falsely, and wrongfully puttest upon us such a deed. And that we
will make good, any of us. Choose which thou list of us when we
are whole of our wounds."

"Ye shall not," said Sir Meliagrance. Away with your proud
language! For here ye may all see," said Sir Meliagrance, "That by
the queen this night a wounded knight hath lain."

Then were they all ashamed when they saw that blood. And,
wit you well, Sir Meliagrance was passing glad that he had the
queen at such an advantage, for he deemed by that to hide his
treason.

So with this rumor came in Sir Lancelot, and found them all at
a great array. "What array is this?" said Sir Lancelot.

Then Sir Meliagrance told them what he had found, and
showed them the queen's bed.

"Truly," said Sir Lancelot, "Ye did not your part nor knightly,
to touch a queen's bed while it was drawn, and she lying therein.
For I dare say my lord Arthur himself would not have displayed
her curtains, she being within her bed, unless that it had pleased
him to have lain down by her. And, therefore, ye have done un-
worshipfully and shamefully to yourself."

"I wot not what ye mean," said Sir Meliagrance, "but well I am
sure there hath one of her wounded knights lain by her this night,

and therefore I will prove with my hands that she is a traitress unto my lord Arthur."

"Beware what ye do," said Lancelot, "for, an ye say so, an ye will prove it, it will be taken at your hands."

"My lord, Sir Lancelot," said Sir Meliagrance, "I rede [advise] you beware what ye do. For, though ye are never so good a knight, as ye wot well ye are renowned the best knight of the world, yet should ye be advised [cautious] to do battle in a wrong quarrel—for God will have a stroke in every battle."

"As for that," said Sir Lancelot, "God is to be dread, but as to that, I say nay plainly—that this night there lay none of these ten wounded knights with my lady Queen Guenevere. And that will I prove with my hands, that ye say untruly in that now."

"Hold!" said Sir Meliagrance. "Here is my glove that she is traitress unto my lord, King Arthur, and that this night one of the wounded knights lay with her."

"And I receive your glove," said Sir Lancelot.

And so they were sealed with their signets, and delivered unto the ten knights.

"At what day shall we do battle together?" said Sir Lancelot.

"This day eight days," said Sir Meliagrance, "In the field beside Westminster."

"I am agreed," said Sir Lancelot.

"But now," said Sir Meliagrance, "Since it is so that we must fight together, I pray you, as ye be a noble knight, await me with no treason, nor none villainy the meanwhile, nor none for you."

"So God me help," said Sir Lancelot, "Ye shall right well wit I was never of no such conditions. For, I report me to all the knights that ever have known me, I fared never with no treason, nor I loved never the fellowship of no man that fared with treason."

"Then let us go to dinner," said Meliagrance. "And after dinner, ye and the queen and ye may ride all to Westminster."

"I will well," said Sir Lancelot.

Then Sir Meliagrance said to Sir Lancelot, "Pleaseth it you to see the estres [apartments] of this castle?"

"With a good will," said Sir Lancelot.

And then they went together from chamber to chamber, for Sir Lancelot dreaded no perils—for ever a man of worship and of prowess dreadeth least always perils, for they ween every man be as they be. But ever he that fareth with treason putteth oft a man in great danger. So it befell upon Sir Lancelot, that no peril dread. As he went with Sir Meliagrance, he trod on a trap, and the board rolled, and there Sir Lancelot fell down more than ten fathom, into a cave full of straw. And then Sir Meliagrance departed, and made no fare as that he nist where he was.

And when Sir Lancelot was thus missed, they marvelled where he was become. And then the queen and many of them deemed that he was departed as he was wont to do, suddenly. For Sir Meliagrance made suddenly to put away aside Sir Lavaine's horse, that they might all understand that Sir Lancelot was departed suddenly.

So it passed on till after dinner. And then Sir Lavaine would not stint until that he ordained litters for the wounded knights, that they might be laid in them. And so, with the queen and them all, both ladies and gentlewomen and other, went unto Westminster. And there the knights told King Arthur how Meliagrance had appelled the queen of high treason, and how Sir Lancelot had received the glove of him—"And this day eight days they shall do battle afore you."

"By my head," said King Arthur, "I am afeared Sir Meliagrance hath taken upon him a great charge. But where is Sir Lancelot?" said the king.

"Sir," said they all, "We wot not where he is, but we deem he is ridden to some adventures, as he is ofttimes wont to do, for he hath Sir Lavaine's horse."

"Let him be," said the king. "He will be founden, but-if he be trapped with some treason."

So leave we Sir Lancelot lying within that cave in great pain. And every day there came a lady and brought him his meat and his drink, and wooed him, to have lain by him. And ever the noble knight Sir Lancelot said her nay.

"Sir Lancelot," said she, "Ye are not wise, for ye may never out of this prison but-if ye have my help. And also your lady, Queen Guenevere, shall be burnt in your default, unless that ye be there at the day of battle."

"God defend," said Sir Lancelot, "that she should be burnt in my default! And if it be so," said Sir Lancelot, "that I may not be there, it shall be well understand, both at the king and at the queen, and with all men of worship, that I am dead, sick, or in prison. For all men that know me will say for me that I am in some

evil case an I be not there that day. And, well I wot, there is some
good knight, either of my blood, or some other that loveth me,
that will take my quarrel in hand. And, therefore," said Sir Lancelot, "Wit ye well ye shall not fear me. And, if there were no more
women in all this land but ye, I will not have ado with you."

"Then art thou shamed," said the lady, "and destroyed for ever."

"As for world's shame, Jesu defend me. And, as for my distress,
it is welcome, whatsoever it be that God sendeth me."

So she came to him the same day that the battle should be, and
said, "Sir Lancelot, methinketh ye are too hard-hearted. But
wouldst thou but kiss me once, I should deliver thee, and thine
armour, and the best horse that is within Sir Meliagrance's stable."

"As for to kiss you," said Sir Lancelot, "I may do that and lose
no worship. And, wit ye well, an I understood there were any dis-
worship for to kiss you, I would not do it."

Then he kissed her. And then she got him and brought him to
his armour. And when he was armed she brought him to a stable,
where stood twelve good coursers, and bade him choose the best.
Then Sir Lancelot looked upon a white courser, the which liked
him best, and anon he commanded the keepers fast to saddle him
with the best saddle of war that there was. And so it was done as
he bade. Then got he his spear in his hand, and his sword by his
side, and commended the lady unto God, and said, "Lady, for this
good deed, I shall do you service if ever it be in my power."

Now leave we Sir Lancelot wallop all that he might and speak
we of Queen Guenevere, that was brought to a fire to be burnt.
For Sir Meliagrance was sure, him thought, that Sir Lancelot
should not be at that battle. Therefore, he ever cried upon King
Arthur to do him justice, other-else bring forth Sir Lancelot du
Lac.

Then was the king and all the court full sore abashed and
shamed that the queen should be burnt in the default of Sir
Lancelot.

"My lord Arthur," said Sir Lavaine, "Ye may understand that it
is not well with my lord Sir Lancelot. For, an he were alive, so he
be not sick or in prison, wit ye well he would be here. For never
heard ye that ever he failed his part for whom he should do battle
for. And therefore," said Sir Lavaine, "my Lord, King Arthur, I
beseech you give me license to do battle here this day for my lord
and master and for to save my lady, the queen."

"Gramercy, gentle Sir Lavaine," said King Arthur, "For I dare say all that Sir Meliagrance putteth upon my lady the queen is wrong, for I have spoken with all the ten wounded knights, and there is not one of them, an he were whole and able to do battle, but he would prove upon Sir Meliagrance's body that it is false that he putteth upon my queen."

"So shall I," said Sir Lavaine, "in the defence of my lord, Sir Lancelot, an ye will give me leave."

"Now I give you leave," said King Arthur. "And do your best, for I dare well say there is some treason done to Sir Lancelot."

Then was Sir Lavaine armed and horsed, and suddenly at the list's end he rode to perform this battle. And right as the heralds should cry, "Laissez les aller!," right so came in Sir Lancelot, driving with all the force of his horse.

And then Arthur cried, "Ho!" and "Abide!"

Then was Sir Lancelot called on horseback tofore King Arthur. And there he told openly tofore the king and all, how Sir Meliagrance had served him first to last. And when the king and the queen, and all the lords, knew of the treason of Sir Meliagrance, they were all ashamed on his behalf. Then was Queen Guenevere sent for and set by the king in great trust of her champion.

And then there was no more else to say. But Sir Lancelot and Sir Meliagrance dressed them unto battle, and took their spears. And so they came together as thunder, and there Sir Lancelot bare him down quite over his horse's croup. And then Sir Lancelot alighted and dressed his shield on his shoulder, with his sword in his hand, and Sir Meliagrance in the same wise dressed him unto him. And there they smote many great strokes together and, at the last, Sir Lancelot smote him such a buffet upon the helmet that he fell on the one side to the earth. And then he cried upon him aloud, "Most noble knight, Sir Lancelot du Lac, save my life! For I yield me unto you and I require you, as ye be a knight and fellow of the Table Round, slay me not, for I yield me as overcome. And whether I shall live or die I put me in the king's hands and yours."

Then Sir Lancelot wist not what to do, for he had liefer than all the goods of the world he might have been revenged upon Sir Meliagrance. And Sir Lancelot looked up to the Queen Guenevere, if he might espy by any sign or countenance what she would have done. And then the queen wagged her head upon Sir Lancelot, as though she would say, "Slay him!" Full well knew Sir Lancelot, by the wagging of her head, that she would have him dead. Then Sir Lancelot bade him rise for shame and perform that battle to the utterance.

"Nay," said Sir Meliagrance, "I will never arise until ye take me as yolden and recreant."

"I shall proffer you large proffers," said Sir Lancelot. "That is for to say, I shall unarm my head and my left quarter of my body, all that may be unarmed, and let bind my left hand behind me, so that it shall not help me. And right so I shall do battle with you."

Then Sir Meliagrance started up upon his legs, and said on high, "My lord Arthur, take heed to this proffer, for I will take it. And let him be disarmed and bounden according to his proffer."

"What say ye," said King Arthur unto Sir Lancelot. "Will ye abide by your proffer?"

"Yea, my lord," said Sir Lancelot. "I will never go from that I have once said."

Then the knights-parters of the field disarmed Sir Lancelot, first his head, and sithen his left arm and his left side, and they bound his left arm behind his back, without shield or anything, and then they were put together. Wit you well, there was many a lady and knight marvelled that Sir Lancelot would jeopardy himself in such wise.

Then Sir Meliagrance came, with his sword all on high, and Sir Lancelot showed him openly his bare head and the bare left side. And when he weened to have smitten him upon the bare head, then lightly he avoided the left leg and the left side, and put his right hand and his sword to that stroke, and so put it on side with great sleight. And then with great force Sir Lancelot smote him on the helmet such a buffet that the stroke carved the head in two parts. Then there was no more to do, but he was drawn out of the field. And at the great instance of the knights of the Table Round, the king suffered him to be interred, and the mention made upon him, who slew him and for what cause he was slain.

And then the king and the queen made more of Sir Lancelot du Lac, and more he was cherished than ever he was aforehand.

"MELUSINE"

THE VERY AND TRUE history witnesseth that Raymondin and Melusine were at merriment, making great joy for the prosperous estate and good fortune of their children. But this joy was soon turned to great sorrow, for as ye have heard how the history saith tofore, that Raymondin promised to Melusine that never on the Saturday he should not enquire of her nor desire to see her that day.

It is truth that on a Saturday, a little before dinner time, Raymondin understood that his brother the Earl of Forest was come to Merment for to see him and his noble court. Whereof Raymondin was right joyous, but sith [later] great mischief came to him therefor, as hereafter shall be shewed. Then made Raymondin great apparel [preparation] and right noble for to receive his brother. And shortly to shew, he came and recountered his brother with noble company and welcomed him honorably, and did much that one of the other, and went to churchward together. And after the divine service was done, they came again to the palace, where all things were ready to dinner. They washed their hands and syne set them at dinner, and they were worshipfully served.

Alas! Then began a part of the dolor and heaviness. For his brother could not keep him but he asked after Melusine, saying in this manner, "My brother, where is my sister Melusine? Let her come, for much I desire to see her."

And Raymondin, which thought none evil, answered, "She is not here at this time, but to-morn ye shall see her and shall make you good cheer."

But for that answer the Earl of Forest held not his peace, but thus said again to his brother, "Ye are my brother; I ought not to hide to you your dishonor. Now, fair brother, wit it that the common talking of the people is that Melusine your wife every Saturday in the year is with another man in avoutery; and so blind ye are by her saying that ye dare not enquire nor knoweth where she becometh or goeth. And also, other men say and make them strong, that she is a spirit of the fairy that on every Saturday maketh her penance. I wot not which of both I shall believe, and for none other cause I am come hither but to advertise you thereof."

When Raymondin then understood these words that his brother him said, he rose fro the table and entered into his chamber. And anon, all esprised [seized] with ire and jealousy withal, took his sword and girded it about him, and syne went toward the place where as Melusine went every Saturday in the year. And when he came there, he found a door of iron, thick and strong. And, wit it well, he had never been tofore that time so far thitherward. And when he perceived the door of iron, he took his sword, that was hard and tempered with fine steel, and with the point of it did so much that he pierced the door and made a hole in it. And looked in at that hole and saw therein Melusine, that was within a great bath of marble stone, where were steps to mount in it and was well fifteen foot of length. And therein she bathed herself, making there her penitence, as ye shall hear hereafter.

The history saith in this part that Raymondin stood so long at the iron door that he pierced it with the point of his sword, whereby he might well see all that was within the chamber. And saw Melusine within the bath, unto her navel in form of a woman combing her hair, and from the navel downward in likeness of a great serpent, the tail as great and thick as a barrel and so long it was that she made it to touch ofttimes, while Raymondin beheld her, the roof of the chamber, that was right high.

And when Raymondin perceived it, wit it well that he was right dolent and sorrowful, and not without cause. And could never hold his tongue, but he said, "My sweet love, now have I betrayed you and have falsed my covenant by the right false admonishing of my brother, and have forsworn myself toward you."

Raymondin then was smitten to the heart with such sorrow and distress that unnethe [scarcely] he could speak. And penseful, with a heavy countenance, returned hastily toward his chamber. And took some wax, wherewith he went and stopped the hole that he had made at the door of iron, and syne came again to the hall, where he found his brother. And then when the Earl of Forest perceived him and saw his heavy countenance, well supposed he that he had found Melusine in some shameful fait [deed], and said to him in this wise, "My brother, I wist it well! Have ye not found as I said?"

Then cried Raymondin to his brother of Forest in this manner, "Void this place, false traitor, for through your false report I have falsed my faith against the most faithfullest and truest lady that ever was born. Ye are cause of the loss of all my worldly joy and of my total destruction. By God, if I believed my courage [impulse] I should make you to die now of an evil death. But reason natural keepeth and defendeth me therefrom, because that ye are my brother. Go your way and void my sight, that all the great masters of hell may conduct you thither!"

And when the Earl of Forest perceived Raymondin his brother, that was in so great ire, he went out of the hall, and all his people. And mounted on horseback and rode as fast as they might toward Forest, right penseful and heavy, repenting him of his foolish enterprise, for he knew well that Raymondin his brother would never love him nor see him.

Here I leave to speak of him and shall shew you of Raymondin, that entered into his chamber woeful and angry.

"Alas, Melusine!" said Raymondin, "of whom all the world spake well! Now have I lost you for ever. Now have I found the end of my joy and the beginning is to me now present of mine everlasting heaviness. Farewell, beauty, bounty, sweetness, amiability! Farewell, wit, courtesy, and humility! Farewell all my joy, all my comfort and mine hope! Farewell, mine heart, my prowess, my valiance! For that little of honor which God had lent me, it came through your noblesse, my sweet and entirely beloved lady. Ha! falsed and blind Fortune, eager, sharp, and bitter. Well hast thou overthrown me fro the highest place of thy wheel unto the lowest part of thy mansion or dwelling-place, there as Jupiter feasteth with sorrow and heaviness the captive and unhappy creatures. Be thou now cursed of God! By thee I slew, against my will, my lord mine uncle, the which death thou sellest me too dear. Alas! Thou had put and set me in high authority through the wit and valor of the wisest, the fairest, and most noble lady of all other, and now, by the false blind traitor and envious, I must lose the sight of her of whom mine eyes took their feeding. Thou now hatest, thou now lovest, thou now makest, thou now undost: in thee is no more surety ne rest than is in a vane that turneth at all winds. Alas, alas, my right sweet and tender love! By my venomous treason I have maculate your excellent figure. Alas, mine heart and all my weal. Ye had healed me clean of my first sore: ill I have now rewarded you therefor. Certainly, if I now lose you, none other choice is to me but to take mine uttermost exile, there as never after no man living shall see me."

Here saith the history that in such dolor and bewailings abode Raymondin all that night till it was daylight. And as soon as Aurora might be perceived, Melusine came and entered into the chamber. And when Raymondin heard her come, he made semblance of sleep. She took off her clothes and then all naked laid herself by him. And then began Raymondin to sigh, as he that felt great dolor at heart. And Melusine embraced him and asked what him ailed, saying in this wise, "My lord, what aileth you? Be ye sick?"

And when Raymondin saw that she of none other thing spake, he supposed that she nothing had known of this fait [occurrence]. But for naught he believed so, for she wist well that he had not entamed [opened] nor shewed the matter to no man. Wherefore, she suffered at that time and made no semblance thereof. Wherefore he was right joyous and answered to her, "Madame, I have been somewhat evil at ease and have had an access in manner of a continue [fever]."

"My lord," said Melusine, "abash you not: for if it please God, ye shall soon be whole."

And then he, that was right joyous, said to her, "By my faith, sweet love, I feel me well at ease for your coming." And she said, "I am thereof glad," and when time required they rose and went to hear mass.

And soon after was the dinner ready, and thus abode Melusine with Raymondin all that day. And on the morn she took leave of him and went to Niort, where she builded a fortress.

And here ceaseth the history of her and returneth to speak of Geoffrey.

APPENDIX

THE FOLLOWING PASSAGES of Latin and French are the sources for the English passages quoted on pages 13 to 21 of the introduction.

DIONYSIUS, "DE MYSTICA THEOLOGIA"

ITERUM etiam incipientes negationes ab altioribus, dicimus quod omnium causa neque est anima, neque mens; neque habet phantasiam inferiorem aut superiorem, neque opinionem, neque rationem, neque intellectum; neque est ratio, neque intellectus; neque dicitur, neque intelligitur. Ex ut decurramus per media ad extrema; neque est numerus, neque ordo, neque magnitudo, neque parvitas, neque aequalitas, neque similitudo, neque dissimilitudo; neque stat, neque movetur. Et ut ad summa per quaedam media revertamur, et in summis negationes terminemus; neque virtutem habet, neque est virtus, neque lumen; neque vivit, neque vita est; neque substantia est, neque aevum, neque tempus; neque etiam intelligibiliter tangibilis secundum essentiam suam, neque scientia, neque veritas, neque regnum, neque sapientia, neque unum, neque unitas, neque bonitas, neque deitas; neque spiritus secundum quod nos intelligimus spiritum, neque filiatio, neque paternitas, neque aliquid aliud plene cognitum a nobis vel ab aliquo exsistente, scilicet homine puro vel angelo. Sed neque Deus est aliquid non exsistentium, aut aliquid exsistentium; neque exsistentia ipsum cognoscunt secundum quod ipse est, neque ipse cognoscit ea secundum quod ipsa sunt in se ipsis, sed secundum quod sunt in Verbo. Neque est ipsius rationalis investigatio, neque nomen, neque cognitio; neque ipse est tenebrae a lumine deficientes, neque est lumen intelligibile, neque est error, neque veritas. Et omnino nulla est ipsius aut positio aut ablatio; sed quum aliqua quaecumque sub ipsa sunt, ponimus vel negando auferimus, ipsum neque ponimus neque auferimus, quoniam et super omnem positionem est perfecta et unica omnium causa, et super omnem ablationem est excessus ipsius ab omnibus absoluti et super omnia eminentis.

"LIFE OF ST. ELIZABETH OF SPALBECK"

(Elements omitted by the English translator are italicized.)
PORRO in provincia Leodiense prope quoddam famosum *et solemne*

328

monasterium virginum, filiarum beati Bernardi primi claraevallensis abbatis, quod vocatur Erkenrode, per sex aut septem leucarum distantiam a Leodiensi civitate remotum, erat quaedam puella nomine Elizabeth, in cuius virginia puritate misericors et miserator Dominus, mirificans misericordias suas, fidei nostrae manifestissima documenta necnon et passionis suae miracula multipliciter et mirabiliter suscitavit, ut incredulos ad fidei firmitatem, *peccatores ad poenitentiam, ingratos ad gratiam, duros et obstinatos ad pietatis et devotionis affectum accersat et invitet, immo quasi cogat invitos.* Quae quidem mirabilia Domina opera cum audissem, ego frater Phillipus de Claravalle, circa partis illas officium visitationis exercens non credebam narrantibus, donec ipse veni et vidi oculis meis, et probavi quod dimidia pars mihi non fuerat nuntiata.

HIGDEN'S "POLYCHRONICON"

Eoque anno Conradus imperator, Lodowicus rex Franciae, comes Flandriae et multi alii cruce signati ad Terram Sanctam iter arripuerunt, qui viam terrae magis quam maris eligentes, transita Hungaria, per dolum imperatoris Constantinopolitam perditi sunt. Nam multi, gustata farina calce mixta, defuncti sunt, ceteri multi aut gladio aut fame propter eorum luxuriam et rapinam consumpti sunt. Rediens tandem Lodowycus de Terra Santa cum ex diutina continentia et coitus defectu, prout medici dicebant, aegritundinem incurreret, suasumque sibi foret per medicos et praelatos ut ob nimiam distantiam reginae puella aliqua uteretur, respondit, "Malo mori castus quam vivere adulter." Et sic totum Deo committens cito convaluit. Dum autem aliquando clericus quidam privilegium papale ei attulisset quod in omni cathedrali ecclesia regni sui primam vacaturam haberet cum fructibus medio tempore provenientibus, ille statim litteras combussit, dicens se malle tales litteras comburere quam animam suam in inferno torqueri.

ALAIN CHARTIER, "LE QUADRILOGUE INVÉCTIF"

Tu diz que je suis cause de ceste tresmaudite guerre et que j'ay pourchacee et bastie par impatience de la haulte prosperité de paix. Tu diz que par ma folle erreur et les partiz que j'ay desloiaument soustenuz est ceste confusion et maleurté souvenue. Si te respons que la folie des mendres hommes est fondée sur l'outraige des plus grans et que les péchiez et desordonnances descendent des greigneurs aux plus petiz. Car, selon ce que les princes et les haulx hommes se maintiennent en

estat et en vie, le peuple y prent sa rigle et son exemple soit de bien ou
de mal, de paix ou d'esclandre.

VULGATE—"MERLIN"

ORE DIST li contes que quant li .xii. message se furent parti del roy
Artu, que li rois Artus remest entre lui et sa baronie moult durement
corecié del mant que li empereres Luce li auoit mandé.

Et Merlins li dist, "Sire, mandés vo gent, car nous navons que de-
morer. Car li empereres s'aparelle moult durement."

"Merlins, biaus dous amis," fait li rois, "jou li serai al encontre plus
tost qu'il ne vaudra."

"Il nous encontrera a son damage. Mais ore adieu, car jou menuois as
barons faire vo message."

Adont se suanui Merlins conques li rois Artus ne sot quil devint. Et
Merlins s'en ala tout premierement en Orkanie et dist le message al roy
Loth, qu'il fust a Logres de cel jour en .xv. jors a tout son pooir. Et
il dist qu'il i seroit volentiers. Et Merlins le commanda a Dieu et s'en
parti d'iluec.

Que vous iroie jou acontant? Il fist a savoir a tous les princes qui
terre tenoient del roy Artu qui fuissent a Logres dedens .xv. jors, fors
seulement le roy Ban et le roy Bohort son frere. Et puis s'en retorna
arriere et trova le roy Artu en ses cambres, si li dist, "Sire, vos messages
est bien fais a tous vos barons, et seront chi de hui en .xv. jors tout
apparellie."

"LA QUESTE DEL SAINT GRAAL"

(Elements omitted by Malory are italicized.)

OR DIT li contes que, quant mesires Gauvains se fut partiz *de ses com-
paignons,* il chevaucha a mainte jornee *sans aventure trover qui a
conter face;* tant qu'il vint a l'abeie ou Galaad avoit pris l'escu blanc
a la croiz vermeille, et li conta len les aventures qu'il avoit achevées.
Et quant il oï ce, si demanda quele part il ert alez, en len li dist. Et il
se mist au chemin aprés lui et chevaucha *tant que aventure le mena*
la ou Melyanz gisoit malades. Et *quant cil reconut monseignor Gauvain,*
si li dist noveles de Galaad *qui s'en ert au matin partiz.*

"Dieux!" fet mesires Gauvains, "*tant sui meschaanz!* Or sui je li plus
maleureus chevaliers dou monde, qui vois suivant ce chevalier de si
pres et si nel puis ateindre! Certes se Diex donast que je le poïsse

trover, jamés du lui ne departisse, *por qu'il amast ma compaignie autant come je feroie la soe."*

C'est parole oï uns des freres *de laienz,* si respondi *a monseignor Gauvain:* "Certes, sire, la compaignie de vos deus ne seroit mie covenable. Car vos estes serjanz mauvés et desloiax, et il est chevaliers tiex come il doit estre."

"*Sire," fet mesires Gauvains, "a ce que vos me dites me semble il que vos me connoissiez bien."*

"Je vos conois," fet li preudons, "mout mielz que vos ne cuidiez!"

"Biau sire," fet Gauvains, "donc me poez vos bien dire, s'il vos plest, en quoi je sui tiex come vos me metez sus."

"Je nel vos dirai mie," fet cil, "mes vos troveroiz par tens qui le vos dira."

En ce qu'il parloient einsi entra laienz *uns chevaliers armez de toutes armes, et descendi en la cort: et li frere corurent a lui por lui desarmer et l'amenerent en la chambre ou mesire Gauvains estoit. Et quant il est desarmez et mesire Gauvains le voit, si conoist que ce est* Gaheriés *ses freres: et li cort a l'encontre les braz tenduz* et li fet joie merveilleuse; *et li demande se il est sainz et haitiez. Et il dit, "Oïl, Dieu merci."*

Cele nuit furent bien servi des freres de laienz; et a l'endemain, *si tost come il ajorna,* oïrent messe *tuit armé fors de lor hiaumes. Et quant il furent monté et apareillié, si se partirent de laienz et errerent jusqu'a hore de prime. Et lors resgardent devant aus et* voient monseignor Yvain *tout sol chevauchant; et il le conoissent bien as armes qu'il portoit. Si li crient qu'il s'arrest. Et il se resgarde quant il s'oï nomer, si s'arreste et les conoist a la parole. Et il li font grant joie* et li demandent coment il l'a puis fet. Et il respont qu'il n'a riens fet, *car onques puis ne trova aventure qui li pleust.*

BIBLIOGRAPHY

TEXTS: These are the editions and manuscripts from which the selections have been taken.

The Abbey of the Holy Ghost, in Horstmann, Carl, *Yorkshire Writers,* 2 vols. London, 1895–96.

Agnus Castus, ed. G. Brodin. Upsala, 1950.

The Prose Life of Alexander. London, Early English Text Society, original series 143, 1913.

An Alphabet of Tales. London, Early English Text Society, original series 126, 127, 1904–05.

Arderne, John, *Fistula in Ano.* London, Early English Text Society, original series 139, 1910.

Berners, Juliana, *Treatyse of Fysshynge,* ed. Piscator. Edinburgh, 1885.

Bosworth, R. J., ed., *Gothic and Anglo-Saxon Gospels.* London, 1865.

Capgrave, John, *The Chronicle of England,* Rolls Series. London, 1858.

Caxton, William, *Reynard the Fox,* ed. E. Arber. Birmingham, England, 1878.

———— *The Four Sons of Aymon.* London, Early English Text Society, extra series 44–45, 1885.

———— Jean D'Arras' *Melusine.* London, Early English Text Society, extra series 68, 1895.

———— Gossouin's *Mirrour of the World.* London, Early English Text Society, extra series 110, 1913.

———— *Prologues and Epilogues.* London, Early English Text Society, original series 176, 1928.

Chartier, Alain, *Le Quadrilogue Invéctif.* Paris, Classiques Français du moyen-age, No. 32, 1923. English translation from Bodleian MS., Oxford.

Chaucer, Geoffrey, *The Complete Works,* ed. F. N. Robinson. Boston, 1957.

The Cloud of Unknowing. London, Early English Text Society, original series 218, 1944.

Dicts and Sayings of the Philosophers. London, Early English Text Society, original series 211, 1941.

A Fifteenth Century Courtesy Book. London, Early English Text Society, original series 148, 1914.

Fortescue, Sir John, *The Governance of England,* ed. C. Plummer. Oxford, 1885.

Gesta Romanorum. London, Early English Text Society, extra series 33, 1879.

Golden Legend. See Butler, Pierce, *A Study of the Legenda Aurea,* Baltimore, 1899.

Gregory, William, *Historical Collections of a Citizen of London,* ed. J. Gairdner. London, Camden Society, 1876.

Hay, Sir Gilbert, *The Buke of the Ordre of Knychthede.* Edinburgh, Scottish Text Society, No. 62, 1914.

Hilton, Walter, *Of Angels' Song,* in Horstmann, Carl, *Yorkshire Writers,* 2 vols. London, 1895–96.

Jacob's Well. London, Early English Text Society, original series 115, 1900.

John of Ireland, *The Choice of Counsellors,* in Smith, G. G., *Specimens of Middle Scots.* Edinburgh, 1902.

Dame Julian of Norwich, *Revelations of Divine Love,* ed. Grace Warrack. London, 1952. *MS.* in British Museum, Add. 37,790 (longer text).

Kempe, Margery, *The Book of Margery Kempe.* London, Early English Text Society, original series 212, 1940.

La Tour-Landry, Geoffrey de, *The Book of Geoffrey de la Tour-Landry.* London, Early English Text Society, original series 33, 1906.

Lavynham, Richard, *A Litil Tretys on the Seven Deadly Sins,* ed. J. van Zutphen. Rome, 1956.

A Book of London English, ed. R. W. Chambers. Oxford, 1931.

Love, Nicholas, *The Mirrour of the Blessed Life of Jesu Christ.* Roxburghe Club, 1908.

Malory, Sir Thomas, *Le Morte Darthur,* 3 vols. (Caxton text), ed. H. O. Sommer. London, 1889–91. See also E. Vinaver, *The Works of Sir Thomas Malory,* 3 vols. (Winchester text), Oxford, 1947.

Mandeville, Sir John, *Travels.* London, Early English Text Society, original series 153–154, 1919–23.

The Life of St. Mary d'Oignies, ed. Carl Horstmann, *Anglia,* VIII, 1885.

Merlin. London, Early English Text Society, original series 10, 21, 26, 112, 1865–99.

Mirk, John, *The Festial.* London, Early English Text Society, extra series 96, 1905.

Paues, A. C., ed., *A Fourteenth-Century English Biblical Version.* Cambridge, 1904.

Pecock, Reginald, *The Repressor of Overmuch Blaming the Clergy,* Rolls Series, 2 vols. London, 1860.

Paston Letters, 6 vols., ed. J. Gairdner. London, 1904.

The Pilgrimage of the Lyf of the Manhode. Roxburghe Club, 1869.

The Book of Quint Essence. London, Early English Text Society, original series 16, 1889.

✓ Rolle, Richard, *English Writings,* ed. H. E. Allen. Ox rd, 1931.

The Stonor Letters, ed. C. L. Kingsford. London, Camden Society, 1919.

A *Talking of the Love of God,* in Horstmann, Carl, *Yorkshire Writers,* 2 vols. London, 1895–96.

Thorpe, William, *Examination,* in A. W. Pollard, *Fifteenth-Century Verse and Prose,* Westminster, 1903.

Tiptoft, John, *The Declamation of Noblesse,* in R. J. Mitchell, *John Tiptoft.* London, 1938.

Usk, Thomas, *The Testament of Love,* in W. W. Skeat, ed., *Chaucerian and Other Pieces.* London, 1897.

The Book of Virtues and Vices. London, Early English Text Society, original series 217, 1942.

Wey, William, *The Itineraries of William Wey.* Roxburghe Club, 1857.

Wycliffe, John, *The English Works.* London, Early English Text Society, original series 74, 1880.

Yonge, James, *Secreta Secretorum.* London, Early English Text Society, extra series 74, 1898.

Discussion and Guides. Some of the editorial matter in the above texts contains useful commentary upon the writers and their work and styles. The following works make significant contributions to the study of prose in the period.

Atkins, J. W. H., *English Literary Criticism: The Medieval Phase.* Cambridge, 1943.

Aurner, N. S., *Caxton.* London, 1926.

Benham, A. R., *English Literature from Widsith to the Death of Chaucer.* New Haven, 1916.

Bennett, H. S., *Chaucer and the Fifteenth Century* (*Oxford History of English Literature,* Vol. 2, part 1). Oxford, 1947.

———— *The Pastons and Their England.* Cambridge, 1922.

———— "Fifteenth-Century Secular Prose," *Review of English Studies,* XXI, 1945.

———— "Caxton and His Public," *Review of English Studies,* XIX, 1943.

———— "The Production and Dissemination of Vernacular Manuscripts in the Fifteenth Century," *The Library,* Series 5, I, 1947.

Buhler, Curt, *William Caxton and His Critics.* Syracuse, N.Y., 1960.

Byles, A. T. P., "Caxton as a Man of Letters," *The Library,* Series 4, XV, 1934.

Cambridge History of English Literature, Vol. II. Cambridge, 1908.

Chambers, R. W., *On the Continuity of English Prose*. Oxford, 1957.

Chambers, Sir E. K., *English Literature at the Close of the Middle Ages* (*Oxford History of English Literature*, Vol. II, part 2). Oxford, 1947.

Chaytor, H., *From Script to Print*. Cambridge, 1945.

Clark, A. C., *Prose Rhythm in English*. London, 1913.

Davis, Norman, "Styles in English Prose of the Late Middle and Early Modern Period," *Langue et Littérature*, XXI. Liège, 1961, 165–184.

Green, V. H. H., *Bishop Reginald Pecock*. Cambridge, 1945.

Gerould, G. H., *Saints Legends*. Boston, 1916.

Jacob, E. F., "Florida verborum venustas," *John Rylands Library Bulletin*, XVII, 1933.

Ker, W. P., *Essays on Medieval Literature*. London, 1905.

Kingsford, C. L., *English Historical Literature in the Fifteenth Century*. London, 1913.

Knowles, D., *The English Mystical Tradition*. London, 1961.

Krapp, G. P., *The Rise of English Literary Prose*. New York, 1915.

Mitchell, R. J., *John Tiptoft*. London, 1938.

Morgan, M. M., "A Treatise in Cadence," *Modern Language Review*, XLVII, 1952, 156–164.

Morley, Henry, *English Writers*, Vols. IV-VI. London, 1887-95.

Mosher, J. A., *The Exemplum in the Early Religious and Didactic Literature of England*. New York, 1911.

Mustanoja, Tauno, *Middle English Syntax*. Helsinki, 1960.

Ohmann, Richard, "Prolegomena to Prose Style," *Style in Prose Fiction, English Institute Essays*. New York, 1959, 1–24.

Owst, G. R., *Literature and Pulpit in Medieval England*. Cambridge, 1933.

Pollard, A. W., *Fifteenth-Century Verse and Prose*. Westminster, 1903.

Prins, A. S., *French Influence on English Phrasing*. Leiden, 1932.

Read, Herbert, *English Prose Style*. London, 1952.

Saintsbury, G., *A History of English Prose Rhythm*. London, 1912.

Schlauch, Margaret, "Chaucer's Prose Rhythms," *P.M.L.A.*, LXV, 1950, 568–589.

Schofield, W. H., *English Literature from the Norman Conquest to Chaucer*. New York, 1906.

Sisam, K., *Fourteenth-Century Verse and Prose*. Oxford, 1921, 1929.

Smith, G. Gregory, *Specimens of Middle Scots*. Edinburgh, 1902.

Stevenson, W. H., "The Introduction of English as the Vehicle of Instruction," *Furnivall Miscellany*. Oxford, 1901, 421–429.

Sutherland, J., *On English Prose*. Toronto, 1957.

Thompson, J. W., *The Medieval Library*. Chicago, 1939.

Vinaver, Eugene, *Malory*. Oxford, 1929.

———— *The Works of Sir Thomas Malory*, 3 vols. Oxford, 1947.

Weiss, R., *Humanism in England during the Fifteenth Century*. Oxford, 1941.

Wilson, R. M., "On the Continuity of English Prose," *Mélanges de linguistique et de philologie Fernand Mossé in memoriam*. Paris, 1959, 486–494.

Workman, S. K., *Fifteenth-Century Translation as an Influence on English Prose*. Princeton, 1940.

Further bibliographical information on texts and criticism will be found in: *The Cambridge Bibliography of English Literature*, Cambridge, 1941-57; J. E. Wells, *A Manual of the Writings in Middle English*, New Haven, 1916, and supplements; L. L. Tucker and A. R. Benham, *A Bibliography of Fifteenth-Century Literature*, Seattle, 1928; and the works listed above by H. S. Bennett, E. K. Chambers, and S. K. Workman.